social class
and
mental
illness:

social class and mental illness:

A

John Wiley & Sons, Inc.   New York • London • Sydney

Community Study

AUGUST B. HOLLINGSHEAD, Ph.D.

Professor of Sociology,
Graduate School, Yale University

FREDRICK C. REDLICH, M.D.

Professor and Chairman, Department of Psychiatry,
School of Medicine, Yale University

in memory of
Bertram H. Roberts

preface

This is the final report of one part of a research project carried out by a team of social scientists and psychiatrists into interrelations between social stratification and mental illness in the urbanized community centered in New Haven, Connecticut. The second part will be reported in a companion volume by Jerome K. Myers and Bertram H. Roberts, entitled *Social Class, Family Dynamics, and Mental Illness,* John Wiley and Sons, New York.

The research reported here focused upon two questions: Is mental illness related to social class? Does a mentally ill patient's position in the status system affect how he is treated for his illness? To answer these questions we studied the social structure of the community, the psychiatric patients in treatment, the institutions where they are cared for, and the psychiatrists treating them.

Stated briefly, we have found that the New Haven community is characterized by a distinct class structure. Each class exhibits definite types of mental illness. Moreover, each class reacts to the presence of mental illness in its members in different ways, and the treatment of psychiatric patients within the various classes differs accordingly. Successive chapters tell the story of how members of the community became patients, how they and their families responded to psychiatric intervention, and the effects of social class on patients and therapists. The book ends with some recommendations on what our society could do about improving socially determined shortcomings of psychiatric practice. The details of linkages between social class and mental illness can be seen only by reading the book.

Although it is a report of scientific research, the writing is directed toward both a professional and a lay audience. Nevertheless, the medical and social science content of the material has been retained. Its findings, conclusions, and recommendations should be of interest to psychiatrists, psychologists, sociologists, nurses, educators, social workers, public health administrators, lawyers, judges, and others who shape public policy in health and welfare. Persons interested in questions of vital concern to all of us, such as how our way of life affects our health and how we are treated when mental illness strikes, will want to read this book.

The two volumes that report the results of this research are the product of ten years of work. In the fall of 1948 the authors of this volume, who are the senior men, began to lay plans for the ensuing research. Betweeen that date and the summer of 1950 they confined their activities to drafting a research proposal with the help of Dr. Ernest Gruenberg, who shortly afterwards left Yale to establish a research group in Syracuse, New York, for the New York State Commission on Mental Health. Our request for a research grant was approved by the National Institute of Mental Health, United States Public Health Service, which supported the major part of this research from its inception to its conclusion. Late in 1950 Bertram H. Roberts, psychiatrist, and Jerome K. Myers, sociologist, joined us. Dr. Roberts, a promising young investigator in social psychiatry, died in an accident on August 12, 1955, but Dr. Myers finished the volume they had started.

For advice at the beginning of the study we wish to thank David Rapaport, and Margaret Mead. During our work we benefited from advice by John C. Eberhart, John Clausen, and Morton Kramer. For most valuable comments and criticism after reading the manuscript we owe our thanks to Norman Cameron, James A. Davis, and Melvin L. Kohn.

At one time or another the following persons were members of the team who worked with the authors of these volumes: psychiatrists L. Z. Freedman, John MacIver, and Leslie Shaffer; psychologist Harvey Robinson; anthropologist William Caudill; sociologists Theodor R. Anderson, Leslie Clark, Robert E. Ellis, Raymond Forer, Fred Strodtbeck, and William W. Vosburgh; research assistants Elizabeth Bellis, Jane Collier, Emily Kirby, Barbara Myers,

Virginia Tenzer, and Catherine Vosburgh; secretarial assistants Elizabeth Banks, Doris Berndtson, Jerry E. Edwards, Lorraine Estra, Lillian Fisher, Anne M. Hollingshead, Ellen M. Hollingshead, Constance Ives, Lillian Smith, and Janet Turk. We are grateful to each person named for the contribution he made to this enterprise.

The success of large-scale research depends on the cooperation of many agencies and individuals who cannot be named. For this co-operation—with rare exceptions, splendid cooperation—we are deeply indebted to professional and administrative staffs of psychiatric hospitals and clinics and to private practitioners whose patients became the subjects of our study. The thousands of our fellow citizens who gave of their time and personal information are also a part of "the team." Without these members of the team the project could not have been completed.

In reporting material obtained from our colleagues' and from our own records we have done everything possible to guard the confidentiality of the source. With the exception of naming the community in which the research was done and Yale University, where we worked, no names are mentioned of patients, respondents, professional persons, or institutions.

Between 1952 and 1957 twenty-five papers on selected aspects of the work were prepared, delivered before professional audiences, and published in psychiatric, psychological, and sociological journals. Some of the data contained in these papers are incorporated in this book and in the forthcoming one by Myers and Roberts, but most of the materials in each book are not in the professional papers.

Finally, we undertook an interdisciplinary sociological and psychiatric study of our community. Part of the results is encompassed in this book. We hope our work will benefit this community as well as other communities.

AUGUST B. HOLLINGSHEAD
FREDRICK C. REDLICH

New Haven, Connecticut
December 1957

contents

scope and methods

part one

part one • scope and methods

Chapters One and Two relate how a sociologist and a psychiatrist selected social class and mental illness as a problem for research and how the data were collected to test a series of hypotheses which assume that the class system of a metropolitan community in New England is connected, on the one hand, with the distribution of mental illness in its population, and, on the other, with the ways mentally ill persons are treated by psychiatrists.

A reader who wishes to gain an understanding of why we studied the social system and the practice of psychiatry should begin with Chapter One. Readers who are not interested in the necessary details of scientific procedures may wish to omit Chapter Two. However, such readers after studying subsequent materials may desire to return to the discussion of methodological procedures in Chapter Two to learn how we collected the data and our reasons for organizing and analyzing them as we did.

the research problem

INTRODUCTION

Americans prefer to avoid the two facts of life studied in this book: social class and mental illness. The very idea of "social class" is inconsistent with the American ideal of a society composed of free and equal individuals, individuals living in a society where they have identical opportunities to realize their inborn potentialities. The acceptance of this facet of the "American Dream" is easy and popular. To suggest that it may be more myth than reality stimulates antagonistic reactions.

Although Americans, by choice, deny the existence of social classes, they are forced to admit the reality of mental illness. Nevertheless, merely the thought of such illness is abhorrent to them. They fear "mental illness," its victims, and those people who cope with them: psychiatrists, clinical psychologists, social workers, psychiatric nurses, and attendants. Even the institutions our society has developed to care for the mentally ill are designated by pejorative terms, such as "bug house," "booby hatch," and "loony bin," and psychiatrists are called "nutcrackers" and "head shrinkers."

Denial of the existence of social classes and derisive dismissal of the mentally ill may salve the consciences of some people. The suggestion that different social classes receive different treatment for mental illness may come as a shock, but to repress facts because they are distasteful and incongruent with cherished values may lead to consequences even more serious than those we are trying to escape by substituting fantasy for reality.

Social Class

American ideals relative to social status are premised upon the "self-evident truth" that "all men are created equal." If our ideals corresponded to reality, there would be no classes in our society. However, students of American society have pointed out on numerous occasions that American ideals and American reality are two different things. More than a half-century ago, Lord Bryce in his astute analysis of our society put the problem succinctly when he said:

> There is no rank in America, that is to say no external and recognized stamp marking a man as entitled to any special privileges or to deference or respect from others. No man is entitled to think himself better than his fellows. . . .
> The total absence of rank and universal acceptance of equality do not, however, prevent the existence of grades and distinctions which, though they find no tangible expression, are sometimes as sharply drawn as in Europe.[1]

In more recent years, Myrdal summed up the disparity between what we profess publicly as members of a democratic society and how we act in private life as "an American dilemma."[2] The observations of these discerning Europeans have been documented many times by the researches of American social scientists. Some 25 years ago, the Lynds [3] in their widely acclaimed books on "Middletown" demonstrated the reality of social classes in the daily activities of Middle Western Americans. In the ensuing years a number of social scientists have published extensive evidence to support the fact that American society is stratified.[4]

Nevertheless, the phrase "social class" is an emotionally provoking symbol to Americans. The idea that people are unequal socially is resisted strongly. Even when Americans privately "draw the line" between one another in subtle ways, they do not like to admit it in public. Our reluctance to admit that we discriminate among our fellow citizens is traceable to the doctrine of equality enunciated in the Declaration of Independence. Publicly we talk about equality; privately we practice inequality. A consequence of this conflict in values is that some of the most highly charged emotional issues facing our society revolve around the everyday practices of some members of our society who behave toward other members in invidious ways. The inconsistency between our public protestations and our private acts presents us with deep moral issues.

This is recognized officially in the area of race and ethnic relations. It is expressed by fair employment practice acts and the efforts of national, state, and local governments to end segregation in the schools and other areas of public life. The official efforts of men and women of good will, however, are resisted mightily by other members of the society. Such actions are based upon the traditional conviction that some men are socially superior to others.

Mental Illness

Our attitudes toward mental illness are also a product of our cultural heritage. Historical evidence indicates that mental "disturbances" have been known in all civilized societies. The severe disturbances of kings, generals, religious leaders, and other personages have been recorded since ancient times. Persons who were not important enough to have their mental aberrations written into the human record undoubtedly also were afflicted, even though their ailments and their numbers have been lost in the mists of time. Although man's mental and emotional maladjustments are not new, the public is more clearly aware of them now than in the past, and responsible leaders have become increasingly concerned with their alleviation.

In the last decade mental illness has been recognized as one of the most serious unsolved health problems facing our society. A few figures will indicate its magnitude. The approximately 750,000 persons who are currently hospitalized in mental institutions occupy some 55 percent of all hospital beds in the United States. Hundreds of thousands of other mentally ill persons are treated by psychiatrists in clinics and in private practice, but the number of hospitalized cases increases year by year. During World War II, 43 percent of all disability discharges (980,000) from the Armed Forces were granted on psychiatric grounds, and 865,000 young men were rejected for psychiatric reasons in Selective Service examinations. Moreover, some 16,000 to 17,000 persons commit suicide each year and, according to the best estimates, there are about 3,800,000 alcoholics in the adult population. We are certain that patients hospitalized in mental institutions in addition to those cared for by psychiatrists in private practice and in clinics represent only a portion of those who are mentally ill. Estimates indicate that there are from seven to eight million other Americans who are less seriously disturbed but who could benefit from psychiatric care if it were available.[5]

Social Class and Mental Illness

Is the presence of mental illness in the population related to class status? Is the treatment received by a mentally ill member of our society an effect of his class position? These questions are crucial to the research reported here. They are even more important from the viewpoint of their scientific meaning and their implications for social policy.

Detailed evidence will be presented in this book to support the answers we have reached. If our answers support American ideals of equality, class status should have no effect upon the distribution of mental illness in the population. Neither should it influence the kind of psychiatric treatment mentally ill patients receive. However, the reader should remember that our ideals and our behavior are two different things.

Both social class and mental illness may be compared to an iceberg; 90 percent of it is concealed below the surface. The submerged portion, though unseen, is the dangerous part. This may be illustrated by recalling what happened when an "unsinkable" trans-Atlantic luxury liner, the *Titanic*, rammed an iceberg on her maiden voyage in 1912. In that crisis, a passenger's class status played a part in the determination of whether he survived or was drowned. The official casualty lists showed that only 4 first class female passengers (3 voluntarily chose to stay on the ship) of a total of 143 were lost. Among the second class passengers, 15 of 93 females drowned; and among the third class, 81 of 179 female passengers went down with the ship. The third class passengers were ordered to remain below deck, some kept there at the point of a gun.[6]

The idea that stratification in our society has any bearing on the diagnosis and treatment of disease runs counter to our cherished beliefs about equality, especially when they are applied to the care of the sick. Physicians share deeply ingrained egalitarian ideals with their fellow citizens, yet they, too, may make subtle, perhaps unconscious, judgments of the differential worth of the members of our society. Physicians, among them psychiatrists, are sensitive to statements that patients may not be treated alike; in fact there is strong resistance in medical circles to the exploration of such questions. But closing our eyes to facts or denying them in anger will help patients no more than the belief that the *Titanic* was "unsinkable" kept the ship afloat after it collided with an iceberg.

RESEARCH PLANS

All research passes through several phases. The principal ones involve preliminary planning, the collection of data, their analysis, interpretation, and, finally, the drafting of a report. Here we are concerned with a brief statement of the first three steps in the planning phases of this project. The theoretical and professional interests of the authors focused our attention on the interrelations between social class and mental illness. The first step in the development of this research was the examination of the literature on this problem.

Examination of the Literature

We found that the question of relationship between an individual's position in the class structure and the kind of mental illness he develops, on the one hand, and the treatment he receives for it, on the other, had not been studied extensively by either psychiatrists or sociologists. Only a few speculative and research papers had dealt with this question before 1950.[7] However, social scientists and medical men had made numerous studies of mental illness from a number of other points of view.[8] Medical researchers early approached the problem from the viewpoint of possible connections between man's mental aberrations and biological, psychological, and physical factors in his environment.[9] Sociologists analyzed the question in terms of ecology [10] and of social disorganization [11] paying little attention to biological factors.

Our study of the literature revealed, also, that no generally accepted theory encompassing the biological, psychological, and social aspects of "normal" and "abnormal" behavior pertinent to our interest was available for test or verification. This statement is made in full cognizance of the attempts of anthropologists, psychologists, and sociologists to formulate unitary theories of behavior which bridge the gap between the individual as an organism and the sociocultural matrix that surrounds him. It is made in the light, also, of the contributions of Freud and his disciples to our knowledge of the psychopathology and psychology of the individual.

Psychiatric theories and social science theories, although presumably based on observation of human behavior, have been developed independently, and few efforts have been made to bridge the gap between the two kinds of theory; even key concepts developed in one discipline are ignored for the most part in the other. This observation is especially cogent because social scientists have been concerned with the concept of social class [12] for more than a century, but psychiatrists until recent years have overlooked it.[13]

Although Sigmund Freud was aware of class as a social fact, he paid little attention to it in his theory. He made a passing reference to the possibility that class status might be a factor in personality development in his *Introductory Lectures*.[14] In this instance, he speculated on the different personalities of the daughters of the landlord and the janitor as developed in J. Nestroy's farce, *On the Ground Floor and in the Mansion*. In this play the landlord's daughter is characterized as a romantic young woman absorbed by feelings of conflict and guilt over a platonic love affair; her compensation is hysteria. The janitor's daughter is lustily engaged in a variety of sexual pursuits without remorse. Personalities, conflicts, and adjustments in the two young women differ markedly, and Freud implies their differences are related to the differential impact of their social class positions. Freud was aware also of class differences in the treatment of patients. Neither he nor his disciples systematically investigated the influence of class on either the development or the treatment of mental disorders. However, Alfred Adler, Karen Horney, Erik Erikson, Erich Fromm, and Abram Kardiner showed some awareness of the problem.

Psychiatry, as a medical specialty, is influenced heavily by conceptions developed in the biological sciences. The chief emphasis in psychiatric theory has been placed on psychological and biological mechanisms. Little attention has been focused on the sociocultural milieu which envelops persons from birth to death. Even psychoanalysis was posited mainly upon biological assumptions. An important sector of Freud's conceptual scheme is built around the idea that the individual in the course of his maturation (ontogeny) passes through three inevitable libidinal phases of development: oral, anal, and genital. This sequence was inferred from the biological doctrine that the individual recapitulates instinctively the needs, drives, and pressures that have been built up in man during his evolutionary development (phylogeny). Freud developed this doctrine in the early part of his life. Later in his career, after he realized that some of his earlier concepts left many questions unsolved, he began to include the individual's relationship to his social world and the effects this had upon personality development in his theories.[15] It was during the later stage of his career that he developed the structural concepts which resulted in the newer ego psychology. However, a fusion of ego psychology and sociocultural theory is a future task.[16]

Today, the individual psychiatrist's knowledge of man's social system comes almost entirely from intuitive ideas, personal experiences, and what patients have told him about their family and community relationships. On the other hand, social scientists have not paid enough attention to the biological and psychological equipment of the human individual. Anthropologists, psychologists, and sociologists have gathered extensive data on family organization, child-rearing practices, recreational patterns, diet and habits of eating, drinking, sex customs, ethical ideas, attitudes, and so on, through an extensive list of human activities and institutions. Social scientists have demonstrated that behaviors differ greatly in different social strata and subcultures of a society, but psychiatric theory gives only passing attention to the sociocultural environment that envelops the human being. This approach to an understanding of the patient isolated from his society is comparable to the position of an astronomer who studies the sun and has only a peripheral interest in the nearest planet, rather than seeing the sun as a small part of an astronomical system.

Our search of the literature indicated, moreover, that verified knowledge of "disturbed" behavior is so limited that we cannot isolate many biological variables from psychosocial and sociocultural factors that are involved in "abnormal" behavior. When theorists do differentiate social from biological factors, they usually fail to assess the importance of each type of variable in the resulting behavior. As psychiatrists, particularly, do become aware of the complexity of interlocking factors entailed in the motivation and perception of behavior and the great difficulty in establishing a hierarchy of importance and sequence of events in personality development, they tend to take refuge in such terms as "the human being as a whole" or, on a more sophisticated plane, they speak of circular and reticular causality. All too often, they dodge the issue by using holistic concepts without any operational reference.

From the viewpoint of theory, it would be desirable to see social factors as events in a causal psychological chain, such as frustration, which directly or indirectly gives rise to maladjusted behavior in the individual. Unfortunately, this is not possible in our present state of knowledge. It is unlikely that single causes of "abnormal" behavior can be identified. Nevertheless, we must attempt relentlessly to isolate biological, psychological, and social factors in their dynamic interactions. We need, among other things, to understand how social events are experienced and interpreted by the person whose behavior we are investigating. To do this, we have to investigate possible functional linkages between sociocultural variables and the development of "disturbed" behavior in the individual. Unfortunately, all too often in the literature, contradictory statements are made about the effect of social factors on psychiatric disorders. For example, Kubie pointed out in a recent paper that wealth is accused as the cause of mental disease as often as poverty, and license is blamed for maladjustments as much as stern discipline.[17]

In sum, our review of the literature indicated that social scientists and psychiatrists in the years before World War II carried on their researches and developed their theories in splendid isolation. When they traveled parallel paths they tended to ignore each other. If their interests took them along the same road, they were careful to take opposite sides. In view of this situation, we desired to bridge the gap between the theoretical positions represented by sociologists and psychiatrists.

Two Research Questions

After several months of preliminary work, the central questions of this research emerged, namely: (1) Is mental illness related to class in our society? (2) Does a psychiatric patient's position in the status system affect how he is treated for his illness?

The first query is related to the etiology of mental illnesses. The psychodynamic concept of unconscious conflict between instinctual forces and the demands of the environment is crucial for many attempts at explanation of most neurotic and psychotic illnesses. Knowing that the different social classes exhibit different ways of life, we conjectured that emotional problems of individuals might be related to the patterns of life characteristic of their class positions.

The second question is focused on treatment. Our observations and experiences with psychiatric treatment led us to think that the kind of treatment a patient receives is not a function solely of the state of medical knowledge which is embodied in the art and science of making a diagnosis and prescribing treatment. Subtle and powerful psychological and social processes appear to be important determinants in the choice of treatment and its implementation. We are interested particularly in finding out whether the various psychiatric treatments patients receive are affected by class status.

Working Hypotheses

The third major step in the formulation of our research plans was taken when we crystallized our thoughts on these questions around a series of tentative hypotheses. Eventually, five working hypotheses were written into the research design. Each hypothesis connected the two major concepts of the research, namely, social class and mental illness, in such a way that the resulting proposition could be tested empirically. The several hypotheses were phrased thus:

Hypothesis 1. The prevalence of treated mental illness is related significantly to an individual's position in the class structure.

Hypothesis 2. The types of diagnosed psychiatric disorders are connected significantly to the class structure.

Hypothesis 3. The kind of psychiatric treatment administered by psychiatrists is associated with the patient's position in the class structure.

Hypothesis 4. Social and psychodynamic factors in the development of psychiatric disorders are correlative to an individual's position in the class structure.

Hypothesis 5. Mobility in the class structure is associated with the development of psychiatric difficulties.

Assumptions

Several assumptions are implied in these hypotheses: First, the social structure of our society is characterized by a system of stratification. Second, individuals living in a given class are subjected to problems of living that are expressed in emotional and psychological reactions and disorders different in quantity and quality from those expressed by persons in other classes. Third, psychiatrists, who are responsible for diagnosing and treating mental illness, are controlled, as members of the society, by its value system. This presumption implies that psychiatrists work with phenomena that are essentially social in origin, and they cope with them in ways that are prescribed, on the one hand, by the professional subculture of psychiatry as a medical specialty and, on the other, by the expectancies, working rules, and values that impinge upon them in their day-to-day professional and lay activities.[18] Fourth, the working rules of psychiatry are practiced in ways that are connected implicitly with class status. Fifth, mental illness is defined socially; that is, whatever a psychiatrist treats or is expected to treat must be viewed as mental illness. This position is based upon the fact that in our society psychiatrists treat individuals whose behavior would be ignored in a second society, punished by the criminal courts in a third, and in still others given over to priests. We agree with Romano that "the conventional conceptual scheme of disease is not applicable to mental disease." [19] Sixth, the class status of individuals in the society is viewed as the independent or *antecedent* variable; the diagnosis of a patient's illness and the treatment prescribed for him by a psychiatrist are considered to be dependent or *consequent* variables. Demonstration of the validity of these assumptions rests upon a systematic examination of the five hypotheses.

Tests of the Working Hypotheses

The formulation of the working hypotheses was a step forward in the development of our research plans, and the next major problem was to decide how we could test them. This brought us face to face with methodological problems and procedures. What these problems were and how we handled them are described in detail in Chapter Two. The results of our examination of the first three hypotheses are presented in this book. Our tests of *Hypotheses 4* and *5* are reported in Jerome K. Myers and Bertram H. Roberts' volume, *Social Class, Family Dynamics, and Mental Illness.**

Each hypothesis was tested with different kinds of data and different research methods. The first three utilize data drawn from the entire community of New Haven, Connecticut. One might call this a "macroscopic" or survey approach. *Hypotheses 4* and *5* are investigated by the detailed study of fifty psychiatric patients and their families who live in this community; one might refer to this as a "microscopic" or clinical approach. The two approaches supplement one another: The survey approach furnishes well-defined quantitative data on a cross section of the community, whereas the clinical approach gives a close view of fine details on individuals and families and permits insights into the origins of maladjusted behavior and responses to treatment under sharply different social conditions.

The urbanized community centered in the city of New Haven was selected as the site for this research for a number of reasons, the first one being that the senior members of the research team are residents; they occupy positions at Yale University which give them access to social and psychiatric data indispensable to tests of the several hypotheses. In addition, New Haven has been identified with the Mental Health Movement since its founding here some 50 years ago. The community, approximately 240,000 in population, is large

---

* To be published by John Wiley and Sons, New York (manuscript in preparation).

enough to enable the researchers to mask easily the identity of any person. However, it is small enough to study in detail.

The data we have gathered may be used as a base line for the accumulation of comparable data in other, but similar, communities. Cross-community comparisons of social structure and the distribution and treatment of psychiatric patients should contribute to the solution of some of the theoretical and practical problems highlighted in this research. Without encroaching upon our findings we may ask: Why is the age- and sex-adjusted rate per 100,000 for schizophrenic patients in psychiatric treatment from the New Haven community over nine times higher in the lowest social class than in the highest one? Why do "lower" class psychiatric patients drop out of treatment after one, two, or three visits to clinics? If similar questions are asked and similar findings are reported from other urbanized communities, social science and medical researchers will have factual data upon which they may base theories and plan procedures for coping with mental health problems.

SUMMARY

Social class and mental illness are two facets of life which members of our society prefer to avoid. We chose to study them because they represent major problem areas in our society. We assumed a functional interdependence between the status structure of the community and a number of different aspects of mental illness and psychiatric therapy. Our principal assumptions were phrased in terms of hypotheses so that they could be tested with factual data and by procedures recognized to be scientific. A number of papers have been published in professional journals on this research,[20] but the data and the discussion presented in subsequent chapters are essentially new. Now that we have traced the background of our interests and defined the research problem, we are ready to spell out in detail the methodological procedures we followed in the development of our research plans.

NOTES

[1] James Bryce, *The American Commonwealth*, The Macmillan Company, New York, 1906, Third Edition, Vol. II, p. 752.

[2] Gunnar Myrdal, *An American Dilemma*, Harper and Brothers, New York, 1944, 2 Vols.

[3] Robert and Helen M. Lynd, *Middletown*, Harcourt, Brace and Company, New York, 1929; ——, *Middletown in Transition*, Harcourt, Brace and Company, 1936.

[4] E. Wight Bakke, *The Unemployed Worker*, Yale University Press, New Haven, 1940; Richard Centers, *The Psychology of Social Classes*, Princeton University Press, Princeton, 1949; Percey F. Davidson and H. Dercey Anderson, *Occupational Mobility in an American Community*, Stanford University Press, Stanford, 1937; Allison Davis, Burleigh B. Gardner, and Mary R. Gardner, *Deep South*, The University of Chicago Press, Chicago, 1941; John Dollard, *Caste and Class in a Southern Town*, Yale University Press, New Haven, 1937; St. Clair Drake and Horace R. Clayton, *Black Metropolis*, Harcourt, Brace and Company, New York, 1945; Walter R. Goldschmidt, *As You Sow*, Harcourt, Brace and Company, New York, 1947; R. J. Havighurst and Hilda Taba, *Adolescent Character and Personality*, John Wiley and Sons, New York, 1949; August B. Hollingshead, *Elmtown's Youth*, John Wiley and Sons, New York, 1949; R. W. Jones, *Life, Liberty and Property*, University of Pennsylvania Press, Philadelphia, 1941; Harold F. Kaufman, *Prestige Classes in a New York Rural Community*, Cornell University Memoir 260, 1944; Alfred C. Kinsey, Wardell B. Pomeroy, and Clyde E. Martin, *Sexual Behavior in the Human Male*, W. B. Saunders Company, Philadelphia, 1948; ——, *Sexual Behavior in the Human Female*, W. B. Saunders Company, Philadelphia, 1953; John W. McConnell, *The Evolution of Social Classes*, American Council on Public Affairs, Washington, 1942; Hortense Powdermaker, *After Freedom*, The Viking Press, New York, 1939; W. L. Warner and Paul S. Lunt, *The Social Life of a Modern Community*, Yale University Press, New Haven, 1941; —— and Leo Srole, *The Social Systems of American Ethnic Groups*, Yale University Press, New Haven, 1945; —— and J. O. Low, *The Social System of the Modern Factory*, Yale University Press, New Haven, 1947; ——, Marchia Meeker, and Kenneth Eells, *Social Class in America*, Science Research Associates, Chicago, 1949; James West, *Plainville, U.S.A.*, Columbia University Press, New York, 1945; William F. Whyte, *Street Corner Society*, The University of Chicago Press, Chicago, 1943.

[5] Kenneth Appel, "Present Challenge of Psychiatry," *American Journal of Psychiatry*, Vol. III, No. 1 (July 1954), pp. 1–12; J. M. A. Weiss, "Suicide: An Epidemiological Analysis," *Psychological Quarterly*, Vol. 28 (1954), pp. 225–252.

[6] Walter Lord, *A Night to Remember*, Henry Holt and Company, New York, 1955, p. 107.

[7] For example, see Robert E. Clark, "Psychoses, Income and Occupational Prestige," *American Journal of Sociology*, Vol. 44 (March 1949), pp. 443–440; ——, "The Relationship of Schizophrenia to Occupational Income and Occupational Prestige," *American Sociological Review*, Vol. 13 (June 1948), pp. 325–330; Kingsley Davis, "Mental Hygiene and the Class Structure," *Psychiatry*, Vol. 1 (February 1938), pp. 55–56; Talcott Parsons, "Psychoanalysis and the Social Structure," *Psychoanalytical Quarterly*, Vol. XIX, No. 3, pp. 371–384; John Dollard and Neal Miller, *Personality and Psychotherapy*, McGraw-Hill Book Company, New York, 1950; Jurgen Ruesch, "Social Techniques, Social Status and Social Change in Illness," in Clyde Kluckhohn and Henry A. Murray (Editors), *Personality in Nature, Society and Culture*, Alfred A. Knopf, New York, 1949, pp. 117–130; W. L. Warner, "The Society, the Individual, and His

Mental Disorders," *American Journal of Psychiatry*, Vol. 94, No. 2 (September 1937), pp. 275–285; Abram Kardiner and Lionel Ovesey, *The Mark of Oppression*, W. W. Norton and Company, New York, 1951.

⁸ For example, see Trygve Braatøy, "Is It Probable that the Sociological Situation is a Factor in Schizophrenia?" *Psychiatrica et Neurologica*, Vol. XII (1937), pp. 109–138; Donald L. Gerard and Joseph Siegel, "The Family Background of Schizophrenia," *The Psychiatric Quarterly*, Vol. 24 (January 1950), pp. 47–73; Robert W. Hyde and Lowell V. Kingsley, "Studies in Medical Sociology I: The Relation of Mental Disorders to the Community Socio-Economic Level," *New England Journal of Medicine*, Vol. 231, No. 16 (October 1944), pp. 543–548; ———, "Studies in Medical Sociology II: The Relation of Mental Disorders to Population Density," *New England Journal of Medicine*, Vol. 231, No. 17 (October 1944), pp. 571–577; Robert W. Hyde and Roderick M. Chisolm, "Studies in Medical Sociology III: The Relation of Mental Disorders to Race and Nationality," *New England Journal of Medicine*, Vol. 231, No. 18 (November 1944), pp. 613–618; William Malamud and Irene Malamud, "A Socio-Psychiatric Investigation of Schizophrenia Occurring in the Armed Forces," *Psychosomatic Medicine*, Vol. 5 (October 1943), pp. 364–375; B. Malzberg, *Social and Biological Aspects of Mental Disease*, N. Y. State Hospital Press, Utica, 1940; William F. Roth and Frank H. Luton, "The Mental Health Program in Tennessee: Statistical Report of a Psychiatric Survey in a Rural County," *American Journal of Psychiatry*, Vol. 99 (March 1943), pp. 662–675; J. Ruesch and others, *Chronic Disease and Psychological Invalidism*, American Society for Research in Psychosomatic Problems, New York, 1946; ———, *Duodenal Ulcer: A Socio-psychological Study of Naval Enlisted Personnel and Civilians*, University of California Press, Berkeley and Los Angeles, 1948; ———, Annemarie Jacobsen, and Martin B. Loeb, "Acculturation and Illness," *Psychological Monographs: General and Applied*, Vol. 62, No. 5, Whole No. 292, 1948 (American Psychological Association, Washington, D. C.); C. Tietze, Paul Lemkau, and M. Cooper, "A Survey of Statistical Studies on the Prevalence and Incidence of Mental Disorders in Sample Populations," *Public Health Reports*, 1909–1927, Vol. 58 (December 1943); ———, "Schizophrenia, Manic Depressive Psychosis, and Socio-Economic Status," *American Journal of Sociology*, Vol. XLVII (September 1941), pp. 167–175; J. W. Eaton and R. J. Weil, "Culture and Mental Disorders: a comparative study of the Hutterites and other populations," The Free Press, Glencoe, Illinois, 1955.

⁹ For example, see A. J. Rosanoff, *Report of a Survey of Mental Disorders in Nassau County, New York*, National Committee for Mental Hygiene, New York, 1916; Ludwig Stern, *Kulturkreis und Form der Geistigen Erkankung* (Sammlung Zwangloser Abhandlungen aus dem Gebiete der Nerven-und-Geisteskrankheiten), Vol. X. No. 2 Halle a. S:C. Marhold, 1913, pp. 1–63; J. F. Sutherland, "Geographical Distribution of Lunacy in Scotland," *British Association for Advancement of Science*, Glasgow, September 1901; William A. White, "Geographical Distribution of Insanity in the United States," *Journal of Nervous and Mental Disease*, Vol. XXX (1903), pp. 257–279.

¹⁰ Robert E. L. Faris and H. Warren Dunham, *Mental Disorders in Urban Areas*, The University of Chicago Press, Chicago, 1939; H. Warren Dunham, "Current Status of Ecological Research in Mental Disorder," *Social Forces*, Vol.

25 (March 1947), pp. 321–326; H. W. Green, *Persons Admitted to the Cleveland State Hospital, 1928–37*, Cleveland Health Council, 1939.

11 R. E. L. Faris, "Cultural Isolation and the Schizophrenic Personality," *American Journal of Sociology*, Vol. XXXIV (September 1934), pp. 155–169; ———, "Reflections of Social Disorganization in the Behavior of a Schizophrenic Patient," *American Journal of Sociology*, Vol. L (September 1944), pp. 134–141.

12 Charles Page, *Class and American Sociology*, Columbia University Press, New York, 1940; Robert L. Heilbronner, *The Worldly Philosophers*, Simon and Schuster, New York, 1953.

13 For a comprehensive statement of this position see R. H. Felix and R. V. Bowers, "Mental Hygiene and Socio-Environmental Factors," *The Milbank Memorial Fund Quarterly*, Vol. XXVI (April 1948), pp. 125–147; Thomas A. C. Rennie, Leo Srole, Marvin K. Opler, and Thomas Langner, "Urban Life and Mental Health," *The American Journal of Psychiatry*, Vol. 113 (March 1957), pp. 831–836; John E. Gordon, Edward O'Rourke, F. L. W. Richardson, and Erich Lindemann, "The Biological and Social Sciences in an Epidemiology of Mental Disorders," *American Journal of the Medical Sciences*, Vol. 223 (March 1952), pp. 316–343; this paper is particularly valuable for the bibliographical references it contains in this field.

14 Sigmund Freud, *A General Introduction to Psycho-Analysis*, Liveright Publishing Corporation, New York, 1920, pp. 308–309; see also *Vorlesung zur Einführung in die Psychoanalyse*, Gesammelte Schriften Vol. VII, Verlag, Leipzig, 1942, pp. 365–366.

15 For example, see Bronislaw Malinowski's criticism in *Sex and Repression in Savage Society* of Freud's ideas in *Totem and Taboo* that society and culture are epiphenomena of man's instinctual needs.

16 Erik H. Erikson, "The Problem of Ego Identity," *Journal of the American Psychoanalytic Association*, Vol. 4 (1956), pp. 56–119.

17 L. S. Kubie in Alexander Leighton, John Clausen, and Robert Wilson (editors), *Explorations in Social Psychiatry*, Basic Books, Inc., 1957.

18 August B. Hollingshead, "Social Behavior and Social Rules," in Iago Galdston (Editor), *Ministry and Medicine in Human Relations*, International Universities Press, New York, 1955, pp. 71–80.

19 John Romano, *Epidemiology of Mental Disorders*, Milbank Memorial Fund, New York, 1950, p. 60.

20 The following papers have been published on selected segments of the research: August B. Hollingshead, "Trends in Social Stratification: A Case Study," *American Sociological Review*, Vol. 17 (December 1952), pp. 679–686; Fredrick C. Redlich, "The Concept of Normality," *American Journal of Psychotherapy*, Vol. 6 (1952), pp. 551–576; H. A. Robinson, F. C. Redlich, and A. B. Hollingshead, "An Investigation of Social Structure and Psychiatric Disorder," *The Psychologist*, Vol. 7 (1952), p. 348; August B. Hollingshead and Fredrick C. Redlich, "Social Class and Psychiatric Disorders," *Interrelations Between the Social Environment and Psychiatric Disorders*, Milbank Memorial Fund, New York, 1953, pp. 195–208; Fredrick C. Redlich, August B. Hollingshead, B. H. Roberts, H. A. Robinson, L. Z. Freedman, and J. K. Myers, "Social Structure

and Psychiatric Disorders," *American Journal of Psychiatry*, Vol. 109 (April 1953), pp. 729–734; August B. Hollingshead and Fredrick C. Redlich, "Social Stratification and Psychiatric Disorders," *American Sociological Review*, Vol. 18 (April 1953), pp. 163–169; Frank Auld, Jr. and J. K. Myers, "Contributions to a Theory for Selecting Psychotherapy Patients," *Journal of Clinical Psychology*, Vol. X (January 1954), pp. 56–60; L. Schaffer and J. K. Myers, "Psychotherapy and Social Stratification: An Empirical Study of Practice in a Psychiatric Outpatient Clinic," *Psychiatry*, Vol. 17 (February 1954), pp. 83–93; August B. Hollingshead and Fredrick C. Redlich, "Schizophrenia and Social Structure," *American Journal of Psychiatry*, Vol. 110 (March 1954), pp. 695–701; B. H. Roberts and J. K. Myers, "Religion, National Origin, Immigration, and Mental Illness," *The American Journal of Psychiatry*, Vol. 110 (April 1954), pp. 759–764; H. A. Robinson, F. C. Redlich, and J. K. Myers, "Social Structure and Psychiatric Treatment," *American Journal of Orthopsychiatry*, Vol. XXIV (April 1954), pp. 307–316; J. K. Myers, "Note on the Homogeneity of Census Tracts: A Methodological Problem in Urban Ecological Research," *Social Forces*, Vol. 132 (May 1954), pp. 364–366; ——— and L. Schaffer, "Social Stratification and Psychiatric Practice: A Study of an Outpatient Clinic," *American Sociological Review*, Vol. 19 (June 1954), pp. 307–310; August B. Hollingshead and Fredrick C. Redlich, "Social Stratification and Schizophrenia," *American Sociological Review*, Vol. 19 (June 1954), pp. 302–306; Fredrick C. Redlich, "The Influence of Environment on Mental Health," *Bulletin of the New York Academy of Medicine*, Vol. 30 (August 1954), pp. 608–621; J. K. Myers and B. H. Roberts, "A Sociological-Psychiatric Case Study of Schizophrenia," *Sociology and Social Research*, Vol. 39 (September–October 1954), pp. 11–17; August B. Hollingshead, R. Ellis, and E. Kirby, "Social Mobility and Mental Illness," *American Sociological Review*, Vol. 19 (October 1954), pp. 557–584; J. K. Myers and F. Auld, Jr., "Some Variables Related to Outcome of Psychotherapy," *Journal of Clinical Psychology*, Vol. XI (January 1955), pp. 51–54; F. C. Redlich, A. B. Hollingshead, and E. Bellis, "Social Class Differences in Attitudes toward Psychiatry," *American Journal of Orthopsychiatry*, Vol. XXV (January 1955), pp. 60–70; B. H. Roberts and J. K. Myers, "Schizophrenia in the Youngest Male Child of the Lower Middle Class," *American Journal of Psychiatry*, Vol. 112 (September 1955), pp. 179–185; August B. Hollingshead and Lawrence Z. Freedman, "Social Class and the Treatment of Neurotics," in *The Social Welfare Forum*, Columbia University Press, New York, 1955, pp. 194–205; J. K. Myers, "An Empirical Approach to the Study of Schizophrenia," *Psychiatric Research Report 5*, American Psychiatric Association (June 1956), pp. 29–48; Lawrence Z. Freedman and August B. Hollingshead, "Neurosis and Social Class I: Social Interaction," *American Journal of Psychiatry*, Vol. 113 (March 1957), pp. 769–775; August B. Hollingshead and Fredrick C. Redlich, "Social Mobility and Mental Illness," *American Journal of Psychiatry*, Vol. 112 (September 1955), pp. 179–185.

methodological
procedures

INTRODUCTION

The principal methodological operations pertinent to the development of the research from its original conception to the drafting of this report are described in this chapter. Briefly, they are: (1) the enumeration of individuals receiving psychiatric care; (2) a sample census of the general population; (3) the placement of the patient and the control populations in the class structure of the community; (4) accumulation of detailed information about the practice of psychiatry; and (5) clinical study of the 50 patients and their families included in the Control Case Study reported in the companion volume by Jerome K. Myers and Bertram H. Roberts, *Social Class, Family Dynamics, and Mental Illness,* John Wiley and Sons, New York. Each of these operations will be described in some detail in succeeding sections of this chapter.

THE PSYCHIATRIC CENSUS

Detailed information derived from clinical psychiatric records was the first requisite for testing the first three hypotheses. Therefore, the enumeration of patients in psychiatric treatment received the highest priority in our plans. The principal steps in the development of the Psychiatric Census are outlined here.

Definitions

Any person in treatment with a psychiatrist or under the care of a psychiatric clinic or mental hospital between May 31 and December 1, 1950, who was a resident of New Haven, West Haven, East Haven, North Haven, Hamden, or Woodbridge, Connecticut, when he entered treatment is defined for our purposes as a "patient." These towns encompass the urbanized community of New Haven. Individuals in hospitals primarily for mental defectives are considered patients only if they are diagnosed as psychotic.

A "psychiatrist" is a person who holds a Doctor of Medicine degree and has completed or is undergoing training in a psychiatric hospital or clinic, in accordance with the criteria of the medical profession.

"Psychiatric agencies" are hospitals or clinics under the supervision of psychiatrists that care for and treat patients with mental and emotional disorders. Such psychiatric agencies are supported by public funds and private resources.

In so rigidly defining a case, we have not counted a significant percentage of mentally ill persons who are in a therapeutic relationship with physicians other than psychiatrists, psychologists, psychiatric social workers, and other accredited persons and agencies. We did not contact clerical counselors or faith healers. Although such "patients" pose an important question for investigation, we do not consider it feasible or desirable to include them in this study. The same principle is followed in the determination of which patients are counted from general hospitals. If a person is treated by a psychiatrist he is counted; if by a physician who is not a psychiatrist, he is not considered to be a psychiatric patient.

The requirement of residence in the community eliminated students whose homes were elsewhere but were under psychiatric treatment in the community. It also excluded psychiatric patients who came to the New Haven area for treatment from other communities. Transients who had been apprehended by the police, referred to a psychiatric agency, and committed to the state hospital from the community but whose residence could be established in other places are not counted. However, transients whose homes could not be allocated to another place are counted. This is not a serious problem as only public agencies are involved in such cases, and every effort is made, usually by an agency concerned, to establish the legal residence of a patient so that town can be charged for the patient's care.

Case-Finding

The problem of locating persons to be enumerated revolved around three questions: first, which residents of the community are being treated by psychiatrists; second, where they are being treated; and third, whether or not private practitioners, clinics, and hospitals responsible for the treatment of these individuals would give us access to their clinical records. Although the research design did not call for direct interviews with the patients, we needed detailed personal and clinical data on each one. The sole avenue of access to the required data was through the psychiatrist, clinic, or hospital responsible for the patient's care. The cooperation of private practitioners and psychiatrists in charge of clinic or hospital patients was essential to the realization of the objectives of the study. If psychiatrists refused to furnish data about their patients, the project would fail, because they were the only persons who knew whom they were treating. If the psychiatrists were willing to cooperate, the project could move forward. Therefore, the problem was to elicit the support of psychiatrists and psychiatric institutions treating patients from the community on the date set for the census.

The practice of well-to-do individuals to leave the community for psychiatric help posed a problem. We had to locate the out-of-town patient and obtain the necessary data about him from the psychiatrist who was treating him. Persons who leave their home communities for psychiatric treatment usually go to private practitioners or private hospitals. Those under the care of a private practitioner generally commute between their homes and the doctor's office. Those who are hospitalized in distant places normally seek well-known treatment centers and go there for therapy. Although the rule of private care applies to most patients who leave home for treatment, it is not taken for granted. We believe that some mentally ill individuals leave home as a symptom of their illness, and they may be found later and brought into psychiatric treatment in a public agency. Thus, we had to weave our case-finding net as finely but as extensively as possible.

The first step in the solution of the case-finding problem was a compilation of lists of private practitioners and psychiatric agencies where residents of the community might receive treatment. Four separate lists were compiled: (1) public hospitals—state and veteran; (2) clinics; (3) private hospitals; and (4) private practitioners. We thought patients in public hospitals would be concentrated in one of the three state hospitals, but we knew some veterans were cared for in veterans hospitals in other New England states and in New York. We thought some patients might be found in state hospitals elsewhere, so state hospitals in New England, New York, and New Jersey were placed on the state hospital list. The clinic list covered all clinics in Connecticut and a few children's clinics in New York City. The clinics were divided into three categories: general clinics, children's clinics, and clinics for alcoholics. The private hospital list included all licensed institutions in Connecticut, Massachusetts, Rhode Island, Vermont, New Hampshire, New York, and New Jersey. In addition, well-known treatment centers from Canada to Florida and as far west as Kansas where individuals from the community might be in treatment were listed. All psychiatrists in private practice in Connecticut and the New York City area were placed on the private practitioner list.

The next step was the preparation of a letter that carefully explained the objectives of the Psychiatric Census. Each letter was typed individually on official stationery and mailed, to every private practitioner and psychiatrist in charge of a clinic or hospital on our lists as a personal communication from F. C. Redlich, M.D., Chairman, Department of Psychiatry, School of Medicine, Yale University. A second letter from Redlich was mailed to each psychiatrist and institution on our lists the last week in November, 1950, stating that we would need to know the number of patients in treatment from New Haven, East Haven, West Haven, North Haven, Hamden, and Woodbridge, Connecticut, between May 31, 1950 and December 1, 1950. Enclosed with this letter were a stamped, self-addressed envelope, a three-by-five card with the doctor's name and address on it, and this printed statement: "I have —— (0, 1, 2, 3, etc.) patients who have permanent residence in New Haven and its suburbs under treatment." The recipient was asked to note the number of patients he had in treatment from the community on the dates mentioned and to return the card as soon after the census date as possible.

We realized that the personal factor was extremely important in what we planned to do, and its success or failure hinged on the willingness of psychiatrists to cooperate with us. Therefore, Redlich, through the summer and fall of 1950, explained the project in personal conversations, professional discussions, meetings, and private letters to psychiatrists in the area. He visited the superintendents of the state hospitals and several veterans and private hospitals in the region. In addition, he called a number of medical directors of clinics and hospitals on the telephone to explain our plans and objectives. Thus, many key professional people had more information about the project than the letters contained.

Copies of the first explanatory letter and the second census-request letter were mailed to 1287 private practitioners and hospital and clinic psychiatrists on our lists of potential treatment agencies for individuals from the community. All public and private hospitals responded to the second letter. Responses were received from all but two clinics. In these instances, Redlich talked to the psychiatrists in charge; these clinics then sent in their reports. Every private practitioner in Connecticut, except for two, responded to our request, but Redlich had to telephone several before the reports were mailed.

Private practitioners in New York City proved to be a special problem. We sent 896 explanatory letters and requests for a patient count to private practitioners in metropolitan New York of which 747 responded affirmatively to the request for the number of patients in treatment from the community by December 15, 1950. The 149 nonrespondents were sent a third letter and an appeal to *please* report whether they had any patients from the New Haven area. This appeal also included a three-by-five printed card and a stamped, self-addressed envelope and elicited 129 additional responses. Telephone calls were made later to the 20 practitioners who had failed to respond to both the invitation to report and the appeal to *please* report any patients they were treating from our community. These telephone calls enabled us to determine whether the nonrespondents had no patients from the area or were not interested in cooperating with us.

Preliminary analysis of the post card reports on how many patients were in treatment in given institutions and with private practitioners indicated that patients from the community were being treated primarily in Connecticut. Six private hospitals outside the state reported one or more patients from the community. Patients in public institutions were entirely in Connecticut except for veterans who were being cared for in Massachusetts and in New York.

Every private practitioner and psychiatric agency who reported one or more patients from the area was sent a third letter stating that simple enumeration was only a preliminary part of the Psychiatric Census. This letter carefully explained that the purpose of the count was simply to locate patients who were being treated. It also pointed out that each treatment agency reporting patients from our area would be visited by members of the research team for personal interviews. During the interview, a census schedule would be filled out on each patient. The principal points on the schedule were mentioned, and the psychiatrist was asked to indicate on the accompanying card his willingness to be interviewed by a psychiatrist on the research team. This letter was also on official stationery, but it was signed by both Hollingshead and Redlich.

All private and public hospitals, all clinics, and all private practitioners except two in Connecticut indicated their willingness to cooperate with us. One Connecticut practitioner who refused to make the necessary data available had reported one patient from the community. Nineteen private practitioners in New York City, who reported that they were treating 30 patients from our area, declined to participate in the census interview. When we attempted to elicit from them their reasons for non-cooperation, ten simply refused to offer any explanation, and three reported that they were going to be out of the country and could not see the interviewer. One physician wrote, "I cannot lay my hands on the records." Another stated, "I have over 2000 patients and I am too busy to search for the charts from New Haven." One's verbalized reason for refusal was, "The project is financed by the government." The remainder wrote letters explaining that their New Haven patients came to New York City to avoid exposure to their associates in New Haven and that to furnish us with the necessary data would be a violation of confidence as their patients could be identified easily.

TABLE 1

Type of Treatment Agencies Who Reported Patients on December 1, 1950, and Were Willing or Unwilling to Furnish Data for the Psychiatric Census

Type of Treatment Agency	Number Who	
	Cooperated	Refused
State hospitals	6	0
Veterans hospitals	5	0
Private hospitals *	11	0
Clinics	7	0
Private practitioners *	46	20
Total	75	20

* One private hospital and four private practitioners were willing to cooperate, but when they were interviewed, we found that they had no patients from the community.

Although the case-finding net was large and tight, we probably missed some residents of the community who were receiving treatment in hospitals or from private practitioners not on the lists we compiled. Also some practitioners who cooperated may have "forgotten" some cases when they were interviewed by the team psychiatrists. We know we lost at least 31 cases through the refusal of practitioners to make clinical data available. We estimate that from 10 to 20 additional cases may have been missed by the case-finding procedures used or the refusal of practitioners to report cases easily recognized by the research team. The total of patients in treatment who were not enumerated for one reason or another ranged, we believe, from 40 to 50. They were probably largely ambulatory cases who sought privacy by leaving the community or enjoining their physicians to silence, and their wishes were respected.

The Patient Schedule

The schedule developed to record the data on patients enumerated in the Psychiatric Census is a compromise between what we desired and what we could obtain from clinical records and interviews with psychiatrists. A number of field trials were made with preliminary schedules in clinics, veterans and state hospitals, private hospitals, and with selected practitioners. The pilot schedules contained more questions than we were able to use in the final schedule (see Appendix 1, pp. 384–386) because of the limitations of clinical records. Gradually the preliminary schedules were modified to the point at which we were convinced we could obtain answers for most of the questions asked from the clinical records and the practitioners. It did not appear prudent to ask questions that could not be answered from the sources available to us.

The final schedule was divided into two parts: sociological and psychiatric. The sociological part focused on the patient's social and family history. The relevant identifying information included the patient's name, address, race, sex, age, occupation, education, place of birth and rearing, his sibling relationships, and a synopsis of his family's history, as well as the national origin, occupation, and marital status of his parents. In the family history we looked for evidence of emotional stability, social mobility or aspirations for social mobility, and evidence of status conflict or little interest in status. We attempted to evaluate success or failure of economic life through learning whether the patient drifted from job to job or was a steady worker. Wherever possible, we elicited evidence of success or failure in education. Any evidences of what is commonly considered to be antisocial behavior, such as alcoholism, sexual promiscuity, or excessive gambling, were included.

The psychiatric portion of the schedule listed the type of referral, whether the patient paid full or partial rates for his care or was treated without any expense to himself, when the patient first saw a psychiatrist, the date when the current treatment was instituted, the number of past psychiatric hospitalizations, when the patient was hospitalized for his current illness, and other relevant material indicating the extensity and intensity of the therapeutic history.

A check list was prepared for information on the type of treatment the patient was undergoing. We allowed for all commonly used procedures and provided space for the addition of any other methods. Because of the ambiguity pervading contemporary thinking in regard to psychotherapy, we found it necessary to establish fairly arbitrary criteria for categorization in this area. *Psychoanalysis* is defined for purposes of this book as the classical Freudian method of treatment practiced by a member of a psychoanalytic society or student of an institute of psychoanalysis recognized by the American Psychoanalytic Association. In this community only *classical* analysis is practiced. There are no adherents of Jung, Horney, Sullivan, etc. The goals of this therapy are maximal realignment of personality forces through analysis of symptoms, conflicts, instincts, defenses, transference, and resistance. Under *analytic psychotherapy*, we subsumed therapy short of classical psychoanalysis, but which included basic psychoanalytic procedures involving the fundamental concepts with less emphasis on pure analytic procedure. From a practical standpoint, we found patients in psychoanalysis were seen at least four times a week; patients in analytic psychotherapy less frequently. We used the term *directive therapies* to include supportive, directive, and suggestive therapy or any combination of these methods. In evaluating hospital treatment, we specified that treatment must be specifically for mental illness, and not to serve some function useful to a person other than the patient. So-called *industrial therapy* which involves working in an institutional setting is considered to serve some function useful to a person or organization other than a patient. Under *organic treatments*, we provided for the most commonly used techniques, such as the various shock treatments, lobotomies, and drug therapies. (It should be noted that the field work was done before the pharmaceutical market was flooded with tranquilizing drugs.) Hospitalized cases where no therapy is administered is categorized as *custodial care*. Cases seen for evaluation, for legal or compensation procedures, or for purely diagnostic purposes are not considered to be in treatment but registered as patients without treatment. The various types of treatment defined here will be described in Chapter Nine where the treatment process is analyzed in detail.

The frequency and duration of the therapeutic sessions were recorded along with the diagnostic impression of the psychiatrist treating the patient. Finally, a brief synopsis of the patient's psychiatric history was compiled by the psychiatrist who gathered the psychiatric data on the case.

Data Collection

The data for each schedule were abstracted from the patient's clinical record by a sociologist and a psychiatrist. A sociologist abstracted the data from the record on social background and family history; a psychiatrist searched the record for the pertinent materials on the patient's psychiatric history, diagnosis, mental status, and treatment. This procedure was modified, however, for the private practitioner's patients. The schedules on the patients of private practitioners were completed entirely by the team psychiatrists who were thoroughly familiar with the procedures of the sociologists.

Abstractor's Reliability

The data recorded on the schedules of the Psychiatric Census came from two sources: (1) direct interviews with psychiatrists treating patients on a private basis and (2) the records of patients who were under the care of institutions. In the first instance, our information was one step removed from the patient; in the second, not only the psychiatrist but also the record stood as intervening factors. Under these circumstances, the reliability of the records used and the reliability of the abstractors should be considered in the evaluation of the data collected. We faced these questions with the realization that we could not, of course, test the reliability of the hospital psychiatrists. Therefore, the data presented in later chapters must be construed as representing the information as it is recorded in the patient's charts. We could test, however, the reliability of the abstraction of these data from the charts. Since one state hospital furnished 50 percent of the patients in the Census, we selected it as the most appropriate place to study the reliability of the sociologists and psychiatrists doing the abstracting of patient data for the Psychiatric Census schedules. To do this, we randomly selected 100 patient records from the hospital's files. We then duplicated the abstracting and recording procedures for each patient with a different team of sociologists and psychiatrists doing the work.

A series of comparisons were made, item by item, of agreements and disagreements between the first and second pairs of sociological and psychiatric abstractors to test the reliability of the abstracting process. Agreements on specific questions between the original and reliability schedules for the 100 patients ranged from a low of 76 percent to a high of 100 percent. Agreement was below 80 percent on only two questions: the number of siblings in the patient's family and the principal psychiatric treatment the patient was receiving currently. The range of agreement on the sociological questions varied from 76 to 100 percent; on the psychiatric questions the range was from 79 to 96 percent. The mean agreement on the sociological items was 90.1 percent; for the psychiatric ones it was 87.1 percent.

Two factors pertinent to the degree of reliability were: first, the subjective judgments required of the readers in obtaining specific data, and second, the ease with which such data were ascertainable in the patient's chart. As would be expected, the greater the evaluative requirement on the abstractor, to the degree that acquisition of the data was not simply a mechanical transmission of items like sex or age, the greater the variation among abstractors. Facts which were regularly, clearly, and unambiguously recorded on uniform charts showed the highest reliability; those in which the recording was irregular or scattered throughout the chart showed the greater disagreement. The psychiatric item, that is, principal form of therapy, which fell below 80 percent agreement illustrates these difficulties. The principal form of treatment had to be abstracted, in many instances, from several kinds of therapies including, for example, group therapy, industrial therapy, and shock therapy. In some cases this was relatively simple, as for a patient who had just been lobotomized a short time before the Psychiatric Census after sitting in a back ward for years. In many cases, however, determination of the principal form of treatment was considerably more difficult. Furthermore, in other cases it was not recorded or was recorded in an indifferent manner.

Although the mean percentage of agreement between the two sets of abstractors varied from 88 to 90 percent, we consider this a satisfactory measure of reliability in view of the kinds of records available in the hospital. These records have been accumulated through the years by a number of different hospital workers with varying social and psychiatric orientations. Then too, there were conflicting statements in particular records. Often, there were duplications; in other instances, what might have been of importance to us was omitted. The researchers were faced with confusion and unreliability in the clinical records. They often faced alternative choices of information to be registered from a confused, discursive, and contradictory record. They attempted to ferret out what appeared to be the most recent, complete, and coherent statement pertinent to the question at hand.

This situation raises questions of the reliability of the clinical records available to us. We accepted them as our one readily available source of information, but it was clear that their validity and reliability for research studies left much to be desired. Thus, the unreliability of the clinical records themselves should be considered in an evaluation of the percentage of agreement and disagreement among abstractors, as well as evaluating material presented in our findings. The net result is the amount of disagreement reported here.

Diagnostic Questions

The Veterans Administration's diagnostic classification was adopted because, at the time of the field work, it was the best classification available and presents contemporary concepts of psychiatric thinking. It also establishes reasonably discrete categories. Furthermore, the equivalents with the standard diagnostic categories adopted by the American Medical Association are clearly presented so that we were provided with a method of integrating contemporary nosological thinking with more standardized diagnostic procedures in use by the majority of institutions and psychiatrists. Finally, it provided us with a reasonably accurate method of integrating the diagnostic categories of analytically oriented clinics and psychiatrists into our study. Although, in the interest of greater efficiency, the psychiatrists on the team selected the Veterans Administration system of nomenclature and the categories and subcategories subsumed within it, where the number of patients was too small for statistical analysis they combined categories into broader groups.

We were concerned with the validity of the diagnoses made by the psychiatrists treating the patients. We were originally of the opinion that the diagnostic label placed upon a patient would vary from practitioner to practitioner. Also, we thought the diagnosis of a patient's illness, in one phase of his history, might not be applicable in a different phase. Therefore, the diagnoses placed upon the patients in the several treatment agencies needed to be scrutinized carefully.

After the Census was completed, the team psychiatrists studied the symptomatology and psychiatric history of each patient and evaluated the diagnosis of the patient which the physician in charge of the case had made. In those cases where the diagnosis of the team psychiatrists differed from that of the psychiatrist in charge of the case, the patient's disorder was rediagnosed in terms of the criteria established by the Veterans Administration schema. However, before a case was rediagnosed, it was read independently by two psychiatrists and the clinical psychologist on the team. It was then discussed and evaluated in terms of the adopted schema as to how it should be diagnosed. Far fewer cases needed to be rediagnosed than had been anticipated originally. Seventeen percent of the cases gathered from private practitioners were rediagnosed, whereas less than 6 percent of the cases gathered from clinics and hospitals were rediagnosed.

Questions on the validity of the diagnosis placed on the case by the treatment agency were concentrated among the psychoneuroses and the schizophrenias. Problems of diagnosis in the psychoneuroses revolved around which specific category of the 28 categories available in the adopted classification scheme was most appropriate for the case. Each case was assigned to a particular diagnostic category, but the psychiatrists were acutely aware of the difficulties entailed in distinguishing between categories.

The striking variations in the subcategories of diagnoses placed upon schizophrenic patients in the different hospitals, especially the state institutions, constituted the largest single diagnostic question we faced. Originally, the schizophrenic patient's disorders were diagnosed as belonging in one of eight nosological categories; the precise diagnosis was recorded on the schedule and punched on the Hollerith cards. The particular diagnostic label placed on a schizophrenic patient appeared to be a product of the normative conceptions of the staff rather than the actual differences in the psychopathology of the patients. We dealt with this problem by compressing all schizophrenic subcategories into one group. However, this step was not taken until we had begun the analysis of the data. The minor differences between subcategories did not appear to be meaningful for analytic purposes so they were ignored in the statistical phases of the research.

THE FIVE PERCENT SAMPLE

Detailed vital and social data had to be gathered on the general population of the community in order to make direct comparisons between the patients and the nonpatients by class position. Although data on age, sex, and race of all individuals in each of the towns were available from the United States Census for 1950, we could not use this resource because census data do not enable a researcher to stratify individuals by the criteria we believed were essential to our study. Therefore, we had to take a sample census of the general population. By collecting pertinent vital and social data on a representative sample of individuals drawn from the general population, we were able to make direct comparisons between the *patient* and the *general population* to determine if the distribution of treated psychiatric disorders is associated with class status.

The Population Sample

Data on the general population are based upon a systematic sample of all individuals resident in 5 percent of the households in the area covered by the Psychiatric Census. Households were selected for the sampling unit because they are the primary dwelling units for practically all residents of the community. Sojourners in hotels, general hospitals, jails, college residence halls, and similar special-purpose residential units were not counted in the Psychiatric Census unless they were bona fide residents of the community and in psychiatric treatment.

The size of the sample was determined by two criteria: (1) the total estimated number of households in the community and (2) the proportion of all households estimated to be in the numerically smallest strata of the population. The total number of households in the community in November, 1950, was calculated from data accumulated by the United States Census Bureau in April, 1950, supplemented with data furnished by the Security Connecticut Insurance Company from its monthly survey of physical structures in the area and by the planning division of the Southern New England Telephone Company. These companies keep up-to-date records on new building in the several towns in the area.

Previous studies indicated that the smallest proportion of the community's households would be found in the highest ranking stratum of the class status structure, or in our terms, class I. We estimated that class I households would comprise some 3 percent of the community's total of approximately 72,000 households, or 2160 dwelling units, but these households would neither be randomly distributed in the several towns of the community nor would they be concentrated in one or two of them. Preliminary knowledge indicated the need for the sample to be a large one so that the range of probable variations in the sizes and types of class I households would be represented by enough instances to ensure reliability in estimates derived from it. We estimated that 100 class I households would be the smallest number that would meet both requirements. A 5 percent sample would yield 108 class I households from the estimated total of 72,000 households; a 4 percent sample would yield 86 class I households; and a 6 percent sample, 130 class I households. A 5 percent sample was the smallest one that would meet our theoretical requirements. To have increased the size of the class I sample would have added to the precision of the estimates of the rates discussed in Chapters Seven and Eight, but it would have increased the cost of the survey disproportionately.

The Sampling Frame

The sampling frame was constructed from the *City Directory* for 1951, supplemented by lists of dwellings constructed in 1950 and electric, water, and telephone services installed by the local utilities companies. These supplementary lists were checked against one another and the *City Directory* to avoid duplication. The *City Directory* was very complete in its listing of new dwellings up to October 1, 1950. New dwellings occupied during October and November were added to the *City Directory* list for sampling purposes. The adequacy of the *City Directory's* coverage of dwellings in the deteriorated areas of the community was tested by 100 spot checks in blocks selected at random. This pilot study indicated that the *City Directory* was in error in from 7 to 10 percent of the time as to who lived in a particular dwelling, but it was in error in only 3 to 4 percent of the cases as to the location of the dwellings.

The *City Directory* makes two listings for each household in the towns covered by our study: the name of the household head and the address of the household by streets. Pilot studies of the adequacy of the *City Directory's* listing of names and addresses showed that the directory was 99 percent accurate on addresses except in deteriorated areas of the several towns and on newly developed lots and subdivisions. Therefore, we decided to draw our sample from the address section of the *City Directory*, supplemented by new dwellings in each town occupied in the last quarter of 1950 and by households randomly selected from blocks in deteriorated areas.

Every twentieth address in the *City Directory* and on the supplementary lists was marked for interview. The first address selected from the *City Directory* and the supplementary lists was determined by numbering twenty small cardboard squares from one to twenty, shuffling them thoroughly, and drawing one number. The first number drawn was nine. We counted down to the ninth address listed on the first page of the address section of the *City Directory* and marked it for the sample. Thereafter each twentieth address was checked for inclusion in the sample. This procedure provided us with a systematic sample of 3383 addresses of households. We supplemented this listing with 225 households living in the poorest areas. This was done to compensate for the known underlisting of addresses by the *City Directory* in these areas.

The Interview Program

Members of households living at the addresses drawn in the sample were interviewed by a representative of the research team during May, June, July, and August, 1951. However, the interval between compilation of the address lists and the completion of the last interviews created problems. Among them were removal of a family from an address, births, deaths, and departures from a household of one or more members.

The problem of removals was handled by substituting the household unit dwelling in the particular address at the time the interviewer reached it for the household in the original sample. The substitution of the household living in a given unit at the date of interview for one living there when the sample was drawn was based upon the assumption that persons living in the household at the time of the interview would not differ essentially in their social characteristics from those living in the unit at the time the address list was compiled. The age and sex composition might be different, but we did not control for this factor. Births, deaths, and departures from a home were also beyond the control of the sampling process. In sum, we sampled a population of dwelling units, that is, whoever was living in the sampled address when the interviewer reached it.

The interviewers of persons in the sample were all college graduates. They were, in the main, graduate students in the social sciences at Yale, but a considerable proportion were school teachers, some were wives of graduate students, and some were students in the Divinity School at Yale University. The interviewers were trained by Hollingshead and Myers. They were supervised directly by Myers. Every sixteenth interview was spot-checked by Hollingshead and a professional woman who had extensive experience supervising field studies for the Bureau of the Census.

The interview program was prolonged beyond original expectancy by the ethnic composition of the population. In some sections of the city of New Haven, households were drawn in the sample where no member could speak or understand English well enough to complete the interview. Individuals had to be found who could speak Italian, Russian, Ukranian, Hungarian, Greek, Polish, Finnish, and dialects of these languages. They then had to be trained as interviewers or, in the case of small ethnic groups, such as Finnish and Greek, taken to the home by an interviewer and the questions on the schedule translated to the respondent. This was a time-consuming task, but one that had to be done well if non-English-speaking persons were to be represented in the sample population.

One hundred and fourteen households drawn in the original sample refused to be interviewed. In addition, 62 substitute households refused to be interviewed in place of the family who had lived at a given address at the time the list was made. Substitutions were made for these 176 refusals by selecting an address at random from the same block, apartment, or tenement house. The interviewer then made a clean approach to the new address, and usually the respondent was willing to be interviewed. In the whole program, slightly less than 5 percent of the households drawn refused to cooperate, and substitutions were made. Finally some 32 dwelling units had been demolished, and 17 could not be located. Thus, of the 3608 household units drawn in the sample, 3559 interviews were completed. The sources of the data on these households are summarized as:

Sources of Data	Number
Husband and wife	158
Wife	2,515
Husband	466
Mother or adult daughter of the "head"	154
Father or adult son of the "head"	64
Male head (single)	45
Female head (single)	124
Unknown	33
Total	3,559

The Interview Schedule

The interview schedule was designed to provide vital and social data on every resident in the sample households. Age, sex, race, occupation, education, marital status, religion, and relationship to the head of every individual were asked and recorded on the schedule sheets. Additional data collected on the household included family income, whether the dwelling was owned or rented, magazines and newspapers entering the household regularly, and other items not related to direct comparisons between the patient and general populations, but of interest in understanding the stratification of the community.

Is the Sample Representative?

The representativeness of the sample was tested by comparing the sex, age, and ecological distributions yielded by the sample with the total counts reported by the 1950 Census for the towns encompassed by the New Haven community. However, before these comparisons could be made, the figures reported by the United States Census Bureau required certain adjustments. The 1950 Census enumerated college students in the population of the town where they were attending college rather than in the population of their home towns. Because their mental hygiene problems were cared for by student health departments, college students were not drawn in the sample or enumerated in the Psychiatric Census, unless they were residents of the community.

Corrections for the presence of students in the Census figures were made in this manner: First, maps of the 1950 Enumeration Districts of all the towns in the area were purchased from the Bureau of the Census. Second, special runs of the population enumerated in each district by age and sex were prepared by the Bureau of the Census. Third, each college furnished the names, ages, sex, and college and home addresses of all students enrolled in 1949–1950. Fourth, the number of students residing in each Enumeration District in 1949–1950 was subtracted from the total number of males or females in the appropriate age groups reported for the district in the special tabulations purchased from the Bureau of the Census. We calculated that 10,050 students whose homes were in other communities had been counted by the United States Census of 1950 as New Haven residents. Some 8500 were males and 1550 were females. Of these, 8031 lived in Yale University's residential colleges, dormitories, and apartments. The remaining students were concentrated in dormitories and rooming houses adjacent to other local colleges. The students enrolled in Yale University were concentrated in special Enumeration Districts around the center of the university, so that no problem was involved in separating them from the remainder of the population. The women in Albertus Magnus and Larson Colleges were equally easy to locate. The students of New Haven State Teachers College were the only ones where difficulty was encountered in the corrections.

After the age and sex corrections had been made for the students, direct comparisons by sex and age were made between Census figures and the population estimates derived from the sample. The percentage distributions by age and sex for the two counts are presented in Table 2.

TABLE 2

Percentages of the Population of the New Haven Community by Sex and Age According to the 1950 Census and the 5-percent Sample

Age Group	Males		Females	
	Census *	Projection †	Census *	Projection †
Under 15	24.7	27.5	22.3	24.7
15–24	11.9	11.3	12.7	11.8
25–44	31.6	30.8	32.8	32.2
45–64	23.3	22.3	22.8	22.7
65 and over	8.6	8.0	9.4	8.5
Total (N)	115,260	115,760	123,413	124,580

* Corrected figures based upon special tabulations by Enumeration Districts furnished by the United States Bureau of the Census.

† These figures are projections from the number of persons in the sample by sex and age. Every person in the households interviewed was multiplied by 20 to attain the estimated figure.

A comparison of the two sets of figures shows that the sample estimate is within 1 percent of the Census count for both males and females above 15 years of age, except for females 65 years of age and over. The sample is 2.81 percent high for males and 2.39 percent high for females below 15 years of age. The overpopulation for boys and girls in the sample is concentrated in the interval under two years of age. This discrepancy between the sample count and the Census count may be attributed to the fact that the sample was taken a year later than the Census and many babies had been born in the interval.

Since the birth rate was higher in the early 1950s than in the late 1930s, the number of children was greater than the number of adolescents who had passed from the age bracket under 15 to the bracket 15–24. Among both males and females in the age groups 15–24, the sample was a lower percentage than the Census reported. These discrepancies are probably conditioned by the growth of the Armed Forces after the outbreak of the war in Korea. Even though there are differences between the percentages of males and females in the several age groups, as reported by the Census and found in the 5 percent sample, these discrepancies are within sampling variability, except below 15 years of age. The point to keep in mind is that these are the years when the impact of psychiatric disorders is not reflected in the rates for the prevalence of treated mental illness because there are so few individuals under the age of 15 who are patients. Chi square tests indicate that the sample does not differ significantly from the census for either males or females in the age groups above 15 years of age.[1] This finding shows that the sample is representative of the general population with exceptions noted, and it may be relied upon in the computation of morbidity rates by sex and age groups.

The sample's representativeness from the viewpoint of the social prestige of ecological areas was tested by comparing the number of households reported in each Enumeration District by the Census with the number of households estimated for the district from the sample. Before this comparison was made, each Enumeration District was assigned the ecological rank of the largest number of residential blocks in it.[2] The entire district was equated with this ecological rank. This procedure resulted in a certain measure of error where an Enumeration District contained more than one ecological level. However, few districts had more than one level represented in them; where there was an ecological difference, it was almost always one level only. The assignment of an ecologically mixed Enumeration District to one ecological level was offset by the assignment of another district to a different level.

When this procedure was completed and comparisons were made among the number of households in each of the six types of ecological areas reported in the Census and estimated from the sample, discrepancies in the two counts appeared:

First, the Census reported 1.8 percent more households in the "best" or *first* rank ecological areas than the sample estimate indicated.

Second, the sample estimate was 1.0 percent higher than the Census for the *second* ranking ecological area.

Third, the sample estimates were 2.4 percent and 2.1 percent higher than the Census figures for the *third* and *fourth* rank ecological areas.

Fourth, the Census figures were 1.0 percent and 1.5 percent higher than the sample estimates for the *fifth* and *sixth* rank ecological areas.

These comparisons show that the largest percentage of underestimation was in the "best" ecological areas rather than in the "poorest." The overestimation of households in ecological levels *two*, *three*, and *four* and underestimation in levels *one*, *five*, and *six* probably reflect trends in the redistribution of the community's population between the time the Census was taken in April, 1950, and the sample in the summer of 1951. Ecological levels *two*, *three*, and *four* are the sites of practically all new housing developments in the area. People have been moving out of *five*- and *six*-level areas into better areas. The "best" ecological areas have been growing slowly, but in comparison with the middle-level areas they have been losing population. Irrespective of the growth trends, the comparisons of the numbers of sample households with the number reported by the Census for the six ecological levels demonstrate that the sample is representative of the total number of households from the perspective of the ecological values of the areas where the sample families live. This finding is important because *the ecological rank of a respondent's residence is a criterion variable in the Index we used to determine a person's class status in the community.*

THE DETERMINATION OF CLASS STATUS

The patients enumerated in the Psychiatric Census and the respondents interviewed in the *5 percent sample* were stratified by the use of Hollingshead's Index of Social Position.[3] The Index utilizes *ecological area of residence, occupation*, and *education* to determine an individual's class status. To obtain a class status score on an individual, one must know his address, his occupation, and the number of years of school he has completed. Each of these factors is given a scale score, and the scale score is multiplied by a factor weight determined by a standard regression equation. The three products are summed, and the resultant score is taken as an index of this individual's position in the community's class system.[4] A detailed statement of the development of the Index of Social Position, how it is used, and how it was validated are given in Appendices Two and Three, pp. 387–397. Here we are concerned only with recording that the patients and the control population were stratified by an objective, operational procedure.

THE CONTROLLED CASE STUDY

The Controlled Case Study was designed to explore systematically interrelationships between sociocultural and psychological factors and the development of psychoneurosis and nuclear schizophrenia in two nonadjacent social classes. The detailed methodological procedures, conceptual frameworks, and findings of this phase of the research are presented in Myers and Roberts.[5] We are concerned here merely in recording the major methodological procedures because we will draw upon some of the clinical observations of this phase of the study in later chapters.

Fifty patients, 25 psychoneurotics, and 25 schizophrenics, were selected from classes III and V for detailed clinical and sociological study. Detailed data were collected on each patient by the psychiatrists and sociologists with a 128-page schedule. This schedule was divided into four parts. The first part was filled out by a team psychiatrist in a series of interviews with the patient; the second was filled out by a team psychiatrist in an interview with the patient's therapist; the third and fourth parts were filled out by a sociologist in interviews with members of the patient's family of orientation and his family of procreation. In addition, considerable material was gathered from the patient's clinical record and the clinical interviews Redlich had with each patient at the end of the interview process as a last step in data collection. The team developed two assessment schedules to evaluate the data systematically. The assessment schedules covered the following areas: psychological history, history of physical illnesses, attitude toward psychiatry and psychiatric treatment, social identification, family dynamics, education, religion, ethnic background, recreation, occupation, housing, and social class.

The 50 patients are white between the ages of 22 and 44. These age limits were imposed because attention was focused upon patients who presumably had reached adult responsibility and adjustment, but who had not entered the involutional period.

The 25 psychoneurotics in the Controlled Case Study and the 25 schizophrenics were compared with the psychoneurotics and schizo-phrenics enumerated in the Psychiatric Census to see if they were representative on the following variables: age, sex, religion, ethnic origin, and class score on the Index of Social Position. No signifi-cant difference was found at the 5 percent level of confidence on any variable when the two diagnostic groups of patients were compared.

SUPPLEMENTARY SCHEDULES

The Psychiatrist's Schedule

An interview schedule was designed for the specific purpose of gathering personal data from psychiatrists about their family back-grounds, their wives and their family backgrounds, their educations and professional lives, their family lives, income, and specific philoso-phy of medical and psychiatric practice. This schedule was divided into ten parts:

1. Parents and siblings
2. The wife and her parents
3. The respondent's education and research experience
4. Children
5. Vacations and use of leisure time
6. Conceptions of class status
7. Participation in community associations
8. Professional and family income
9. Professional practice, research, and teaching
10. Opinions on psychiatry and psychiatric patients

Each part was organized around a protocol of semistructured ques-tions designed to elicit facts and attitudes that would enable us to gain some understanding of the respondent as a person, a family man, a member of society, and a professional practitioner. The schedule was pretested on both psychiatrists of the research team and psychia-trists in other communities who were not to be interviewed in the study.

Forty psychiatrists who participated in an earlier phase of the re-search were interviewed by a psychiatrist on our research team. The respondents included private practitioners, clinic psychiatrists, state hospital psychiatrists, Veterans Administration psychiatrists, and pri-vate hospital psychiatrists. The schedule was designed for a one-hour interview to fit the organization of the psychiatrist's time sched-ule, but most lasted an hour and one-half, and a few ran to three hours. The factual data were recorded as the respondent gave them, but much of the material on attitudes was recorded in detail later by the interviewing psychiatrist from notes made on the schedule while the interview was in process.

The Agency Schedule on Treatment Costs

The data on costs of treatment (discussed in Chapter Ten) were gathered from private practitioners, public hospitals, private hospitals, and clinics in which the patients enumerated in the Psychiatric Census were in treatment by the use of a schedule designed specifically for the purpose. This schedule asked detailed questions on the costs of administering the agency, professional salaries, nonprofessional salaries, the costs of particular types of treatment such as electro-convulsive therapy, surgical procedures (for example, prefrontal lobotomy), medicines, food, housekeeping, physical plant, and insurance. We also asked sources of support, the amounts patients paid, special fees for specified types of therapy, discounts given to patients, and so on, in elaborate detail.

DATA PROCESSING

The information gathered on the individual patient's schedules in the Psychiatric Census and the Household Schedules of the 5 percent sample was edited, coded, and punched on Hollerith cards for processing on International Business Machines. However, before any schedule was edited, the authors with other members of the research team prepared a memorandum on editing. Precise editorial instructions were prepared on general procedures as well as on specific questions. For example, one item on general procedure states:

> Where a question is applicable to a patient, but the actual answer (the datum we want) is "none," the editor shall in all instances place a blue zero. For example, Question 21 (on the Patient's Schedule) concerns the number of children which the patient may have. If the patient is married but has no children or if the patient is single and it is reasonable to assume, since there are no evidences to the contrary, that he does not have any illegitimate children, the actual answer to the question is "none," and if "none" is written on the schedule the editor shall substitute a blue zero in the answer space.
>
> The above conventions are necessary in order that it will be evident to the coder that the editors have examined *every* question on the schedule and have either found the information appearing therein to be sufficient or have indicated the insufficiency of the data or the changes to be made in blue pencil.

In addition to the general editorial instructions illustrated by the foregoing excerpt from the Memorandum on Editing the Psychiatric Patients' Schedules, specific instructions were given for individual questions. An illustration of editorial procedures is the instruction we prepared for dealing with Question 24 on the marital status of the patients' parents.

> Where the marital history is an involved one, the editor shall attempt to make a separate listing for father and mother in the space below the question, that is, following out the exigencies of the father's various marriages, divorces, and separations, and also those of the mother. If the answer is "Widowed," but there is no way of telling from the rest of the schedule whether it is the father or the mother that died, then the editor must consider this as insufficient information and place a blue question mark on the schedule. Equally, if the question is answered by saying that both parents are dead, this is not an answer to the marital status of the parents because we do not know what this status was before one or both of the parents died; thus the editor must again place a blue question mark on Question 24.

The detailed instructions in the memoranda for the editors enabled them to edit the individual schedules in a uniform way.

The schedules were not coded until after they were edited. All coding was done with a red pencil. The coder worked from the blue pencil marks of the editor. Each schedule was coded with an identifying number that was punched into the Hollerith card. This was done so that at any phase of the analysis we could return to a schedule to check on a punch mark in a card. After the coding was completed, the code numbers were punched into the Hollerith cards, and the cards were verified against the schedules. When these operations had been completed, we were in a position to begin the statistical manipulation of the thousands of discrete items we had punched into the cards from the Psychiatric Census and the 5 percent sample.

THE USE OF STATISTICAL TECHNIQUES

We are concerned throughout the study with testing the hypotheses on relationships between class status and various aspects of psychiatric practice. We are interested in seeing, in the main, what happens if the independent variable, class status, is varied in terms of each of the three major hypotheses under study: (1) prevalence of treated psychiatric disorders, (2) the distribution of various types of psychiatric disorders, and (3) characteristics of treatment. In most analyses, we work with *attributes* such as class status, diagnostic categories, treatment agencies, type of treatment, and so on. We may wish, for example, to see if varying class status results in different proportions of cases in the two principal diagnostic categories, neurotics and psychotics. In this instance, we would work as follows:

	Diagnosis		
Class	Neurotics	Psychotics	Total
I–II	x	x	...
III	x	x	...
IV	x	x	...
V	x	x	...
Total	...	...	

$$\chi^2 = \ldots, 3 \; df, \; p > < .05$$

Each of the cells of the table now marked with an x would be filled with the appropriate number of patients who are in this category. We proceed to *test* each hypothesis as follows: First we set up a "null hypothesis." This states that there is no relationship between class status and type of mental illness. If this is true, we would expect to find the same proportions of neurotics and psychotics in each of the classes. For example, if in the total group of patients 50 percent are neurotics and the null hypothesis is true, 50 percent of the class I-II patients should be neurotic, 50 percent of the class III patients should be . . . , and so on. However, if the *observed* proportions in the different classes differ greatly from this *expected* proportion, we reject our null hypothesis and conclude that there is a relationship between class status and type of mental illness.

The chi square test enables us to determine whether the observed deviations in the eight cells of the table used for illustrative purposes are larger than the figure which would be produced by sampling error alone, hence something must be working on the observed data besides sampling error. We shall use the 5 percent probability level throughout this study as the minimum for the determination of significance. If a probability value is high enough to reach or exceed the value required for significance at the 5 percent level, we express this value in these terms: $p < .05$; the expression ($p < .05$) indicates that the observed distribution of psychotic patients in the several classes would occur, by sampling error alone, no more than 5 times in 100. When the chi square value is larger than we could expect by chance, less than 5 times in 100 successive samples, we conclude that they result from sampling errors alone, and there is probably no true relationship between class status and the data under analysis.

Some of the analyses are concerned with the relationship between the attribute *class status* and a *variable,* such as the number of years the patients have been in psychiatric treatment. Some of these relationships have been examined by means of chi square with the variable reduced to a small number of categories, such as *less than 2 years, 2–5 years,* etc. In other instances, the continuity of the variable is retained. When this procedure is followed, analysis of variance is used.

In the analysis of variance, instead of frequencies of categories, we have a series of "scores" or numerical values representing each case within the class. By means of analysis of variance, we can test whether the variability *between* the classes is significantly greater than the variability *within* the classes at a given level of probability.

We found it necessary in some analyses to hold one or more factors constant and examine the relationship between class and the selected aspect of psychiatric disorder with the third factor controlled to avoid confusing the class status factor with some related, but indirect, factor that is operating in the data under study. For example, the relationship between class status and the type of treatment is analyzed with the treatment agency "controlled." This is done by making separate chi square tests for cases in treatment with private practitioners, clinics, and public hospitals. In this analysis, we are concerned with learning if class status is a pertinent factor in determining the kind of treatment the patients receive within each treatment agency.

The confounding of the relationship between class and some continuous variable by a second continuous variable is handled in some instances by *covariance analysis.* For example, the relationship between the number of years patients have been treated and class is confounded by the patient's age. Age in this instance is the second factor that is related to both the number of years in treatment and the class status of the patients. By means of covariance analysis, corrections are made in the data on the basis of the age factor, and the analyses are carried out on the resulting adjusted data.

The number of mentally ill persons in class I under the care of psychiatrists is too small for statistical analysis. Therefore, we combined class I with class II in the tabular presentations and the textual discussions. However, when we have occasion to illustrate a point by reference to a particular case, the exact class status of the patient is given.

SUMMARY

The pertinent methodological procedures necessary to the gathering of the data to test the five working hypotheses around which this research is designed have been outlined in this chapter. We have taken the reader step by step through the planning phases of the Psychiatric Census, the 5 percent sample, the Controlled Case Study, and the study of psychiatric practice. The Index of Social Position used to place patients and the control population in the class status structure also was described briefly. The reader has been shown how we elicited the cooperation of psychiatric agencies and individual psychiatrists in the study and how we checked the data they gave us for coverage and reliability. We have related how the data in the 5 percent sample were gathered and tested for representativeness. Finally, the nature of the statistical procedures used to test the first three working hypotheses were outlined and illustrated by an example. In addition, some statements are based on extensive experience in sociological theory and field study and intensive clinical work in psychiatry and psychoanalysis.

NOTES

[1] The Census figures were used as the *expected;* the actual numbers in the sample were used as the *observed.* This procedure gave a χ^2 of .96 for the males and a χ^2 of 6.869 for the females, 3 *degrees of freedom, probability* $>$ .05.

[2] The ecological evaluation of the entire community had been made by Jerome K. Myers as a part of the stratification procedure discussed in the next section.

[3] For a detailed statement of the development of this *Index* and its statistical characteristics, see Appendix 2, pp. 387–397.

[4] Validation of the Index of Social Position by the use of factor analysis is demonstrated in Appendix 3, pp. 398–407.

[5] Jerome K. Myers and Bertram H. Roberts, *Social Class, Family Dynamics, and Mental Illness,* John Wiley and Sons, New York (manuscript in preparation).

the social setting

part two

part two • the social setting

The social setting in which the psychiatrists, the patients, and their families live is described in Part Two. Each chapter is focused on a particular dimension of social reality. Chapter Three traces the history of the community's status system from its establishment in America to the present. Chapter Four is a systematic analysis of the subcultures associated with each of the classes in the social system. Chapter Five describes the institutions we have developed which care for the mentally ill and places the psychiatrist in the social setting.

the social structure in historical perspective

chapter
three

The social structure of the New Haven community is a product of the development and change of cultures brought to these shores from Europe. For an observer to understand it, he needs to place the factors time has brought to bear upon the community in historical perspective and focus his attention upon the emergent profile. When this is done, one may see cultural values and practices from a past age reflected in the behavior of people today. Viewed from the present, the history of the community may be divided into three parts: the Colonial Epoch, the Age of Industrialization and Immigration, and the Acculturation of the Immigrants. The first era stretches from the settlement of New Haven to the drafting of the Constitution of Connecticut in 1818; the second covers the years from 1818 to the outbreak of World War I in 1914; and the third extends from 1915 to the present.

THE COLONIAL EPOCH (1638–1818)

The community was founded in 1638 by English Puritans who brought their social institutions and cultural values to an inlet on the north shore of Long Island Sound. In England, the founding fathers had been accustomed to a hierarchical social system characterized by status inequalities protected by law. Every man had his appointed place in a corporate order; he knew where it was and was expected to abide by the laws applicable to his place. The status order was accepted as morally and legally right, if not ordained by God.

The King, as head of church and state, was the final authority for all enterprises. From him came all charters, honors, valuable offices, and preferences of one kind or another. The New Haven Colony came into existence by the royal action of Charles I and was incorporated into the Connecticut Colony by Charles II in 1662. Before this date, certain principles underlying English social organization had been written into the laws of the New Haven Colony.

The New Society

The founding fathers established the colonial society on the principle of differential privileges associated with a man's "quality." They expected the lower ranks to accord the same respect to them they had received in England; however, they did not want a peerage above themselves. This is understandable, as the leaders of the New Haven Colony belonged to the merchant and professional classes in England, not the peerage. The Reverend John Davenport, the first clerical leader, was an Oxford graduate, and Theophilus Eaton, the merchant leader, came from a middle class family according to English standards.

The original settlers differed also from the authorities in England on religious questions; they earnestly desired to "purify" the Anglican church by returning to the scriptures as they interpreted them. Even though the original settlers did not recognize the legitimacy of the Anglican church, they believed in the inseparability of church and state. Thus, they incorporated an established church within the fabric of the colony's government and created a theocracy after the pattern prevailing in England.

The linkage of church and state assured the perpetuation of ranks in the new colony. Everybody had to attend and support the Congregational Church, but not everyone could be a member, nor could everyone have a voice in the government. Only freeholders, who subscribed to Puritan doctrine and were recognized church members, had political rights. They chose from among themselves the governor, the deputy governor, and their assistants. This elite group formed a General Court which possessed all official power in the colony. The General Court ruled on religious, political, educational, economic, and social affairs. It determined where a church could be built, who could be installed as minister, and who was to hold political offices and enjoy the privileges associated with them.

The Early Rank Order

In the formally recognized status system, the first rank was composed of shareholders in the company who were church members. The second rank was made up of church members who had money to pay their passage to the New World, but not enough to invest in the company. The third rank included persons who had paid their passage to the New World, but were not members of the church. The fourth rank included church members who had come to the colony as indentured servants for periods of three, four, or five years. The fifth rank was composed of bond servants who were not members of the church. The third, fourth, and fifth ranks were neither "admitted inhabitants" nor "freeholders"; thus, they were disenfranchised. The bottom stratum was occupied by Negro slaves who were in the community from the earliest years, but were outside the white status order.

A man's rank was part of the legal title by which he was recognized officially. Old records in the probate judge's office show a man's rank with his signature—whether he was a gentleman, a cleric, a yeoman, an artisan, a bond servant, or a slave. The seating charts of the "First Church" show numerous ranks in the congregation. Moreover, laws passed by the General Court explicitly stated what a man or woman of a given rank could do, wear, or eat, and violators of the sumptuary laws were punished according to their rank.

The Standing Order [1]

By the end of the seventeenth century, the status structure had crystallized to a point where position was more a matter of hereditary right than of individual achievement. The Standing Order, as it came to be called, was produced by a number of different factors: First, the community was small; as late as 1760 it had no more than 6,000 inhabitants. Second, almost all the residents were descendants of the English settlers who came between 1638 and 1685. In such a small community, everyone tended to know everyone else and, of particular importance, one's status was known. Third, the British origin of the population provided a homogeneous cultural base. In 1790, 96 percent of the white population was of English stock, 3 percent was Scottish, and 1 percent was Scottish-Irish and Irish stock. Fourth, the community was oriented toward England by the nature

of the colonial system and looked to England for its finished goods
and a market for its produce.

Social Mobility

From the beginning of the settlement, wealth was respected as the
measure of a man's ability. If a man could make money, he could
move up in the status system, but official rank took precedence over
wealth. Thus, the status structure was relatively stable for almost
two centuries, although there were always some individuals and
families who were upward mobile or downward mobile. Ambitious
young men left farms and small villages, particularly after 1740, to
earn a living in New Haven and other shore towns. These "country
boys" were not welcomed by the "town-born" who had been in the
community for several generations. For example, James Hillhouse
and Roger Sherman, who played leading roles in the town, state, and
nation during the Revolutionary War era, were among those labeled
as "interlopers" by the town-born when they came to New Haven
as young men. These interlopers made good, and a generation later
they were the respected old men accepted by the town-born aristocracy. Their sons were sent to Yale College, and usually their children married into the aristocratic families. Economic success combined with an approved marriage assured an upward mobile family
a firm position in the higher reaches of the status system in the next
generation.

The Standing Order and the American Revolution

Historical events leading to the Declaration of Independence had
few immediate effects on the status structure. After the American
colonies declared their independence in 1776, the Supreme Council
of Connecticut passed a resolution of approval. However, the Royal
Charter of 1662 continued in force, except that Connecticut was declared to be independent of the British Crown.

The common people of Connecticut played an important part in
the Revolutionary War, but the oligarchy in power did not accept
the democratic ideals in the Declaration of Independence. After the
war, the small groups of families who had ruled the colony since its
founding continued to make and to enforce the laws. Only nominal
assent was given to the Articles of Confederation, and the Constitution of 1789 with its appended Bill of Rights was rejected by the government of Connecticut.

The national government hardly touched the lives of ordinary citizens. The farmers carried out their daily and yearly routines; the merchants continued to venture in goods and land and grew richer as the years passed. The great families continued to rule the town in the name of Congregational orthodoxy, the status quo, and their own interests; neither the successful interlopers nor the town-born were desirous of changing the Standing Order. Finally, the conservatives reaccepted into their social circles Revolutionary leaders who had risked their lives and fortunes in the late war.

Opposition to the Standing Order

From the end of the Revolution until 1800, there was no challenge to the Standing Order. Only some 2 percent of the adult white males had the franchise, and they were not interested in extending it to others. Practically everyone voted for the nominees of the families of "quality"; dissenting votes were usually for personal rather than political reasons. After 1790, the conservative interests of the aristocracy were represented by the Federalists.

Organized opposition to the established order first appeared in the election campaign of 1800. Critics of the status quo, mainly Episcopalians and disgruntled Congregationalists, realized that Connecticut was governed by feudal principles, and they focused their attack upon the pillars of the Standing Order: aristocratic families, the established church, the special privileges of the Congregational clergy, and Yale College. Debate between the Jeffersonian group and the Federalists led to acrimonious charges that "atheistic riffraff" were stirring up "class hatreds." The chief spokesman of the Jeffersonians, Abraham Bishop, claimed Connecticut was either an "elective despotism" or an "elected aristocracy." [2]

Although the Federalists were challenged in 1800, the limited franchise enabled them to control completely the state election machinery, the public press, the pulpit, and the town meetings. As a consequence, they elected the seven representatives to the Federal Congress and the governor, and they controlled the General Assembly.

The Jeffersonians organized the Republican party before the election of 1804; their platform included a written constitution for Connecticut congruent with the Federal Constitution, but they lost the election. After 1804, the Republicans made the people conscious that they were subjects of Connecticut under the Royal Charter of 1662 and not citizens as defined in the Federal Constitution. Under the Charter of 1662, the executive, legislative, and judicial branches of the government, as defined in the Federal Constitution, were integrated in a Supreme Council. The Supreme Council, composed of fourteen members of the aristocracy, met in secret to determine policy and to hand down judicial decisions. However, it was not until the War of 1812–1815 brought widespread economic depression and political dissatisfaction that the opposition was able to make a successful stand against the Federalist Party. Merchants, ship-owners, and manufacturers had been hit hard by the Embargo of 1808, and they were hit harder by the British blockade and raids of shipping along the Connecticut coast after 1812. The War of 1812 was extremely unpopular among the Federalists who called it "Mr. Madison's War." In the fall of 1814, Federalist representatives, along with influential leaders from Massachusetts, decided the time had come to make their position known in the national capitol. Thus, they met in Hartford on December 15, debated the issues in secret, and in January, 1815, issued a declaration of policy.

The convention demanded redress against its grievances and implied that Connecticut would secede from the Union unless the Federal government recognized its claims. Its grievances included the domination of the country by the "Virginia Dynasty" and infringements against state sovereignty by the national government. A committee was sent to Washington to make the findings of the convention known to the President and the Federal government. To the discomfiture of the Federalists, the war was brought to a successful conclusion while the committee was on its way to Washington. In spite of popular approval of the outcome of the war, the Federalists and the newspapers stood by the Hartford Convention.

When the declaration of the Hartford Convention became known in the state, the opposition to the status quo seized upon it as the issue. Men whose fathers and grandfathers had fought in the War for Independence, and who themselves had been in the ranks during the War of 1812, were dissatisfied with the Standing Order. A Toleration Party was soon formed from dissident groups dedicated to breaking the power of the oligarchy. To quiet popular clamor for reform, the Federalists extended the franchise in 1816; as a consequence, in 1817 the Toleration Party elected the governor and an overwhelming majority of the representatives in the legislature.

The Connecticut Constitution

Toleration Party leaders, after their election in 1817, set out to break the power of the Standing Order. They called a Constitutional Convention in 1818. Connecticut's first constitution disestablished the Congregational Church and gave freedom to "any organized Christian sect." (Note, however, this toleration was limited to Christians.) It eliminated the Congregational tithe collected by the towns. In addition, it incorporated provisions of the Bill of Rights of the Federal Constitution and separated the powers of the state into legislative, judicial, and executive branches. Finally, it extended the suffrage to a wider segment of the population. However, representation in the lower House of the General Assembly was by town rather than by population. This concession to the old Standing Order continues in force to the present. In effect, it enables the small towns of the state, with relatively homogeneous Yankee populations, to control the State Legislature.

The election of the Toleration Party in 1817 brought the colonial era to an end in Connecticut. It also marked the beginning of the decline of the oligarchical families who had dominated New Haven for more than a century and a half. The transition from aristocracy to democracy, however, was much slower than the political actions which led to the legal eclipse of the Standing Order. Even though the official privileges of the aristocracy and the Congregational Church ended in 1818, the great families continued to exercise power privately through ascribed status, the financial control of economic enterprises, and the monopolization of legal talent.

The Status Structure at the End of the Federalist Period

Some eight to nine generations of Americans matured on the local scene between the founding of the New Haven Colony in 1638 and the Constitution of 1818. Throughout the colonial era, the vast majority of the population were subjected to the decisions of the small, self-perpetuating oligarchy who controlled economic affairs, political activity, religious worship, education, and personal behavior.[3] This was the Standing Order, but what comprised it?

The "Quality"

The Standing Order was headed by an aristocracy of forty or fifty families called the "quality." Families of quality for the most part were direct descendants of the early settlers. Their number, however, had been augmented by a few men of talent and ability who had come to the community mainly from other Connecticut towns. The heads of these families were owners of merchant ships; they shipped local produce such as pork, beef, grain, lumber, and oysters to England and the West Indies, and they imported finished goods:

rum, rope, molasses, sugar, iron, salt, spices, cloth, and wines. They
also bought large tracts of land for resale in smaller parcels at hand-
some profits. Their wealth, it is estimated, varied from a low of
$50,000 to a high of approximately $1,000,000. The men were mainly
graduates of Yale College; their wives had attended young ladies' finishing schools. The great families were almost exclusively Congregationalists. There were no Methodists or Baptists among them; however, there were some Anglicans. Their members had intermarried
through the years so that they were interrelated in complex ways. In
this, as in any aristocracy, wealth guaranteed privilege, privilege guaranteed power, and power conveyed status. The trappings of privilege included the family's place in church and town meeting, clothes,
home, the son's social rank in Yale College, and the right of men to
offices in the government. The Wolcott family is a fair example of
connections between these families and the offices they held in the
Colonial Era. A single female member of this family, Ursula Wolcott
(1724–1788), was the daughter of a Connecticut governor, wife of a
governor, mother of a governor, sister of a governor, and the grand-
mother of a governor. In addition, she was a blood relative of sixteen
other colonial governors and fifty-six judges. And, to add to the
irony of history, a nephew was the first governor of Connecticut
elected under the Constitution of 1818.[4]

The "Better Sort"

Yale professors, Congregational clergymen, lawyers, and doctors
headed the second status rank, families of the "better sort," as they
were called. Like the quality, the better sort were oriented toward
England, English society, and the Standing Order. The Congregational clergy and Yale professors, the majority of whom had been
Congregational ministers before they became professors, ranked
above lawyers and doctors. The lawyers tended to be spokesmen
and retainers for the great families. By 1820, there were some fifty
families in this stratum.

The "Middle Sort"

Families who owned retail shops, where goods brought to town by
the merchant venturers were sold, represented a third stratum. These
families were known as the "middle sort." Their shops were largely
in lean-tos on the sides of their houses or in front rooms of their
homes. Most shopkeepers were literate, as they had completed
"common" school. In religion, they tended to be Congregationalists,

but a sprinkling of Anglicans were found among them. A number of the shopkeepers were also part-time farmers.

Farm-owning families who had the right to vote in town elections ranked along with the shopkeepers. They represented a substantial part of the population. Their homesteads were on the arable lands surrounding the town and the river bottoms in the back country. Some farmers were able to read and write simple English and follow the Scriptures. In the main, they were Congregationalists, but there were Anglicans and Methodists among them.

The artisans, or mechanics, composed a distinct stratum that ranked below the middle sort, yet they were not generally recognized as being of the "lower sort." They had learned trades as apprentices under journeymen, masons, wheelwrights, carpenters, and so on. A strong tradition of rights, duties, and "status honor" inherited from the medieval guilds prevailed among them. Usually they worked either by the day or on a contract basis, but they owned little real property, and few had the franchise. Some were able to read and do the arithmetic associated with their work, but at best they had a meager education. They lived in humble homes located away from the Green, or central park, around which New Haven is built. Religiously, they were divided among Congregationalists, Anglicans, Methodists, Baptists, and other Protestant sects of English origin. They were respected for their steady habits, responsibility on the job, knowledge of tools, and mechanical procedures. However, a sharp difference existed between the artisan and the property-owning groups because of the high values the society placed on real estate.

The "Lower Sort"

Casual day-laborers, sailors, and fishermen were at the bottom of the free-rank system. They were definitely of the "lower sort." They were, in the main, without property, skill, or calling. They were not generally "admitted" inhabitants of the town; thus, they did not enjoy the franchise. To be admitted as a citizen of the town gave a man and his family a definite social and legal standing because he had the right to vote in town meetings, but not in state elections. Only admitted inhabitants who were freeholders could vote in state and national elections. Many individuals in this stratum drifted to the town from villages or isolated woodland areas. Some were woodcutters for the charcoal pits that furnished fuel for the bog iron bloomeries along the shore. Many had been indentured servants, or were descendants of indentured servants. They were, on the whole, a rough, illiterate group, commonly referred to as "numb-skulls," "lubbers," and "riffraff."

The bottom stratum of white society was composed of two elements: indentured servants and the town's poor. Men and women who voluntarily entered into a contract with ship-owners or merchants to work for five, six, or seven years in return for passage to the New World were in a distinct group, legally and socially, from all other whites. The town's poor, mainly debtors, were sold in public auctions on the Green periodically until the middle of the 1820s.

Negroes, both free and slave, were an important but minor element in the population from the community's earliest days. Free Negroes were used as servants, laborers on the docks, and in rough work in general. Slaves were owned by the aristocracy from the middle 1640s to as late as 1825. As the aristocracy gained wealth and sought to pattern its way of life after the English gentry and the planters of the West Indies, more slaves were bought. At the end of the Revolutionary War, almost every great family owned one Negro slave; some owned two, three, and four, but there were no large slave-holders. In 1790, 116 slaves and 144 free Negroes were enumerated by the United States Census. The Negro population, slave and free, comprised 3.2 percent of the total population at that time. The free Negroes, from the beginning, lived in a "quarter" of the town immediately behind the homes of the aristocratic families northwest of the Green. By 1820, Negroes had increased to 4.9 percent of the population; they had organized a separate church and developed other social organizations of their own, but only a very few had the franchise. Whether slave or free, the Negroes lived outside the white status structure.

To summarize a few salient points of this first period:

(1) Status differentiation was an integral part of early American culture; colonial Americans were a status-conscious people.

(2) Social relations were organized in terms of rank. A man's status determined where he belonged in the community and in the larger society. Moreover, his standing in life often was perpetuated in death. For example, in a local cemetery is the epitaph, "James ——, departed this life April 21, 1817. Born a man, died a cobbler."

(3) The homogeneous descent of the settlers from British society, combined with ingrown localism after 1685, gave rise to a relatively close society where status awareness and identification were of primary importance.

(4) The status dimension was as much a part of the culture of the people as the language they spoke or religious beliefs.

INDUSTRIALIZATION AND IMMIGRATION (1820–1914)

The years between 1815 and 1820 mark the beginning of the second epoch in the community's history. During these years, the Toleration Party successfully challenged the Standing Order and forced the aristocracy from its legally privileged position. New Haven continued, however, to carry on its old ways for another decade, but larger historical forces were to transform the seacoast town into an industrial city in the years ahead.

The community, at the end of the Revolutionary War, was a sprawling town of 8000 people. New Haven, with a population of 3350, was the center of activity. After 1815, the emigration of Connecticut Yankees to western New York and the virgin flatlands of northern Ohio drained the population from inland towns, as thousands of individuals and families left the "land of steady habits" and sought a brighter future. The outlying villages of East Haven, West Haven, North Haven, Hamden, and Woodbridge lost population. Those who left the local scene, as well as those who remained, were mainly descendants of the English pioneers who settled in the area in the seventeenth century. This English stock had more than replenished itself generation after generation. It was ingrown, interrelated on each status level, and proud of its English origin. This pride was to be its hallmark in the years ahead, and was to set the Yankees apart from the immigrants who came to the city between 1825 and 1915.

New Haven City began to grow rapidly after 1830 when steamboats, turnpikes, canals, and above all the railroad to Boston and New York opened up new markets and sources of raw materials. After 1815, the heads of the great families turned from merchant-venturing and land speculation to new enterprises. A number became manufacturers of clocks, buttons, brass fixtures, carriages, woolen cloth, and guns. A few saw that the community's future growth lay in the development of transportation. As a consequence, some men became interested in developing turnpikes from New Haven to such points as Hartford, New York, and New London; others promoted steamship lines, canals, and, after 1830, railroads. A few became bankers and financial promoters. In these and other ways, the great families of the earlier era put their capital to work in new ventures designed to bring them more capital.

The rise of factories created a need for an abundant supply of cheap labor; at the same time, the westward migration from the back country drained off the hands so badly needed. Had labor been available, the factory owners could have provided the goods which developing western areas needed. To meet their labor needs, the New Haven manufacturers sent long black wagons called "slavers" to the outlying villages to lure workers, mainly girls, to the mills.[5]

Labor-recruiting, however, did not provide enough hands to man the factories; the industrialist had to look to European immigration to solve his labor shortage. From the late 1820s to World War I, first hundreds and then thousands of peasants were recruited annually from European countries to fill the unskilled factory and pick-and-shovel jobs connected with digging canals, paving streets, building railroads, and constructing the factories and tenements where they were to work and live. Immigration changed the population from the homogeneous British stock of 1820 to one of mixed ancestry by 1914. With the new populations came new cultures and new transplantations of European status structures to these shores.

Construction of a canal from New Haven to the Connecticut River, begun in 1825, brought the first group of unskilled laborers from southern Ireland; other unskilled laborers followed the first group, so that by 1832 there were enough Irish in New Haven to form a Roman Catholic parish, the first non-Protestant church in the community. The antagonism of New Haveners to it was so great that the *New Haven Register* openly advocated "court-martial" of the Yale Divines for allowing Roman Catholics to gain a foothold in this Protestant land.

The number of Irish immigrants increased greatly in the 1840s as the potato famines squeezed the peasants from the land. By 1854, the Irish had increased in numbers and group assertion to the point that a petition was presented to the still aristocratic Common Council requesting that some Irish be made constables. This request was tabled, but the Irish were not to be so easily denied some participation in the official life of the city. Before another generation passed, they succeeded in capturing the police force, and the Common Council itself was under pressure from upward mobile Irish politicians who wanted to sit with the Yankee elite.

German immigrants, who began to arrive in the late 1830s, were in great demand in the factories, carriage works, and boat yards. The Germans were not a culturally homogeneous group; there were a few Bavarian Jews in the first contingent, and the remainder was further divided by Catholic and Lutheran religious doctrines. By 1840, there were enough Jewish families to establish the first synagogue in the city. Political refugees from the Revolution of 1848 arrived in 1849. This group differed from earlier German settlers in that several brought considerable capital and knowledge of industrial processes and organization to the community, and they proceeded to establish businesses and small factories. Throughout the 1850s, the number of German and Irish immigrants settling in the city increased year by year.

During the Civil War, immigration ceased, but as soon as the war was over, Irish and German immigrants came in larger numbers than before. In addition, Swedish immigrants began to settle in the area in the late 1860s. In 1870, 28 percent of the population were foreign-born. Of this group, 67 percent were Irish, and 17 percent were German. This was far different from the 0.2 of 1 percent of foreign-born persons in the population in 1820. The immigrants continued to come in increasing numbers, particularly from Germany, Sweden, and Denmark throughout the 1870s; then the source of immigration shifted to southern and eastern Europe.

In 1880, there were about 500 Italians and some 350 to 400 Russian and Polish Jews in the city. After 1890, Russian and Polish Jews and Italians came in increasingly large numbers until the outbreak of World War I. Finally, in the early 1900s, Poles began to settle in the city in appreciable numbers. The Polish Jews formed a synagogue in 1881, and the Roman Catholic Poles formed their own parish in 1904.

The Yankee Core Group and the Immigrants

The "Yankees," although they comprised only a small percentage of the population by 1915, looked upon the community as a structure which they had fashioned out of a wilderness through their own relentless efforts. This proud, uncompromising minority looked down upon the immigrant groups; few Yankees were willing to accept immigrants socially. They believed in a way of life encompassed by Protestantism, profits, privilege, and pride in an English origin. The elite Yankee minority set the pattern for the immigrant stock who aspired to realize American ideals of equality of person and position. What is particularly important from the viewpoint of status is that the Yankees possessed the culture the immigrants had to acquire before they could become "Americans" in the eyes of their children, of themselves, and of the Yankees. The Yankees firmly held the levers of power; they were willing to have others work for them at their direction and in their interest, so long as they did not attempt to seize control. Moreover, old Yankee families controlled the city of New Haven and the suburban towns politically, financially, industrially, and professionally, as well as socially.

Social distance between the Yankees and the immigrant groups was heightened by the fact that the immigrants first settled in run-down, congested sections of the city and were, on the whole, non-Protestant. In addition, differences were formalized by the establishment of churches and other institutions that tended to bind each nationality group into an ethnic enclave which was patterned, as nearly as circumstances permitted, after the society of its homeland.

Salient Points of the Second Era

To summarize a few major points of the second era:

First, between 1820 and World War I, the New Haven community was transformed from a small town with a homogeneous population of English descent into a metropolitan center with a heterogeneous population from many lands.

Second, in 1820, it was a local commercial center and its few small factories produced goods for a relatively local market. By 1914, it had become a wholesaling center for southern and central New England; its factories had increased in size, number, and complexity, and its market was world-wide.

Third, large industrial enterprises developed in the city between the Civil War and World War I. Sargent and Company opened its plant in 1864, and the Winchester Repeating Arms Company began operations in 1867. With the development of large-scale enterprises came the structuring of human relations in the plants around an elaborate bureaucracy of ownership, management, and industrial workers.

Fourth, the manufacturers before the Civil War were Yankee-born and bred; many were descendants of the old aristocracy. After the Civil War, a few Germans began to manufacture corsets, cigars, and pianos. Before the end of the era, some Irish became owners of retail stores, wholesale outlets, and construction companies; Swedes became boatbuilders and small contractors; Eastern Jews entered the needle trades, and a few Italians became contractors and food-processors. While some leaders in each ethnic group entered businesses, others moved into the professions: law, medicine, the ministry, engineering, and teaching. The rise of these new families in status and power created stresses in the social structure which had to be met by adjustments in the traditional status system.

Fifth, each immigrant group held itself apart from the others. Thus, the community was separated into a series of almost self-contained subcultures and societies.

Sixth, every immigrant group came from a European class society; therefore its members were already accustomed to the concept of status. They soon learned that the Yankees looked down upon them and they, in turn, tended to accept the Yankees' judgment and to retreat into their own social organizations. Thus, the necessary conditions were present for the development of parallel social structures in the community. The flowering of this process was to characterize the years ahead.

THE ERA OF ACCULTURATION (1915 TO THE PRESENT)

World War I was a turning point in the historical development of the community. From 1820 to August, 1914, industrial growth was accompanied by unrestricted immigration from European countries. Between 1840 and 1860, the population of New Haven more than doubled, and the value of its industries multiplied fourfold. From the Civil War to World War I, the curves of population and industrial growth in the central city swept upward, but the surrounding towns remained rural for the most part. The central city has not grown since World War I, but the adjacent towns have become urbanized as population has moved into them in ever increasing numbers.

The immigrants who came to New Haven between 1830 and 1915 provided the basis, in the main, for the present population. In 1920, the community had a population of 190,000 with 162,000 resident in New Haven. Twenty-nine percent were foreign-born, and an additional 35 percent were native-born of foreign parentage. Thus, approximately two residents of three were either immigrants or the children of immigrants. The Irish were still the largest group, but foreign-born Italians outnumbered the Germans, and the Russian and Polish groups were nearly as large as the German-born portion of the population. In 1950, the community had a population of some 237,000. The various population elements by national origin were distributed as follows: Italian—30 percent; Irish—25 percent; Russian-, Polish-, Austrian-, and German-Jewish—11 percent; British-American —12 percent; German—7 percent; Polish—5 percent; Scandinavian—3 percent; other European stock—3 percent; and Negro—4 percent. The growth of 47,000 population between 1920 and 1950 was produced largely by the increase of births over deaths.

The diverse cultural roots of the population are exemplified by the identification of individuals and groups as Irish-American, Italian-American, and so on, throughout the community. The tendency to identify various national origins is growing in political circles where the two major parties bid for the votes of individuals by appealing to historical backgrounds, both in the formation of slates of candidates and the content of their local political appeals. Today, members of the several ethnic groups think of themselves as Americans, but they are keenly aware that their ancestors were Irish, Italian, Russian, German, Polish, Hungarian, or Greek.

In spite of isolating factors previously discussed, the immigrant stocks were brought under the influence of American culture through their jobs and schools. On the job, the immigrants came into direct contact with the Yankees, for most enterprises were owned by them, and their supervisory personnel were either Yankees or partially acculturated individuals from an earlier immigrant group. Sooner or later, all ethnic groups were brought under the influence of the public schools, either through adult citizenship classes or, what was more usual, through compulsory attendance of their children. As the process of acculturation has taken its course, members of ethnic groups have acquired American culture patterns and values. Among them are beliefs in the equality of man and the equality of opportunity. Also, they have acquired personal knowledge of the inequalities associated with being members of out-groups, as the second and third generations of ethnic groups have been rebuffed by the Yankees. Thus, they are keenly aware of the American status dilemma: the public profession of equality and the private practice of inequality.

The differences in time of arrival for the several immigrant groups has given rise to differential distribution of their descendants in the status structure. This was produced by the fact that each immigrant group entered the occupational pyramid "at the bottom" or "near the bottom." As its members became acculturated, they tended to "work up" in the socioeconomic system. The Irish, as we pointed out above, were the first non-British group to settle here. They were hired as muckers on the canal, later as laborers on the railroad tracks, and as "unskilled hands" in the newly founded and expanding factories. The Yankees were given the more skilled jobs and supervisory positions. When the Germans came, a few proved to be an exception, in part, to the custom for immigrants to start "at the bottom" because some of them were well-to-do merchants, manufacturers, and artisans who had left Europe for political reasons. German refugees, who brought their wealth with them, established businesses and sent back to Germany for workmen. Thus, from the beginning, the Germans were divided into owning and working strata. Likewise, some of the Scandinavians who came in the late 1860s and 1870s were craftsmen who were engaged immediately in cabinet-making, boatbuilding, carriage-making, and carpentry rather than unskilled labor. Nevertheless, the vast majority of the Germans and Scandinavians began their American work careers in manual jobs of little skill. Almost every immigrant from southern and eastern Europe who came in later years worked first in hard, unskilled, or menial jobs. As a new immigrant group entered the occupational system, the members of earlier ethnic groups moved up a notch. Thus, different ethnic groups occupied different positions in the economic system when large-scale immigration ended.

Today, the majority of the members of each ethnic group occupies positions in the social system relative to its phase of acculturation. This principle has been demonstrated by two independent studies of the status positions of different ethnic groups in the community during the present era: The first, by McConnell,[6] analyzed the ethnic background of 1633 heads of households selected at random to see if ethnic origins were linked to socioeconomic status. It was found that approximately two thirds of British-American heads of households are in nonmanual occupational pursuits, whereas exactly two thirds of the Italian and Polish are in manual occupations. What is more striking is the discovery that 64 percent of the professionals and business executives are British-American, whereas only 4.5 and 3.4 percent are of Italian and of Polish origin, respectively. The Irish are concentrated in public service jobs and white-collar clerical work. The Russian and Polish Jews are concentrated in retail trade and the professions of law and medicine. The Germans are spread from the highest executive positions to the skilled crafts, but very few are in the semiskilled and unskilled categories.

The second study, by Myers,[7] is an exhaustive analysis of the assimilation of Italians in the community. Myers found that only a small percentage of Italians have moved into higher occupations; the vast majority are manual workers. These studies reveal that the difference in the time each ethnic group has been in the community, coupled with the way it was regarded by the old Yankee elite, set the stage for the current system of stratification.

The Present Status Structure

The community's current status structure is differentiated both *vertically* and *horizontally* by lines of cleavage which hold some groups together, while they simultaneously separate them from other groups. *Vertical cleavages* follow along racial, ethnic, and religious lines. Around the sociobiological axis of race, two separate social structures have evolved: one for whites, the other for Negroes. The white social structure is subdivided further into Catholic, Protestant, and Jewish segments. Within these major religious divisions, there are numerous ethnic subdivisions. For example, Polish Catholics maintain a religious and social life separate from Irish Catholics.

Each of these vertical divisions is transected by a series of horizontal cleavages which divide the community into social strata in ways reminiscent of the Standing Order of the eighteenth and early nineteenth centuries. The horizontal lines of status differentiation, which cut across the vertical cleavages, are based upon commonly shared values which our culture attaches to one's occupation, education, place of residence in the community, and associations irrespective of his position in the vertical divisions of the social structure. For example, a surgeon ranks high in the status structure of the community whether he is a Catholic of Italian, Irish, or German descent or a Reformed Jew of German or Polish descent. In like manner, an unskilled sweeper in a factory is assigned a low status value which is independent of his religion or ethnic origin. In brief, the vertically differentiating factors of race, religion, and ethnic origin when combined with the horizontally differentiating ones of occupation, education, place of residence, and so on, produce a social structure that is highly compartmentalized.

The integrating factors in this complex are twofold. First, each stratum of each vertical division is similar in its cultural characteristics to the corresponding stratum in the other divisions. Second, the cultural pattern of each stratum, or "class," was set by the old Yankee group. This *core group* provided the master cultural mold that has shaped the status system of each racial, religious, and ethnic group, within the larger context of the group's standing in the community.

The development of parallel class structures within the limits of race, ethnic origin, and religion may be illustrated by the fact that there are six different "Junior Leagues" in the white Gentile segments of the New Haven community for appropriately affiliated young women. The top-ranking organization is the New Haven

Junior League; it draws its membership from old Yankee Protestant families whose daughters have been educated in private schools. The Catholic Charity League is next in rank; its membership is drawn mainly from Irish-American families. In addition, there are Italian and Polish Junior Leagues within the Catholic segments of the population with high class status. The Swedish and Danish Junior Leagues are for properly connected young women in these groups, but they are Protestant. Jewish families have exclusive social organizations comparable to the Junior Leagues in the Gentile segments of the community, but they avoid the term "Junior League." The Negroes have a Junior League for their top-drawer young women. Its name: The Junior League of New Haven.

The evolution of parallel class structures within the vertical cleavages of race, religion, and ethnic origin has been a major trend in the social structure of the community during the twentieth century. Parallel institutions for a given class level, by religious, ethnic, and racial groups, proliferate throughout the community. The implications of this structure for individuals may be seen after the cultural characteristics of the several classes extant in the community have been described.

NOTES

[1] For a detailed, carefully documented, comprehensive history of the community, see Rollin G. Osterweis, *Three Centuries of New Haven,* Yale University Press, New Haven, 1953, especially pp. 108, 196–202.

[2] *Ibid.,* p. 198.

[3] For a documented analysis of this position in the colonial towns, see Carl Bridenbaugh, *Cities in Revolt,* Alfred A. Knopf, New York, 1955.

[4] Chandler Wolcott, *Wolcott Genealogy,* The Genesee Press, Rochester, New York, 1912. This is the best single source to trace the ramifications of this famous family. See especially pp. 57 and 110.

[5] Robert Austin Warner, *New Haven Negroes, A Social History,* Yale University Press, New Haven, 1940, pp. 13–14; see also Samuel Koenig, *Immigration Settlements in Connecticut,* Connecticut State Department of Education, Hartford, 1938, p. 15.

[6] John W. McConnell, "The Influence of Occupation upon Social Stratification," Unpublished Ph.D. Thesis, Sterling Memorial Library, Yale University, 1937.

[7] Jerome K. Myers, Jr., "The Differential Time Factor in Assimilation: A Study of Aspect and Processes of Assimilation among the Italians of New Haven," Unpublished Ph.D. Thesis, Sterling Memorial Library, Yale University, 1949.

class status
and cultural
characteristics

chapter four

INTRODUCTION

The preceding chapter traced the development of the community's social structure from its founding to the present. This chapter systematically presents the cultural characteristics of its principal social classes. The position of each class in the social structure is designated by a Roman numeral. The highest is class I, and the lowest is class V.

Individuals and families are placed in classes by Hollingshead's Index of Social Position. This Index is premised upon three assumptions: (1) that social stratification exists in the community, (2) that status positions are determined mainly by a few commonly accepted cultural characteristics, and (3) that items symbolic of status may be scaled and combined by the use of statistical procedures so that a researcher can quickly, reliably, and meaningfully stratify the population.

The three indicators of status utilized by the Index of Social Position to determine class position are: (1) the residential address of a household, (2) the occupational position of its head, and (3) the years of school the head has completed. Each of these items is evaluated by a scale (given in Appendix Two, pp. 387–397). The scaled items are combined and weighted by statistical procedures into a single score. To estimate the class status of a household one must know its address and its head's occupational position and education. For example, let us say that Richard Roe lives with his wife and four children at 123 Low Street; he is the manager of a chain store; he was graduated from high school and has completed one year of business college. To determine the class status of Richard Roe and his family, we would convert the three items indicative of social position into scale scores thus:

Factor Item	Scale Score	Factor Weight	Scale Score × Factor Weight
Address	4	6	24
Occupation	3	9	27
Education	3	5	15
Index of Social Position Score =			66

The Index of Social Position score is translated into a *class status* score by procedures described in Appendix Two, pp. 387–397. We would assign Richard Roe and the members of his household to class III.

The operationally determined "class" which emerges from the use of the procedures prescribed in the Index of Social Position is presumed to be a reasonably accurate estimate of status positions which persons occupy in the community. The reader should remember that the Index of Social Position is simply a procedure for *conceptualizing* and indexing the population into categories that have relevance in everyday behavior. The assumption of a meaningful correspondence between the estimated class status of persons and their social behavior was validated by the use of factor analysis. The evidence to support this assumption is presented in Appendix Three, pp. 398–407.

When persons or families are arranged on the ordinal scales included in the Index of Social Position, namely, place of residence, education, and occupation, and their positions on these scales are compared with other cultural items, such as the newspapers they read or the television programs they view, their positions on the Index are correlated significantly with their behavior in regard to most items. Persons who possess particular patterns of consumption, taste, attitudes, and other identifiable sociocultural characteristics that are correlated with the three factors built into the Index of Social Position are the constituent units in the population aggregates which we identify as "social classes." In short, classes, as delineated by the Index of Social Position, are characterized by distinct subcultures. The principal constellation of cultural traits associated with each class will be traced in the ensuing sections of this chapter. The rich details of the subculture for each class are based upon a series of studies Hollingshead and his students have made in the last decade supplemented by data collected for this study.

The specific subcultural traits more or less common to the members of a class are learned through participation in the behavior system peculiar to it. The identification of persons with other persons who share similar cultural values, attitudes, beliefs, and customs produces group solidarity as well as group differences. Persons in a particular class learn almost unconsciously, in the course of their lives, a subtle series of cues which enable them to recognize one another and to identify even strangers as equals or unequals; cues shown by persons in other classes are shared as well. Those who are marked by out-group stigmata are viewed with suspicion, if not with hostility or denegation. Differences in patterns of subcultural traits, and the recognition of them by members of the community, set each class off from the others.

Social Mobility

Social mobility involves a change in the class status of individuals during the course of their lives. The class position occupied by an individual's parental family during his childhood and early adolescence is the base line against which mobility may be measured. Viewed theoretically, an individual either goes through life occupying the class position he inherited from his parental family, or he acquires a different class status through the instrumentality of his own activities. An individual who does not change his class is viewed as being intergenerationally *stable*. An individual who changes his class position is *mobile*. A person who achieves a class status higher than that of his parental family is defined as being *upward mobile*. A person who fails to hold the status occupied by the parental generation and acquires a class position lower than his parents' in the status structure is identified as being *downward mobile*. Generally speaking, upward mobility in the American social structure is approved behavior and downward mobility is unapproved behavior. Mobile behavior is learned in the course of an individual's life, but the details of how mobility or stability are acquired are far from being clear.

The principal requisites for achieving upward mobility are skill, education, and knowledge, particularly in males, and physical beauty, charm, and talent in females. The particular choice of goals of upward mobile persons—power, wealth, or fame—depends on specific values of the individuals concerned.

CLASS I

Status Awareness

Each respondent in the control sample was asked a series of questions designed to elicit his awareness of status. The first question asked was: "Do you think classes exist in the community?" The second was: "What things determine one's class?" Each respondent made his own decision as to his belief in classes and the criteria that placed a person in a class. After responses were recorded from these questions, the interviewer asked, "To what class would you say you belong?" The interviewer then read slowly eight choices: "upper," "upper-middle," "middle," "lower-middle," "working," "lower," "do not know," and "I do not believe in classes."

The direct questions on "class" brought into focus incongruity between a person's response to a question involving values in the publicly professed dimensions of the culture, particularly if it involves democratic beliefs, and his actions in situations involving in-group codes. A class I matron, who was startled by the questions but who identified herself as "upper" class, provided insight into this facet of the social ethic with the acid comment, "One does not speak of classes; they are felt." In spite of such incongruities, over 98 percent of the class I respondents think there are "social classes" in the community: 37 percent identify with the "upper" class, 56 percent classify themselves as "upper-middle" class, and 5 percent as "lower-middle" class. The remaining 2 percent do not believe in classes.

Whereas class status brings its members into contact with one another in many functional relationships in the maintenance of the community's general social life, ethnic and religious differences segment the 3.4 percent of the community's population placed in class I (by the Index of Social Position) into internally organized, almost self-contained, social worlds. A *core group*, composed of pace-setting, commonly recognized "old families," enjoys the highest prestige and power positions in the status system. Revolving around it are satellite groups composed of persons who have "arrived" recently in the business and professional worlds and, in the words of an *arriviste*,* "Yale professors who try to play the game on $10,000 a year." Although there are distinct differences in the ability of different groups to "play the game," all groups respect and, in many ways, emulate those who sometimes satirically are referred to by members of fringe groups as "proper New Haveners." "Proper New Haveners" are truly "at the summit" [1] of local "society." Members of these families have been at the summit for two, three, and more generations, and some have been in the "nuclear group" [2] since colonial times.

Fifty-three percent of the adults in this class are stable through two and more generations and 47 percent are upward mobile from their parental families. Stable members of the core group possess a complex subculture which aspirants must acquire before they are admitted into the group. Those who are accorded "accepted" status are the "gatekeepers"; they decide which "new people" are invited into their exclusive organizations. Conversely, the gatekeepers "drop the black ball" on those they do not approve.

Economic Orientation

Executives and professional men head class I families. Those in business are major office holders, such as on boards of trustees, presidents, vice-presidents, secretaries, and treasurers in the larger industries, construction and transportation companies, stores, banks, brokerage houses, and utilities. Two thirds of the men in the professions are in independent practice—lawyers, physicians, engineers, architects, and certified public accountants; the other one third are salaried—professors, clergymen, and engineers for the most part. A few executives receive from $40,000 to $50,000 a year, but more earn from $20,000 to $30,000. The modal range for mature free professionals is from $20,000 to $25,000 per year. However, the median reported family income, where the male head is the only one gainfully employed, is $10,000. This median is conditioned in large part by the presence of Yale University and its large, comparatively low-paid faculty, as well as the presence of young professionals, widows, and retired people in the sample. In the 8 percent of the households where a wife is engaged in business or a profession, the median income is $15,025 a year.

* By "*arrivistes*" we mean persons who are upward mobile, who have achieved class I positions through their own efforts rather than by inheritance, usually in the current generation. The connotation of unscrupulousness usually associated with the word does not apply in these discussions.

Families in the core group are, on the whole, wealthy, but there are large differences in their economic positions. A few families are multimillionaires; other families may possess only a quarter- to a half-million dollars. The wealth of the core group has been inherited by two, three, and more generations, whereas that of the *arrivistes* has been acquired during the present or previous generation. Inherited wealth is accorded a higher social value within the core group than "made money." Several generations of inherited wealth attests to the genuineness of the patina on the family's pecuniary escutcheon. A family which possessed the ability to make money in the first place, and to hold it and add to it through the generations, has demonstrated its "true" worth.

A cardinal principle in established families is that capital funds should not be squandered. Each generation should live on income only and add to capital by conservative management. Squandering of capital funds results in the next generation's being faced with the problem of earning its living. An inherited income assures a high standard of living without undue effort of a family head to support his family of procreation. Men are expected to look after their inheritances and those of their wives, but estate managers may be employed and trust departments of large banks relied upon for counsel, if not actual management of securities, trusts, and properties. A man should have an occupation or a profession, although he may not rely too heavily upon it for income. Income from inherited wealth supplemented by income from salaries and fees earned by the male head is the most general pattern.

Persons with private incomes are careful to see that the dollar sign is muted on their possessions and on the things they do. The dollar sign and interest in the dollar sign are stigmata of newly rich strivers. Individuals who accumulate wealth view money as *the* requisite of high social position; those who have inherited wealth look to other things as the sine qua non of position. The core group is not ostensibly interested in money, but a substantial income is necessary to their way of life. This point was brought to our attention sharply by an elderly member of a distinguished family who, in response to a question on income, reported with indignation, "We have it."

Ethnic Origin

Persons able to pass the core group's test of financial means are faced with a more crucial barrier—the lineage test. Lineage is used to protect the group from "social climbers" who are attempting to reach "the summit" on the basis of personal achievement. The upward mobile nuclear family with the right ethnic background is the most serious threat to privileged position, and they are a target for the group's hostile and biting remarks. For example, a man in the core group was discussing local families and their estates when the interviewer commented on the purchase of an estate by an *arriviste* of mixed Irish and Yankee descent in the respondent's neighborhood. The respondent, who was interviewed in his office, straightened in his chair, tapped the desk with a forefinger, and stated emphatically, "Money does not count up there (a hill in a suburb covered with estates). Family background, who you are—these are the things that count." This man overlooks the simple fact that these families could not live on their estates without wealth. An *arriviste* may manage to purchase an estate "on the hill" and be isolated from the social life of the families who accept one another as equals. The question of who one is, ethnically, places acceptance in the group in a different dimension of the social structure from economic competence. A person is able to do something about his role and function in the economic system, but he is powerless in the ethnic dimension of his life. Here he is dependent upon his ancestors.

The core group ascribes a different and lower status to persons from disapproved ethnic backgrounds—Jews, Irish, Italians, Greeks, Poles, and others from southern and eastern Europe. Core group members tend to lump these national origin groups together; all are undesirable. An industrial leader, when asked why New Haven has such a diverse population, stated, "I should say largely it was an overflow of great tidal waves of these races—Italians, Irish, Jews, Germans, and so on—reaching New York and sliding on to the next place. These races are very gregarious, and they are coaxed easily by a roll of money." A prominent core group matron thought that the "Italians just swarmed into this area. It seemed to be the happy hunting ground. New Haven has become an Italian colony. It's amazing." Another emphasized, "The Poles and Italians gave us our vicious gangs." A prominent attorney accused the "Jewish traders" of "gobbling up fine old companies in trouble" and continuing "their Sheeney ways."

Chronologically, wealth comes first; then one's family background is discovered, and the importance of wealth is pushed into the background. The number of generations a family has been prominent *and* resident in the community is important to the elderly arbiters of power and status. This point was well put by a distinguished

matriarch while we were discussing the importance of some famil\
in the life of the city over a number of generations. Such a family
was named as an illustration. The respondent closed her eyes,
thought for a few moments, and resumed the discussion with, "The
——— are not really old New Haveners. They first settled in Say-
brook (a pioneer settlement on the Connecticut coast) in the 1640s,
but the family did not move to New Haven until 1772."

The core group is composed of extended families who trace their
ancestry directly to the colonial period and then to England, Scotland, the Netherlands, or to French Huguenot refugees. These well-
known "old Yankees" represent 59 percent of this stratum. Persons
of Irish descent, who through the years have accumulated wealth
and established family positions but have maintained their identifications with the Roman Catholic Church, are a group apart and
compose 11 percent of this class. Descendants of other immigrant
stocks—German (6 percent), Scandinavian (2 percent), and Italian
(9 percent)—who are accumulating wealth through business enterprise and successful professional practices, represent other subgroups.
Jews (13 percent) represent a separate hierarchy from the Gentile
groups. German-Jewish families as a rule occupy higher prestige
positions in the Jewish segment of class I than Jews of Polish and
Russian descent.

Religious Affiliation

Ethnic origins and religious affiliations are highly correlated.
Viewed over-all, the three major religious groups are divided as follows: Protestants—61 percent, Roman Catholics—24 percent, Jews—
13 percent, and mixed or no affiliation—2 percent. Within the
Protestant group, 61 percent of the families are Congregationalists,
17 percent are Episcopalians, 7 percent are Lutherans, 5 percent are
Baptists, 2 percent are Methodists, and other denominations comprise
the remaining 7 percent. In each religious group—Protestant, Catholic, and Jewish—the membership is concentrated in a small number
of congregations. For example, there are 24 Congregational churches
in the community, but over 93 percent of the core group members
belong to three of these churches. Episcopalians are clustered in 2
of 19 parishes in the area, and Roman Catholics are concentrated in
4 parishes. Among Jews, the greatest clustering is in the Reformed
Congregation. As Russian and Polish Jews have moved upward in
the class structure, they have left the Orthodox and Conservative
congregations and affiliated with the Reformed Temple founded by

German Jews who came to the community a century ago. As these *arrivistes* have become affiliated with the Temple, the descendants of its Germanic founders have tended to withdraw from its affairs except for important ritualistic occasions and high holy days.

Although 98 percent of the respondents claim affiliation with three religions, from 8 to 33 percent are not members of any specific congregation and do not attend services. For practical purposes, these people are "unchurched." Approximately 25 percent of Protestant men and women and 38 percent of Jewish men and women have no congregational ties; only 15 percent of the Roman Catholic men and 8 percent of the women are in this category. These people probably had nominal connections with their claimed denominations at one time in their lives, but currently they are outside the religious participation pattern. The percentage of "unchurched" persons is significantly higher in class I in comparison with the other strata.[3] The "unchurched" men and women in each major religion are upward mobile in significantly larger numbers than those who are stable socially. However, a considerable number of upward mobile persons function actively in selected churches and thereby aid their mobility strivings in a positive way.

Religious identification rather than affiliation and active participation is a salient factor in the organization of this stratum's social life. If a person is identified as a Jew, most Gentile doors are closed to him; moreover if he is a Roman Catholic, lines are drawn around him in Protestant circles, but not so openly. Conversely, Jews and Roman Catholics react in negative ways to Protestants. The three parallel hierarchies of Protestant, Catholic, and Jew, around which the social life of the community, at all levels, is organized, have crystallized in class I with signal force. A core group member made this very clear when he stated, in response to a question about his relationships with Jews, "We have business dealings with them. I sometimes sit next to an eminent Hebrew at a business luncheon." When asked if Hebrews were ever invited into his home, he bristled and said coldly, "In my living room there is never a Hebrew, no matter how eminent he is in professional or business life. Hebrews know."

A distinguished member of a prominent Jewish family described in detail how his family has been discriminated against in its attempts to be accepted into "restricted" clubs and associations. With particular reference to having the "black ball dropped" on his application for membership in a beach club, he remarked with feeling, "My ass is not good enough to sit on their sand."

A housewife whose husband changed his name legally from an easily recognizable Polish-Jewish one to a distinguished New England Yankee one about thirty years ago in the hope that it would enable him, in her words, "to cross over," told how this move failed. They then joined the Temple and became leaders in the Jewish community. She feels strongly that her religion is her "social gospel" but it does not help her make contact with the "white Protestants" who are "the privileged group in New Haven society."

A male member of the "privileged group" who was nominally a Congregationalist but attended church on Easter, Christmas, and only a few other times, did not think religion was too important in his way of life. He commented, "The churches are becoming women's and children's organizations, and, outside of paying the bills, the men don't seem to have much control."

Education

Class I is the most highly educated segment of the population. The median years of school completed by the male heads of families is 17.6. The median for the wives is 14.4 years. One wife in five has the same amount of education as her husband; 43 percent of the husbands have had at least four years more education than their wives, but only 7 percent of the wives have had at least one more year of education than their husbands. The distinct difference in the amount of education between husbands and wives is an outstanding characteristic of this class.

Formal schooling, after the eighth grade, normally is received in a private institution patterned after the English public school. Secondary education in a public school is frowned upon by all segments of the core group; many in this stratum refuse to send their children to the public schools from the earliest years. The core group families send their sons to distinguished New England boarding schools where they spend from four to six years preparing for an Ivy League College. Daughters are sent to well-known boarding schools to prepare them for entrance into a select women's college. Families who cannot afford to send their children to boarding schools enter them in one of the accepted single-sex day schools in the community.

The country day and boarding schools are staffed by an elite corps of headmasters and headmistresses of approved Yankee lineages and Protestant faiths, from "upper class" families, who were educated in the aristocratic-value system and are dedicated to preserving and transmitting it. They may close the educational gates to persons who cannot pass both the means and lineage tests, but other criteria are used to justify such actions. They attempt to hire teachers with backgrounds similar to theirs; as this is difficult today, their staffs tend to be made up of upward mobile individuals who have identified with the core group's value system.

Private secondary schooling is preparatory, if not a requisite, to entrance into a one-sex "name" college. The "big three," Yale, Harvard, and Princeton, are the dominant preference for men. The smaller men's colleges occupy secondary positions in the local value hierarchy—Amherst, Williams, Dartmouth, Brown, and Wesleyan. Women should be sent to Smith, Vassar, Wellesley, Bryn Mawr, Mount Holyoke, or Radcliffe to be acceptable in the social world under discussion. Coeducational private colleges such as Swarthmore or Oberlin are respectable but do not carry prestige. Attendance at a state university marks a man or a woman as an *arriviste;* the state university graduate is at best a "fringer" in the elite groups. The vast majority of the upward mobile family heads, whether from old American stock or ethnic groups, were trained in whole or in part at state universities, but they generally do everything within their means to see that their children attend private secondary schools and name colleges.

Lessons to teach the individual how to act in various social situations and how to use leisure time in approved ways are extremely important in the way of life of this stratum. Professional functionaries who sell their skills and talents to class I families run classes for ballroom dancing, tennis, golf, sailing, music, and so on. Several years of formal training in leisure time pursuits prepare the young person for the core group's way of life, as well as the parallel one prevailing among the fringe groups.

Family Constellation

The nuclear group of husband, wife, and dependent children constitutes the primary family and common household unit. This group normally passes through a family cycle [4] which begins with marriage, extends through the childbearing and child-rearing years, and ends in old age through the death of one of the parental pair. Each marriage brings into being a new family cycle. Upon the birth of their first child, the nuclear pair becomes a family of procreation, but for the child this family of origin is his family of orientation. Thus, each individual who marries and rears children has a family of orientation and a family of procreation.

Each nuclear family is related to a number of other nuclear families by consanguinal and affinal ties. Also, each family in the kin group occupies a position in the status system which may be the same or different from the others. The differences are produced by the mobility of some families. This movement of the individual nuclear family in the status system, while it is approved and often lauded as "the American way," has important effects on kin group relations.

One's ancestors and relatives count for more in the core group than what one has achieved in one's own lifetime. Background is stressed most heavily when it comes to the crucial question of whom a member may marry. One of the perennial problems of the established family is the control of the marriage choices of its young men. Young women can be controlled more easily because of the more sheltered life they lead and their more passive role in courtship. The relative passivity of the female, coupled with sex exploitation of females from lower social positions by high level males that sometimes leads to marriage, results in a significant number of old maids in established families. Strong emphasis on family background leads to the selection of marriage mates from within the old-family group in an exceptionally high percentage of cases and, if not from the old-family group, then from the new-family segment of this stratum. The degree of kinship solidarity, combined with intraclass marriages, results in comparative stability in the class, in the extended kin group, and in the nuclear family within it.

The core group family is basically an extended kin group, solidified by lineage and a heritage of common experience in the communal setting. A complicated network of consanguinal and affinal ties unites nuclear families of orientation and procreation into an in-group that rallies when its position is threatened by the behavior of one of its members, particularly where out-marriage is involved; this principle will be illustrated later. The nuclear family is viewed as only a part of a broader kin group that includes the consanguinal descendants of a known ancestral pair, plus kin brought into the group by marriage. Divorce is avoided if possible; when it occurs the entire family looks upon it as a disgrace, if not a scandal. The solidarity of the kin group is markedly successful in keeping divorce to a minimum. The ratio of widows and widowers to divorced persons is 27 to 1. This is the highest ratio in the population.

An important factor in the established family's ability to maintain its position through several generations is its economic security. Usually a number of different nuclear families within a kin group are supported, in part at least, by income from a family estate held in trust. Also, because of the practice of intramarriage within the core group, it is not unusual for a family to be the beneficiary of two or more estates held in trust. For example, one extended family group is the beneficiary of a trust established a century ago that yields something over $300,000 annually after taxes.[5] This income is divided among 37 different nuclear families descended from the founder, 28 of whom live in the home community; 23 of these families are beneficiaries of one other trust fund, and 14 receive income from two or more other trust funds. These different nuclear families regard themselves as part of the "Scott" family;[6] moreover, they are so regarded by other established families, as well as by persons lower in the status system who know something of the details of the family history.

The Scott family has maintained its social position for more than two centuries by a combination of property ownership, educational, legal, and political leadership, and control of marriages. Its members are proud that it has never had a non-Protestant marriage in seven generations; only five divorces have been traced, but these are not mentioned; one desertion has been hinted but not confirmed.

The family tradition of Protestant intermarriages had a severe test in recent years. A son of one nuclear family, who had spent four years in the Armed Forces in World War II, asked a class II Catholic girl to marry him. The engagement was announced by the girl's family to the consternation of the Scott family, who immediately brought pressure on the boy to "break off the affair." After several months of family and class pressure against the marriage, the young man "saw his error" and broke the engagement. A year later he married a family-approved girl from one of the other "old" families in the city. Today he is an officer in his wife's family's firm, and his father has built him a fine suburban home.

This case illustrates a number of characteristics typical of the established core group family. It is stable, extended, tends to pull together when its position is threatened—in this instance by an out-marriage—exerts powerful controls on its members to ensure that their behavior conforms to family and class codes, and provides for its members economically by trust funds and appropriate positions.

The *arriviste* family is characterized most decisively by phenomenal economic or professional success during a short interval of time. Its meteoric rise in the social system is normally the personal triumph of the nuclear head of the family. If the head is a businessman, he is busy making a "million bucks"; the family purchases the symbols associated with the wealthy American family: a large house, fine furniture, big automobiles, and expensive clothes. The new tycoon knows the power of money in the market place, and he often attempts to buy high position in the status system. In a professional family, the head is intent on making a "name" in his profession and acquiring some wealth. His family follows the same general pattern of purchasing the outward symbols of success but in a more modest fashion. The new family is able to meet the means test, but not the lineage test of the established families. Consequently, it is generally systematically excluded from membership in the cliques and associations of greatest prestige. This is resented especially by the wife and children, but less often by the tycoon or professional man.

The new family is unstable in comparison with the established family. It lacks the security of accepted position at the top of the local status system—a position that will come only with time; it cannot be purchased. The stabilizing influence exerted by an extended family group, as well as friends, on the deviant individual is absent. Then too, the adults in the new family are self-directing, full of initiative, believe in the freedom of the individual, and rely upon themselves rather than upon a kin group. (Many upwardly mobile individuals break with their kin groups to aid their mobility.) The result is, speaking broadly, conspicuous expenditure, insecurity, and family instability. Thus, we find divorces, broken homes, and other symptoms of disorganization in a significantly large number of new families. The ratio of widows and widowers to divorced persons is only 5 to 1; this is significantly lower than in the core group. In like manner, the percentage of children under 17 years of age living in broken homes is decidedly higher in the new families (18 percent versus 3.4 percent). Because new families are so conspicuous in their consumption and behavior, they become, in the judgment of the general population, symbolic of "upper class" actions and values to the resentment of established families who generally frown upon such behavior.

Family Homes

Single-family houses valued by the tax assessor from $30,000 to $50,000 are owned by 81 percent of their occupants; 95 percent are valued for tax purposes at above $20,000, and some homes are valued above $100,000. The "small" house has 8 to 10 rooms, whereas a "large" one may have 25 to 30 rooms. The modal house has from 12 to 15 rooms. It is located on spacious, carefully landscaped grounds designed to give privacy and is set off by the beauty of the structure in the "best" residential areas. These tend to be hills and ridges in the suburban towns, but there are still "pockets" of fine homes in the city. To be socially correct, and to enhance one's prestige, a second home is essential for core group families. It is a "cottage" located at fashionable beaches along Long Island Sound, the Maine Coast, on Cape Cod, or one of the offshore islands, for example, Martha's Vineyard. If a family prefer the mountains, their "cottage" is found in exclusive areas of the Berkshire, White, or Green Mountains. Summer "cottages" are generally in colonies protected by incorporated private associations whose members decide who may buy into the area or to whom an owner may rent his "cottage." Some are small homes of 5 rooms, but others are estates of 15 to 20 rooms with large landscaped grounds, multiple-car garages, a small stable, and a tennis court.

The family seat, or town house, is occupied from nine to ten months each year. The "cottage" is used during the summer, usually from Fourth of July until Labor Day. This is The Season when a family is expected to be out of town. Core group families usually own or have access to a third home—the lodge. The lodge is occupied for only two or three weeks during the year: a fishing lodge in Maine or New Brunswick during the trout season; a hunting lodge in the same areas during the deer, moose, and bear seasons. The fishing and hunting lodges are owned privately, but the owners generally belong to an association so that large areas of water or land can be controlled at relatively nominal costs to each member. Some of these sportsmen's associations are a century old, and have members in the same family to the fourth and fifth generations.

Exclusiveness is attained in the "best" areas by rigid zoning requirements which insure a certain amount of uniformity in the size of the grounds and the structures. These areas are separated from adjacent areas by shubbery and large lawns. Within the home, entertainment rooms are separated from the bedrooms, and the family quarters are isolated from servants' quarters. The accent is upon privacy for the family and its individual members in and around the home. The day of many servants has passed but a family normally has either one full-time or a part-time cleaning woman, and often both. A domestic cleaning service may do the heavy house-cleaning each week, and a complete house-cleaning two, three, or four times a year. The housewife does a good bit of the day-to-day light housekeeping—shopping and other maintenance chores—but the heavy work is done ordinarily by hired help. When a core group family is pinched financially, it places a higher value on a part-time servant than on expensive entertaining and expensive automobiles. The home grounds are landscaped and maintained by contract gardeners; only families with the larger estates employ a full-time gardener. However, families try to keep the servant complex intact through the one maid-of-all-work, even if she is employed part-time, and specialists who do contract work, such as washing windows and polishing floors.

An automobile is a necessity, but a few conservative individuals do not own and have never learned to drive one. At least 99 percent of the families own one automobile, and over half own two. The preferred family car is a Cadillac, but Chryslers, Oldsmobiles, Buicks, and station wagons of the more popular brands are acceptable. The car tends to be under three years of age; some families will drive automobiles for ten years or more, but they are carefully polished and maintained. If the family owns a country place, it is customary to letter its name on the station wagon. Another folkway is to possess a two- or three-numbered marker (license plates in Connecticut are markers and they are permanent) or to have only one's initials on the marker. A family with two initials on its marker usually rates higher than one with three or four letters. One family owns several automobiles; each marker in the three generations represented has one given initial of a family member and the initial of the family's surname. The ceremonial car of the family head, a custom-built black Cadillac sedan, bears the initials of a noted ancestor who lived a century ago.

The Club System

A family's class status can be determined most accurately by its club memberships because the private clubs of the area are graded according to the prestige of their members. Conversely, a man, woman, or a nuclear family is ranked by those conversant with the elite's system of values in terms of the clubs to which one belongs. Memberships in appropriate clubs are evidence of validated status and they symbolize for the initiated "who one is." Socially acceptable people belong to approved clubs; those who are unacceptable or have been in the community too short a time to have established a "toe hold" do not hold memberships. All private clubs are self-perpetuating associations, managed by a board of governors, the inner circle who represent the value structure of those in power in the club. The members and the board of governors in particular determine who is admitted; in sum, they are the gatekeepers of the accepted elite.

Three distinct types of clubs characterize this stratum: the one-sex club, the family club, and the special interest club. "Gentlemen's" and "ladies'" clubs represent the first type. The family club is designed to meet the social and recreational needs for all family members. The special interest club is for persons with particular tastes and hobbies. Three "gentlemen's" clubs maintain club houses where the members may meet, relax, read, have a drink at the private bar, or eat with their equals. Two of these clubs are "exclusive"; the acknowledged members of the core group, the Gentile professional and business elites, are divided between them. No exclusive "ladies'" club maintains a club house. Their members meet in private homes, parish houses, or other clubs. The most exclusive one meets in the home of some member. It has no name other than the one its members have traditionally accorded themselves, namely, Our Society. This is truly a core group of equals where memberships are passed down from mothers to daughters and daughters-in-law with few exceptions. There are a half-dozen acceptable family clubs in the community, but Gentile members of the core group are concentrated in one, the *arrivistes* are clustered in another, professional families in two others, and Jewish *arrivistes* and professionals in another. Several yacht, fishing, hunting, and beach clubs are maintained by Gentile families; in like manner groups of Jewish families maintain beach and country clubs.

Some 97 percent of the class I families have at least one club membership and 75 percent belong to two or more clubs. The husband belongs to a men's club, the wife to a ladies' club, and the family to a family club. A relatively small number of leisure time interests are represented in the special interest clubs—tennis, golf, polo, sailing, fishing, and hunting among the men and the raising of flowers and purebred livestock or thoroughbred horses among both sexes.

Mass communication media reach class I persons in a selective way. Practically every home is equipped with a radio, but only 50.5 percent owned television sets as late as the fall of 1952. Among the television set owners, there are sharp differences between the core group and the *arrivistes*. Only one third of the core group own television sets—usually these are families with younger children. Over four out of five *arriviste* families own television sets, large and expensive ones. Television viewing is very selective among core group adults; they are partial to drama, serious music, and news programs. The *arrivistes* too view these programs but they include also variety, comedy, and quiz programs.

The local evening newspaper is subscribed to by 99 percent of class I householders. In addition, 26 percent subscribe to the local morning newspaper. Both of these daily newspapers are owned and published by the same family. Approximately 51 percent of the class I families subscribe to *The New York Times* regularly, and 26 percent receive *The New York Herald Tribune*. News magazines, like *Time* and *U.S. News and World Report*, reach 31 percent of the homes; 17 percent of the homes receive trade or professional journals; 39 percent subscribe to such educational and literary magazines as *Harper's*, *The New Yorker*, and *Saturday Review*. At least four such "quality" magazines come into over 53 percent of the class I homes.

Philanthropy

A sense of social obligation in relation to those they "fear are not so fortunate" is a commonly held value among mature individuals. Both men and women spend hundreds of hours each year serving on the boards of many welfare organizations. They set policy, raise money, and hire and fire personnel as the occasion demands. Their only compensation is the knowledge that someone has to be responsible for these community activities. Generous amounts of money are given to the United Fund, special charities, the hospital, and various health drives like the March of Dimes and the Heart Fund. The younger women, in particular, give freely of their time and generously of their money to help maintain philanthropic activities sponsored by each of the seven Junior Leagues or associations of similar type. Support of the symphony, art center, schools, and colleges are also prominent in the obligation pattern of this stratum.

The Social Ethic

Formal recognition of a Gentile family's position in the elite is achieved by inclusion in the *Social Directory;* over 95 percent of class I Gentile families are listed, but less than 5 percent of class I Jewish families. Listing in the *Directory* is a symbol of acceptance into the higher brackets of the class structure, but not into the inner circle. A family must belong to the Cotillion or the Assembly to be in the inner circle. This requires the possession of all the traits that make a "lady" or a "gentleman" by local standards. The means, the lineage, and the breeding tests must be passed before a family is acceptable to the core group. Elements in the breeding test include "character," "good manners," "personal grooming," and evidence of "culture." Pretense is a cardinal sin; to pretend is as vulgar as an attempt to buy one's way. One must never accept hospitality unless he can return it in the same spirit it was given. Proper clothes for the occasion are stressed heavily. Personal grooming is important for both sexes at all times and at all ages. A woman may acquire the finest imported gowns but have a mouthful of crooked teeth and a "blatant Midwestern voice" which mark her origins and block her efforts to be accepted. In sum, the cardinal characteristics of this stratum's cultural pattern include wealth, lineage, and "good breeding." There are no substitutes; those who enjoy the coveted qualities of high status and acceptability possess this trinity; those who aspire to be accepted in the core group must acquire them. A distinguished elderly gentleman whose ancestors were founders of a western Massachusetts city has lived in the city for over 70 years. While discussing the "New 'Haven" attitude he observed, "If my grandchildren live to be old men and women, they may be looked upon as New Haveners," by those we have referred to as "proper New Haveners."

A salient characteristic of some numbers of the core group is an ardent amateur's interest in avocations such as sailing, polo, golf, breeding of purebred livestock, and the collection of book plates. Their assured private incomes enable them to indulge their hobbies and idiosyncrasies to an extent undreamed of by middle and working class persons. Their whimsical personalities combined with wide experiences make many of them delightful sophisticates and charming companions.

Summary

Class I is composed of the community's business and professional leaders. Its members live in those areas of the community generally regarded as the "best"; the male heads are college graduates, usually from famous private institutions; their wives have completed from one to four years of college. Incomes are the highest of any stratum, and many families are wealthy; often their wealth is inherited. This is true particularly of a core group of interrelated families who have lived in the area for several generations. Members of the core group are descendants of the pioneers who settled in New England three centuries ago. These families dominate the private clubs that play so prominent a part in this group's use of leisure time. The core group family is stable, secure, and, from the viewpoint of its values, socially responsible for its members and the welfare of the community.

The core group's business and professional supremacy is challenged by the upward mobile *arrivistes*. Men and women in this segment of class I are educated, able, aggressive, and, in a word, leaders. Relations between the core group members and *arrivistes* represent an area of tension, particularly in social affairs and community activities. The upward mobile families are "new people" to the community; most are descendants of "old immigrants," but some are from "new immigrant" stocks. The nuclear family is not as stable as the core group family; separations, divorces, and remarriages are not too unusual. We infer that separations and divorces are evidences of "acting out" inner tensions, associated with their mobility and feelings of rejection by the core group. Although the *arrivistes* are still a minority in class I, many core group members feel threatened by them and the vigorous leadership they show in community affairs.

CLASS II

Status Awareness

Nine percent of the community's population is placed in class II by the Index of Social Position. This is the most status-sensitive stratum in the population. Ninety-six percent of the respondents know that there are classes in the community and can identify their own positions in the class structure. Nineteen percent believe that they are upper class; 54 percent place themselves in the upper-middle class; 18 percent identify themselves as middle class; 3 percent see themselves as working class; and the remainder are not sure of their identification beyond "somewhere in the middle class."

Status sensitivity in class II stems from the pivotal positions its members occupy in the social structure. They are close enough socially to established families and elite community leaders to know how they think and act, yet many know the problems of "less fortunate" people—small business owners, white-collar workers and blue-collar workers—as they have lived with them at one time. Seventy-four percent of the class II adults have been upward mobile in the course of their lives. Their mobility has brought them into contact with subcultures of the higher classes and has moved them away from the values of their families of orientation. They have had to make new identifications and associations and have had to learn a complex of usages different in quality and often in form from those learned unconsciously as children in lower positions in the social system. To achieve their aspirations, many have moved from their home community to another community, only to be shifted to still other communities by their ambitions. Each advance in geographical and/or social space has taken these families from accustomed milieus and forced them to put down new roots.

Seventy-one percent of the mobile families are headed by men employed by national organizations with offices in cities throughout the nation; an additional 10 percent are salaried professionals. Both executive and professional employees tend to move from job to job to realize success goals. Many feel isolated from the community in which they live for only a few years. A district manager for a national merchandise chain who had moved eight times in nineteen years said, "My friends, people I have picked up with, are all over the country—Lord knows where they are! We are displaced people in our own country." These people are extremely sensitive to how they must behave to succeed in a new situation in order to continue to move upward in the managerial hierarchy.

Economic Orientation

The quest for success and security is a hallmark of upward mobile persons. A young male looks forward to the time when he will be at the top of his chosen profession or high on the executive ladder. He thinks he will earn $15,000, $25,000, or as much as $50,000 a year and will help make decisions, not just carry out those made by others. Middle-aged and older men, however, are more concerned with "holding on." A 50-year-old third-line executive states, "There is nothing ahead for me in the company. My job is to hold on." This man has learned to relinquish further success as measured by promotion in the executive hierarchy for security. Security is realized also by saving part of one's income against possible future hazards.

Forty-nine percent of the male family heads are business managers who execute rather than formulate policy; 31 percent are lesser ranking professionals—engineers, teachers, social workers, pharmacists, opticians, and accountants; and 20 percent are proprietors of business worth between $35,000 and $100,000.[7] The managers and professionals are salaried employees; the owners rely upon profits for their income. These families have no backlog of wealth, but 12 percent earn over $10,000 per year. When there is one worker in the family, the male head, the median yearly income is $6500. One sixth of the wives are gainfully employed as teachers, social workers, office managers, secretaries, or in clerical and sales occupations. The working wife contributes $3500 a year to the family income. Families with two incomes earn $10,000 a year.

The typical family balances its need to present a "good front" with its efforts to save for years to come. Thus, most of its income is spent on current living with some part saved first in insurance policies, second in the family home, and third in securities. As much life insurance as the family can afford is purchased for the protection of the wife and children. The family home is secondary to the insurance program and the purchase of stocks and bonds and annuities is further back in the family's financial plan.

The Family Home

Newly married couples usually begin their family life in a small apartment in New Haven or some more distant city, but their planning is directed toward a home in the suburbs. Generally, as soon as savings meet minimal mortgage requirements, the family buys a house. The home is viewed as a symbol of the family's success in realizing a major life goal, and its selection is a major enterprise. However, only 55 percent have title to their homes; the other 45 percent rent houses or apartments located in New Haven city. When a home is bought, it must be in the "right" area in a "good" school district. Older homes in established districts are considered more desirable by many families than the ranch type common in newly developed areas.

Widespread application of this viewpoint leads to the infiltration of younger families into established "better" areas in the suburbs. Eighty-eight percent want to leave the city to settle in two desirable suburbs. Here they are frequently "over-housed," and the mortgage payments are a continuous strain. This point is illustrated by a housewife who had three children in the suburban school generally considered to be the "best" in the community.

> Out here there is a background of ease though none of us really have a great deal of money. I think the people next door and our neighbors across the street have probably more than any of us. I mean as far as we are concerned we just hope and pray the mail comes through at the right time each month so we can pay the next round.

The suburban areas populated largely by class II families are located on the lower slopes of the hills and ridges where the class I's live. The homes of both classes are single-family, but the class I homes are on larger lots and are screened from one another and the street by more shrubbery. Also the houses are larger, usually 10 to 15 rooms, whereas the class II homes contain 6, 7, or, at the most, 8 rooms. The homes of the class II's are maintained by the wife and husband rather than cleaning women, landscape gardeners, and general servants.

These families believe in zoning and independent action to protect their residential areas from invasion by "undesirables"—primarily ethnically identified individuals who have enjoyed financial success in recent years. Restrictive clauses are illegal, but informal "gentlemen's agreements" operate to locate Jews in selected areas, Italians in others, and Protestants in still others. These arrangements are given force by real estate brokers who work with the sellers and their neighbors to maintain the "quality" of the "better" neighborhoods. Real estate brokers believe that they must "fit the right kind of people into a neighborhood." [8]

Characteristically, the husband commutes by private car or bus to his office in New Haven five or six days a week. The wife, as family executive, manages the home and children while the husband fulfills his economic functions in the city. Except for weekends, holidays, and vacations, the family schedule revolves around the commuting member.

Education

Class II adults differ from those in class I in the type and amount of education they have experienced. They have been educated in public schools from the elementary grades throughout the college and university years. A small minority were educated in parochial schools; very few attended private elementary or secondary schools. Class II adults have not had as much education as class I's. However, 71 percent of the men and 38 percent of the women are college graduates; 19 percent of the men and 8 percent of the women have graduate degrees. An additional 16 percent of the men and 21 percent of the women experienced from one to three years of college. The remainder are largely high school graduates. Educationally, class II has one thing in common with class I; the men are better educated than the women. In 61 percent of the homes, the husbands have had one or more years of education than their wives. The median years of school completed number 15.5 for the men and 13.7 for the women.

Most adults attribute their success to the education received in their formative years. Some feel further success is blocked by the amount or type of education they received. For example, a 53-year-old executive in a large concern who is fourth generation Irish and a devout Catholic believed his future is limited because he attended a Catholic college. He stated, "The vice-presidencies go to Protestant Yankees who have Yale degrees." This man sent his two sons to a local private secondary school and then to Yale. However, he discouraged them from joining his company because he felt their future would be better in some other corporation. The need for a "good education" for their children is emphasized by parents who attribute their success to education or who believe their mobility strivings are limited by the wrong kind or amount of education. Many of these parents project their strivings for higher status upon their children.

The children attend public elementary schools but when high school is reached, about one fourth are sent to private day schools in the community. As children progress through school strong emphasis is placed on grades; the college preparatory course is taken in secondary school, because the parents feel the need of a college education for their children. They know they will have little property to leave to them, and if the children are to build upon the foundation they have laid, they must have a college education, and possibly additional training.

Secondary and collegiate education places a heavy burden upon family finances. The minimal cost for secondary public education is $600 to $700 a year, and college education is at least $1600 a year in a municipal or state institution. The minimal annual cost in the Ivy League colleges is $2500. The class II family with two or three children will spend consequently $25,000 to $50,000 to educate its children. Clearly, this is a heavy burden for a family with an income of $7000 to $10,000 a year. The winning of scholarships to defray the cost of college is part of the educational plan in these families; also the boy or girl is expected to work during the summer vacations and possibly part time during the school year. However, a college education is believed to be "worth the price" for it compensates the struggling parents for their anxiety over insecurity.

Ethnic Origins

Upward mobility is linked closely to ethnic heterogeneity in class II. Yankee or "American" stock households are in the minority; they comprise only 20 percent of this stratum. Fourteen percent are of English-Scottish or Welsh ancestry; 12 percent are from northern European countries, such as Germany, Scandinavia, the Netherlands, France, and Austria; 20 percent are of Irish origin. Russian and Polish Jews from the "new immigration" are the largest ethnic element, 26 percent; 8 percent of the household heads are of Italian descent. Ethnic origin combined with upward mobility means that a relatively small proportion of adults are stable intergenerationally.

Religious Affiliations

Ethnic origin is associated closely with religious affiliation. Therefore, Catholics, Jews, and Protestants are represented in unequal numbers. Protestants comprise 45 percent of the class, Roman Catholics 29 percent, and Jews 26 percent. Congregationalists represent 34 percent of the Protestants, and Episcopalians 30 percent; the remainder are largely Methodists, Presbyterians, Lutherans, and a few Baptists. Roman Catholics are of Irish, Italian, German, Austrian descent, and a few are of English origin. The Jews are in large part members of Reformed and Conservative congregations; there are few Orthodox Jews. Some 20 percent of the men and 16 percent of the women have no local church affiliations.

Mixed marriages are rare (less than 7 percent of the households). When they occur they involve, in more than 19 of 20 cases, a Catholic and a Protestant. Less than 4 percent of the cross-religious marriages involve a Protestant and a Jew, and less than 1 percent a Jew and a Catholic.

The vast majority of Protestants, Catholics, and Jews are active in their churches, but a considerable number in each religious group indicate they think people with more power and higher prestige take advantage of them. A Congregational wife states her complaint in these terms:

> When the church wants something done, they have a church dinner. First they sell you a ticket. I have to buy because the wife of my husband's boss sells it to me. We go, and in the dullness of our after-dinner indigestion, we have the riot act read to us on what must be done. Either that or they get us to sign for some contribution. You always feed a Christian a good hearty meal [said with considerable cynicism], then you make him work. It is usually spaghetti, but it might be pot roast. You are never quite sure.

A Jewish businessman voiced his resentment toward continuing drives to raise money for one Jewish charity after another:

Lift up your heart, close your ears, shut your eyes, and open that pocketbook. I'm not belittling these people, but I have the bee put on me all the time, and I can't brush it off. When they want me to give them the business I get tired.

An upward mobile mother of French and German extraction married to an Irishman summed up her position on the church as: "I'm through with nuns and priests." She said she has had too many things told to her and demanded of her by the church throughout her life. The daughter attends a Protestant private school and the mother hopes the daughter will make the break with the church that she herself wants to make but has found impossible so far.

These excerpts from tape-recorded interviews indicate that although the vast majority attend church, for many attendance is to meet external pressures and obligations rather than in response to a genuine need for religion. Those who feel their religion is onerous are looking for moral and emotional security in some other type of activity, but they have not found it.

Family Constellation

Similar ethnic and religious origins of husband and wife combined with geographic and social mobility after marriage give rise to a nuclear family constellation different from those in either higher or lower strata. Class II households are composed predominantly of married adults and their minor children; 97 percent of the adults have been married, and 85 percent are currently; the remainder are widowed, divorced, or separated. In households where the head is not married the ratio of widows and widowers to separated or divorced persons is 9 to 1. This ratio indicates clearly that the family cycle is broken by death far more frequently than by voluntary action of the marital partners; nevertheless, the ratio of widowed to separated or divorced is different from that of both segments of class I. The predominant family constellation is a father, mother, and their minor children under 17 years of age living in a one-family residence. Only 5 percent of the families with children under 17 years of age are broken or have an aged relative, usually a grandparent, in the home.

Two marriage patterns are discernible. Couples married before 1940 were some three years older at the time of marriage than those married afterwards. In the older group, the husband had finished school and been employed for some years before marriage. His wife, too, had finished school and often had been employed for two or three years before marriage. In this group, marriage occurred in the middle and late 20s for the men and in the early and middle 20s for the women; the typical husband is from two to four years older than his wife. Among the couples who married after 1940, both the husband and wife tend to be in their middle or early 20s. There is little difference in their ages. Approximately 20 percent of these couples married while the husband was in service or in school.

Newly married husbands and wives plan for the realization of three major life goals—children, a home, and success. Normally both are employed at the time of marriage; they continue to work until they have saved enough for the wife to leave her job and assume the planned role of mother. A child is desired by 94 percent of the couples within three years of marriage, but they want a child only when they are prepared for it. An unplanned child is a rare occurrence, particularly in the first year of marriage.[9] No differences exist between Catholics, Protestants, or Jews relative to planning families. The size of completed families in the older group was ascertained in order to learn if planned parenthood has been a general practice in this stratum for at least one generation. The analysis revealed that the median number of children per completed family is 1.7. These families, without question, have planned their size. These figures also indicate that this segment of the population has not replenished itself.

Organizations for Leisure

Formal and informal associations are joined by the family as a unit and as individuals. Their memberships include neighborhood clique groups, associations for mutual protection against "undesirables," local church organizations, political clubs, fraternal societies, social clubs, business organizations, the Boy Scouts, the Girl Scouts, and Parent Teacher Associations. The women are committed heavily to welfare activities where they give much time but little money. They routinely ring doorbells and carry on telephone campaigns to raise money for the United Fund, the Red Cross, the Heart Fund, the March of Dimes, the Cancer Drive, the Girl Scouts, and other "drives" to keep "worthy causes" alive. They also will organize on little provocation to block some action they consider "objectionable."

Ninety-three percent of the adults belong to one organization; 84 percent of the women and 79 percent of the men belong to two or more associations. Fifty percent of the men and 57 percent of the women either attend meetings regularly or hold office in their organizations. Seventy-one percent of the men and 67 percent of the women report that their weekday evening recreation is most likely spent in active participation in social clubs, lodges, and community associations. Obviously, a large part of the social life of these people is spent in these organizations.

Recreation in the home revolves around the television set or reading. Families with children accepted television early, but 47 percent voice strong objections to children's TV programs. Variety programs are accepted by adults as appropriate entertainment, but they object to programs of violence. Newspapers and magazines are read extensively, but few books. Almost every family reads the *New Haven Evening Register* and 56 percent read *The New York Times* or *The New York Herald Tribune;* only 11 percent read the *New York Daily News* or the *New York Daily Mirror.* Some 45 percent subscribe to *Life,* 30 percent to *Time,* and 39 percent to the *Reader's Digest.* Forty-two percent read the *Saturday Evening Post,* 41 percent read various women's fashion magazines, and 19 percent read home improvement magazines like *House Beautiful.* Relatively few read literary magazines like *Harper's* or the *Saturday Review.*[10]

Several social clubs are maintained largely by class II families. The core group in each is Yankee or "Old American" in origin. These clubs impose subtle restrictions against upward mobile families of recent ethnic origin. Jews are "restricted" and, as a consequence, they have developed their own clubs. Family clubs are important because here all ages have a place to play tennis, swim, bowl, dance, play bridge, and meet as equals without concern for the "unwashed." Club privileges are denied to nonmembers and sharp lines are drawn between families who are members and those who are not.

The Social Front

Maintenance of the social front is a continuous strain on many families. They want the "best" but they cannot afford it. They may present a placid front to their employers and acquaintances. To their intimates, and in a relaxed mood, they may give vent to deeper feelings. One middle-aged housewife whose husband belongs to a golf club in addition to the approved family club in the area for "business and social" reasons voiced her resentment:

> Golf is a silly damned game. You hit the ball, go after it, hit the ball, go after it; besides it's the 19th hole that's expensive. You can play 18 holes fairly inexpensively, but when you get to the 19th hole you are done. It becomes very sociable then and expensive.

The husband defends himself by pointing out that his golf partners give him a "nice clear feel for business relationships." Good relations at the 19th hole are a means to a valued end—business or professional success.

The desire for success has motivated the efforts of upward mobile men and women. While young, they lived in the future: "The next five years will bring us where we want to be." However, the five years may have stretched out to ten, fifteen, and twenty years, and the still striving, third-line executive realizes the future is not going to be too different from the past; another man may receive the counted-on promotion. In mid-life, he takes stock and realizes that his youth has slipped away, his mental and physical capacities have been taxed to their limit in the struggle to get ahead, and that he is only holding his own. When such a crisis comes, a man or woman who has sought success in vain may slip into a depression. Again, he may decide to hang on grimly and "try to work out his years in the company," because as one said, "We have a fine retirement system." This is a life preserver to men who see that they are not likely to move into the next higher level of the executive or professional hierarchy.

Summary

Almost all adults in the class II stratum have had some formal education beyond high school. The males occupy managerial positions; many are engaged in the lesser ranking professions. The class II members live in one-family houses in the better residential areas. These families are well-to-do, but there is no substantial inherited or acquired wealth. Class II persons are sensitive to status factors perhaps as a consequence of the fact that four in five are upward mobile. The aspirations of these people have taken them away from their parental families and in many cases from their home communities. Upward mobility is closely linked with ethnic heterogeneity and religious affiliation. About one half of the families are Protestants; the remainder are divided rather equally between Roman Catholics and Jews. The nuclear family is composed predominantly of married adults and their minor children. Only 5 percent of the families with children under 17 years of age are broken or have an aged relative, usually a grandparent, in the home. Family members of all ages are "joiners." Their memberships include neighborhood clique groups, associations for mutual protection against "undesirables," local church organizations, political clubs, fraternal societies, business associations, the Boy Scouts, the Girl Scouts, and Parent Teacher Associations. In addition, about half of these families belong to lesser ranking private clubs in the area.

Tension points in class II generally revolve around the striving for success—economic, educational, and social. The younger adults are oriented toward the future, the time when they will "reach the top." Middle-aged men and women are more aware that they have not quite "made it." Older persons know they will not "make it"; they are resigned to things as they are, but there is an underlying fear that sickness, war, or depression will impair their ability to "hold on."

CLASS III

Status Awareness

The 21.4 percent of the community's population who are in class III have a working conception of the status system and how they function in it. Ninety-three percent believe there are social classes; 1 percent do not think so, and 6 percent "do not know." Of those who are aware of classes, 31 percent place themselves in the "upper-middle class," 36 percent in the "middle class," 20 percent with the "lower-middle class," and 12 percent with the "working class." One percent conceive of themselves as "upper class" but not a single person identified with the "lower class"; these figures show that this stratum is keenly aware of status, and its members place themselves with considerable accuracy in the class structure.

Economic Position

Three in four male heads are employees. Fifty-one percent are engaged in various salaried administrative and clerical pursuits; 24 percent own small businesses; [11] 9 percent are semiprofessionals or technicians; and 16 percent are plant supervisors or skilled manual workers. Administrative personnel include men and women who are section heads in federal, state, and local governmental offices, and large business offices as well as employees, such as shop, service, and chain store managers. Bank tellers, bookkeepers, claims examiners, and secretaries are examples of clerical workers. Semiprofessional and technical pursuits encompass photographers, physiotherapists, draftsmen, and trained technicians of one kind or another.

Class III women are an important element in the labor force. Young married women fill many clerical, sales, and technicians positions. Older women, married and unmarried, hold responsible supervisory positions in offices and stores. Unmarried adult females work for a living throughout the productive years. Twenty-eight percent of the class III wives are gainfully employed; 59 percent are concentrated in clerical and sales jobs, and 11 percent are technicians or elementary school teachers. The remainder either own or help run small family businesses. The employment pattern for females includes those with children; 11 percent of all mothers with children under 17 years of age are gainfully employed outside the home. Small family businesses are generally operated by the wife with the help of the husband evenings and weekends. In this way, the family has an income in addition to the husband's salary. A number of little businesses are run by widows or divorcées. In general, a class III woman is working at the time of marriage and continues her job until she begins a family. She may re-enter the labor market when her children are in school and demands are made that the father's income cannot meet.

Family incomes are not so large as in the two higher classes; neither is the range as wide. The median family income in 1950 was $4929 where the household head was the only earner. Among families with a single income, 32 percent report incomes over $5000 a year, but only 2 percent report more than $10,000. Family incomes are thickly clustered in the $4000 to $5000 bracket. In families with multiple incomes, the median is $7538. In families where the husband and wife work, the husband's median income is $550 less than where the wife does not work. Households headed by working women have a median income of $3151.

Savings are invested in homes, insurance policies, savings accounts, and government bonds; few families own common stocks. Small business owners invest in real property significantly more often than employees. Median liquid savings per family is $2900, that is, readily available cash other than the family's investment in real estate and life insurance.

Economic orientation is related to the socioeconomic group of the family head. The small businessman is concerned with business success, the measure of which is profit. A "good" businessman belongs to his neighborhood trade association and to the Chamber of Commerce. There are numerous neighborhood and district trade associations composed of small businessmen in the community which look after the interests of the neighborhood or business district. The little businessman and his trade association exert pressure in elections because they can and do make contributions to candidates who promise to meet their demands. A small businessman verbalizes his self-interest as "community interest" and "service to the public."

Salaried administrative employees identify themselves with the executive hierarchy rather than with the clerical workers or plant supervisors. They dislike unions, are unorganized, and have few associations or spokesman to protect their interests in the company, the labor market, or the community. They are respected by clerical and blue-collar workers, but they are not viewed as equals by small businessmen. The major bulwarks to an administrative worker's self-esteem and prestige are his right to wear a business suit while working, his authority over clerical employees, his desk and his place in the office, and his hope of climbing the executive ladder. The hope of advancement is a motivating factor among young men, but the middle-aged men look back at the time when they dreamed of "moving up," and the older men feel they are caught in the bureaucratic net and will not move.

Supervisory personnel in the plant, key employees in the production process, are marginal men insofar as they are neither management nor labor. They are identified by administrative and clerical workers with labor, but they do not have independent unions to speak for them. They have little protection in labor struggles because they are largely an adjunct of management. Off the job, they tend to be treated as factory workers by professional workers and businessmen. They usually tend to identify themselves with management and its desires.

Semiprofessionals and technicians, in large part women, are almost exclusively salaried employees in big business organizations or some government unit. This group eschews labor unions as beneath its dignity. They may belong to service organizations like the Business and Professional Women's Club, but their organizations are quasi-social and essentially powerless in the labor market and political arena. These employees link their interests with business values. They resist unionization and rely upon their technical knowledge as a bulwark against their relatively low pay and lack of authority on the job. Their self-esteem is helped by the conditions under which they work; however, they are unhappy about their pay.

The labor market for the types of occupations represented in class III is relatively stable, and employees feel secure in their jobs. They pay a high price for this security as there is little opportunity for advancement with respect to either salary or achievement. A middle-

aged trusted employee of one of the large banks who started to work
in 1926 summarized this neatly when he said:

> I have had a job in the bank since the day after I graduated from
> high school. I've never had to worry about a job. I've been fortunate
> enough to have a job, but unfortunately, I'm underpaid.

Most of these people held their positions during the prolonged depression of the 'thirties, but worked for relatively low salaries. In
the 1940s and the years since, their incomes have not risen fast enough
to keep up with the rise in the cost of living. These people feel the
pressure of prices on their paychecks, and there is a widespread feeling among them that they have lost ground financially. The only
segment of this class that does not feel the pressure of prices is the
small businessman. He knows, however, that business has been shifting toward large national concerns and the chains are creating intolerable competitive conditions for many of them. Their fear of the
future is justified for they know that each year some business in their
neighborhood is forced to close its doors.

Education

The typical class III man or woman is a high school graduate. The
median years of school completed for husbands is 12.4 and for wives
is 12.1. These figures indicate relative educational equality between
men and women. In 46 percent of the families both the husband and
wife have the same amount of education, but in 32 percent of them
the husband has had one year more than the wife. To balance this,
17 percent of the wives have had one year more than their husbands.
More than two years difference between the education of the marital
partners is unusual; less than 2 percent in each sex are in this category.

Children attend public school, for the most part, during elementary
and secondary school years; a few attend parochial day schools.
Approximately 89 percent of the boys and girls graduate from high
school; of these slightly less than 70 percent begin postsecondary education. The remainder go to work immediately after high school.
Publicly supported colleges claim the largest number of young men
and women from class III. They enter the local State Teachers College, the State University, and junior colleges. A minority enter religious colleges and a few are admitted to "name" colleges in New
England. Although these young people start college, about one third
leave after one year, and another one fourth drop out after two years.
The men leave college in significantly larger numbers than the women.
Normally the class III boy begins to work part time and summers

during high school. He may have some money saved when he starts college and may work part time during the school year. But if his family cannot help to support him so that he may have a car, belong to a fraternity, spend money, and do all the other things that go with being a collegiate male, he has a tendency to leave college and get a job. A girl has an easier time finding a part-time office job while in college than a boy. If necessary, she will live and work for her room and board in the home of a family near the college. In extreme cases, she may leave school, work and save money for a year, and re-enter. After she finishes her course, she may marry a college graduate immediately, enter the teaching profession, or go on for advanced work. Women from class III families appear to have more motivation to climb the social ladder than the men.

Residence

Where one lives in the community is important to adults in this stratum. They are aware of the evaluation of residential areas and desire to live in "good" sections. Seventy-two percent of the families report that they "feel at home" in their neighborhoods, but 61 percent prefer a different neighborhood. Some 6 families in 10 in New Haven City hope to be able to move to the suburbs or the "country" in a few years, and about 11 percent would like to leave the area completely for one reason or another.

The modal residence is a five- or six-room single-family house located in a "good" residential area in the suburban towns. Some 74 percent of these single-family houses were built over thirty years ago. They are concentrated on narrow streets with lots thirty-five to fifty feet in width. The houses are close to the street and not so well landscaped as the homes of class II families. The newer single-family homes have been built on larger lots, mainly in developments that have sprung up since World War II, but they are smaller in size and cost considerably more than the older houses. Young families headed by veterans have bought these homes under G.I. benefits. In spite of the numbers who have bought homes since the war, only 58 percent have title to their homes, and a minority of 32 percent have finished paying for them. A significant number of class III families have moved into developments where the houses sell for $16,000 to $20,000. The 42 percent who rent their residences live in apartments and multiple-family houses mainly in New Haven City.

Class III families are probably not housed as well today as thirty years ago. This stratum was squeezed by reduced incomes during the depression years; in the 1940s it was caught in the efforts of government and business to hold the line on salaries while prices crept higher. In more recent years, real estate values have risen two or three times faster than their incomes. In consequence, the six-room ranch house on an acre lot in the suburbs has remained a dream.

Ethnic Origin

Some six in seven family heads trace their ancestry directly to some European country rather than to "old American stock" of the pre-Revolutionary era. The largest proportion trace their ancestry to the old immigration of 1830–1870. The Irish are the largest single national group, comprising 34 percent of the family heads in class III. Persons of German and Scandinavian origin comprise 13 percent, and those of English, Scottish, and Welsh descent, 7 percent. The remainder are descendants of immigrants who came to the community after 1880. Fifteen percent are of Italian origin followed closely by Polish and Russian Jews, 14 percent. Poles, Greeks, and other nationalities of southern and eastern Europe represent the remaining 2 percent.

Descendants of immigrants who came to the United States four and five generations ago are, on the whole, acculturated to American society. They think of themselves as Americans and only secondarily of their Irish or Scandinavian descent; they identify with the American ideal of complete acculturation and socialization. There is a minimum of ethnic identification and little economic or social differentiation among these individuals and those whose ancestry is traceable to Yankee stocks. The newer immigrant stocks have not become thoroughly acculturated, nor are they assimilated in the job or social structure. Persons from the newer immigration have been upward mobile in their own lives. They have moved from the social and cultural conditions characteristic of first and second generation immigrants from southern and eastern Europe to a way of life popularly associated with the "American middle class." During the course of their mobility, they have left much of their European cultural baggage behind them, but have retained some of it. This is known in the community; and it tends to set them apart as hyphenated Americans.

Religious Affiliation

Some 47 percent of the families are Roman Catholic, 14 percent are Jewish, 39 percent are Protestant. This distribution is a result of the high association between religion and national origin. The old American stock, Scandinavians, Germans, English, Scottish, and Welsh are predominantly Protestant, whereas the Irish, Italians, and Poles are Roman Catholics. The Jews are predominantly of Russian and Polish origin.

The identification of upward mobile individuals with Protestant religious denominations is an interesting phenomenon. As individuals have moved toward middle class status, they have become either leaders in the Roman Catholic Church or members of Protestant denominations, principally Congregational or Episcopal, which has raised the percentage of Protestants in this stratum above what the figures on ethnic origin would indicate. There has been no comparable movement of individuals of Yankee, Scottish, English, Welsh, or Scandinavian origins into the Roman Catholic Church. We infer that upward mobility has led to greater defections from the Roman Catholic Church than is true of either Protestants or Jews. The Jews are predominantly members of conservative congregations, but a few are orthodox, and the remainder are reformed. Only 13 percent of the men and 17 percent of the women do not belong to some congregation.

Males and females active in all denominations take religion seriously; they belong to a church, go to it regularly, support it financially, and participate in its organizations. In short, they are practicing Jews, Protestants, or Catholics—the "backbone of God's work."

Family Constellation

The modal family includes a father, mother, and minor children but no other relatives or nonrelatives, and this accounts for 48 percent of all households. The next most frequent unit is a husband and wife without children or other persons—24 percent. There are significantly more families where one or more parents of the family head or his spouse are living with their adult children than in either class II or class IV. This is the traditional pattern of children taking care of aged parents, but there are few children of the household heads in these families. The result is a much smaller percentage of three generation families under one roof than one would expect in comparison with class IV. Approximately 93 percent of adults in class III have been married at some time, and 79 percent are currently married. The remainder are widowed, divorced, or separated. Among the formerly married heads, the ratio of widows and widowers to separated or divorced persons is 6 to 1. This ratio indicates more class III adults are prone to divorce or separation than class II's. A more meaningful figure, indicative of differences in these classes, is the percentage of children under 17 years of age who live in broken homes. In class III, it is 10 percent, whereas in class II less than 5 percent live in broken homes.

The median age for marriage is twenty-two years for males and twenty years for females. Approximately four of five couples are engaged from six to eight months, and three in four are married in a church or chapel. Immediately after marriage, about half of the couples move into the parents' home, usually the wife's; about 40 percent move into "rents" of their own, generally apartments; the remainder make various kinds of adjustments. The "living in" arrangement continues for a year or two, but neither party is satisfied. Although the young couples do not want to live with parents, many are forced to do so until they locate adequate housing in areas where they feel they can live.

Planned parenthood is the rule. In completed families the mothers report a median of 3.4 children; in families where the wives are under 45 years of age, the median is 2.1. The younger parents report a desire of 2 to 4 children. No significant differences appear in the various religious groups with regard to the number of children desired. However, among younger Protestants, significantly more couples have no children than among either Jews or Catholics; but Catholics have more 1-child families than either Protestants or Jews, and Jews have more 2-child families than Catholics or Protestants.

Leisure Time Activities

Persons from 7 to 70 belong to community organizations of one kind or another—fraternal orders, church couple's clubs, church auxiliaries, church guilds, benefit societies, fraternities, sororities, veterans organizations, Boy Scouts, Girl Scouts, athletic clubs, political associations, women's clubs, Parent Teacher Associations, and so on through a long list of neighborhood, community, and nationally affiliated associations. However, the most ubiquitous memberships for men are in religious-related lodges or veterans groups, and church-related associations for women. 'Eighty-two percent of the men and 87 percent of the women belong to at least one formal association. Sixty-eight percent of the men and 71 percent of the women belong to two or more organizations. Both sexes are active in their associations; they report that they attend meetings more or less regularly and hold, have held, or are willing to hold office. They believe in the importance of taking part in community associations to work for the "good of the community."

Home recreations include television, reading, visiting friends, or relatives, and do-it-yourself projects. Some 76 percent have television; the remainder have radios. Drama, variety, news, and comedians are the accepted fare for viewing. They accept adult programs but are critical of children's programs, especially those built around violence and crime. Some 55 percent with children and television sets are critical of children's television programs.[12]

Practically all households subscribe to the *New Haven Evening Register*, and 53 percent read one additional newspaper; 26 percent read *The New York Times* or *The New York Herald Tribune*, and 19 percent read the *New York Daily News* or the *New York Daily Mirror*. The *Reader's Digest* is the most popular magazine and is read by 37 percent of the families. *Life* is next and reaches 36 percent. The *Saturday Evening Post* is close behind with 32 percent, whereas *Time* is read by 15 percent. Literary and information magazines such as *Harper's*, *Atlantic Monthly*, and the *Saturday Review of Literature* are read by less than 8 percent. Home improvement magazines like *Better Homes and Gardens* and women's magazines like the *Ladies' Home Journal* are standard fare in a significant number of homes in comparison with class II homes.

Summary

Significantly more men and women are dissatisfied with their present living conditions and less optimistic about the future than are the class II's. However, the majority have a positive view of the future. They look forward to the time when the home will be paid for or their income higher, and things will be easier. Some two out of three husbands and wives under 40 years of age believe that their chances of achieving a desired standard of living within the next ten years are "almost certain" or "very good." They expect to double their income within 15 years.

Men and women over 40 years of age are concerned about the maturing of their children, the maintenance of their neighborhood, and their health. Many are disturbed by reports of corruption in business and government, especially at the local level. Others are disturbed by the encroachment of Negroes into their neighborhoods; the feeling that people do not recognize moral responsibilities to their children, their neighbors, and their associates disturbs others; many middle-aged persons wonder about their "place" in life.

The realization of the gulf between what they think life might be and what it is for them is a point of stress for many beyond the middle years. Years of striving for their ideals has taught them to forego pleasures of the day for spiritual, moral, and social gains of tomorrow. As the years pass, and the realization that hoped-for goals have slipped away, or moved farther into the future, many adults have become resigned to the realization that they must adjust to things as they are.

CLASS IV

Group Identification

The Index of Social Position places 48.5 percent of the community's households in this stratum. These people believe that there are classes in the community, and they place themselves in the class structure with a fair degree of accuracy. The 88 percent of the respondents who say there are classes identify themselves in these terms:

Self-Identification	Percent
"Upper-middle" class [13]	4
"Middle" class	18
"Lower-middle" class	22
"Working" class	53
"Lower" class	3

Our respondents clearly have a greater awareness of class than of where they, as individuals, are in the status system. However, their sense of generalized social reality tells them that there are differences between people, and it enables them to estimate their approximate location. The important point is this: over one half of the people categorized as class IV identify themselves as working class, and another 40 percent see themselves as lower-middle or middle class. Few perceive their social positions as being lower class or upper-middle class. Relatively accurate insights into the status structure and where a person thinks he is in it are important factors in the maintenance of the system.

Comparisons between the occupations and educations of the parental and present generations of household heads show that 71 percent are intergenerationally stable. These people are satisfied with their "way of life" and are not making "sacrifices to get ahead." They have a sense of personal dignity and self-esteem which sustains them in their "life position"; they also identify themselves with the working class in significantly large numbers. On the other hand, 77 percent of the 31 percent who moved upward from class V positions have "sacrificed" to "better" themselves. They identify in significantly large numbers with the middle class rather than the working or lower-middle classes; no one in this category sees himself as being in the lower class. These strivers are less satisfied with their accomplishments and roles in the community; also, they expect more from the future than stable persons who tend to be content with things as they are. Their orientation is a sustaining force in the present; it is also a goad to action and a reward for self-denials from day to day.[14]

Economic Orientation

Thirty-five percent of class IV males are skilled manual employees. Fifty-two percent are semiskilled employees, 12 percent are clerical and sales workers, and 1 percent are petty proprietors.[15]

The skilled trades range from auto body repairers, electric welders, heat treaters, linemen, linotype operators, masons, and typographers, to yard superintendents on the railroad. The semiskilled workers are concentrated on the assembly lines of large manufacturing concerns. They are employed also in small plants scattered throughout the industrial areas of the community. Semiskilled workers not on production lines are employed as checkers, receivers, repairers, truckers, and wrappers. There are fewer skilled than semiskilled workers in a given establishment; therefore, the skilled workers are employed in a larger number of establishments.

Skilled workers feel more secure in their jobs and in their homes; they express fewer worries about the future and the possibility of another depression than do semiskilled workers. Many are enthusiastic about their work and are sure it is giving them what they want out of life. Only some 7 percent of skilled workers feel their work is "just a job," but 59 percent of the semiskilled workers exhibit some degree of dissatisfaction with their work. Skilled and semiskilled workers look to the union and economic conditions in the country for their security rather than to the good will of their employers. The two thirds who are in organized industries believe their greatest safeguards against economic insecurity are "the union" and state and federal legislation.

Practically all women who are not too old, too ill, or dependent upon a husband are in the labor force. Among the wives, 37 percent without children or with children 17 years of age and over are gainfully employed. Eighteen percent of the mothers with children between 6 and 16 years of age are employed outside the home as are 6 percent of the mothers with preschool children. The largest proportion of females employed in manufacturing industries is drawn from this stratum. Young females take jobs as semiskilled factory workers, clerical, or sales workers as soon as they leave school and continue to work after marriage until pregnancy forces them to leave. These wives stay home to rear their children, but as the children grow older a considerable percentage go back to work.

Family income is relatively low in comparison with the higher classes. The median family income is $3812 per year where the male head is the only employed member of the household. In this category, 64 percent earn less than $4000, and 27 percent earn between $4000 and $5000; 9 percent earn more than $5000. When there are two or more incomes in the household, the median earnings are $5763.

The Family Home and Savings

Savings are invested in a home, furniture, clothes, and the family car. Forty-six percent have title to their homes, but only 19 percent of these "home-owning" families have paid for their homes completely. The remainder are buying them on a monthly payment plan. Seventy-nine percent of the home-owning families live in two- or three-family houses. The two-family, three-family, or multiple-family home owners live in working class sections of the city. The one-family home-owning families live mainly in three suburban towns.

Single-family dwellings, particularly among first and second generation immigrant stocks, are viewed as financial burdens. Experience has taught them that, in the long run, a "working man" has periods of unemployment and two- or three-family homes "pay for themselves." In multiple-family houses, the owner lives downstairs and rents the upstairs. The owner gets his quarters rent free, whereas the renter pays for the house and its upkeep. However, third and fourth generations of immigrant stock prefer a single-family house in the suburbs to a two-family house in the city.

Family income is expended for the most part as it is earned. The pay check goes for food, clothes, health, recreation, shelter, and the many expenditures attendant upon family maintenance. The typical family tries to save, but is not able to lay away, under normal conditions, more than $10 to $15 a month. Even this small amount is often expended in an emergency, as, for example, the purchase of a major piece of furniture or an automobile. Few families are able to save enough cash to pay for a new car on delivery or for a substantial payment on a home.

Expenditures are made in chain stores or small independent stores located in working class areas where the family feels it can get the most for its money. Most major purchases, such as refrigerators, washing machines, or sofas, are made on the installment plan. Factory workers tend to be paid in cash, and usually on bill-paying day the wife takes the bus to the center of the city and walks from place to place to pay in cash the monthly installment and utility bills. Money that is saved is usually banked in one of the building and loan associations in the city, but cash hoards are hidden away carefully in the homes of some first and second generation families. Commercial banks are seldom used by class IV families, and there are significantly fewer checking accounts in comparison with class III. The median amount of cash savings approximated $550; but 3 percent reported having more than $1000 in a bank.

Education

The educational pattern of class IV is distinctly different from that of class III. The median years of school completed by the husbands is 9.4 and by the wives 10.5. Only 2 percent of the wives have completed two or more years of school than their husbands. Conversely, only 2.3 percent of the husbands completed two or more years of education than their wives. There is a balancing of education between husbands and wives in this class. But what of the children? They are remaining in school longer than the parental generation did, but not much longer. The median years of school completed by adult children in these households is 11 for men and 11.4 for women. Forty-seven percent of the adult daughters and 63 percent of the sons did not graduate from high school.

Children attend public elementary and high schools, in the main, but a considerable percentage attend Roman Catholic schools. Private schools are beyond their expectations except in very unusual cases, as with a boy of high school age who is a promising athlete. Some higher status person may take an interest in such a boy to see that he receives a "scholarship." Practically all children finish the ninth grade, but the legal school-leaving age is 16, a hurdle many barely cross, and after it is passed adolescents leave school in ever-increasing numbers. High school graduation is the goal of most parents and children, but many do not attain it; only a minority of parents and children think seriously of additional education.

The 20 percent of high school graduates who enter educational institutions beyond the secondary level enroll in the State University, the local State Teachers College, community, and religious colleges. "Big name" colleges are beyond the expectations of the typical high school graduate; however, the proximity of Yale is an inspiration to some young men. Each year some are admitted to Yale and to a few other "name" colleges. These exceptions to the educational pattern in this stratum keep alive the ideal that the "best" colleges are open to men from humble homes, "if they are worth it." A considerable number of girls enter nursing schools, secretarial schools, and one- or two-year technician's training courses. Some young men enter proprietary schools for diesel engineers, draftsmen, air-conditioning, and other technical pursuits associated with direct training for a position in industry.

Ethnic Origin

Partially assimilated European ethnic stocks compose the majority of the heads of households. Only 7 percent trace their ancestry to Yankee stock. The ancestors of these individuals have been in the United States, on the average, eight generations. The remaining 93 percent are descendants of the diverse emigrant stocks who came to the United States in either the old or the new immigrations. They know when their ancestors arrived here and where they came from in Europe. Nine percent trace their ancestry to England, Scotland, and Wales; this group ranges from the first to the fifth generation in the United States. Irish stocks in the first through the fifth generations compose 17 percent of the family heads. Scandinavians— Swedes, Norwegians, and Danes—represent 13 percent; they range from first through the fourth generations. Persons of German descent represent 7 percent; their modal generation in the United States is the third.

Immigrants from southern and eastern Europe and their descendants make up almost one half of the family heads. Italians comprise 30 percent; in the main, the head is the second generation in the United States and usually in this community. Polish and Russian Jews, largely in the second and third generations, represent 7 percent. Roman Catholic Poles, chiefly in the first and second generations, represent 6 percent; Greeks, Hungarians, Lithuanians, Bulgarians comprise 4 percent. Many older individuals among the newer immigrants come from Europe, but the children and grandchildren who were born in the United States represent the modal generation.

More than 9 out of 10 individuals are in process of being assimilated to American society. The process of acculturation is going on apace, but there are strong elements of European cultures associated with each group. The acculturation process has been slowed by the tendency of each ethnic group to settle in particular sections of the city, to develop ethnic organizations, and to marry within the group. The first and second generations maintain the language and value system characteristic of Europe, but, as the third and fourth generations mature, the European language is lost in large part, and the young people develop American practices, beliefs, and values through the public schools, newspapers, radio, television, and jobs. The present generation is moving out of the Italian, Irish, Scandinavian, and Polish sections of the city into new housing developments in the suburban towns where not much attention is given to ethnic origins. Here the hyphen associated with ethnic status is dropped, and the individual thinks of himself as an American of a particular European descent. When this phase of the assimilation process is reached, it is not unusual for the family to ignore publicly European cultural characteristics associated with its private life such as the preparation of "old country" dishes for special occasion meals.

Religious Affiliation

Ethnic origins are reflected in religious affiliations. Sixty-three percent are Catholics, 7 percent are Jews, and 30 percent are Protestants. The Catholics are divided among individuals of Polish, Italian, and Irish origin. The Poles have their own parishes; the Italians and Irish have theirs. Poles, Italians, and Irishmen in the older generations do not like to hear mass from priests who are not members of their ethnic group. However, as the younger people move into the suburbs, there is a mixing of ethnic stocks in the newer parishes. Nevertheless, a strong tendency persists for Polish individuals to go to Polish parishes, Italians to Italian parishes, and the Irish to attend in their own parishes.

Jews of Polish and Russian descent are members of Orthodox or Conservative synagogues; practically none are Reformed. The Protestants are mainly Methodists, Lutherans, Presbyterians, Baptists, and less well-known American sects. Congregationalists and Episcopalians are found in significantly smaller numbers than one would expect. These Protestants attend church less frequently than the class III Protestants. The Irish and Polish Catholics are more devout than the Italian Catholics. The Catholics and Protestants belong in excessively large numbers to churches located in working class areas.

Family Constellation

The typical family constellation differs from class III in four significant ways: first, there are more broken homes; second, more households have boarders and roomers; third, the family is larger; and fourth, there are more three-generation stem families living under one roof.· Each of these facets of family structure will be discussed in some detail. Eighty percent of the families are headed by married men; 18 percent are headed by widowed, separated, or divorced individuals, largely females; and 2 percent are headed by single individuals who never have been married. Unmarried adults, as a rule, do not set up households of their own. They either live at home with a relative or rent a room and board with a family to whom they are not related. Roomers and boarders are a typical pattern among an appreciable number of families. Although 92 percent of the adults report that they have been married and 81 percent are married, among the unmarried the ratio of widowed persons to divorced or separated persons is 2 to 1. This ratio is radically different from the one prevailing in classes II and III; in class II, the ratio is 9 to 1 and in class III, 6 to 1. The low ratio of widowed to divorced or separated persons is an index of the amount of disorganization prevailing among a considerable proportion of class IV families. During every age period the number of broken homes is significantly greater than in class III; of particular importance is the fact that 18 percent of the homes with children under 17 years of age are broken.

The completed family is significantly larger than in class III. Mothers 50 years of age and above have borne a median of 4.1 children. Families married since 1940, however, are planning to rear not more than 3 or 4 children; the median these wives have had is 3.3 children. The discrepancy between the number of children these younger parents report they plan to have and the number already born leads us to infer that they are not planning families to the same extent as are class III's and II's. Many couples "let nature take its course," until after they have had several children. When the problems of rearing several children surround them day after day, conflicts may develop between religious doctrines and realities. A realistic approach to family size is being taken by an undetermined proportion of younger couples who have 2, 3, or 4 children, but there are significantly more children than in the same age group in the higher strata.

The extended family characteristic of southern European countries was transplanted to this community by the immigrant stocks. The common pattern is for a great-grandmother, a great-grandfather, one or two grandparents, and children to live under a single roof. The different generations and nuclear families may or may not have separate apartments. Usually the European language of the elderly matriarch or patriarch is spoken in the home, but English is spoken outside the home by all members except the first generation immigrants. If an extended family is headed by a man, he usually speaks English in addition to his native tongue. Old immigrant women often speak little English, and if so, with difficulty. Many conflicts are engendered over differences between European values held by elders and the desires of younger persons who have become acculturated to a greater or lesser extent to American values.

The Use of Leisure

Leisure time is used in distinctly different ways from the higher classes. Far more hours are given to the many chores associated with the maintenance of the living establishment. The men and women are accustomed to doing their work themselves rather than hiring a specialist. When the combined skills of husband and wife, brothers and sisters, sons and daughters, fathers-in-law, and other relatives cannot do a particular job, an artisan may be hired, but this is a last resort. The currently popular do-it-yourself movement has long been the pattern among the manual workers. Masons, plumbers, painters, paper hangers, glaziers, landscape gardeners, garage mechanics, or other workmen are not hired to do a job the men can do themselves. Women do time-consuming and expensive jobs that specialists do for individuals in the higher classes, such as making curtains or dresses. The family saves money by doing its own work and thereby raises its standard of living. These home activities take time and energy and they leave few hours free in the day.

Eighty-nine percent of the families own television sets, 96 percent have radios, and 82 percent subscribe to telephone service. These communication and entertainment devices are used every day. The most popular home recreational activity is watching television on weekday and weekend evenings. The wife may watch television

during the day if she has some free time; the radio is more likely
to be turned on while she does her household chores. The telephone
enables her to communicate with her relatives and friends and keep
up with what is going on in the family and the neighborhood.

Reading is not a prominent feature of the leisure pattern. Seven
percent of households do not subscribe to or buy any newspaper.
The *New Haven Evening Register* is read by 93 percent, 30 percent
read either the *New York Daily News* or *New York Daily Mirror*,
less than 12 percent read either *The New York Times* or *The New
York Herald Tribune,* even in the Sunday editions. Barring the *Register,* the most widely read newspaper is the *Bridgeport Herald,* a weekly
specializing in sex, crime, and sensational exposés in the community.
It is brought into 32 percent of the households. Twenty-five percent
neither subscribe to nor read any magazine regularly. The remainder report subscribing to or regularly reading one to three magazines. *Life* is the most popular magazine; 25 percent of the households report that they read it regularly. *Reader's Digest* is read by
20 percent, but practically no one reads *Time, Newsweek,* or *U.S.
News and World Report.* Home improvement magazines, like
Better Homes and Gardens, are read by some 13 per cent of these
families.

The figures in the preceding paragraphs indicate clearly that television and radio are more popular vehicles for entertainment and
the communication of ideas than are magazines. Far more time is
spent in viewing television than in reading.

Formal associations play only a minor role among individuals of
all ages. Class IV people are not joiners in the legendary American
tradition. Twenty-seven percent of the households report that no
one in them belongs to any formal association. For 64 percent there
is one membership—in the labor union. Only 9 percent of the adult
members of the households belong to associations, such as fraternal
orders, veterans groups, political clubs, card clubs, and athletic clubs.
Two thirds of this 9 percent belong to one additional association.
Although the labor union is the most frequent membership held,
many respondents point out that they belong to it as a condition of
their job. They do not attend meetings regularly, and they do not
participate in the union's social activities more than once or twice a
year. Except for a few individuals, the union is an impersonal, distant organization that "looks after our rights" in a contractual way.
In a crisis, the members are rallied by the union stewards and other
key officials.[16]

Family-centered activities utilize most of the leisure time of adults and children of all ages and ethnic groups. The typical nuclear family has many relatives in the same stratum. Visits with relatives and friends may be by invitation, but far more often they are spontaneous. Family members drift in and out of the houses and apartments at irregular hours and upon impulse. Most of the visiting, however, takes place in the late afternoon, early evening, and on weekends. Visiting with relatives takes precedence over visiting with friends to the ratio of 5 to 1. The visiting pattern is aided by the proximity of relatives and friends. It also stems from the still viable European village and extended family patterns. This should not be overemphasized, however, for the same general behavior prevails among the "Yankees" in this stratum.[17]

Short outings during the summer to the local amusement park or to nearby state parks, public beaches, and semicommercial recreational activities, like the plant's baseball games in local parks, are another facet of the recreational pattern. During the standard two-week summer vacation, the family may make an automobile trip to some point of interest, such as Niagara Falls or the White Mountains, but more often it will visit a brother, sister, or relative. These families do not own summer homes on the seashore or in the mountains, and very few rent "summer places." This behavior is out of their range of expectancy, and if it is not they cannot afford the expense. Thus, their recreational pattern is centered around productive work in the home, watching television, occasionally reading a magazine article, visiting with relatives, and rare visits to an amusement center or the seashore.

Summary

The modal family may be summarized in general terms. The husband who is 44 and the wife who is 42 years of age are members of an ethnic group—if Italian, second generation; if Irish, third. They were married after an engagement of five months in a Roman Catholic church when the husband was 21 and the wife was 19 years of age. When the couple married, they moved into a "rent" of their own in the dwelling owned by the husband's family. They now live in a two-family home, are satisfied with their housing, but hope to buy a single-family home in the suburbs some day. They have 4 or 5 children; the younger ones are in elementary and high school; the oldest one has finished school and is working on the production line of a local factory, or, if a male, is in the armed services. The husband and father has been working since the age of 17. He worked at his first job for about a year and a half, then changed to one he thought was better; however, he is still a semiskilled worker on a production line. His wife, too, began to work in the factory when she was 17 years of age, but she may have tried sales or clerical jobs as well. She worked at her first job about two years. She was working when she was married and continued to work until her first pregnancy was well advanced.

The recreation of the parents consists of "working around the place," viewing television, occasionally listening to the radio, some reading, and family visiting. The children spend more time with television, the radio, and the movies than do their parents. In addition, they go to local athletic events and visit the amusement park two or three times during the season. The husband belongs to "the union" but no other organization. The wife belongs to no formal organizations, but she is a member of an informal neighborhood women's group.

Their effective family income after withholding taxes, union dues, social security, and hospital insurance is approximately $65 a week, and they are able to save about $5 of it. Their savings are used periodically to pay for emergencies or the purchase of desired consumer goods. At present they feel economically secure, but they are not wholly satisfied with their living conditions; the children are dissatisfied. The parents believe that their marriage has been a "good one" and it has been aided by the cooperation and mutual interest they have held through the years. The parents look forward to a happy future, especially to when they will be able to save enough to buy their "dream house." They believe that their chances of obtaining it are "good" now that the children are "out from underfoot." The husband expects to continue to earn a "good income." He thinks his "best years" will come in his "late fifties" when he will be earning "about $100 a week."

CLASS V

Status Awareness

The Index of Social Position places 17.7 percent of the households in this, the bottom, stratum of the class structure. Class V respondents are least verbal about the class system; 65 percent believe there are "social classes" in the community, but 35 percent "don't know" or are confused. Respondents aware of classes realize that they rank low in the status structure, but almost three in four identify with class positions higher than those we assign to them. Fifty-four percent say that they belong to the working class; 19 percent think that they belong to the lower-middle class; only 27 percent identify with the lower class. The 35 percent which we categorize as not believing that there are classes represent several viewpoints. Some are unable to conceptualize what the question means, others really "don't know," and still others find the question too painful to answer directly and easily. The majority of these respondents recognize that the problems they live with are related to the questions, but they are uncertain of their answers.

A considerable number of respondents reacted negatively to the questions about classes. That this is a part of the defenses of this stratum became apparent when we probed for underlying feelings. A middle-aged second generation Polish woman who worked in a shirt factory responded to "Do you think there are classes in New Haven?" with the remark that she did not know what we meant. However, she proceeded to tell the interviewer: "I'm working class, no more than that." A few sentences later she pointed out that she was much better off than her brother "Steven" who is not able to pay his bills and is on relief periodically. By both working, she and her husband are able to pay their bills and stay off relief. According to her value system, this definitely places them in the working class. By implication, people who do not pay their bills and go on relief are either lower class or, as she phrased it, "in the relief class." This woman has a working conception of status factors and what determines one's position in the status structure, but she is reluctant to use the word "class" except in her own frame of reference.

There is a strong tendency for individuals to identify with higher positions in the status structure. This is in accordance with the American value that we are all middle class. People high in the status system refuse in large part to identify themselves as upper class, but will say that they are upper-middle class. On the lower end of the status scale, persons are just as unwilling to call themselves lower class. Only a minority see themselves and their surroundings as an integral whole. These are the bitter realists who identify themselves as "lower class slum dwellers."

Economic Position

Employable adult males are semiskilled—52 percent, unskilled—46 percent, and those who do not have and never have had a regular occupation—2 percent. Members of the latter group will do "anything" when they are able to work. Jobs in class V are low-paid, require long hours six or seven days a week, and, in the main, are in industries that are not unionized. Older men and women began to work as soon as they were old enough to hold down a job; it was common practice to leave school at 12 to 14 years of age. Today, the boy or girl does not go to work until 16 years of age, possibly older. Normally their work careers begin on unskilled "blind alley" jobs, such as messengers, stock boys, bus boys, janitors, or whatever they can get; later they may "graduate" to semiskilled work, but most remain unskilled. One "swamp Yankee" in the prime of life who identified himself as working class had started to work at 14. He stated with mingled pride and bitterness: "I've shovelled snow all night in blizzards. I've pushed the broom on Dixwell Avenue [this is the lowest indignity to which a white man, particularly of Yankee stock, can subject himself inasmuch as it involves cleaning the gutters in the Negro quarter of the city]; I've cleaned out septic tanks; I've not been fussy what I did. Usually I've been able to feed the wife and [four] kids, but sometimes I've had to take the scraps that were thrown me."

Significantly more wives and mothers are gainfully employed outside the home than in class IV; 48 percent in contrast to 37 percent. Fifty-six percent work at semiskilled factory jobs; the remainder are employed at unskilled jobs such as maids, cleaning women, sorters in the laundry, maids in the hospital, and scrub women in offices. Almost 34 percent of the mothers with children between 6 and 16 years of age are gainfully employed part time or full time, and some 17 percent with children under 6 years of age are employed.

The median income of families supported by the male head is $2659 per year; 27 percent earn under $2000, and 51 percent earn between $2000 and $3500. Where husband and wife are employed, the median income is $4350, but less than one half of 1 percent of these families earn $5000 and over. A man or woman earns as much at age 26 as at 45. The income curve rises slightly between 16 and 25 years of age, but after 25 it levels out and continues to be level until the middle fifties. After age 55, income drops consistently until the man or woman goes on relief, old age assistance, or social security. This is the only class where young men and women are worth more economically than middle-aged persons. These people are paid by the hour, the piece, or the job, and they earn only while they are working. Their jobs tend to be seasonal or cyclical, so that there are long periods of unemployment and underemployment. These are periods of "hard times," and over the years the family income has to be supplemented by unemployment compensation, state aid, and direct relief. Some 87 percent of the class V families and individuals were listed on the Social Service Index of the Council of Social Agencies when it was still active. One third of these families have been known to several social agencies for one reason or another through two and three generations.

Low and intermittent incomes preclude systematic saving; 62 percent report that they have no savings, and 38 percent report that they have some money saved. The median amount of cash saved by these families is $150. These figures are surprising, but the balance between the pressure of bills and a low income is a difficult one to maintain. One housewife who has only a few dollars saved posed the question neatly: "How can I save on $48 a week and 5 kids?"

Insurance is owned by 83 percent of the families, but 17 percent have none. The median value of their insurance is $1200; no one reported more than $10,000. Few veterans maintained their policies, and only 3 percent maintained the face value of $10,000. A veteran who keeps his G.I. insurance usually retains $1000, $2000, or $5000. Typical insurance is an industrial policy which provides accident, death, and sickness insurance under stipulated circumstances. Normally, the husband will have $500 to $1500 worth of insurance, the wife, $1000, and perhaps $500 on each child. These expensive package policies are sold by "industrial agents" who collect for them weekly or semimonthly. Beyond their meager savings and insurance policies, there are no financial resources. Money can be borrowed on furniture, clothes, and a car; there are frequent debts and installments to be met out of the paycheck.

Money for the necessities of life is an ever-present problem. Food is purchased mainly from the neighborhood grocery, but families with cars go to super markets located on the periphery of the tenement areas where these families are concentrated. The family car may be anything from a Cadillac to a Chevrolet, but only 57 percent own cars. The median age of their cars is 12 years. Refrigerator, television, car, and clothes are the major expenditures and are bought on the installment plan. The wife handles the money that is brought home or that she earns herself. Payments are made in cash as the banks are not used except for Christmas Club plans and savings.

Economic Orientation

Older men and women, who are first generation immigrants, are resigned to struggling for a living. They made the adjustment from Europe to America with difficulty and they have no hope that they will be able to better themselves in comparison with what they have achieved in the last 20, 30, or 40 years. Resignation and reliance upon the "breaks" are clear in the following words: "I'm well tonight. Tomorrow morning I get up and go to work at 4, and I'll be all right unless I get sick or something. I am happy; my wife is happy; and my kids (six) are getting along by themselves." His wife is thankful they have their health and are able to "pay their way" even if "the old man" has to get up early to clean the plant, where he is a sweeper, before the other men come to work. The husband feels "lucky" their children can make their own way.

Almost one half, 45 percent, of the adults under 40 years of age are inured to the grueling hardships they experience. These people live from day to day; as one man stated: "We take what the tide brings in." He and his wife work, although they have three small children. After the war, this man sat out his veteran's relief for a year because "I had it coming to me." He takes his life and his pleasure the same way. The 55 percent with a measure of optimism about the future are not too hopeful of achieving a higher standard of living within the next ten years. They feel they are much better off now than they were as children, and if everything "goes along" as it has for several years, they will be able to pay their debts and perhaps buy a little home in a suburban area. Some parents in this group, particularly mothers, hope "there's a better shake [of the dice] for the kids than for us." But others feel their chances of getting a "better shake" are less than "fifty-fifty." Economic insecurity is widespread in all ages; only 19 percent think their jobs are secure. Four in five have money problems which they think can be solved only by a regular and higher paying job. Over 35 percent are overwhelmed by the economic demands that society has made upon them.

The Family Home

Over two thirds of class V live in crowded old tenement areas of the city. These wooden and brick structures were built 60 to 80 years ago. A field worker describes them in the following words:

The typical flat is in an ancient building with a facing of brick or composition shingles. It is built on the sidewalk leaving no space for a front yard. The house is built so close to the house next door that the residents, when sitting in their rooms, can almost reach across to touch its begrimed clapboards. If there is a backyard, grass will have been succeeded by gravel, mud, broken bottles, and rusty bits of old metal. An old car with the tires cracked away from the rims may be gradually disintegrating as is the whole neighborhood. The approach to the building is up some broken wooden steps. The door which is gouged and defaced with the names and initials of occupants and which has lost great slivers of its wood is swinging on its hinges so that it cannot be fully closed. A lock which once was set in it has been removed leaving a round hole by the latch. It has been painted several times but at no time recently, for the grime is thick upon it. There has been glass in the door, but it has been replaced by plywood roughly tacked on. Just inside the door and along one wall are mail-boxes with only a few bearing a name.

The interior is ill-lighted by a gloomy sky-light set far above the floor and covered by chicken wire. The linoleum on the entrance floor is worn through to the scuffed wood beneath and littering it are scraps of newspapers and cigarette butts. The old brown wallpaper has been torn off in many places. It bears drawings and initials. At intervals, holes have been broken in the plaster showing the stripping underneath. These holes may be replastered but not recovered with wallpaper or paint. It is a startling white against the filth of the hall. Up a rickety stairs and along another hall may be found the homes of several families. In the poorest buildings there may be no light at all. In the pitch black the only way one can find the family he wishes to see is to light a match and feel his way. The poorest buildings will have on each floor two toilets standing with doors open at the end of the hall.

The doors to the flats open into the kitchen—the family living room. The kitchen usually contains a refrigerator of an old vintage but still in good condition outwardly. From the ceiling hangs an old light fixture from which one bare bulb is burning. In other sockets are extension cords. One leading to a radio which is blaring and the other to the iron the housewife is using. In one corner of the kitchen is one section of a U.S. Army double-deck bed. Off the kitchen one can look into the bedroom which is crowded with sway-backed beds. Flies are buzzing around even in late fall. The breakfast set is of plastic and chrome, but the plastic is worn through and the chrome is rusted in spots. On the rare occasions where there is a living room, there are usually a few tables and the room is sparsely furnished with davenports and chairs so broken down that one sits very close to the floor when using them. Prominent in the living room will be the ever-present huge television set. The floors are often covered with odd pieces of linoleum on which the design has been completely defaced. These are sometimes tacked on the floor and may be interspersed with pieces of corrugated iron roofing which have been pounded as flat as possible and nailed to the floor. In some places the covering underneath shows worn depressions on its surfaces.

The walls are bare except for the presence of a picture the size of a postcard. These pictures may be framed in carved wood frames and some, at least, were purchased or won during tours of the local carnival center. Nailed to the walls will be cheap crucifixes or religious statuettes in Catholic homes. There are few exceptions to this pattern.

These tenements may house from 10 to 50 families. A typical pattern is for several related families to live in the same building. They may have individual "rents" but they run in and out of one another's flats at will. Each flat rents for $25 to $30 per month; some are more expensive, but few are cheaper.

The city, years ago, recognized some sanitary problems associated with tenement living and built two public bath houses. An individual may obtain a bath with fresh soap and a clean towel for five cents. The bath houses are patronized annually by approximately 150,000 bathers. Many come week after week and some families have been using municipal bath houses for 50 years. Patrons are almost exclusively class V individuals.

Sanitation is a chronic problem for there may be only two toilets in a twenty-family tenement or five toilets if it is a fifty-family tenement. A serious sanitary problem associated with living in these tenements was brought to our attention by a respondent who told, much to the interviewer's disbelief, that "the —— piss out the windows." Near the end of the interview, the man slapped the interviewer on the knee and said, "Look, there's one of the bastards doing it now." The interviewer saw the respondent's story come to life before his eyes.

Single-family dwellings are located almost exclusively in two suburban towns. Here are large areas of woodland, swamp, and rocky ground where individuals have bought parcels of land and built small homes. Almost all of these homes have been built by the owners often from salvaged material. Normally, the building process takes two, three, or four years. These homes are small, irregular combinations of clapboard, tarpaper, used brick, and cement blocks. There is no sewage except privies or septic tanks, the roads are not paved, and, in many cases, the streets are not surveyed.

Education

Class V's have the poorest educations in the population. The median years of school completed is 6 for men and slightly less than 8 for women; 54 percent of the men and 39 percent of the women have less than seventh grade educations. Few have completed ninth grade.

Private schools are beyond the experience of the parents. They think in terms of public schools which 9 out of 10 children attend. Although class V is predominantly Catholic, and there are many Catholic schools in the community, less than 10 percent of the children attend them. The parents give a number of reasons for not sending the children to parochial schools: "It costs too much," "They are too narrow," "Nothing is taught but religion," "A kid gets a broader education in the public schools."

Parents expect the schools to teach their children how to stay out of "trouble" and prepare them for a "good job." They expect that a boy or girl will finish junior high school; high school is beyond their own experience, but most parents hope their children will go through high school. They are not sure what value it has beyond the connection between an "education and a good job." A mother who is working in a shirt factory so that her two sons and a daughter can "graduate from high school" summarized her conception of a "good job": "No hard labor to it. Something that's easy and well-paying."

This woman's husband has been a laborer on the "bull crew" of local construction companies since he was 14 years of age. In the course of 30 years he has done all kinds of heavy manual labor in all seasons and under trying circumstances. He has been hurt a number of times, and he has developed arthritis and other ailments due to his rough outdoor work. It is easy to understand why the mother wants "easy" and "well-paying" jobs for her sons. Her dream is to see the day when they are "linemen" with the "telephone company" and her daughter is "in the office." She thinks that if they can be persuaded to finish high school, they will be able to obtain work with this well-regarded concern.

Parents who "plead" with their children to finish high school are counterbalanced by those who see little connection between formal education and a "good job." This group looks upon experience as the prime consideration—"Experience is the thing that counts." A semiskilled machine worker who has had steady work for the past seven years claims that men have come and gone with his company but he manages to "stay on. . . . Where other fellows try to do everything by the book, I do it by common sense. You can't do everything by the book."

Ethnic Origins

Yankees and other Americans of pre-Revolutionary ancestry are a minority of less than 4 percent. These people are proud of their long history in America. Each has at least one ancestor he can trace in fact or fantasy back to the colonial period and who has been built up to heroic proportions in family legend and myth. It is unusual to encounter a person who actually can trace his lineage to the ancestor claimed, but some can. For example, an elderly woman living in a deteriorated four-family house on the waterfront told proudly how her home had come down through five generations and how she was descended from a number of first families. She went into the corner of the lopsided sitting room and bedroom pulling from her bosom a brass key tied around her neck with a shoelace and unlocked an ancient barrel trunk. The trunk was filled with old documents, letters, pictures, and genealogical charts. This woman showed that she was related to several "aristocratic" local families, and stated: "Time has passed my family by." Such persons will not tell you, although many realize, that they are looked down upon by their neighbors and contemptuously referred to as "swamp Yankees" by "Yankees" higher in the status structure. Swamp Yankees hold themselves aloof from Italians, Poles, Jews, Greeks, and other new immigrants, but have closer ties with the older immigrant groups. Throughout the last century there has been marriage among these stocks, and in the current generation intermarriage with Italians and Poles has begun.

One fourth of the respondents are representatives of the old immigration. Some 10 percent are Irish; English, Scottish, and Welsh comprise 9 percent; Scandinavians and Germans, 6 percent. There is a heavy loading of immigrants in this group, but there are individuals whose ancestors have been in the United States for four generations. French-Canadians, mainly first and second generation migrants to the community, comprise almost 4 percent. Seventy percent of this stratum is made up of new immigrants and their descendants: Italians— 48 percent, Poles—12 percent, Slavs (Lithuanians, Finns, Ukrainians, Hungarians)—6 percent. All these ethnic groups have in them first generation immigrants. In the main, middle-aged individuals are second and younger people third generation Americans.

Most class V persons are isolated from the rest of the community by their location in the slums and their recent arrival in America. In addition, each ethnic group tends to be concentrated in a particular area. Italians are concentrated in two areas, Poles in another, Lithuanians, Finns, Jews, and Hungarians in still other areas. Outside of the hours spent on the job and the years young people are in school, most social activities take place within the narrowly confined enclaves of each ethnic group.

Religious Affiliation

Religious affiliations reflect ethnic origins in class V in the same general way that they do in the higher strata. Seventy-three percent are Roman Catholics, 23 percent are Protestants, and 4 percent are Jews. Individuals often report that they are Roman Catholics but additional discussion indicates that they are not practicing their religion with care. When they were children, their families were affiliated with the church, but as adults the respondents are often in difficulty with the parish priest. Antagonism toward the church is widespread; the interviewees bristle with hostility. Mixed marriages performed outside the Roman Catholic church are a source of conflict between the individual and the church. This is brought into focus by the case of a Polish man who is married to a swamp Yankee woman. The marriage was performed by a justice of the peace, but it is illegal from the viewpoint of the Roman Catholic church.

A middle-aged second generation woman of Polish descent was bitter about the church's demand for money and how some priests sanctioned immoral behavior to obtain money. She summarized her tirade with "It's hypocrisy, that's all it is." A second generation Italian who had spent three years overseas in the Army thinks priests use the church to get rich personally. He claimed that a priest left an estate of $45,000 which had been accumulated in irregular ways. He summarized his hostility by saying, "The only thing the priests are active in is collecting." Such beliefs and feelings are used by class V people to justify their behavior in relation to the church. Proportionately fewer practice the precepts of the church than in the higher classes, but they explain this class-linked behavior on individual grounds. The general antagonism of class V persons to institutional officers of all kinds will be discussed later.

The Baptist church has the largest single group, 31 percent, of all class V Protestants. The Methodists are a poor second, followed by Lutherans, Jehovah's Witnesses, Seventh-Day Adventists, and a number of small store-front churches. Significantly few Protestants claim to be Congregationalists or Episcopalians. These churches are oriented toward the higher social strata.

Jehovah's Witnesses and the Seventh-Day Adventists are zealously

proselytizing in class V residential areas. Their members make religion an active part of their lives; they attend church, belong to
church-related organizations, and work together for the promulgation
of their beliefs. On the other hand, Baptists and Methodists are poor
participants. Many are distrustful of the motives of the ministers and
"the church." One swamp Yankee Baptist woman stated she had attended church when she first came to the community seven years before, but was not made to feel welcome. She said that she had asked
the minister to call which he did after some months. The husband
reported that after the minister found that they lived in a three-room
tarpaper shack on the sandflats, he seemed uncomfortable and did not
stay long. The wife claimed that the next time she went to church,
the minister avoided her.

The Polish and Russian Jews who live in an old area of first settlement worship in small Orthodox synagogues. Unlike the Catholics
and Protestants, they are practicing members of their faith. Feelings
of skepticism and hostility toward the church and religious activities
do not pervade the interviews with these people.

Family Constellations

The five types of family constellations found are categorized as
(1) the nuclear family, (2) the stem family, (3) the broken nuclear
family, (4) the residual nuclear family, and (5) the mixed family.
The nuclear family of father, mother, and children comprises 44 percent of the households. The three- or four-generation stem family
follows with 23 percent. Broken nuclear families of one parent and
minor children encompass 18 percent of the households. Residual
nuclear families are made up of husbands and wives only, widows or
widowers. Most of their members are persons beyond middle life
whose children have left home or couples who have never reared children. A small minority are young couples who have not started their
families. Eleven percent of the households are in the residual nuclear
family category. Mixed family constellations include a parent, children, roomers and/or boarders, and common-law families. Four percent of the households are in this classification.

Forty-one percent of the children under seventeen years of age live
in homes that have been disrupted by death, desertion, separation, or
divorce. In most of these families the mother stays with the children;
however, desertion of the family by the mother is not too unusual.
When this occurs, the father normally takes the children and moves
in with some relative of his or the wife's. The majority of three-

generation stem families are broken in one way or another; most of them involve families in which an adult child with children returns to a parental home upon the break-up of his marriage. There is little difference in these homes from the broken family type, where one family maintains a home for the children of the disrupted marriage except that there are three generations in the household.

Socially and psychiatrically the three-generation *stem family*, the *broken family*, and the *mixed family* may be viewed as pathological types. A broken family where three or four generations live together ordinarily contains elderly persons who are first generation Americans. Their children are second generation, the parents of the children are third generation, and the children are fourth generation. Inevitably, there are differences in acculturation, socialization, and generational behavior patterns. Conflicts between the generations are heightened by their nearness to one another. The first generation elderly immigrant adheres to the values, beliefs, and practices of his homeland. The parental generation is caught in the bicultural conflict of partially assimilated American practices versus those of the immigrant generation. In turn, there is conflict between the middle-aged parents or parent and the younger parent of the children. A parent who returns to a parental home because of a broken marriage is faced with further conflict. The children are a part of this constellation and are inevitably involved in the conflicts, anxieties, and tensions which engulf the household.

The mixed family would appear to be particularly fertile ground for the development of psychopathology. Here we find a conglomerate of broken homes where two or three generations live together, where boarders and roomers, in-laws, and common-law liaisons share living quarters. Laws may be broken and the moral standards of the higher classes flouted before the children's eyes day after day. This is especially the case in common-law family groups, as illustrated by an example from the tape-recorded interview series. The speaker, a man, was described to the interviewer by the female (nominally) head of the household as a boarder. During the interview, his real position in the home became apparent.

> Personally, I'll take off my hat to a man that's married to a common-law wife and brings up a family. I think such a man has a lot more character than anybody—not anybody that's married, but the average person that's married. I admit it. What is a marriage license? It is nothing. It is just a piece of paper that is trying to hold you on the straight and moral track. It's the same reason that you need police—

because you have weak people who will go astray, who have no respect for anyone but their own desires and their own likes. That's the way I look at it. There is no difference. If a man has enough moral character to love a woman, to live by her, to bring up the children respectably, what's the difference? A marriage license is a mere piece of paper!

This man has been a "boarder" in the family for five years. He is helping to support three children of the wife's by a former marriage, and one from the present liaison. Unfortunately, his brave words about "bringing up the family" in a respectable way were challenged three days after the interview by the arrest of the sixteen-year-old "stepson" who was accused of stealing a car, driving while intoxicated, driving without a license, and breaking and entering.

The ratio of widows and widowers to separated and divorced persons is further evidence of family disorganization. It is 1 to 1.3; this is significantly higher than in class IV. The brittleness of family ties evidenced by this ratio may be produced in part by age differences between husbands and wives. Thirty-two percent of the husbands are 6 or more years older than their wives. This significantly large age difference is a product of the lower status male's tendency to roam around the country, go to sea, join the army, and work at casual labor for a number of years before he marries. A high percentage of older men are first generation immigrants who came to the United States as young men, worked for a number of years, and either sent back to their homeland for wives or married women on the scene who were younger than themselves.

The circumstances surrounding marriage are significantly different from those prevailing in class IV. Future marital partners meet and begin to date in casual ways. Their courtship is brief and takes place largely in public places: roller skating rinks, drive-in theatres, dance halls, taverns, and the woods and beaches in season. Some 30 percent of the couples marry without an engagement period; when engagements occur, the median length is 4 months. Today the median age for marriage is 23 for males, 19 for females. Fifty-nine percent are married in church by a minister, but 27 percent are married by a justice of the peace which usually involves a mixed marriage, marriage where one partner has been married before, or the urgent need for speed and relative secrecy. The pertinency of a swift marriage is linked to the fact that 40 percent of the girls are pregnant before marriage. The "You don't buy a pair of shoes without trying them on first" proverb was quoted to the interviewers by several men.

One couple who paid a justice of the peace $30 to marry them because the girl was Catholic and the husband Methodist and they wanted it over "in a hurry" related how they decided to marry. The husband remarked, "I must have been drunk that night to say 'yes.'" The wife answered tartly, "He didn't say 'yes,' he said, 'I will.'" The husband responded with a grin, "I remember the night you told me." The wife let out a long embarrassed giggle and said, "We sure have a nice little son out of it."

Marriages performed by justices of the peace end in divorce in significantly large numbers; this kind of marriage usually implies trouble between the young couple and the family of one or both of the marital partners. For example, one couple decided to marry as soon as the girl realized she was pregnant. The couple went to the girl's home and told the mother they planned to be married the following Saturday. The mother threw a tantrum and ordered the couple from the house; she refused to go to the small wedding because of her anger and "disgrace." A month after the child was born, a reconciliation was made between the mother and the daughter; the young father had "taken off" and abandoned his wife and child.

Doubling up at marriage with parents, relatives, or friends is a common source of friction. Seventy-seven percent of newly married couples move into homes of relatives, in-laws, or friends; whereas 23 percent move into their own "rents"; none own homes. Couples who move in with their families remain until interpersonal relations make it impossible to live under the same roof. When this stage of frustration is reached, the couple "moves out" or the husband "takes off" if the couple is living with the wife's family; the wife may stay with her relatives or go with the husband to seek a "rent" of their own. This is not easy in the over-crowded areas where these people live.

Leisure Time Activities

Low educational level combined with recent ethnic origin is correlated with a paucity of reading in all ages. Eleven percent of the adults do not subscribe to any newspaper or magazine, nor do they use the public library. These people read nothing except an occasional local or ethnic newspaper. An additional 25 percent subscribe to the local newspaper but to nothing else. Twenty-eight percent report that they occasionally read the *New York Daily News*, the *New York Daily Mirror*, or the *Bridgeport Herald*.

Magazines are read by approximately 2 persons out of 5; 43 percent report reading no magazines; 11 percent read from 1 to 3 magazines. *Life* is the most popular magazine; it is viewed by 18 percent of the respondents. Some 16 percent report reading escape fiction. The most popular escape fiction read by women are magazines of the "true confessions" variety; men read western escape fiction rather than confession magazines.

Television is preferred to radio, and 76 percent of the homes boast television sets; 93 percent own a radio. In television homes the radio, which the wife listens to during her working hours, is usually found in the kitchen. During the afternoon and evening hours, particularly on weekends, the television set will be turned to high volume until the last person goes to bed at night. This creates bedlam as the thin partitions carry the sound from apartment to apartment. One disgusted man who worked an early morning shift and wanted to sleep in the evening said:

> I can listen to the wrestling matches every Saturday night from the fellow next door on this side. I can listen to the fights with the fellow on the other side of me on Friday night. We live too close down here. Their bedroom joins ours. We practically live in the same room. Down here, that leads to trouble. Everybody is spatting all the time. As far as I'm concerned, I can live by myself with less neighbors.
> Here you have to be a little standoffish if you want any privacy at all; otherwise they move right in.

Class V people approve of TV and enthusiastically view its programs. Some 83 percent of the parents with children under 17 years of age are favorable to children's programs. However, some parents think there is too much violence and that it has a bad effect upon children.

Seventy-six percent of the families are completely isolated from formal community associations—unions, social clubs, lodges, political associations, and so on. Only 19 percent of the men and 12 percent of the women belong to labor unions; most are nominal members who joined to obtain and hold their jobs. Their dues are collected by the check-off system, and they seldom attend union meetings. Some persons are strong supporters of the union but do not participate in its activities. Others support the union by attending meetings and talking "union" to their associates. A service worker on the railroad who was interested in giving the interviewer a good impression of the union said:

> The union is all right. If it wasn't for the union we wouldn't be making much money. They've helped us a lot. They've raised the wages more than they would have. You need somebody to fight for you in a place like that. Seniority doesn't mean much at all. I'm a union man.

This man attends union meetings, but he is not an official and does not think he ever will be. Nevertheless, he believes the union is the one strong protecting force of the "laboring man" in the community. "Working women" are less active in the unions than the men.

The lack of clubs and organizations with facilities where the members can meet combined with over-crowding in the home leads to either the use of commercial recreational facilities or simply spilling out into the streets. Favorite out-of-home recreations include movies, going to the amusement park, the beaches, or a small nearby park or square. The children play games in the streets, alleys, open areas around the factories that may not be fenced or locked, and in parking lots. Older children move in gangs in the downtown area, to parks and beaches, and on "exploring" expeditions to other communities. Also they patronize roller skating rinks, the amusement park, and roam around selected sections of the community. Adolescent boys frequently come into contact with the police; they may be sent home or arrested as juvenile delinquents. Older boys and girls go to public amusement spots, make dates, and drift away to petting spots and other amusements. Young married couples tend to stay home and watch television or visit with one another. Middle-aged and older people, in the main, stay home, visit around the neighborhood, or go downtown or to a city park for entertainment.

Older persons report few social contacts outside their immediate families. A second generation Irish laborer summed up his social world quite well when he stated:

> That's one thing around here, the neighbors, they're all pretty busy about different things. They don't get together too much. Because like the fellow next door, he works; he works in the rolling mills in Winchester's; he works funny hours, and when I'm home he's working, and when I'm working, he's home. We don't get together very often. When we do, we get out in front on the stoop and talk by the hour. But the people on this side, we hardly ever see. Because they are older people. They come and go very little. You don't see them at all, and the people across the hall you hardly ever see anyone come in or out of the apartment. Whatever they do, I don't know. You don't see them around very much.

Long hours, not articulated with the 8-to-5 routine, isolate this type of person from his community, friends, and family. When he has any leisure he is content to sit, talk with an associate, have a can of beer or a glass of wine, look at television, and sleep. Formal organizations have little attraction for him.

Social Orientation

A deep-seated distrust of authority figures pervades class V persons from childhood to old age. Suspicion is directed toward police, clergymen, teachers, doctors, public officials, public health nurses, and social workers. A class V respondent had finished a tirade on police efficiency when he switched to doctors. He told of a neighbor's wife who had developed a side reaction from a sulfa drug prescribed by a clinic doctor:

> That's a doctor for you. I wouldn't take my dog to one. To prescribe 100 pills like that for a working man's wife and not even find out if she had ever had sulfa. I can't see doctors. Maybe this one was in league with the druggist. Maybe he sells sulfa pills on the side for all I know.

Politicians are believed to operate a machine designed to exploit poor people. Non-Italians think this machine is run by Italians, "just like a gang." This statement by a person of Irish descent is typical. "The Italians stick together. The Irish don't stick together, so they can't run the machine like they used to. The machine is mostly one nationality, that is Italian." Protestants made the allegation that New Haven was run by the Catholics: "The Italians and the Irish got together with the Poles and ran the town for their advantage." Others claimed the machine politicians had "sold out" to the Catholic church and "the rich people."

Institutions for care of the disabled and the ill are believed to be run for money and one has to have "pull" to get into them. A family with a feeble-minded four-year-old child claimed that its efforts to have the child admitted to the state home had failed because of their lack of influence.

Hostility against official representatives of society is linked to convictions that they are being exploited. Some believe they have to live in the slums because the state is taking advantage of them. One veteran living in a three-room flat in a dilapidated tenement stated:

> Like in other states, where a project is for a veteran who can buy his own home without such a hard down-payment. They have nice

homes and we have to live like this. There's nothing in Connecticut— that somewhere, somehow—they can do things so that you don't have to live like this.

Another believed the city officials were taking advantage of the veterans living in an "emergency" housing project. He told how a child from the project had been drowned a few days before because a hole had been torn in the fence surrounding the area. The police had not made the responsible construction company repair the fence. He also explained how dredging in the harbor had led to sand being blown into the houses day after day. The interview was made shortly after the Fourth of July, and although fireworks were banned, many people came to the park and fired various types. He said:

> Fireworks are banned. But they stay down here for a whole week and they shoot off fireworks until 2 or 3 in the morning. These places are tinderboxes [rows of tarpaper-covered lumber houses]. I was here last week. She was working. I was minding the baby. I see a rocket land on the roof, red hot. There is a law against fireworks, but no, these people will be out throwing salutes at 2 or 3 in the morning. I'll go out and tell them to cut it out or else I'll call the police. I'll call the police and they don't stop them. Then I send my wife out.

(This man had many facts on his side: The child had been drowned in the harbor a few days before. Fireworks had been shot in the area, and a few fires had been started. The houses were a continuous structure, and, if a strong breeze had been coming in from the bay and a fire had started from the illegal use of fireworks, approximately 100 families could have been burned out in a few minutes. The sand and dirt blown from dredging the harbor was a constant irritation.)

The complainant was asked why he and his neighbors did not appeal to existing community groups. "They wouldn't do it. You know what I mean. They each have their own friends, and they don't seem to bother with anybody else." Manifestations of a feeling of exploitation were encountered among families in other housing projects scattered through the area. In a low-cost state housing development, we were told that the people were not getting much for their money, but that nothing could be done about it.

> What are they giving us in this project? And the people, they won't say anything because if they do, what happens? They get thrown out. They (the state officials in the housing office) make life miserable for you so you have to move. You will probably have to move into something worse. What I mean is, well, people today, they won't work together for anything.

The conviction that people will not work together gives rise to the widespread belief that every man has to "rely on number one" and "trust to luck and your common sense." "Look out for yourself and wait for the breaks," was expressed by a man when he said, "You can't get any place unless you're lucky and look out for yourself." This attitude carried over to the political area. A middle-aged second generation American indicated in response to the question on his voting practices:

> Anybody who votes straight Party is ignorant. I wouldn't care if I was listed as a Democrat or as a Republican, because when I go in there, I wouldn't care. I want to know what's in it for me when I vote for a man. That's what I'm voting for.

A commonly encountered viewpoint is "live today, let tomorrow take care of itself." This is impulse gratification; it frequently leads to trouble for men and women in this stratum as police, teachers, and neighbors know. An amusingly tragic situation will be used to illustrate some facets of this philosophy of the "man lower down."

Pasquale's name had been drawn from the control sample in one phase of the study, and it was necessary to locate his whereabouts. Pasquale was listed for an address in a congested tenement area. The interviewer went to the street and was told the Pasquales had moved away. The informant thought Mrs. Pasquale was living with a stepaunt in another section of the city. This woman was under the impression Pasquale had gone to Bridgeport to take a job and as soon as he found a place to live, he would send for his wife. The interviewer then went to the address of the stepaunt. No one was at home; a woman across the hall said Mrs. Pasquale was at a clinic for expectant mothers. The interviewer was given Pasquale's mother's address. At this address, a back flat in a forty-family tenement, he asked for Pasquale. The stepfather who answered the door took the interviewer into the kitchen where Pasquale's mother was ironing. The interviewer asked the mother where Pasquale was living, and she said, without embarrassment, "245 Whalley Avenue." The interviewer wrote this down and was trying to close the interview when the mother said incredulously, "Don't you know that's the County Jail?" Then she and the stepfather laughed with obvious enjoyment at their private joke and the interviewer's embarrassment.

The stepfather told the interviewer something of his stepson and daughter-in-law. Pasquale is a third generation American of Italian descent whose mother had been deserted when Pasquale was a small boy. In recent years, the mother had married the current stepfather, her third husband, who is a second generation American of Polish extraction. Pasquale was reported to have had a "chip on his shoulder" since he was a small boy. He ran away from school and joined the Army when he was fifteen, expecting to see the world and have a good time, but "he got something he didn't expect—hard work." After his return from the Army, he stole goods from a store and was caught running from the scene. Before he accidentally tripped and fell, he outdistanced three policemen. He was nick-named "Lightfoot" because of this incident. "Lightfoot" had been sentenced to the State Reformatory for this theft. His current difficulty with the law was associated also with the gratification of an impulse when his wife was some five to six months pregnant. According to the stepfather and mother, "Lightfoot" had been without work and was at home alone with the wife's stepaunt one afternoon; he attempted to rape her, but she fought him off and called the police.

No one would go "Lightfoot's" bail; his stepfather summarized the situation: "He won't be in circulation for some time." The stepfather reported he had tried to help his stepson until "Lightfoot's" wife, Edna, interfered with his family affairs and "pulled" him into trouble. Edna told us in a later interview that she had attempted to help her stepfather-in-law become interested in something that would keep him off the street and out of trouble. The stepfather has a record of petty misdemeanors stretching over a period of many years. Edna, in the course of her efforts to rehabilitate the stepfather, "talked" him into subscribing to an "art correspondence course." Edna said that in her judgment the stepfather had considerable artistic ability which he exercised by drawing on the walls of the apartment, on the fences of alleys, and wherever he thought he had a subject. According to Edna, the stepfather worked on the "art correspondence course" until he had received all the materials from the school. Then he refused to pay. The art school turned the account over to collectors, but he continued to refuse to pay and, in his words, "they gave me the works." He later stated, "This finished me with Edna." It was at this point that the mother and stepfather had "kicked 'Lightfoot'" and Edna out of their apartment, and they had gone to live with Edna's stepaunt. In the meantime, the pregnant Edna was working to support herself and "Lightfoot" who was unemployed. She reported that she had no money to pay for the "art correspondence course." Later she left work because of her pregnancy, and Lightfoot attacked the stepaunt.

A different facet of the tendency toward impulse gratification was illustrated by a tenth generation "Old Yankee" who claimed to be a direct descendant of Elder Brewster of Plymouth Colony. This man stated his philosophy of life in these terms:

There's only one basic rule that you've got to learn. It's taken me 48 years to learn it . . . if I ever learn it. You've got to learn to enjoy what you've got and to enjoy it to the utmost of it and to have absolutely no envy of the next fellow. If you can afford a 1939 car, learn to go out in that car on a Sunday and really enjoy yourself. You're looking at the same scenery as the fellow who is riding in a $5000 brand new fish-tailed Cadillac. And then too, you've got to get envy out of your system. Because you're only making $2000 or $3000 and Johnny Jones is making $7000 and the President is making $137,000 and the president of the Life Insurance Company is making $237,000—your life is so spent in envy and jealousy that you don't have time to enjoy what is at hand.

I'll give you a good theory of that. In the summertime where I go fishing, there's a Jewish lawyer who's worth about a million bucks. He must be awfully close to it in securities, cash, business, and such. Anyway, this lawyer is pretty well set. He goes fishing with four other fellows and spends $35 a day. He doesn't get any more out of his fishing than I do. I could lose an awful lot of sleep and an awful lot of happiness because he has the million bucks and I don't. By his rules, I can't afford to go fishing, but by my rules, I can.

The preceding examples from the tape-recorded interviews reveal class V respondents are individualistic, self-centered, suspicious, and hostile to formal institutional controls. These character traits lead to further isolation and discrimination. In their social relations with one another, their feelings of distrust and suspicion hold sway when tension develops between them. Consequently, their social relations are brittle, often transitory, and emotionally unsatisfactory.

Summary

Occupationally, class V adults are overwhelmingly semiskilled factory hands and unskilled laborers. Educationally, most adults have not completed the elementary grades. Individuals and families are concentrated in the "tenement" and "cold-water flat" areas of New Haven and in semirural "slums" in two of the suburban towns. Immigrants from southern and eastern Europe, their children, grandchildren, and great-grandchildren compose the vast majority of this stratum, but about 4 percent are swamp Yankees; and 25 percent are descendants of the "old immigrants" from northern and western Europe.

Five types of family constellations exist in class V: the nuclear family of father, mother, and children, the three- or four-generation stem family, the broken nuclear family of one parent and minor children, residual families consisting of widows, widowers, or elderly couples whose children have left home, mixed families of one parent, children, roomers and/or boarders, and common-law groups. Forty-one percent of the children under seventeen years of age live in broken homes. There are a few more separated or divorced adults in class V than there are widows and widowers. Family ties are more brittle in class V than in the higher classes.

Only a small minority of the family members belong to and participate in organized community institutions. Their social life takes place in the household, on the street, or in neighborhood social agencies. Leisure time activities vary with the several age groups, but in all ages they tend to be informal and spontaneous. Reading either for information or pleasure is not a prominent feature of their activities. Television viewing is a major activity at all ages. Out-of-the-home recreations involve commercial amusements or trips to public places. Adolescent boys, in particular, tend to roam the streets and highways in search of adventure. This often brings them into contact with the police and the courts.

The struggle for existence is a meaningful reality to these people. Their level of skill is low, their jobs are poorly paid, and they have no savings to carry them over a crisis. Adults are resentful of the way they have been treated by employers, clergymen, teachers, doctors, police, and other representatives of organized society. They express their resentments freely in the home and in other primary groups. Children hear them, believe them, and react to the targets of the parents' hostility in ways that are generally approved by the parents. This means that the children fit into the mold provided for them by their parents. Their own experiences with representatives of the higher classes reinforce the attitudes they bring into the situation. As a consequence, hostility breeds more hostility; but in order to survive the class V child or adult must repress his feelings and attitudes. These, however, tend to be expressed by acting out against society, members of the family, or the self. The psychopathological implications of the class V subculture should become clearer as we present data on the psychiatric side of the picture.

NOTES

[1] Edna Woolman Chase, *Always in Vogue*, Doubleday and Company, New York, 1954, p. 208.

[2] *New Haven Evening Register*, May 23, 1956, pp. 1–2, "Group Formed to Oppose Site for East High."

[3] For a thorough discussion of the "unchurched" in the community, see Everett C. Parker, David W. Barry, and Dallas W. Smythe, *The Television-Radio Audience and Religion*, Harper and Brothers, New York, 1955, pp. 70–78.

[4] For a discussion of this concept, see Paul C. Glick, "The Family Cycle," *American Sociological Review*, Vol. 12 (April 1947), pp. 164–174.

[5] A beneficiary of this trust is a respondent, but the trust was founded in another eastern city.

[6] All names are pseudonyms; they are used because some of the quotations have meaning only in terms of them.

[7] This evaluation is taken from Dun and Bradstreet's rating.

[8] This system of class and residential segregation is described in detail by Stuart H. Palmer, "The Role of the Real Estate Agent in the Structuring of Residential Areas," Ph.D. Thesis, Sterling Library, Yale University, 1955.

[9] Couples married in 1948, 1949, and 1950 report that they are planning when they will have children and how many. Two follow-up interviews three and six years after marriage, indicate that they have been successful.

[10] No significant differences were found between the reading habits of Catholics, Protestants, or Jews.

[11] Small business is defined as an establishment evaluated by Dun and Bradstreet as worth from $6000 to $35,000.

[12] For a detailed discussion of this question, see "Parents, Children, and Television," *Information Service*, Vol. XXXIII, No. 17 (April 24, 1945), pp. 1–8.

[13] Less than 0.5 percent identify themselves as "upper class."

[14] This inference is drawn from qualitative data in the depth interviews.

[15] Businesses rated as worth less than $5000 or not listed by Dun and Bradstreet.

[16] Our data are in accord with those of Dotson who studied a working class area in New Haven. See Floyd Dotson, "Patterns of Voluntary Association Among Urban Working-Class Families," *American Sociological Review*, Vol. 16 (October 1951), pp. 687–693; ———, "The Associations of Urban Workers," unpublished Ph.D. dissertation, Yale University, 1950.

[17] For some details of this pattern among "Americans" in the "working class," see Dotson, *op. cit.*

psychiatric
facilities

chapter five

INTRODUCTION

Psychiatric facilities functioning in the community today are also a part of the cultural heritage. Some knowledge of the historical forces that have shaped psychiatric institutions locally will enable the reader to place current practices and organizations in perspective. With these ideas as a point of departure, this chapter first traces the main outlines of treatment rendered locally to mentally ill persons from the community's founding to the present. Then it describes the five types of psychiatric facilities now available to members of the community. It ends with a discussion of the psychiatrist's position in the social structure.

HISTORICAL BACKGROUND

Delinquents, Demons, Distraught

When the early settlers were faced with the problem of dealing with mentally ill persons, they acted according to customary English practices. At that time, the nature of mental illness was not understood; the "distraught" and "insane" were believed to be possessed by demons, the Devil, or witches, and they were regarded with fear. Often they created civil disturbances and were driven from their

homes and towns or jailed along with beggars and criminals. The
family of any person mentally ill was legally responsible for his care.
Where a family was able to keep a deranged member at home, the
sick person was locked and often chained in a barred room. When
the family would not or could not care for its "insane" member, he
was placed under the control of the King's peace officers. When the
King's officers were forced to intervene, the individual was taken to
jail. If witchcraft was suspected, torture and occasionally hanging
followed.

Incidents involving mentally ill persons were recorded in the first
decade of the community's history. In 1645, a "distraught" woman
was turned over to the town marshal to care for "so far forth as her
husband is not able to do it." [1] Three years later the marshal still
had the good wife, and the court ordered her husband to take her
back or to find someone else to care for her. This woman was luckier
than a contemporary, Mary Johnson, who in 1647 was accused of
witchcraft and hanged.[2] Other unfortunates landed at the stake and
gallows in different colonial towns until the witchcraft hunt reached
its peak in Salem, Massachusetts, in 1692. During the seventeenth century, uncounted mental patients throughout the American colonies
suffered, and many died, from lack of treatment and from maltreat-
ment.

In 1699 the Colony of Connecticut passed an "Act of Relieving
Idiots and Distraught Persons" which recognized that "distracted"
persons are different from ordinary delinquents; however, it did not
establish any machinery whereby "distracted" persons should be
treated differently from "rogues," "drunkards," "night walkers," and
the "indigent poor." This law stated:

> Whenever a person should be wanting of understanding so as to
> become incapable of providing for himself, or herself, or should be-
> come insane and no relative appear that will undertake the care of pro-
> viding for them, or that stand in so near a degree as that by law they
> may be compelled to; in every case the selectmen or overseer of the
> poor of the town or particular place where such person was born or
> is by law an inhabitant and thereby are empowered and enjoined to
> take effectual care and make necessary provisions for the relief, sup-
> port, and safety of such impotent or distracted persons at the charge
> of the town or place where he or she of right belongs; if the party
> has no estate of his or her own the income whereof shall be sufficient
> to defray the same. And the Justice of the Peace within the same
> county at their county courts may order and dispose the estate of such
> impotent or distracted persons to the best improvement and advantage
> toward his or her support and also put the person to any proper work

or service he or she may be capable to be employed in at the discretion of the selectmen or overseers of the poor.

This law provided the basis for two widely accepted customs that lasted throughout the eighteenth century. One was to dump an insane person, usually in the dead of night, into another town to avoid caring for him at town expense. Great pains were taken to "warn out" of each town's borders all persons without visible means of support. The other concerned those who were unavoidably the town's responsibility; these persons were sold at an annual auction to the lowest bidder.[3] The low bidder took his chattels to his farm, maintained them as cheaply as possible, and worked them as hard as he could in the hope of making a profit on the sick persons' labor.

More than a century after Mary Johnson was hanged as a witch, a distraught woman became the subject of debate in the colony's General Assembly under the law of 1699.

There is now at Wallingford a strolling woman that has been sometimes wandering from town to town, who is so disordered in her reason and understanding that she passeth from place to place naked without any regard for the laws and rules of decency.[4]

The assembly ordered the selectman of the town to clothe the woman and commit her to the care of "some discreet person that she may labor for her support." The assembly agreed to pay the difference between the price of her earnings and the cost of her maintenance. This action was a recognition of the responsibility of the Colony to care for an indigent, "distraught" person whose residence could not be determined.

Late in the eighteenth century, a Workhouse similar to those in England was established in the city. The Workhouse was a combination "poorhouse" and jail operated by the city, the multiple functions of which are clear from the 1792 Bylaws of the City Workhouse. These laws state that any Justice of the Peace can send the following types of persons to the Workhouse for not more than three months:

. . . rogues, disorderly persons, all runaway stubborn servants and children, common nightwalkers, pilferers, all persons who neglect their callings, mispend earnings and do not provide for their families, and all persons under *distraction*, unfit to be at large, and not cared for by their friends or relatives.[5] [Italics ours.]

The able-bodied inmates labored under the direction of the Workhouse overseer to contribute to their upkeep. The overseer was em-

powered by another Bylaw to "punish with fetters and shackles, and
by whipping on the naked body not more than 10 strikes at a time,
or with close confinement without food or drink," [6] those who did
not follow his orders. For three quarters of a century, during the
Workhouse Era, all kinds of unfortunate persons "enjoyed asylum"
at the city's expense in this "Benevolent Institution." Surrounding
towns either sent their "distraught" townsmen to the City Workhouse
or continued to sell them at the annual public auction. The Workhouse was an improvement over the auction system, although it did
not completely replace that practice; at best, it was the substitution
of disciplinary barracks for the auction block. The insane were not
separated from the delinquent and the indigent until the state hospital
was opened. [7]

Insane Asylums

The first institution for mental patients in the state was chartered
by the General Assembly in 1822 after petition and representation
from a committee of the Fellows of the State Medical Society who
surveyed in 1821 the need for an "insane asylum" in the state. The
Medical Society's committee concluded that there were 1000 insane
persons in the state, and it recommended that a private institution
under medical direction be chartered by the Legislature. It also recommended that the new institution be the reverse of everything
usually associated with a "madhouse." It was not to be a jail ". . .
nor should it be merely a hospital where they may have the benefit
of medical treatment for without moral management the most judi-
cious course of medication is rarely successful." [8]   The purposes
of the proposed asylum were: "(1) to diminish the number of insane
in the state, (2) to relieve the state of public danger, (3) to cure the
curable, (4) to afford sympathy and comfort to the incurable, (5) to
provide economic means of care at public expense, and (6) to be a
valuable school of instruction for . . . medical men."

At a meeting in our city, the committee reported $12,000 had been
subscribed in support of the proposed institution. Some 2062 individuals in the state were listed as subscribers; 29 persons in other states
subscribed less than $400. One subscription was for $30, payable in
medicine; another was for one gross of bilious pills, price $30; of two
lottery tickets subscribed, valued at $5, one drew a blank and the
other a prize, bringing a net gain of $17. Individual subscriptions
eventually totaled $14,000.

The new institution was patterned after the famous York Retreat that William Tuke had founded in England. It received its first patients in April 1824, and until 1868 it was the only asylum for the insane in the state. Although the Retreat was chartered as a nonprofit private institution, it accepted both privately and publicly supported patients. By 1840, however, friction had developed between the Trustees of the Retreat and the selectmen of towns over the amounts the Retreat claimed it cost to care for a patient and what the selectmen were willing to pay. This quarrel was aggravated by the Retreat's limited facilities. The Retreat had no difficulty filling its rooms with private patients who were willing to pay $3 a week. The selectmen wanted to send more public patients than the Retreat could handle and wanted to pay only from $1 to $1.50 per week for the care of each one.

The dispute between the Retreat's trustees and the selectmen of the towns was complicated further by the number of distraught persons wandering over the state whose residency could not be determined. In 1841 a committee of the General Assembly was appointed to examine this question. As a result of its report, the General Assembly, in 1842, appropriated $2000 to defray the cost of caring for wandering insane persons and named the Governor as "Commissioner of the Insane Poor." [9] The Governor soon contracted with the Trustees of the Retreat to care for 40 insane poor at $2.50 per week.

This action did not solve the problem, and the following year the General Assembly empowered the Governor to negotiate with the Trustees of the Retreat to construct facilities to care for the state's insane poor and appropriated $10,000 for this purpose. The Governor, however, was unable to draw up a contract acceptable to the Trustees of the Retreat. As the problem became more acute, the General Assembly increased the annual appropriation for the care of the wandering insane poor from $2000 to $5000 in 1844.[10] By 1846 the number of state-supported patients at the Retreat had increased to 100. Because the $5000 appropriated the previous two years for their support was insufficient, the Governor drew upon the public treasury to meet the deficit.[11]

Each year the number of "indigent insane" increased, but the General Assembly refused to raise the appropriation above $5000. It met the problem of increasing needs by cutting down on the amount paid the Retreat for the care of state patients. In 1842, the Governor as Commissioner for the Insane Poor, had contracted with the Retreat to pay $2.50 per week for each state patient's care. By 1850, the state had cut its support to $1.50 per week for each patient.

The Governor, in his report to the General Assembly in 1851, pointed out a number of pertinent facts: First, the state was paying less than half of what it cost the Retreat to support a patient for a week; second, the number of insane in the state was increasing; third, the Retreat did not have adequate facilities for the insane who needed care; and fourth, the annual appropriation needed to be increased.[12] The Assembly failed to act on the basis of these facts, and 15 years elapsed before some effort was made to modify the situation.

In 1865 a commission was appointed by the General Assembly to study the problem of the insane poor. The commission reported in 1866 that there were 706 indigent insane poor persons in the state; 202 were at the Retreat, 204 were in Workhouses, and 300 were at large in the towns. The commission recommended that care should be provided for the 300 persons at large in the towns, as well as those in the Workhouses and the Retreat, in a single, state-owned and supported asylum. Supported by the Governor, the commission, and an awakening public opinion under the stimulus of such leaders as Dorothea L. Dix,[13] the General Assembly in 1866 approved an act to establish a state mental hospital and appropriated funds to build it. The first state hospital began to receive patients in 1868.

A plan to build a second state hospital to relieve overcrowding in the original one was recommended to the General Assembly in 1890. Nothing was done, however, until 1897 when $100,000 were appropriated. This hospital was opened in 1903. Some 30 years later, a third state hospital was authorized by the General Assembly, and the cornerstone was laid in June 1931. Today, a fourth state hospital, a treatment center, a hospital for the criminal insane, a child study home, and a home for senile psychotics are needed to ease over-crowded conditions in the present public hospitals.

The state hospital was viewed, from the day it was opened, as a "dumping ground" for chronic cases. This attitude was fostered by psychiatrists at the Retreat, as well as by enlightened professional opinions of the time which held that there should be two types of mental institutions: hospitals for the acutely ill and asylums for the chronically ill.[14] Physicians at the Retreat had claimed a phenomenally high percentage of "cures" among their patients, at one time as high as 95 percent. They had never wanted public patients because, they claimed, they were "incurable" chronic cases, who at best could only be kept in seclusion and restraint. Many institutional physicians in the post-Civil War years believed that if the acutely ill were segregated in one institution where they could be treated by "moral management" and medical procedures, most of them could be "cured." They believed also that those who could not be "cured" should be put in an asylum where they would receive custodial care. The state actually experimented with this idea. In 1877 the General Assembly passed an act to convert a state orphanage into an asylum for chronically insane persons. However, public opinion would not tolerate this open stigmatization, and the chronically ill and acutely ill remained in the same state hospital.

The widely held belief that commitment to the state hospital disgraced the family of the patient played into the hands of physicians and businessmen who operated small proprietary sanitoria in the state in the last quarter of the nineteenth century. Caught between the humiliation of the state hospital and fear of the insane, a family able to pay the fees, even for a short time, preferred a private institution to the state hospital. Mentally ill persons entrusted to some of the inferior private hospitals were treated often little better than the indigent poor in the public hospitals. Nevertheless, the private institutions protected the families of their patients from the stigma of the state hospital.[15]

Extramural Treatment

The public's awareness of the nature of mental illness may be traced directly to the educational program launched a half-century ago by the mental hygiene movement. As the public's awareness of the characteristics of mental disorders increased, a demand was created for medical specialists to treat emotionally disturbed persons before their illness necessitated hospitalization. Ambulatory care, stimulated by new concepts of the nature of mental illness and the discovery of new therapeutic procedures, became as characteristic of the twentieth century as the insane hospital was of the nineteenth.

Clifford Beers,[16] a native of our community, founded the Mental Hygiene Society in 1908 after his recovery from a long mental illness. Its stated purposes were: (1) to disseminate material related to the care of mental disease and the prevention of mental disease through pamphlets and lectures, (2) to improve the care of the mentally ill in mental hospitals and almshouses, (3) to secure better laws on commitment, (4) to establish psychiatric wards in general hospitals, and (5) to receive cases in their earliest and most curable stages. Beers' passionate devotion to this cause grew into a national and international movement of great force.

The creation of public clinics can be accredited especially to the efforts of lay and professional members of the Society for Mental Hygiene. In addition, legislation, public surveys, and the creation of a Bureau of Mental Hygiene in 1920 and of the State Department of Mental Health in 1955 are results of its activities. When the Society for Mental Hygiene was organized, no psychiatric clinics existed and only a few neurologists practiced in the state. Psychiatric office practice was discouraged and belittled by the superintendents of the two state hospitals.

The first psychiatric clinic in the community was opened in 1913 under the auspices of the Society of Mental Hygiene. One psychiatrist from the state hospital spent one half-day per week in the clinic. The patients were mostly persons "on parole" from the state hospital. In 1915, 96 patients were seen in this clinic. During the First World War, very few patients were examined, but after the war the number of consultations rose sharply. This clinic functioned throughout the 1920s, but it was closed in the early 1930s as there were no funds to support it.

A school of medicine has been associated with Yale University since 1812, but only a rudimentary course was offered in psychiatry until 1927. The first full-time professor of psychiatry was appointed a year later. This was not an unusual situation in American schools of medicine; until recent years psychiatry was a neglected subject.

Private practice began a half-century ago, when a pioneer neurologist and psychiatrist opened an office in the city. This physician gained a measure of professional recognition as a translator and interpreter of Kraepelin's writings and theory. Before World War II, only three psychiatrists were in full-time practice in the city. It was not until after World War II that the private practice of psychiatry was firmly established.

The last decade has been marked by a rapid growth in the number of private practitioners. The importance of psychotherapy was demonstrated in the Armed Forces during World War II, and a strong demand for practitioners of psychotherapeutic methods resulted. In 1950, there were 16 psychiatrists in full-time private practice, most of them practicing psychotherapy. In addition, six other men were prescribing other types of psychiatric therapy. During the last decade also, there has been a shift in the theoretical and therapeutic orientations of these private practitioners. The few practicing before World War II had an organic orientation and practiced directive psychotherapy, if any. Today, psychoanalysis and psychoanalytic therapy are the therapeutic methods prescribed by most private practitioners. The psychoanalysts have gained in comparison with other types of psychiatric practitioners, particularly among the younger generation who are strongly attracted to psychoanalytic theory and practice. In 1947, there was only one recognized psychoanalyst who, incidentally, spent only a fraction of his time in practice. In 1950, there were 11 psychoanalysts in private practice, and moreover, a psychoanalytic society and a psychoanalytic institute were in the making.

Major Developments in Psychiatric Therapy

The idea that "distraught" persons are sick and are amenable to treatment began to be accepted in medical circles early in the nineteenth century.[17] The classification of the mentally ill into particular types of disorders received great impetus through the systematic work of Kraepelin (1855–1926). He described in detail the signs and symptoms of mental disorders, classifying them into types and subtypes comparable to what his contemporaries had succeeded in doing in the fields of internal medicine and pathology. Based on his own description, Kraepelin ventured to determine classes of disease with definite prognosis. Although he was aware that the etiologies of the major disease categories he had outlined were unknown, he believed that they would be explained in the future by methods of neuropathology, endocrinology, and genetics. Perhaps more than anyone else, Kraepelin succeeded in bringing mental diseases into the realm of medicine.[18] Because Kraepelin believed so strongly in the constitutional basis of mental illness, he took a pessimistic attitude toward therapy. One of his contemporaries, Eugen Bleuler (1857–1939), was more optimistic in regard to methods of treatment but he, too, believed in the predominance of organic factors in the etiology of mental disease. The impact of Kraepelin and Bleuler in this country was modified and mitigated by Adolf Meyer (1866–1950) who broadened the etiological scope and therapeutic armament of mental disorders along pragmatic lines. Although most public psychiatric institutions have changed somewhat since the introduction of organic and psychological treatment methods, they still derive their basic theoretical orientations largely from Kraepelinian thoughts.

The greatest changes in psychiatric theory and practice in the last half-century are directly traceable to Sigmund Freud (1856–1938). Freud was trained as a neurologist and retained to a certain degree a definite constitutional perspective about psychoses and, to a lesser extent, about neuroses throughout his life, although he disproved more than anyone else the relative importance of constitutional predisposition. His monumental contributions to present-day psychiatry include a comprehensive theory of normal personality development and, above all, a rational method of treating hitherto untreatable emotional disorders. What used to be a medical specialty dealing mainly with psychoses became, in the words of one of its most effective spokesmen, Harry Stack Sullivan, "a science of interpersonal relationships."

The newer conception of the psychiatrist as a student of psychological, social, cultural, constitutional, and organic factors entailed in the etiology and treatment of mental disorders has stimulated considerable controversy as to whether psychiatric treatment should be a prerogative of the medical profession. The issue raised here is this: Is psychotherapy strictly medical or is its scope and nature broader? There are many very influential psychiatrists who claim that psychologists, social workers, and trained lay analysts must be barred from the practice of psychotherapy. Are psychiatrists who practice psychotherapy certain about their own mission? All too often they cannot agree on the question of whom to treat, when to treat, and what to treat. The many opinions held by the experts range from sweeping optimism and the omnipotent feeling that any emotional problem may be tackled with the tools of modern psychiatry to nihilistic pessimism that no cures are possible. We shall discuss these questions at length in Chapter Twelve.

PSYCHIATRIC AGENCIES

The State Hospital

Sixty-eight percent of the patients in this study are committed to state hospitals; 82 percent of these patients are in the oldest state hospital. This results from the division of the state into three geographic districts of approximately equal population. The oldest state hospital (1866) is so overcrowded that the steel cots are placed in long rows with the head of one touching the foot of the adjacent cot. The aisles between these columns of beds are so narrow that only single-file passage is possible. Sanitation, not to speak of comfort, is difficult to maintain. All wards where chronic patients are housed are permeated by the odor of sweat, urine, paraldehyde, and, in the male wards, tobacco. In the chronic wards, the visitor sees scores of aging men and women sitting idly in long dark hallways, pushing mops purposelessly, or trailing, like a flock of hungry chickens, behind the doctor when he walks through the wards. The acute wards are more hospital-like; here a definite effort is made to study and treat each patient's problem so that he may be released and not add to the seriously overpopulated chronic wards. Unfortunately, the patient population increases year after year.

The aim of the state hospital is to treat new cases and care for chronic ones. Over 90 percent of the patients come to the hospital with an emergency certificate, signed by a physician, which permits the authorities to keep the patient for 30 days. When a more prolonged stay is necessary, which is usually the case, the patient is "committed" to the hospital by a Probate Court acting on the statements of two physicians. Any resident of the state who is in need of psychiatric care may go or be sent to the state hospital.

Each state hospital is under the direction of a Board of Trustees, usually prominent citizens who serve without compensation. Their office is honorary; some of them render excellent services, but a number of them are appointed by Governors more for political reasons than for professional competence or any interest they may have in the institution. The Boards of Trustees function more as advisors and trouble shooters, when the administration and professional staff need support and protection from the Legislature, state government, or the press, than as effective governing boards. However, in each hospital the Trustees exercise power in appointing or discharging the superintendent.

The medical staff consists of superintendent, assistant superintendent, clinical director, staff psychiatrists, and psychiatrists in training. The nonmedical professional staff includes clinical psychologists, psychiatric social workers, occupational therapists, and nurses. Each of these groups is far too small to provide adequate medical care. The nurses are assisted by a large corps of untrained attendants, usually recruited from the "lower" social strata, who have direct charge of patients. Clerks, craftsmen, farmers, and police make up the nonprofessional staff. The hospital patients do a considerable part of the institution's daily chores, such as dishwashing and working on the coal gang, in the dairy, the gardens, and so on.

The superintendent, a psychiatrist, is the "mayor" of the hospital community. He represents the institution to the public, the Legislature, the Governor, and the Board of Trustees. The superintendent is aided by an assistant superintendent, a business manager, and a clinical director. The clinical director advises the superintendent on methods of treatment and care, as well as on research and medical

education. Once certain medical and psychiatric policies and procedures are adopted, it is the clinical director's responsibility to see
that they are carried out.

Each state hospital's employees form a community of their own,
because most of the professional staff and many other regular employees live on the hospital grounds. These families have few contacts with the nonhospital community. Even after long terms of service, they participate little in the town's activities or associate with the
citizens of the nonhospital community, whose members often look
with a certain suspicion and lack of sympathy at the "insane hospital."
Isolation in the hospital community often creates psychological
stresses and drives good professional persons from the institution. It
unquestionably contributes materially to the chronic understaffing
of the hospital.

TABLE 3

**Number of Specified Personnel Employed in the State Hospital, Ratio of
Staff to Patients, and the Median Salary Paid in 1953**

Type of Personnel	Number	Ratio	Median Salary
Administrator	2	1,515	$13,200
Psychiatrists, full-time	18	168	8,000
Medical consultants, part-time	3	1,010	8,333
Other professional staff	31	98	4,192
Registered nurses	76	40	4,124
Attendants	450	7	2,567
Clerks	38	80	2,413
Kitchens, dining rooms, etc.	88	34	2,586
Total	736	4.1	$ 2,580

Although some professors from the University lecture regularly at
the hospital, there is not close enough professional contact between
the School of Medicine and the state hospital. On the surface, leading members of both institutions try to cooperate, but confidence
in one another is lacking. Some Trustees feel that psychiatrists in
the School of Medicine want to dictate policy and use the hospital
for their own purposes without understanding its problems. The
University psychiatrists think some of the hospital psychiatrists are
opposed to modern psychiatry and are unwilling to learn. These
feelings become verbalized at times, and some staff members are referred to in uncomplimentary terms. Joint appointments to hospital
and University staffs have resulted in progress; one measure of progress is a Postgraduate Seminar in Psychiatry and Neurology under the

sponsorship of the State Department of Mental Health and Yale University. Persons of good will recognize that these efforts are important but that progress is apt to be slow. What Weir Mitchell said to the state hospital superintendents in 1894 is, to a certain extent, true today:

> . . . you began to live apart and you still do so. Your hospitals are not our hospitals. You live out of range of the critical shot; you are not preceded or followed in your work by clever rivals or watched by able residents fresh with the learning of the school.[19]

This "standing apart" is felt by all professionals involved—psychiatrists, psychologists, social workers, nurses, and the auxiliary therapists—but it is most serious in the cases of psychiatrists. The psychiatrists are required to care for all ordinary medical problems of the patients from colds to broken bones and major operations, in addition to their responsibility to prescribe and administer specialized psychiatric therapies for each patient under their care. They have few contacts with psychiatrists outside the hospital and also little contact with nonpsychiatric medical specialists, for outside consultants are used sparingly. Isolation is coupled with overwork, low pay, and having to cope with "bureaucrats upstairs." In addition, antagonisms among psychiatrists, clinical psychologists, social workers, and nurses lower staff morale; they also have adverse effects on the patients.[20] All this adds up to general frustration on the part of staff members who care and to indifference among those who do not.

In spite of the heroic efforts of some professional persons, the state hospitals are not apt to solve the problems they face without more adequate public support. Although their professional staffs are composed, for the most part, of men and women who face the difficulties of their work with quiet dignity, the low salaries, limited professional opportunities, low prestige of their jobs, and isolation do not add to their morale. They are asked by the state to do too much with too little. The effects of meager appropriations for patients committed to the state hospitals will become clear in later chapters. When one considers the difficulties and hardships the professional and lay staffs of the state hospitals face in their day-to-day tasks, it is surprising what an excellent job they do. Truly the state hospital personnel are the infantry in the army of mental health workers.

Veterans Hospitals

Approximately 4.2 percent of the patients enumerated in the Psychiatric Census are in Veterans Administration Hospitals. Over three fourths of the veterans are in neuropsychiatric hospitals populated largely by psychotics. Veterans from World War I are concentrated largely in a single hospital in an adjoining state. Those from World War II are in a different hospital in another adjacent state. Hospitalized neurotic patients, at the time of our field work, were cared for in the neuropsychiatric service of a general hospital.

Conditions in the veterans hospitals are different from those in the state hospitals. The veterans hospitals are newer, and they are maintained according to higher standards. Their psychiatric staffs are larger; they have a ratio of one psychiatrist to eight patients, whereas in the large state hospitals the ratio is one psychiatrist to 168 patients. (See Table 3.) In addition, the staffs are paid better and there was not—until recently—the general air of frustration in the professional staff that is so common in the state hospitals. In the new general Veterans Administration Hospital located in the community, there is close collaboration in teaching and research with the School of Medicine.

The veterans hospitals are well run, active in their therapeutic program, and interested in research. Public support of the Veterans Administration has enabled its physicians to create a progressive psychiatric service. If public support continues, the type of psychiatry practiced in the veterans hospitals may have a beneficial effect on the state hospital system. However, this will cost money and, to date, the General Assembly has shown no indication to appropriate the funds necessary to improve care and treatment in the state hospitals to a level even slightly approximating the standards of the veterans hospitals. The differences between the cost of psychiatric services in the local general hospital of the Veterans Administration of approximately $20 per patient per day compared to $3.70 per patient per day in the state hospital is one measure of the disparity between the two services.

Private Hospitals

Less than 2 percent of the patients in the study are cared for in private hospitals. The private hospitals are small institutions except one which has over 300 beds. They are scattered widely; only one is located in the community Their accommodations range from luxurious cottages on carefully landscaped country estates to dismal decaying old mansions that are almost as poorly maintained as the state hospital. In the most "exclusive inns" the hotel costs, combined with the fees for therapy and personal services, come to more than $20,000 per "guest" per year. In the smaller sanitaria, the costs approximate $7000 per patient per year. In these latter institutions the emphasis is also upon "gentility," but they simply cannot maintain the "exclusive" air of the "upper class inns" and "country retreats."

The aims of private hospitals are identical with those of public hospitals: to cure or to care for patients. Beyond their avowed general purposes, public and private institutions have little in common. The responsibility of the private hospital ceases when the patient or his family is unable to pay the bill.[21] After a patient's financial resources are exhausted, in practically all cases he is either discharged or transferred to a public hospital. "Pay or get out" is the rule.

Therapeutic orientations differ from hospital to hospital. In one exclusive and expensive country retreat, only psychoanalysis and analytic psychotherapy are practiced. In another equally expensive establishment, which prefers to be thought of as an inn, the guests are "rehabilitated" by suggestion, advice, and deliberate planning of their lives. A third retreat specializes in psychotic patients. This hospital combines to a certain degree dynamic psychotherapy with organic methods. In some hospitals organic treatment is the predominant method. In these institutions, the psychotherapies are looked upon as inferior and impractical therapeutic methods. This type of hospital is known in dynamically oriented psychiatric circles as a "shock mill."

The private hospitals have a much higher ratio of employees to patients than the state hospitals. This is clear from a comparison of the data presented in Tables 3 and 4. From the viewpoint of therapy, the greatest differences between state and private hospitals are in the low ratio of psychiatrists to patients in the state institutions. The salaries of psychiatrists in the private hospitals are at least double those in the state hospitals.

Some private hospitals are personal businesses run strictly for profit; others are chartered "nonprofit" but patient-supported institutions. To establish clearly what is meant by nonprofit is difficult. The principal practical effect appears to be that the nonprofit institution enjoys a tax-exempt status. After examining this question at some length, we concluded that tax exemption depends as much upon public relations as upon the activities of the institution. In some nonprofit hospitals, educational and research aims are interwoven with therapeutic and patient-care programs. In others, such programs exist only on paper.

TABLE 4

Number of Specified Personnel Employed in a Typical Private Mental Hospital, Ratio of Staff to Patients, and the Median Salary Paid in 1953

Type of Personnel	Number	Ratio	Median Salary
Administrator	1	38	$25,000
Psychiatrists, full-time *	5	8	16,000
Internist, full-time	1	40	7,000
Other professionals	5	8	5,082
Registered nurses	9	4	3,515
Attendants	20	2	2,459
Kitchen and dining room help	11	3	1,530
Housekeepers	6	7	2,548
Clerks	6	7	2,506
Chauffeurs and handymen	1	38	3,000
Bookkeepers	1	38	4,800
Groundskeepers	6	7	2,309
Total	72	2.1	$ 2,507

* With limited private practice opportunity.

A private institution with an educational program may be recognized by the Specialty Board for residency training. This is highly coveted by most private hospitals, but residency training programs create serious problems for the institutions that have them. The principal problem stems from the need to train more psychiatrists in the theory and techniques of psychotherapy. To entrust mental patients to beginners in the difficult art of psychotherapy, even under careful supervision, is hazardous at all times and creates special problems when patients come from core group families in class I and high fees are being paid for their care. This problem has been particularly acute in one teaching hospital where it was found that private patients could be entrusted to third-year residents only, and, even then, supervision has to be strict. Another problem which besets this hospital is the reluctance of the senior staff to deal with administrative and service problems. At times this question has jeopardized the best care of patients.

Psychiatric treatment in a private mental hospital is so expensive that only a small percentage of the population can afford even the cheapest ones for more than a few months. Nevertheless, families make great sacrifices to keep mentally ill members in private institutions as long as possible. Unfortunately, some institutions exploit persons who prefer a private place to commitment to a state hospital, even though the level of care they receive may be no better. When the public and the medical profession become more aware of psychiatric values received, profit-seeking hospitals may have a more difficult time convincing their clientele of the superiority of their services. However, the exceptional private hospital that makes an effort to practice the best kind of psychiatry is also having increasing difficulty maintaining its "standards" as a considerable proportion of the clientele that patronized it in past years is being treated by private practitioners at far less cost. The changing nature of psychiatric practice, that is, the use of two polar methods, drugs and psychotherapy, may force the "better" hospitals to broaden their "exclusive" orientation. In the long run, all "good" hospitals will need public support to enable them to become truly "therapeutic communities."

Public Clinics

Eight percent of the patients enumerated in the Psychiatric Census are seen in clinics. Emphasis on the importance of clinics is growing. Five of the seven clinics caring for these cases are located in the central section of the city. The two clinics located outside the community are supported by the Veterans Administration and are used by veterans from our area as diagnostic and consultation centers. Each of the clinics in the community is designed to care for particular segments of the population. One is located in the community hospital. More than one half of all patients who come to clinics each year are seen in this clinic. Its financial support comes from various sources: the state, the hospital, and the Federal government; the community proper contributes very little through the United Fund. This clinic provides diagnostic and treatment services to adults through the hospital and the School of Medicine's psychiatric residency training program. The therapeutic orientation in this clinic is analytic-psychological. A second clinic is located in a sectarian general hospital in the city. From 30 to 40 adults are treated here each year by volunteer physicians who administer electro-convulsive and other organic therapies, drugs, and the briefest kind of directive psychotherapy. The State Commission on Alcoholism maintains a clinic for alcoholics. The therapeutic emphasis is upon psychotherapy with organic therapies viewed as adjunctive. There are two children's clinics; one is supported by the community and the state, and the other is operated by the University. The therapeutic orientation in the community's children's clinic is undefined; in the children's psychiatric clinic of the University, it is psychoanalytic.

The large clinic in the community hospital is staffed by a physician-in-charge, an assistant, and 12 residents.[22] Supervision is carried on by trained psychiatrists, mostly paid from University funds, who hold full-time and part-time appointments in the clinic. The other clinics operate on a small scale. The children's mental hygiene clinic employs one full-time psychiatrist, a psychiatric social worker, and a psychologist.

The Department of Psychiatry in the School of Medicine at Yale University is interested in maintaining the large adult outpatient clinic in the community hospital primarily for teaching and research purposes and, secondarily, for the services it renders to patients. This dual orientation, combined with the fact that several agencies contribute to its finances, results in the vexing question: "Who pays for what?" Community spokesmen maintain that the University should underwrite the clinic's deficits of $60,000 to $70,000 a year because the clinic is used for training psychiatric residents and clinical psychologists. The University claims that the community should pay for the services rendered to clinic patients by residents and staff members. A similar argument exists between the two children's clinics. In spite of these running disputes over finances, the two University clinics work closely with social agencies in the community and are effective in providing consultations to the agencies when called upon for help. Most problems connected with reconciling service to individuals and responsibilities for instruction and research are worked through to the satisfaction of all parties. Since three of the five clinics are in hospital settings, their ties with hospital services, dispensaries, and other clinics are strong compared to their ties with social agencies and private practitioners. There is a definite trend to place psychiatry in general hospitals. Nevertheless, working relations of the clinics with practicing psychiatrists, other specialists, and general practitioners are reasonably good.

To be admitted to a clinic, though theoretically simple, is at times a struggle for "a place in the sun." The demand for treatment far exceeds its availability, and the scarcity of psychiatric time has forced the clinics to give preference to patients from the community. Also, clinics operate during the day, and patients who work find it difficult to avail themselves of the service offered. To cope with this problem, evening hours have been added but without much success.

Private Practice

Nineteen percent of the patients studied are treated by 42 private practitioners. Twenty-two psychiatrists are engaged full time in private practice in the community, and eight others are devoting part of their time to private practice. Twelve of the private practitioners treating patients in the study are located in other cities, mainly in New York, to which the patients commute.

Two distinctly different therapeutic orientations are represented by the 30 practitioners who live in the community. We divide these practitioners into those who have an analytic and psychological orientation (referred to as A-P group) and into those who have a directive and organic (D-O group) orientation. At first, we referred to the D-O group—following common usage—as eclectics. However, most of these practitioners are not real eclectics. One psychiatrist who falls into the D-O group once declared, "To help a patient I would do anything, even stand on my head if necessary." He might do that, but he would not practice psychoanalytic therapy for two reasons: He is opposed to it, and he has never learned the technique. There are a few outstanding specialists, particularly in the psychosomatic field, who master all available methods, true eclectics—we prefer to call them individualists—but today most practitioners, including psychiatrists in university centers and other institutions, fall into one group or the other. We recognize that this division, like any other, is somewhat arbitrary, and there are considerable variations. We also hope that this division will not last forever, and that *one* scientific psychiatry will emerge. In this particular community, the University psychiatrists belong largely to the A-P group, and the public hospital psychiatrists largely to the D-O group.

Our division is based on two criteria: the principal method of therapy and training for such therapy. We find that there is a definite division in theory and practice between the analytic-psychological approach and the directive-organic approach. The analytic approach consists essentially of analyzing behavior, relationships, and conscious and unconscious motivations according to psychoanalytic theories. The classical psychoanalytic approach consists of analyzing symptoms and defenses, transference and resistance, with the purpose of strengthening the ego through insight into unconscious forces, particularly into those which are apt to produce psychopathology. The so-called dynamic psychotherapeutic approach follows this general line with less rigor and greater flexibility. The emphasis is on gaining insight and applying insight and not on manipulation or direction unless this is absolutely necessary because of a weak ego; whenever directions are given they must at least be based on analytic insights of the therapist. The approach is almost entirely psychological; organic methods of diagnosis and treatment are extraneous to it and are rarely employed by its practitioners.

The directive approach consists of changing attitudes, opinions, and behavior of the patient by means of directive and supportive methods such as assertion, suggestion, reassurance, advice, manipulation, and even coercion. It is usually not based on analytic insight but on the therapist's judgment and what is called clinical experience and evaluation of the patient's problems and situation. Depending on the therapist and the patient, the therapist may try to buck up the patient's low esteem, convert him to the therapist's own philosophy of life, give him a stern lecture, friendly advice, tell him to go to a resort, to take it easy or work harder, to treat his wife kindly or get a divorce. The success of any of these maneuvers, and they can be quite successful, depends on the wisdom and strength of the therapist rather than on his technical knowledge and also on the suggestibility and the ego strength of the patient. The directive approach requires, besides clinical experience, and even more urgently than technical knowledge, broad human experience and a willingness to assume authority.

Directive techniques are often combined with organic medical techniques, both diagnostic and therapeutic. D-O practitioners are likely to do medical and neurological examinations, carry out laboratory tests, prescribe drugs, administer shock treatments, and refer their patients to neurosurgeons or even carry out, themselves, "minor" neurosurgical procedures, like transorbital lobotomies. Many of their explanations, to themselves and to their patients, are couched in medical or pseudomedical terms. Although D-O practitioners have a general interest in psychology and the social sciences, their knowledge of these disciplines is, in practice and theory, weaker than that of the A-P group. What interest and knowledge they have are overshadowed by their stronger biological and medical interests. Hence, we refer to one as psychological and to the other as organic. Another basic difference is that the A-P group holds the expressed belief that the etiology of most mental illnesses, with the possible exception of a few organic disorders, is primarily psychological and that treatment, too, should be psychological.

The training of the two groups is different; the A-P group goes through full or partial psychoanalytic training and orientation; their set of axioms stems from Freud's theories and recommendations. Their postgraduate training in the basic biological and clinical sciences tends to be secondary and minimal: Little neurology, for instance, at one time psychiatry's fraternal twin, is known and learned by the average member of the A-P group. The D-O group has a strong affinity to the organic medical approach and is more apt to be trained in neurology and its basic biological sciences.

The A-P group includes those psychiatrists who are fully trained psychoanalysts, among them some of the leaders in the field, as well as those who had some psychoanalytic orientation in their residence training, for instance, or therapeutic experience by way of their own psychoanalysis or intensive psychotherapy. Members of the group not fully trained usually consider the trained analysts as persons of higher professional status and consider themselves as second-class citizens in the hierarchy. Among the A-P group, the members of the American Psychoanalytic Association usually point with pride to their intensive training in the field and consider themselves as the outstanding representatives of classical psychoanalysis; when the discussion turns in that direction they look down their classical analytical noses at their colleagues who have a Jungian, Horneyan, or Sullivanian orientation.

Those we call the D-O group also represent a spectrum. At one end are those who employ psychotherapeutic methods such as reassurance, persuasion, suggestion, advice, and support, based on insights mixed with their personal philosophies. Treatment among these men varies from patient to patient and depends largely on attempts of the therapist to teach the patient to look at problems in the therapist's way. A certain measure of organic treatment may be used by these therapists, as, for example, the prescription of tranquilizing drugs. On the other end of the spectrum are those who prescribe an almost exclusively organic therapy, such as drugs, shock therapy, and psychosurgery.

Although there are minor differences among individuals in each therapeutic orientation, for present purposes we will group the A-P practitioners in one category and the D-O practitioners in a second category. As we compare and contrast the two groups, we will not differentiate within a group unless there is a particular point to emphasize.

The A-P psychoanalyst works regular hours, mornings and afternoons, and sometimes evenings; he does not make house calls. The D-O therapist makes house calls, works uneven hours, and accepts emergencies as part of each day's work.[23] The psychoanalyst charges from $20 to $35 for each visit; a few patients pay less, and some pay $40. The D-O practitioner uniformly charges from $10 to $20 per visit. The analytic practitioner sees his patients longer and more frequently than the D-O practitioner. Patients in psychoanalytic treatment are seen for a "50-minute hour" four or five times a week. The D-O therapist sees his patients for 15 to 30 minutes once a week, perhaps only once a month, or as one practitioner stated, "when they drop in for a pill and a little advice." Another "external" mark of difference is this: The D-O practitioner generally wears a white coat in the office and hospital; the A-P psychoanalyst wears a business suit in his work.

The analytic practitioner may sit behind his patient who lies on a couch; the D-O practitioner never does. "One almost needs a special license to have a couch," one D-O practitioner sighed. The A-P analyst listens to the patient's free associations and is relatively less active than the D-O therapist; his main job is to "analyze" with his patient the patient's unconscious conflicts, resistances, and transferences. The D-O practitioner may get involved in Socratic dialogues, actively advise, suggest, and prescribe. At times he prescribes and administers drugs and electroshock treatments to his patients either in his office or in the hospital where he has privileges to treat. The analysts and the analytically oriented practitioners, as we mentioned before, almost never make physical and neurological examinations; among D-O practitioners such medical examinations are the rule. They perform medical procedures such as venous and lumbar punctures, whereas the analyst refers a patient who needs such an examination to an internist or neurologist.

The local Psychoanalytic Institute is the polar attraction for analytically oriented practitioners and for most university psychiatrists from the senior men to the newest residents. Instruction in the Institute is in great demand among psychiatrists who want to become psychoanalysts or get experience in the field to become better practitioners, teachers, and investigators. Membership in the Institute is a coveted honor, both among the younger men and those who are fully trained. The Institute is rigidly organized; each student is brought under the professional influence of the senior instructors for several years. Few schools have such strong impact on and control over their disciples. The most important figures in the Institute are the senior training analysts. To be a training analyst is considered a high distinction by all analytically oriented psychiatrists. Most of the patients of the training analysts are psychiatrists-in-training; thus, the training analysts exercise a decisive influence on their disciples and a strong indirect influence on the profession.

The analytically oriented psychiatrists have a local Psychoanalytic Society that is more inclusive in its membership than the psychoanalytic institute, but privileges of membership in this society are still very strict and primarily based on complete and proper analytic training except for a few "friends" of analysis who are "extraordinary" members. At one meeting of the Psychoanalytic Society, the question of inviting the D-O group to a joint meeting of the two groups was raised, but it was coolly received and nothing was done. Most of the members of the Psychoanalytic Society belong to the American Psychiatric Association and to the State Medical Society, but the local Psychoanalytic Society is probably as "exclusive" as any professional organization can be. The D-O practitioners belong to local medical societies and the State Society for Psychiatry and Neurology which is a branch of its national organization. The analysts rarely attend medical society meetings, and most of them are little interested in the Mental Health Society of the state and the local psychiatric society. The analysts barely know the D-O practitioners; only a few meet socially and then on rare occasions when circumstances happen to bring individuals together.

Psychiatrists with an analytic orientation read markedly different journals from those with a directive-organic orientation. The analysts read primarily professional analytic journals; the D-O group read journals with an organic orientation such as the State Medical Journal, the Journal of the American Medical Association, and the neurological journals. Both groups read the American Journal of Psychiatry, the trade journal of the profession. Neither the A-P group nor the D-O group read, as a rule, psychological, sociological, and general scientific publications.

The analytic group impress us as being more "inner-oriented," introspective, and psychologically sensitive than their D-O colleagues. The A-P group believe they were impelled to become psychiatrists by their childhood and adolescent experiences. For example, one fully trained psychoanalyst stated that his interest in psychiatry developed from an attempt to solve a hateful or, at best, ambivalent relationship with his father. Another believes his choice of profession was determined largely by a wish to help his mother solve her neurotic problem. We think motivations in the D-O group are hardly different, but the D-O practitioners do not appear to be aware of them or state them in such frank ways. The D-O practitioners are inclined to attribute their occupational choices to factors such as "fine opportunities in a new field," or a "chance to help where help is badly needed." They stress therapeutic needs of other persons rather than their own impulses and identify more with the acknowledged tasks of the medical profession.

When the respondents discussed their professional satisfactions with the interviewer, the analytically oriented physicians emphasized the personal gratifications they gained from understanding the complexities of human behavior; the directive-organic physicians stressed the opportunities their training and ability opened to them to help other people. In the area of professional disappointments, the analysts regret how little they know about individual motivation of behavior; this did not bother the D-O group. They are more concerned with the administrative tasks of their practice and the economic obstacles their patients face when they try to obtain psychiatric care. In short, the analysts stress the unsolved theoretical problems; the D-O practitioners stress practical obstacles which need to be overcome.

Differences in theoretical orientations and practices are accompanied by professional jealousy and a certain hostility between the two groups. Moreover, each group is keenly aware of the other's shortcomings and weaknesses. The D-O practitioners reproach the A-P group for their "doctrinaire" and "unmedical" attitudes and, when tempers rise, "quackery." The analysts view the directive-organic group as "ignorant," "low-brow," and, when they use predominantly organic methods, as "shock artists." A screen of "professional" dignity usually covers such differences of opinion, attitudes, and facts; the public seldom gets a glimpse of these "border wars" within the profession. These feuds and splits may become milder as our knowledge of the nature of mental illness advances; they may even disappear, but they are prominent, if publicly well-masked, elements in the practice of psychiatry today.

All private practitioners have completed work for the degree of Doctor of Medicine in approved medical schools, and most have served general internships in hospitals. In addition, most of them have had residency training required by the Specialty Board in Psychiatry; more than half of them have been certified by the Board. If psychiatry were compared with other medical specialties, it probably would be found to be essentially similar in training, accomplishments, and internal organization. Psychiatrists, as members of a new specialty, tend to be self-conscious and defensive about their work and its difficulties and possibilities. Both the A-P and D-O groups believe in the importance of their work and think that, although psychiatrists are not the most revered specialists in the medical profession, they have the broadest background and are the most intellectual members. They point with pride to the impressive growth of the specialty in the last thirty years.

Very few psychiatrists extend "professional courtesy" for prolonged treatment to colleagues in psychiatry and other branches of medicine and their families. Psychiatrists may reduce their fees in the case of professional patients, but very few are treated free of charge for any length of time. When psychiatrists are asked by their colleagues to justify this position, they point out two factors: First, their income would be drastically reduced especially when their practice consists of a large percentage of professional persons who are in long term therapy, and second, many psychiatrists, particularly analysts, claim that patients must bring a "financial" sacrifice for their treatment or it will not be successful. The reluctance of psychiatrists to participate in the widespread medical folkway of "professional courtesy" generates intense feeling among the other medical specialists who participate in the etiquette of the profession toward psychiatrists. In our opinion, there is no evidence that psychiatrists are "greedier" than anybody else. They are hard-working professionals who more than anyone else, including the complaint office of the department store, have to face a relentless barrage of hostility, dependence, and raw impulses; this is hard to take and requires defenses and rewards of its own.

PSYCHIATRISTS AND THE SOCIAL STRUCTURE

Ninety-five percent of the psychiatrists who live in the community are categorized as members of class I and 5 percent are class II.[24] Placing a psychiatrist in class I or II is a result of the ecological evaluation of the residential area where he lives. Those who live in the "best" areas receive higher social position scores than those who live in "good" areas. But, as the percentages given above indicate, few psychiatrists live in other than the "best" areas. Even though practically all psychiatrists live in "exclusive" or "good" neighborhoods, have attained the highest educational level, and belong to a high status profession, none is a member of the core group within class I, and only two are on the fringes of cliques composed predominantly of persons in the core group.

The A-P group are acutely aware of social stratification and eagerly respond to questions on their notions of the determinants of class position. On the whole the D-O group deny the existence of classes and tend to react with embarrassment when the question is raised. They respond to direct questions on whether they think there are social classes in the community with such remarks as, "I do not care for such snobbery," "I don't like to think too much about this," and, "They're prejudices and biases from a bygone age." The University psychiatrists, by way of contrast, will discuss social stratification as an everyday fact which one needs to consider as one goes about one's work. This reaction is traceable, probably, to their frequent contacts with social scientists through the years. Some five out of six psychiatrists consider themselves to be upper-middle class, some see themselves as middle class, and 5 percent think they are upper class. These self-conceptions are close to the mode of other class I persons.

The median net take-home income of psychiatrists is appreciably higher than the average class I families in the community. The range, however, is not so great as it is for a cross section of class I families. The range of net income, as reported by the fully trained psychiatrists, varied from a low of $10,000 per year to a high of $40,000. The D-O group in private practice have a net take-home income of $25,000; the comparable figure for the A-P group is $22,000.[25] Individually and collectively, the D-O practitioners earn more in their practices than the A-P practitioners.

The cleavage between the A-P group and the D-O group reappears when the social and cultural backgrounds of individuals in the two groups are examined. Only 8 percent of the analytically oriented group are from old American stock; on the other hand, 44 percent of the D-O group come from old American stock. This means that the number of generations persons in each group have been in America is linked to their theoretical orientations. Fifty-eight percent of the analytically oriented group are first or second generation Americans; the comparable percentage for the D-O group is 38.

Religious backgrounds are linked closely with national origin and ethnic backgrounds among psychiatrists as among other members of the community; thus, we are not surprised to find that 83 percent of the analytically oriented group, but only 19 percent of the D-O group, came from Jewish homes. However, 58 percent of the analytic group who came from Jewish homes have no contact with organized religion today. The remainder have nominal affiliation with either Jewish or Protestant congregations. Whereas only 12 percent of the analytic group came from Protestant backgrounds, 75 percent of the D-O group have Protestant origins. One person with a Catholic background reports nominal affiliation with a parish, and another reports that he is "more or less" active. Those with Protestant backgrounds report no religious affiliations. The religious activity pattern is not too different within the D-O group. Fifty-five percent of those from Protestant backgrounds report that they have no religious affiliation now. Twenty-seven percent say that they have active religious affiliations, and 18 percent nominal affiliations. Three D-O practitioners are Jewish in background; two have no religious affiliation today, and one is active in a Reformed Temple. In sum, psychiatrists from Catholic, Jewish, or Protestant backgrounds are seldom active in religious affairs.

The paucity of religious activity in the present generation is in sharp contrast to what the psychiatrists report about their parents' religious behavior. Practically all of the analysts say that their fathers and mothers were active in the religious life of their community. The motivations for the withdrawal of the present generation is a matter of speculation. Doubt and confusion is apparent in their response to questions on how they would like to have their children trained religiously. The greatest amount of conflict on these questions is shown by psychiatrists who either do not practice their ancestral religion or who have changed to another religion.

The differences in ethnic origin which we have discussed indicate that the analytically oriented psychiatrists are geographically more mobile than the D-O group. When we examine the data on the two groups from the viewpoint of social mobility, we find that as a group the A-P practitioners have moved upward much farther in the class structure than the D-O group. Seventy-three percent of the A-P group have moved upward one or more classes from the positions occupied by their fathers.[26] On the other hand, only 42 percent of the D-O group have moved upward one or more classes when measured against their father's positions. Also, the analysts have outdistanced 83 percent of their brothers and 79 percent of their brothers-in-law in their ascent of the class status ladder. The D-O group have not achieved as much comparatively: 26 percent have moved farther than their brothers, and 31 percent have moved farther up the class scale than their brothers-in-law. The analytically oriented group are clearly "over-achievers" in comparison with the D-O group.

The psychiatrists are family men; all in our sample are married. The analysts, however, exhibit a different pattern of mate selection from the D-O's. Some 64 percent of the analysts contracted mixed religious marriages. Most of these mixed marriages are between men with Jewish backgrounds and women with Protestant backgrounds; the remainder involve Jewish men and Catholic women. Thirty-eight percent of the D-O group contracted mixed religious marriages; the majority of these marriages involved Protestant men and Catholic women. Marriages between persons of the same faith reveal an interesting pattern when the class statuses of the wives' families are compared with those of the husbands': In these marriages, the husband and wife either come from families of approximately equal status or the wife comes from a higher status family than her husband. These patterns appear in the marriages of both analytical and directive-organic groups and in each religious group. In mixed marriage, the wife comes from a family that is one class above the class of the man she marries, but at the time of the marriage the husband had achieved a higher position than the wife's family of orientation. This pattern reveals that in mixed marriages, both the husbands and the wives are motivated by strong feelings for upward mobility. The A-P group also have experienced a significantly higher percentage of divorces and remarriages than the D-O group.

All psychiatrists have high ambitions for their children. In the A-P group especially there is commonly an intellectual conception of permissiveness in the supervision of their children's careers, but the tendency to take charge and push cannot be suppressed. For example, a typical response to "How much education do you want for your children?" is "As much as they want; college is the minimum." In both groups, the vast majority of those with children are sending them to private schools. They expect them to do well in school, and plan to send them to "name" colleges. After college, they hope that their children will marry well and that the sons will follow economically rewarding and socially prestigeful occupations. The mothers are as ambitious for their children as the fathers. (Psychiatrists' families do not differ in this respect from comparable professional groups.)

Psychoanalytically oriented psychiatrists lead lives that are isolated for the most part from community activities. This is most pronounced among the psychoanalysts in private practice. These men belong to the fewest organizations, participate the least in community affairs, and know the least about the community and its activities; however, there are a few notable exceptions. The D-O psychiatrists belong to more community organizations, participate in more activities, and are more interested in the community than the analysts. As a consequence, the D-O practitioners, with the exception of the few psychoanalysts who have become noted outside the community, are known more widely in the community outside strictly psychiatric circles than the A-P practitioners. In addition, the wives of the D-O group participate in many more social activities than the wives of the analysts. In short, the D-O practitioners living in the community are more a part of the social life going on around them than the analytically oriented psychiatrists. When the analysts participate in social activities, their recreational patterns conform to their class status, if they are not barred by ethnic restrictions.

We mentioned some possible reasons, social and psychological, conscious and unconscious, why psychiatrists and analysts choose this particular career and what their profession "does for them." Another possibility, usually overlooked, is a strong upward mobility drive and its gratification. Like all phenomenally upward mobile persons, those who have achieved their present class positions largely through their own efforts and abilities have passed through a social, possibly also a psychological, transformation. Their pursuit of the American ideal of personal success and self-advancement has taken them away from the subcultures they learned as children. A large percentage of these men rebelled against the socially approved and the traditional, as well as against their families in childhood and adolescence. Commonly they sought relief for their inner turmoil in activities different from those of their parental families; to gain the goals they sought they had to look elsewhere for guidance. They found it in the theories of dynamic psychiatry. The ideas of Freud and his disciples gave them personal solace, a way of life, and a tool they could apply to earn their livelihood. Their study of Freud's thoughts brought them together; gradually they became members of a tightly knit group of disciples. In some of them, the acceptance of purely psychodynamic interpretations of human motivations tends to isolate them from the main currents of social life. Ironically, in some cases professional success has brought them into contact with high status persons who reject them socially.

SUMMARY AND CONCLUSIONS

The treatment of mentally ill persons in our community has passed through at least three phases. From the community's founding until after the American Revolution, the "distraught" or "possessed" were not regarded as sick persons. In those years they were sold at public auction along with criminals and the indigent, if their families or friends could not or would not care for them. From the end of the eighteenth to the middle of the nineteenth century, the work-house replaced the auction block for the distraught poor, but not much change occurred in the treatment of those who were not public charges. In the second quarter of the nineteenth century, men and women of good will began to realize that distraught persons in all walks and conditions of life were sick people. They also believed that if the insane were to recover, those responsible for their care had to treat them differently. At least, they should be cared for as different from delinquents and the indigent. As a consequence, the first mental hospital in the state was chartered by the Legislature as a private nonprofit institution in 1821. It was found to be inadequate for the large number of mentally ill in the state less than a half-century later; the next step was the founding of a state hospital. The state hospital was soon filled, and two more had to be built. Today, more public hospitals of a modern type are needed. In the last quarter of the nineteenth century, several small private mental hospitals were founded as proprietary enterprises.

Shortly before World War I, the mental hygiene movement gained momentum. This movement gave rise to mental hygiene clinics where ambulatory patients are treated before their illnesses require them to be hospitalized. Since World War II, the private office practice of psychiatry has grown very rapidly. Changes in theoretical orientation within psychiatry from a directive-organic medical one to an analytic-psychological and, gradually, to a comprehensive one combined with the increasing effectiveness of psychiatric therapies led to a marked increase in private office practice.

In recent years, clinic and office practice has attracted the attention of an increasing number of psychiatrists, while hospital psychiatry, except in general hospitals, has become less interesting and less challenging, particularly to younger psychiatrists. This shift in the place of treatment has been accompanied by a demand by physicians entering into residency for training in psychodynamics, intensive psychotherapy, and, whenever it can be obtained, in psychoanalysis. The vast majority of these young men and women plan to enter private practice when their training is completed.

Fifty years ago the superintendent of the state hospital was the representative psychiatrist; today it is the private practitioner. The private practitioner has become a person of civic importance, a man who is consulted on problems in education, crime, and social issues, not to speak of problems in mental health in the narrow sense. Nevertheless, his role has not crystallized because society's mandate to psychiatry is not clear. His position in the community is the topic of serious comment as well as humorous, and at times not so humorous, attacks. His income, which is almost as great as that of other nonsurgical medical specialties, at times surpasses his professional prestige. As a consequence, he is the target of envious remarks by his less well-heeled colleagues in academic positions and in the public mental hospitals and by the public. Criticisms of the private practitioner's "high fee" is, perhaps, an expression of a social mistrust psychiatry encounters in medical and lay circles. People are willing to pay for surgical or medical techniques, but the technical skills of the psychiatrist are not so widely understood and accepted.

NOTES

[1] Albert Deutsch, *The Mentally Ill in America,* Doubleday and Company, New York, 1937, pp. 47–48.

[2] *Ibid.,* p. 32.

[3] Rachel M. Hartley, *The History of Hamden, Connecticut, 1786–1936,* Hamden, 1943, p. 106.

[4] *Public Records of Connecticut,* Vol. 10, February 1756, p. 464.

[5] Rachel M. Hartley, *op. cit.,* p. 107.

[6] *Loc. cit.*

[7] *Ibid.,* p. 311.

[8] *Report of a Committee of the Connecticut Medical Society Respecting an Asylum for the Insane,* Hartford, 1821, pp. 8–9.

[9] *Report of His Excellency Chauncy F. Cleveland, Commissioner of the Insane Poor to the General Assembly, May, 1844,* New Haven, Babcock and Weldman (printers), 1844, p. 4.

[10] *Ibid.,* p. 6.

[11] *Report of the Governor as Commissioner to Carry into Effect the Appropriations for the Insane Poor, the Deaf, and Dumb, and the Blind,* New Haven, 1864, Osborn and Baldwin (printers), p. 3.

[12] *Report of the Commissioner for the Insane Poor to the General Assembly*, Hartford, 1851, pp. 9–13.

[13] Albert Deutsch, *op. cit.*, pp. 158–185.

[14] Ibid., p. 237.

[15] For an intimate view of one of these institutions in our state, see Clifford Beers, *A Mind that Found Itself* (Fifth Edition), Longmans, Green and Company, New York, 1921, pp. 41–61.

[16] *Ibid.* Presents a graphic description of conditions in a small proprietary mental hospital in our state, the Retreat, and the first state hospital discussed before, about 1900.

[17] Gregory Zilboorg, *A History of Medical Psychology*, W. W. Norton and Company, New York, 1941; see especially pp. 319–341.

[18] *Ibid.*, pp. 450–464.

[19] Quoted from Deutsch, *op. cit.*, p. 279.

[20] Alfred H. Stanton and Morris S. Schwartz, *The Mental Hospital*, Basic Books, New York, 1954, pp. 342–362.

[21] Exceptions to this principle include the very unusual case where endowment or research funds support a free bed. The more common adjustment to lack of funds is a reduced fee; we will discuss this in some detail in Chapter Ten.

[22] This was the size of the staff at the time of the Psychiatric Census.

[23] Henry A. Davidson, "The Structure of Private Practice in Psychiatry," *The American Journal of Psychiatry*, Vol. 113 (July 1956), pp. 41–44.

[24] The state hospital, Veterans Hospital, and most private hospital psychiatrists live in other communities.

[25] Psychiatrists on the full-time staff of the University had median net take-home incomes of $12,000. These incomes are for 1954. The incomes for the cross sectional sample of households discussed by class in Chapter Four are for 1950.

[26] For this comparison, the class positions of the psychiatrists and their fathers are determined by A. B. Hollingshead, *Two Factor Index of Social Position* (privately printed), New Haven, 1957, pp. 1–12.

social status and psychiatric illness

part three

part three • social status and psychiatric illness

Part Three analyzes relationships between class status and how mentally "disturbed" persons become psychiatric patients. The data on patients and non-patients which we gathered for testing *Hypotheses 1* and *2* are set forth in detail. Interrelationships between class position and the amount of *treated* mental illness in the population and also associations of class status to several kinds of mental illnesses are traced in the next three chapters.

paths
to the
psychiatrist [1]

chapter six

INTRODUCTION

Every person who follows a path that leads him eventually to a psychiatrist must pass four milestones. The first marks the *occurrence* of *"abnormal" behavior;* the second involves the *appraisal* of his behavior as "disturbed" in a psychiatric sense; the third is when the *decision* is made that psychiatric treatment is indicated, and the fourth is reached when the *decision is implemented* and the "disturbed" person actually enters the care of a psychiatrist. Due to the limitations of the data available to us because of the nature of our research design, the paths between the first two milestones will be sketched only in outline and illustrated by typical cases. The paths between the third and fourth milestones will be traced in detail with statistical materials accumulated on all cases in the study. In our discussion of the events that link each milestone, we will focus attention upon the question: Is class status a salient factor in the determination of what path a person follows on his way to a psychiatrist?

"Abnormal" Behavior

"Abnormal" behavior is used here to indicate actions that are different from what is expected in a defined social situation. Thus, abnormal acts can be evaluated only in terms of their cultural and psychosocial contexts. Homicide, for example, is abnormal in a peaceful community; it is normal when inflicted on the enemy during war.

Viewed psychiatrically, the range of abnormal behavior is very great, covering in intensity mild neuroses to severe psychoses, and in duration from acute, transient "disturbances" to chronic reactions. It encompasses such well-defined phenomena as various types of schizophrenia, and many psychosocial maladjustments that never bring most persons to the attention of psychiatrists.[2] "Abnormality depends" upon appraisal.

"Appraisal"

The perception and "appraisal," by other persons, of an individual's abnormal behavior as psychiatrically disturbed is crucial to the determination of whether a given individual is to become a psychiatric patient or be handled some other way. By appraisal we mean the evaluations of family members and proximate groups of abnormal behavior of persons. The appraisal of behavior as psychiatrically abnormal precedes decisions concerning therapeutic intervention. Appraisal is carried on by individuals and groups through the interpretation of interacting responses. It may be conscious, preconscious, or unconscious; usually, it is a combination of all three. It is both interpersonal and intrapersonal. As a lay response, appraisal corresponds to the professional diagnosis. As an intrapsychic process, it designates how the prospective patient perceives his actions, particularly his disturbed actions. Appraisal, as an interpersonal process, entails how a disturbed person and his actions are perceived and evaluated by the individual and by other persons in the community. Appraisal will determine what is judged to be delinquency, bad behavior, or psychiatric troubles.

Class Status and Appraisal

Inferences drawn from clinical practice, the tape-recorded interviews with persons in the 5 percent sample, and patients and members of their families in the Controlled Case Study and the Psychiatric Census indicate that class I and II persons are more aware of psychological problems than class IV and V persons. Class I and II persons are also more perceptive of personal frustration, failure, and critical intrapsychic conflicts than class IV and V persons. Perception of the psychological nature of personal problems is a rare trait in any person and in any class, but it is found more frequently in the refined atmosphere of classes I and II than in the raw setting of class V. As a consequence, we believe that far more abnormal behavior is tolerated by the two lower classes, particularly class V, without any awareness that the motivations behind the behavior are pathological, even though the behavior may be disapproved by the class norms. We will illustrate these points by drawing upon the clinical histories of several patients in our study.

The first patient is an example of a higher status person who is able and willing to utilize the help of a psychiatrist to overcome self-perceived disturbances. This patient is a 25-year-old graduate student, the son of a salaried, minor professional man in an established class II family. The patient's chief complaint is a feeling that he is not able to work to his full capacity. He first noted this difficulty as an undergraduate in a state university near his home. He discussed this problem with a college friend who was being treated by psychotherapy and, upon his friend's advice, consulted the psychiatrist in charge of the college mental hygiene clinic. However, he did not enter treatment at that time. He knew little about psychiatry when he went to the clinic, but he began to read Freud, Horney, and others; after a period of conscious aversion, he found the materials interesting. The information gathered from them led him, after he had entered graduate school, to discuss his feelings with his friend. Upon this occasion he entered treatment. He was skeptical about psychiatric help in the first weeks of therapy, but he convinced himself that obtaining psychotherapy does not mark a person as "crazy." From this point on he was able to profit from psychiatric treatment. In the course of several months of psychotherapy, he was able to discuss with the therapist his relationships with a stern, driving father and a brother who had disgraced the family on many occasions. The discussions made him realize he was far too critical of himself and inordinately ambitious; unconsciously he was identifying with his stern father while competing with and outdoing the "bad" brother. Gradually, he realized that his unconscious motivations were related to his depression, anxiety, and inability to do graduate work the way he desired.

The patient we shall use to illustrate the lack of sensitivity to psychopathological behavior in the lower segments of the status structure is an elderly class IV man. This man's clinical history indicates that he had exhibited psychopathological behavior throughout his life, but it was not interpreted as such by his family or his associates. A few incidents will clarify the lack of appraisal by the family. In 1940, he took his thermos bottle to a chemist for examination to see if his wife was trying to poison him. Every night before his wife went to bed she secreted butcher knives and other sharp instruments to keep them away from him. He did not trust his daughter to measure medicine "prescribed" for him by a corner druggist, and he accused her of trying to poison him to get his money. He entered his daughters' bedrooms while they were dressing or undressing unless they locked their doors. He kept a razor-sharp hunting knife in the cellar. A daughter and son-in-law knew about the weapon and his constant preoccupation with sharpening it, but no action was taken. The man became violent whenever anyone told him to stop cursing or stop anything he might be doing. When this occurred, he would shout and pound on the walls; on numerous occasions he broke the plaster with the force of his blows. The family avoided bringing any liquor into the home because the father became unmanageable when drunk.

The day before Christmas, however, he requested a bottle for the holidays, and the eldest daughter and son-in-law, in order to humor him, bought a fifth of whiskey. On Christmas Eve, he drank too much, became angry, and used his full vocabulary of obscenity and profanity on the family. The daughter and son-in-law put him to bed and removed his weapons from the room. The next morning he demanded to know what had happened the previous evening, and when he was told he began to yell and curse until the entire building of flats where the family lived was aroused. His daughter in desperation called the police who took the man to the city jail. He was held until after New Year's Day before he was tried, found guilty of breach of the peace, and was sentenced to sixty days in the county jail. After transfer to the jail, he became violent, and a psychiatrist was called to the jail by the sheriff. The psychiatrist recommended commitment to the state hospital.

This man had been in the state hospital two years at the time of the Psychiatric Census. His family did not want him in the home, but they did not feel it was right for him to remain in the state hospital. His eldest daughter, who took charge of the situation, did not think he was "crazy." However, she made no active plans to care for him or to have him discharged. While the study was in progress, the man died in the state hospital.

Although the patient presents a lifelong history of hostility, suspicion, and extreme lack of consideration of others, so far as we are able to determine neither his family nor others in his environment—even when his behavior became violent—considered him a "psychiatric problem." Such an appraisal of behavior is more typical of class V than of class IV, although people in all strata have blind spots regarding psychopathological implications of unusual behavior or even deliberately avoid thinking about them. The lower status patient will attribute his troubles to unhappiness, tough luck, laziness, meanness, or physical illness rather than to factors of psychogenic origin. The worst thing that can happen to a class V person is to be labeled "bugs," "crazy," or "nuts." Such judgment is often equal to being sentenced for life to the "bughouse." Unfortunately, this sentiment is realistic.[3]

The case histories of two compulsively promiscuous adolescent females will be drawn upon to illustrate the differential impact of class status on the way in which lay persons and psychiatrists perceive and appraise similar behavior. Both girls came to the attention of the police at about the same time but under very different circumstances. One came from a core group class I family, the other from a class V family broken by the desertion of the father. The class I girl, after one of her frequent drinking and sexual escapades on a weekend away from an exclusive boarding school, became involved in an automobile accident while drunk. Her family immediately arranged for bail through the influence of a member of an outstanding law firm; a powerful friend telephoned a newspaper contact, and the report of the accident was not published. Within twenty-four hours, the girl was returned to school. In a few weeks the school authorities realized that the girl was pregnant and notified her parents. A psychiatrist was called in for consultation by the parents with the expectation, expressed frankly, that he was to recommend a therapeutic interruption of the pregnancy. He did not see fit to do this and, instead, recommended hospitalization in a psychiatric institution to initiate psychotherapy. The parents, though disappointed that the girl would not have a "therapeutic" abortion, finally consented to hospitalization. In due course, the girl delivered a healthy baby who was placed for adoption. Throughout her stay in the hospital she received intensive psychotherapy and after being discharged continued in treatment with a highly regarded psychoanalyst.

The class V girl was arrested by the police after she was observed having intercourse with four or five sailors from a nearby naval base. At the end of a brief and perfunctory trial, the girl was sentenced to a reform school. After two years there she was paroled as an unpaid domestic. While on parole, she became involved in promiscuous activity, was caught by the police, and sent to the state reformatory for women. She accepted her sentence as deserved "punishment" but created enough disturbance in the reformatory to attract the attention of a guidance officer. This official recommended that a psychiatrist be consulted. The psychiatrist who saw her was impressed by her crudeness and inability to communicate with him on most subjects. He was alienated by the fact that she thought masturbation was "bad," whereas intercourse with many men whom she hardly knew was "O.K." The psychiatrist's recommendation was to return the girl to her regular routine because she was not "able to profit from psychotherapy."

This type of professional judgment is not atypical, as we will demonstrate in Chapter Eleven, because, on the one hand, many psychiatrists do not understand the cultural values of class V, and on the other, class V patients and their families rarely understand common terms in the psychiatrists' vocabulary, such as neuroses, conflict, and psychotherapy. The lack of communication between psychiatrist and patient merely adds to the hostility felt toward the psychiatrist and fear of what will happen to a member of the family if he is "taken away." A lack of understanding of the psychiatrist's goals occurs, in part, because lower class persons are not sufficiently educated, but also their appraisal of what is disturbed behavior differs greatly from that of the psychiatrist.

In class V, where the demands of everyday life are greatest, awareness of suffering is perceived less clearly than in the higher levels. The denial, or partial denial, of the existence of psychic pain appears to be a defense mechanism that is linked to low status. Also, class V persons appear to accept physical suffering to a greater extent than do persons in higher status positions. This may be realistic and in keeping with the often hopeless situations these people face in day-to-day living. In classes I and II, by way of contrast, there is less willingness to accept life as unalterable. Consequently, there is a marked tendency to utilize a psychiatrist to help ease subjective malaise or disease. Nevertheless, the individual usually tries to hide his "shame" until it is no longer concealable. Even members of the immediate family may not be told that the patient is in psychiatric treatment. For example, in an extreme case, a middle-aged class III Jewish woman takes great pains to let nobody except her favorite sister know that she is a patient. The sister, who usually brings the patient to the psychiatrist's office, insists that the patient be administered anesthesia before she receives electro-convulsive therapy. She does not think the patient should know about her "shameful" treatment.

Social Factors and Appraisal

The social factors influencing appraisal fall into two major categories: (1) access to existing technical knowledge and (2) sociocultural values. There is little doubt about the first point; without any knowledge of psychiatric therapy there can be no therapy, but prescription and application of therapy depend upon a group's access to knowledge, particularly in a popular form. The consequences of this, however, have not been understood. Only recently has health education in mental illness begun to be developed by mass communication media. We mentioned in Chapter Five that 300 years ago psychotics were considered to be witches and sorcerers. Even today, symptoms of neurosis and psychosis are thought to be caused by the "evil eye" by many class V Italians in this community. Naturally, such appraisal determined by culture is not compatible with modern psychiatric treatment.

We have begun barely to understand the appraisal process and the effects it has on who is treated by a psychiatrist and by what therapeutic techniques. A number of different things enter into it. The process of appraisal depends on individual factors of specific personality development and experience; it depends also on the values of our culture and the specific class subcultures as well as the knowledge and techniques which are available to the expert and to others who perceive and evaluate behavior in a given social situation.

Where people take their "troubles" depends on the value orientation of the individual which, in turn, depends upon group appraisal. Both interpersonal and intrapersonal appraisals are influenced by psychosocial and sociocultural factors. For example, a class I or II person who informs himself about diagnosis and treatment and who has access to the best medical opinion will appraise himself differently from the way in which a poorly informed class IV or V person will. The reasons for such differences in self-appraisal may be "deep" or "superficial." At this point, we are less concerned with individual differences than with responses to abnormality which are an integral part of a group's way of life.

Speaking broadly, a community can function adequately only by controlling members who create troubles of one kind or another for themselves and for other members of society. Through the years, special institutions have been developed to deal with particular types of chronically recurring troubles or dysfunctions, such as delinquency, poverty, and disease. Delinquency is handled by police, lawyers, judges, probation officers, and other legal functionaries. Poverty is alleviated by public and private welfare agencies. Medical institutions have been assigned the function of caring for personal crises that society defines as illness.

This neat tripartite separation of common dysfunctions works well so long as society makes clear judgments as to what agency is to care for what dysfunction. When lines of responsibility and function are unclear, as at present, problems arise. The objectives and responsibilities of psychiatric institutions often overlap with those of older welfare, legal, and medical institutions. Psychiatrists and psychiatric institutions are often asked to solve problems that involve several areas of social dysfunctions. Because of their characteristics which are as yet unclear, psychiatric institutions may be viewed as bridges between older institutions that have evolved to cope with social dysfunctions. When legal, economic, organic, and emotional factors play concomitant roles in an individual's troubles, that person may be referred to a psychiatrist mainly because traditional welfare, legal, and medical institutions have failed to handle the individual's multiple problems, possibly because no one institution is so equipped. In this sense, the psychiatrist is a community trouble shooter without a clearly defined role in relation to traditional institutions whose functions are more clearly defined and commonly accepted.

A person whose behavior is acceptable to his family, the community, and to himself is not likely to come to the attention of responsible institutional officers—parents, teachers, police, social workers, physicians, or such medical specialists as psychiatrists. However, when behavior is viewed as abnormal and a threat to the community, an individual may be brought to the attention of some official. For example, an adult male who exposes himself in public will not be tolerated by the community; at present, however, it is a moot point whether he will become a psychiatric patient or a legal case, inasmuch as our values assign the control of this kind of behavior to both penal and mental institutions. For another kind of behavior, that of a mildly hysterical class I or II female, the physician may recommend psychiatric care, but resistance to psychiatrists is so strong in our community that the chances are high she will not follow his advice. However, should she attempt suicide, she is likely to be brought forcibly into psychiatric treatment, for the class I and II subcultures attribute motivations toward self-destruction to psychopathology in the individual. In short: *Abnormal behavior that is appraised as being motivated by psychopathological disturbance in the individual is the province of the psychiatrist.*

Whether abnormal behavior is judged to be disturbed, delinquent, or merely idiosyncratic depends upon who sees it and how he appraises what he sees. To be sure, normal behavior is occasionally appraised as disturbed. Persons who perceive and appraise behavior may be classified into a number of categories: (1) the prospective patient, (2) members of the prospective patient's family, (3) friends, co-workers, neighbors, persons supplying and selling commodities, as well as leaders in community associations such as lodges and clubs, (4) professionals in the field of health (physicians, nurses, medical and psychiatric social workers, clinical psychologists), (5) professionals outside the field of health (ministers, lawyers, teachers, family case workers), and (6) officers of the community (police, attorneys, judges, and various other functionaries). Although there is some overlapping in these groups, they represent the major types of persons who perceive and evaluate behavior as normal or abnormal. Above all, these are the persons who decide whether abnormal behavior is delinquent or disturbed and who make referrals to psychiatric agencies.

Appraisals and Decisions to Act on Them

What is done about abnormal behavior that is appraised to be of psychogenic origin depends upon a number of factors. These include the assumed danger the behavior has for the disturbed individual as well as for other members of society, the attitudes, conscious and unconscious, of the individual and his family toward psychiatric treatment, and the availability of treatment. The implementation of appraisal is social, in large part, because the behavior of the persons involved, patients, therapists, or second parties, is defined in terms of cultural norms.

Among professional persons there are sharp differences in the ways behavior is perceived and appraised. Professionals—lawyers, ministers, teachers, physicians—also differ in their judgments from the perceptions and appraisals of lay persons. For example, conflicts are apt to occur when psychiatrists are asked to evaluate delinquent behavior among children and adolescents who are brought before juvenile courts. The judge may think that a child should be punished for his acts, whereas the psychiatrist may take the position that the child is disturbed and in need of treatment, not punishment. Such professional disagreements lead to fundamentally different ways of dealing with abnormal behavior which may block or delay a decision that a person is in need of psychiatric help. This is especially true when the evaluation of the expert does not coincide with "common sense" opinion.[4] Even minor professional disagreements block the implementation of a decision by a competent person that an individual ought to be treated by a psychiatrist.

These disagreements are accentuated by the ambiguous role the psychiatrist plays in our society. Law, custom, and tradition have assigned the care of the obviously psychotic person to the medical profession, but the much broader area of deviant and maladjusted behavior, although viewed as abnormal by some members of society, is not accepted fully by the public as an appropriate area for psychiatric treatment. Psychiatrists, particularly those with a dynamic orientation, consider this not only a legitimate but a most important area of professional activity.

When a psychiatrist enters the area of maladjusted behavior, he works with problems not clearly defined as being within the traditional province of medicine. As a "social" practitioner, the psychiatrist shares the appraisal of abnormal behavior with the lawyer, the clergyman, the teacher, the social worker, and the psychologist on the professional level and with parents and volunteer advisors on the lay level. The psychiatrist's role as a therapist is complicated further by the vague definitions of what facets of abnormal behavior should be handled by what agencies in the society. To be specific, delinquency as a legal problem is in the province of the courts and the penal system. Dependency is assigned to public and private welfare agencies. Yet both delinquency and dependency may be symptomatic of emotional disturbance and therefore amenable to psychiatric treatment. This is one of the areas in the society where the role and function of the psychiatrist are least clear.

Closely related to this issue is the question: Should a sex deviant be prosecuted via the courts and prison system, or should he be regarded as ill and treated in a psychiatric setting? Historically, the sexually deviant individual has been viewed as a legal case and punished by the judicial system. In more recent years some lawyers, social workers, and parole officers have held that deviant sex behavior is a psychiatric problem, but this is a minority viewpoint. What actually happens to a sexual deviant may be determined more by his class status than by what is defined by the law or by the most enlightened theory of social scientists or "progressive" dynamically oriented psychiatrists.

The differential impact of class status on what is done about disturbed behavior after psychiatrists are consulted is clear-cut when an individual's abnormal behavior has come to the attention of the police and the courts. In such cases, offenders in classes I and II are far more likely to retain a psychiatrist to protect them from the legal consequences of their acts than are offenders in classes IV and V. While this research was in progress, a class I married man, whose wife was pregnant, was arrested for exposing himself to a little girl. He was referred to a psychiatrist to avoid a possible prison sentence. This accused man retained a shrewd lawyer, well acquainted with persons in high political circles and also with the judge, a political appointee, who tried the case. The lawyer's primary expectation of the psychiatrist was to make a statement in court that would, in his words, "get his client off the hook." The accused was found guilty of breach of the peace and "sentenced" to two years of psychotherapy. From a psychiatric viewpoint, this is not a miscarriage of justice, but an enlightened sentence. The point is that such "sentences" are given rarely to the class IV and V sexual deviates, alcoholics, and drug addicts who face higher and lower courts but usually land in prison, not on a psychoanalyst's couch. Class IV and V sex delinquents, if found by psychiatric consultants to be disturbed, are committed, at best, to public mental institutions rather than sent to jail.

The generally negative attitudes toward psychiatrists and psychiatric agencies in all social strata result in persons turning in many directions for help before they go to a psychiatrist. Often this is a last resort, "a cry for help." [5] To see a psychiatrist is a rather desperate step for most persons; it is taken reluctantly after other resources, mechanisms, and compensations have failed and when the suffering person feels at "the end of his rope." Even then the patient and his associates must overcome various resistances, individual and familial; these are often linked with class status. A physician may advise a patient to see a psychiatrist, and the patient may be willing to follow the physician's advice; however, the patient's family may object strongly because they fear the social criticism that will result, or because they do not believe in it or are unfamiliar with the practice of psychiatry. On the other hand, they may want the patient committed to a mental hospital to get him out of the family, even though they fear the resulting stigma. In most cases, the motivation to obtain psychiatric help involves ambivalent feelings and conflicting evaluations among the several persons involved.

The decision to turn to the psychiatrist is made generally only after there has been a serious breakdown in social relationships. Even when a person seeks help for a very circumscribed problem, there usually is more personality disintegration than surface manifestations may indicate. To be sure, there are differences between individuals as to the amount and kind of stress that lead to despair. There are also class-linked differences in perception of what one may do to relieve conscious and unconscious feelings of displeasure, disease, or malaise. Accordingly, in all classes there are many instances of outright refusal to cooperate to the point of physical violence among both neurotic and psychotic patients.

Awareness of disease or malaise, psychosocial sensitivity to it, and the ability to express one's feelings regarding disease are the antecedents of the action to cope with the causes of distress. In trying to understand subsequent actions, it is also important to know how psychological suffering is viewed in the several strata. It will make a difference whether suffering is considered a result of ill fate, as it tends to be in class V, or something amenable to remedial action as in the higher classes. Only when the suffering is viewed as remediable is it compatible with therapeutic intervention. Actual knowledge of the causal factors by the suffering person may be small—and need not be large—so long as the psychiatrist is accepted as a person who can help him.

A physician may form an opinion about a person with psychiatric difficulties; he may advise him to see a psychiatrist, or he may force him to enter a mental hospital by the use of an emergency certificate. The patient, though not consciously, may want the physician to do this in order to extract him from a difficult, threatening, and frustrating situation. Underlying motivations may include escape from an unbearable situation, a vague wish for love and support, and, probably less frequently, a constructive desire to work through a problem with the aid of a competent doctor.

Implementation of Decisions to Seek Psychiatric Help

A decision to obtain psychiatric help is not identical with the implementation of that decision. Implementation may not be possible because the help which is sought is not always available. Many persons who want psychiatric help or who are referred to psychiatrists are seriously frustrated when they learn that, for geographic, social, and economic reasons, psychiatry is not available to them. We want to note here, however, that the data we will present in this chapter are limited to cases where the decision to refer an individual to a psychiatrist or psychiatric agency *was* implemented by the person's entry into treatment; instances where the decision was not implemented are not included in our figures.

Sources of Referral

The decision that a person's behavior is disturbed and is amenable to psychiatric treatment may result in a recommendation for action. For our purposes, a decision made by any person that an individual, who later became a patient and was counted in the Psychiatric Census, needed psychiatric care is called a *referral*. The name of the person responsible for the referral, ascertained from the clinical record of each patient, was entered on the Psychiatric Census schedule. We pointed out in a previous paragraph that one or more of six types of responsible persons ordinarily makes the decision that a person exhibiting disturbed behavior be treated by a psychiatrist. Each type of referral will be characterized briefly before we investigate class status as a significant factor in the question of *who* makes the decision to refer disturbed persons to psychiatrists.

1. SELF-REFERRALS. An individual who has enough knowledge of psychiatry and insight into himself to realize he is emotionally disturbed may decide to consult a psychiatrist about his problems. Such an individual is motivated by self-perception to seek relief through psychiatric treatment. Self-referrals are associated primarily with individuals who later are diagnosed as psychoneurotics.

2. FAMILY REFERRALS. Family perceptions of disturbance mean that some member of the immediate family recognizes the nature of an individual's symptoms and recommends psychiatric treatment. The individual may or may not accept the family's decision. When the sick individual refuses to accept the family's view of his difficulty, a psychiatrist may be called to the home or the patient may be brought forcibly to a psychiatrist's office. On the other hand, if his behavior is not considered too severe by his family and associates, nothing may be done until the patient's behavior becomes intolerable. The realization that a person is emotionally disturbed may be made by friends and close private associates; for present purposes, such referrals will be included with the family referrals.

3. MEDICAL REFERRALS. Medical perception of psychiatric illness usually occurs when an individual or some member of his family realizes that the person is ill but is not aware of the nature of his illness. The patient and his family may assume that the difficulty

is organic and should be treated by a general practitioner or a medical specialist other than a psychiatrist. In this case, a general practitioner or a specialist concludes that the individual's difficulties are not within his domain and recommends psychiatric help. The general practitioner or specialist usually acts as an intermediary between the patient and the psychiatrist. Medical and psychiatric social workers and visiting nurses are the persons who frequently refer patients of the lower classes to psychiatric agencies.

4. Nonmedical Professional Referrals. Nonmedical professional personnel may observe an individual's behavior and, on the basis of their knowledge of emotional involvements, decide he needs psychiatric help. Guidance teachers in the school system and family case workers are the most common nonmedical professional persons making referrals. Ministers and lawyers may observe the behavior of disturbed persons, but lawyers make singularly few referrals.

5. Official Referrals. Policemen, of all community officials, are the most likely to perceive that a psychotic individual is disturbed or in need of psychiatric care. This may occur when an officer is called to a home to calm or take charge of a violent individual or where a disturbed individual is being disorderly in a public place. When police officers come in contact with a disturbed individual in classes IV and V, they usually arrest him and hold him in jail until a psychiatrist examines him; if the individual is particularly disturbed, he may be taken to the Emergency Room of the community hospital.

Usually when the police arrest a disturbed individual, they perceive the nature of his difficulty before his family does. The family may know the individual is "difficult," "quarrelsome," "ornery," "abusive," "vulgar," or "profane," but seldom realizes that the individual is mentally ill. The police officer's perception and evaluation of an individual's behavior is crucial in deciding whether the individual is to be sent to jail or to the state hospital. If the police in their investigation decide that the patient is responsible for his behavior, he will be held for trial and, in all probability, sentenced to a term in a local jail or the state penitentiary. On the other hand, if the police conclude that the individual does not understand the nature of his behavior, and therefore is not psychologically responsible for what he has done, the chances are high that he will be turned over to psychiatric authorities. Policemen are Very Important Persons in the process of "diagnosing" severely disturbed and antisocial behavior. We believe that police officers, especially in their training schools, should be given systematic training in the nature and recognition of mental illness. They should be taught also something of the reactions of frightened relatives and what is to be done with a disturbed person.

Let us examine the question of interrelationships between class status and who refers whom to psychiatric agencies. Our discussion is limited to patients in their *first course of treatment* because it is impossible in most cases to determine who made the original referral for patients who have experienced a previous course of psychiatric treatment. Also we are interested in who made the decision that first brought the disturbed person into psychiatric treatment. The data on referrals of patients in their first course of treatment are presented according to the two major groups, neurotics and psychotics. Among the psychotic patients, the schizophrenics are treated separately because of the size of the group and their referral patterns.

Sources of Referrals for Neurotics—by Class

The sources of first referrals among neurotic patients are divided, for purposes of presentation, into medical and nonmedical. Medical referrals are subdivided, in turn, into those made by private physicians and those made by clinic physicians. The nonmedical referrals are tabulated according to the typology described in the preceding section. All first referrals for neurotic patients are summarized in Table 5. Examination of the data presented in Table 5 shows a direct relationship between class status and the percentage of referrals to psychiatrists by private physicians. On the other hand, referrals from clinic physicians show an inverse relationship to class status. Although referrals from private and clinic physicians form class-linked gradients that run in opposite directions, there is no appreciable difference in the percentages of referrals to psychiatrists by clinic physicians between classes I–II and III, but there is a sharp increase in clinic physician referrals at the class IV level of the social hierarchy. Here the increase is from 9.2 percent in class III to 29.1 percent in class IV. Class V referrals from clinic physicians are essentially in the same proportion as in class IV. The percentage of referrals to psychiatrists from private physicians traces a distinctly different gradient, as a glance at Table 5 will show. However, the reader should keep in mind that clinics are associated with people in the two lower classes, whereas, private practice is correlated with persons in the higher classes.

Referrals by nonmedical persons reveal an interesting series of

TABLE 5

Percentage of Referrals from Specified Sources for Neurotics Entering Treatment for the First Time—by Class

Source of Referral	Class			
	I–II	III	IV	V
Medical				
Private physicians	52.2	47.4	30.8	13.9
Clinic physicians	7.2	9.2	29.1	27.8
Nonmedical				
Police and courts *	0.0	1.3	5.1	13.9
Social agencies	1.4	5.3	4.3	36.1
Other professional persons	2.9	5.3	6.8	2.8
Family and friends	20.3	13.2	17.1	0.0
Self	15.9	18.4	6.8	5.5
$n =$	69	76	117	36

$$\chi^2 = 74.26, 9 \ df, pn < .001$$

* χ^2 computed with *courts, social agencies,* and *other professional persons* combined; also with *family* and *self* combined.

variations from class to class. There is a definite class-linked gradient in police and court referrals; the higher the class, the lower the percentage of referrals, with a heavy concentration of referrals in class V. A few referrals are made by family and welfare agency social workers and teachers from classes I–II through IV. In class V there are more referrals from social agencies and public health nurses than from all other nonmedical persons combined. Only clinic physicians approach officials in social agencies in the frequencies of referrals of class V persons to psychiatrists. If we view the clinic physician as a "community professional" along with teachers, social workers, and nurses, then we see that almost two out of three referrals in class V are made by professional workers in the community agencies. When official referrals that are made by the police and courts are added, the proportion becomes approximately four out of five. Few referrals in any class are made by lawyers and clergymen. Referrals by family members and friends are important in the four higher classes but not in class V. Self-referrals are almost as important as referrals by family members and friends in classes I–II and III, but in class IV there are distinctly fewer self- than family referrals; there are as many self-referrals in class V as in class IV. The chi square in Table 5 reveals that *who* decides to refer disturbed persons later diagnosed as neurotic to psychiatric agencies is linked definitely to class status.

Sources of Referral for Psychotic Patients—by Class

The sources of referral for disturbed persons who are diagnosed as psychotic are more strongly associated with class status than for those who are diagnosed as neurotic. Moreover, the percentage of referrals by particular types of persons is sharply different. Both private physicians and clinic physicians make relatively fewer referrals of patients who are diagnosed later as psychotic in comparison with those who are neurotic. In classes III and IV, private physicians make the highest proportion of referrals. In class I–II, some four out of five referrals are made by the patient, his family, or his friends. There are few self-referrals in class III. The family makes about one in six, but family physicians make some three referrals out of five. Other professionals and the police make a few referrals. In class IV, clinic physicians, the police, and the courts make more referrals; social agencies play a minor role. Class V psychotics, unlike the higher classes, are referred in the same general ways as the class V neurotics, except that the percentage of referrals by clinic physicians and social agencies is lower, whereas the proportion of police and court referrals is over three times higher. A close study of Table 6

TABLE 6

Percentage of Referrals from Specified Sources for Psychotics Entering Treatment for the First Time—by Class

	Class			
Source of Referral	I–II *	III	IV	V
Medical				
Private physicians	21.4	59.4	44.1	9.0
Clinic physicians	...	6.2	16.3	13.0
Nonmedical				
Social agencies	...	...	7.4	19.6
Police and courts	...	4.8	18.9	52.2
Family and friends	42.9	17.2	8.1	2.0
Self	35.7	6.2	2.6	...
Other professionals	...	6.2	2.6	4.2
$n =$	14	64	270	378

$$\chi^2 = 243.16, 12 \; df, \; p < .001$$

* Classes I–II and III were combined for the computation of χ^2 because of the small frequencies in classes I and II.

will show that in each class there is a concentration of referrals from one or two types of persons. The patient and the family are the major sources of referral in class I–II. In class III, private physicians and the family are the two principal sources of referral. In class IV, the family and clinic physicians share the decision with the police. In class V, the police and the courts, social agencies, and clinic physicians make practically all referrals.

The class-linked gradients on self-referrals and referrals by family members and friends in Tables 5 and 6 corroborate the generalization stated earlier that persons in the higher classes are more perceptive of disturbed behavior and of the potential help psychiatry offers than persons in the lower classes. For example, in class IV, only 24 percent of the neurotic patients and 11 percent of the psychotic patients entered treatment through appraisal of the patient or other persons in the primary group that the patient was disturbed. In class III, by way of comparison, the comparable figures are 32 percent for the neurotics and 23 percent for the psychotics. When we compare class V referrals by various members of the primary group with class IV referrals, we see even a greater difference than when we compare the class III's with the class IV's. In class V there are no family referrals among neurotics, and only 2 percent of the psychotics are brought into treatment by members of their families. In class V, persons outside the family and friendship groups make practically all referrals. In this class, responsible community agents make almost all appraisals of disturbed behavior. Consequently, they are the sources of effective referrals.

Sources of Referrals for Schizophrenics—by Class

The sources of referral for schizophrenics were studied separately to determine if they are different from all psychotics. We found that schizophrenic persons in each class are referred to psychiatric agencies in almost the same ways as the total psychotic patient population. This might have been expected because the schizophrenics compose some 53 percent of all psychotics in treatment for the first time. The sources of referrals for the schizophrenic patients are recorded in Table 7. Perhaps the most striking thing about these data is that there are no self-referrals from class I–II. In these strata we might expect to find enough insight to impel a disturbed person who is diagnosed later as schizophrenic to seek out a psychiatrist; but this is not what happens. In classes I and II, most referrals are made by the family after some member realizes that the patient is ill and in

TABLE 7

Percentage of Sources of Referral for Schizophrenics Entering Treatment
for the First Time—by Class

Source of Referral *	Class			
	I–II	III †	IV	V
Medical				
Private physicians	45.5	66.7	35.3	10.6
Clinic physicians	...	3.7	23.3	12.5
Nonmedical				
Police and courts	...	7.4	24.8	52.3
Social agencies	...	...	3.8	17.6
Other professionals	...	3.7	1.5	3.7
Family and friends	54.4	11.1	9.8	3.2
Self	...	7.4	1.5	...
$n =$	11	27	133	216

$$\chi^2 = 129.68, 8 \; df, \; p < .001$$

* The χ^2 was computed with social agency and other professional referrals
combined, and self-referrals combined with family and friend referrals.

† In this analysis, cases in class I–II and III were combined.

need of psychiatric care. When an appraisal is made that a member's
behavior is disturbed the family brings the patient to the psychiatrist
or calls the psychiatrist directly. Usually class I and II persons are
brought to psychiatric treatment by their families after heated discussions at home. In one instance, a patient became so violent that
a psychiatrist had to be called, and male members of the family held
the patient while he was subdued by sedatives. The patient was then
taken to a private psychiatric hospital under sedative. Ordinarily,
however, the patient is aware that he is being taken to a psychiatrist
or mental hospital, and violent disturbance is the exception.

Five schizophrenic patients in class I–II were referred to psychiatrists by private practitioners. Three of these referrals came from
general practitioners and two from specialists. In one case, a woman
went to her family physician for difficulties described as nervousness
and visceral aches and pains. The physician treated her for three
weeks before he came to the conclusion she was psychiatrically disturbed; then he referred her to a private psychiatrist. This woman
resisted referral but after discussing the situation with her husband,
her sister, and a friend in the medical profession, she went to the
recommended psychiatrist. The other two persons attempted suicide.

The family physicians were called by their families, and the physicians referred them to private psychiatrists. Suicidal attempts in the higher classes provoke rather drastic, often dramatic, action. The two specialists who made referrals were internists; their referrals were made after preliminary treatment for the patient's real or imagined symptoms.

Class III schizophrenics were referred by all types of persons except social agencies. Two persons, both students, went to psychiatrists as a result of their own feelings. One, in the premedical course, came to the conclusion that his difficulties were psychiatric in nature and, as he said, "turned himself in" when he realized he was "out of contact" with reality. He was hospitalized immediately. Three patients were perceived to be ill by their families and friends. One was taken to a psychiatrist after a friend had convinced her husband that she was mentally ill. The husband and friend took this woman to a psychiatrist who previously had treated the friend. The woman accepted the situation and began ambulatory treatment. Most referrals in class III involved situations where the sick member's behavior became so disturbed that the family could no longer cope with it and called a physician. The police brought two class III persons to the attention of a psychiatrist. In one case, a young man was wandering along the street at three a.m. when he was stopped by a police car. The police realized that he did not know what he was doing and took him home. The father called a physician who examined the young man and referred him to a private psychiatrist. This case is interesting in that the man was not arrested but was taken home by the police who realized that he was ill. We infer that this action was related to the policeman's perception of the man's middle class status.

Class IV individuals are referred to psychiatrists by all types of decision-making persons, but the greatest number are seen first by private practitioners. Clinic physicians and public officers see about an equal number. Outside the family there are few referrals from any one source.

In class V, the police and courts, social agencies, and clinic physicians make over four out of five referrals. The police and courts alone make over half the referrals. The general sequence of events in these cases is as follows: The disturbed individual attracts the attention of the police, often by breach of the peace or by molesting other persons. After a complaint has been made, the police arrest the disturbed person and take him to jail where he usually remains until a psychiatrist is brought into the case. If the prisoner is obviously psychotic, the police may take him directly to the Emergency Room of the community hospital where he is seen by a psychiatrist who is on call at all times. Social workers and public health nurses make referrals when they perceive a person who is in need of psychiatric attention. This recommendation is often resisted by the patient. Schizophrenic individuals in class V often come to the attention of physicians when they come to the dispensary of the community hospital for some physical ailment. Upon examination, the physician may decide that they are in need of psychiatric care and personally take the patient to the psychiatric clinic; experience has shown that otherwise the patient may simply walk out. Systematic observance of practices in the Emergency Room of the community hospital shows that when lower status persons attempt suicide, little attention is given to the possibility that they may be disturbed. If the patient can be treated medically or surgically without being admitted to the hospital, this is done. Such a patient is discharged without a referral having been made to the psychiatric service. If the patient has to be admitted to the hospital, because of the near success of the suicidal act, a referral may be made to the psychiatric service. However, before the referral is made, the suicidal act must be appraised as the act of a disturbed individual by some responsible person in the hospital. One of our class V patients came to the attention of a clinic physician when he reported for work as an orderly. The physician realized that the man was psychotic and took him to the psychiatric dispensary. Within a matter of hours, he was in the state hospital.

SUMMARY AND CONCLUSIONS

In this chapter we have discussed the milestones a person passes on his way to the psychiatrist. We illustrated the first three milestones with clinical materials drawn from the study. We stressed that the *appraisal* of abnormal behavior as disturbed, in a psychiatric sense, depends on four kinds of variables: (1) the tolerance of the individual and the society for certain kinds of behavior, (2) the general sensitivity of persons and groups to psychological components in behavior, (3) the attitudes of different responsible persons in the community toward psychiatry (this includes the type of treatment psychiatry has to offer the individual and the community to help handle abnormal behavior traceable to psychogenic or sociogenic disturbances), and (4) the class status of the persons whose behavior is appraised as disturbed.

The implementation of a decision that a person should be treated by a psychiatrist for his disturbed behavior is linked to class status. There is a definite tendency to induce disturbed persons in classes I and II to see a psychiatrist in more gentle and "insightful" ways than is the practice in class IV and especially in class V, where direct, authoritative, compulsory, and, at times, coercively brutal methods are used. We see this difference most frequently in forensic cases of mentally ill persons who are treated often according to their class status. The goddess of justice may be blind, but she smells differences, and particularly class differences. In sum, perception of trouble, its evaluation, and decisions about how it should be regarded are variables that are influenced in highly significant ways by an individual's class status.

It is common knowledge that there are not enough psychiatrists to treat all psychiatric patients and far too few to administer psychotherapy skillfully for all the neurotic and psychotic persons who need help. There are few good psychiatrists available even for the minority who can afford to pay the $10 to $40 per treatment or who are fortunate enough to find someone competent and motivated to carry on psychotherapy in a public hospital or clinic. Patients also know this, even if only unconsciously, and psychiatrists know, too, that they are dispensing a scarce commodity and therefore try to select what they call a good patient. We are not sure what attributes a good patient must have, but they include sensitivity, intelligence, social and intellectual standards similar to the psychiatrist's, a will to do one's best, a desire to improve one's personality and status in life, youth, attractiveness, and charm. Rarely will such standards be admitted by psychiatrists. On the contrary, psychiatrists claim that the selection for treatment is based on purely psychiatric criteria, but the figures we will present in the next chapter on where patients are treated first indicate how important social criteria are.

NOTES

[1] We are indebted to Dr. John Clausen, Chief, Socio-Environmental Laboratory, National Institute of Mental Health, for this phrase.

[2] For an extensive discussion of this question, see F. C. Redlich, "The Concept of Normality," *American Journal of Psychotherapy*, Vol. 3 (July 1952), pp. 551–576.

[3] This class V lay judgment will be supported with statistical data in Chapter Nine when we discuss duration of treatment by class status.

[4] In a paper, "The Concept of Health in Psychiatry" [Leighton, Clausen, and Wilson (editors), *Explorations in Social Psychiatry*, Basic Books, Inc., 1957], Redlich cites a striking example from the court-martial scene in Herman Wouk's *The Caine Mutiny*.

[5] Verbal communication by J. Rakusin.

class and
prevalence
of disorders

chapter
seven

INTRODUCTION

This chapter focuses on the systematic presentation of the data and the statistical tests with which we determined the validity of *Hypothesis 1*. This hypothesis postulated that the positions which individuals occupy in the class structure of the community are related significantly to the prevalence of treated mental disorders. Before we turn to the analysis of the data assembled to test *Hypothesis 1*, we shall discuss certain theoretical and methodological problems connected with it.

The concept of prevalence was contributed to the medical sciences by epidemiology. Briefly, epidemiology may be defined as the study of diseases and phenomena associated with them in defined populations. Epidemiology is one of the three principal methods devised by the medical sciences and arts to help man to understand and treat diseases. The others are the clinical and experimental methods. The clinical approach is built upon direct observations of individuals with symptoms of disease. The experimental method is focused upon the examination and manipulation of data, associated with disease in the laboratory or in clinical practice. The epidemiological approach studies disease and associated conditions in entire populations.[1] Each of these ways of approaching phenomena observed or assumed to be associated with disease has contributed to man's knowledge. Furthermore, each one is related to the others, and persons working in one discipline draw upon the ideas and techniques of those in the other two. For example, in epidemiological theory and practice the point of departure is the clinical case.[2] Likewise, in clinical and experimental medicine the case with active symptoms is the focal point of thought and action.

The first step in the study of a disease by epidemiological methods "is to determine the broad nature and extent of the problem," [3] that is, the number of "active" or "clinical" cases in a given population at some point in time.[4] When a population is studied during a specified interval of time, "the cases of illness which are identified can be classified with respect to time, thus:

1. Existing prior to the beginning of the interval, continuing throughout the interval, and still existing at the end of the interval.
2. Existing prior to the beginning of the interval and terminating during the interval.
3. Arising during the interval and still existing at the end of the interval.
4. Arising during the interval and terminating before the end of the interval.[5]

These four categories take into consideration the dynamic factors of additions to and subtractions from the number of clinical cases of a specified disease in a given population. When these categories are combined, they represent the total number of persons known to be sick in the population during an interval of observation. All of them are necessary for the determination of prevalence.

Prevalence is defined as the number of cases of a specified disease present in a population aggregate during a stated interval of time. In an epidemiological study, the criteria that define a *case* need to be stated carefully. The size and characteristics of the population aggregate have to be specified. Finally, the time interval has to be stipulated. The interval of prevalence may be one day, one week, one month, one year, or some other determined period.[6]

The cases arising during the interval of observation may be studied separately, that is, categories three and four. These categories may be combined to determine how many new members are added to the population of sick persons during the interval of observation. The number of new cases of a disease developing in a population within a specified interval of time is defined as *incidence*.

Prevalence and *incidence* are *related* concepts, but prevalence differs from incidence in that all known cases of a given disease active in a population during the specified interval are included. Whereas, only the new cases are encompassed in incidence. Prevalence and incidence are fundamental concepts in epidemiological theory, but they apply to different aspects of the problem of the distribution of disease in a population. Prevalence may be said to be a measure of the extent of suffering, irrespective of the length of time persons have been sick. Incidence is a measure of the way the disease attacks those who have not suffered from it previously.

Prevalence of Mental Illness

Determination of the number of mentally ill persons in a defined population is the first requisite to intelligent planning of how to cope with the problem.[7] This has been recognized by epidemiologists and public health officers for a long time. To this end, national censuses in a number of different countries have attempted to gather statistical data on inhabitants who are mentally ill; none of these efforts has been successful. The studies that have been made of both prevalence and incidence of mental illness in particular populations have not been made carefully, or they are not comparable.[8] The net result is this: satisfactory data do not exist on the extent of mental disorders in any society.

The computation of prevalence or incidence figures in mental illness is extremely difficult for a number of reasons. Among them, on the one hand, is the fear of mental illness, and on the other, the lack of a criterion against which mental health or mental illness can be measured. In spite of various attempts by psychiatrists to draw a clearly demarcated line between who is well and who is sick, the boundary between mental health and mental illness remains indeterminate.[9] Unfortunately, psychiatry lacks a standard measure of what is normal and what is abnormal. A standard measure of normality and abnormality would enable researchers to determine the presence or absence of mental illness in a population. It also might enable them to estimate the proneness of some persons to mental illness. In sum, the lack of criteria for dividing the sick from the well presents great obstacles to investigators who desire to make studies of incidence or prevalence of mental illness. With these ideas before us, we will turn to the presentation of the data relative to *Hypothesis 1.*

The Problem

The questions posed in *Hypothesis 1* are: (1) How much *treated* mental illness is there in the population of the New Haven Community? (2) Is the distribution of mental illness linked to class status? To answer these questions, from an ideal theoretical viewpoint, we should have data on untreated as well as treated cases of mental illness. However, as we pointed out in the preceding section, the determination of the extent of mental disorders in a defined population is dependent upon the development of standardized criteria for measuring normality and abnormality of psychological and emotional functioning. If this could be done, a research team might be able to examine either a total population or an adequate probability sample. The next problem would be to decide whether prevalence, incidence, or both measures were necessary for the problem at hand.

To make a true or endemic study of prevalence of mental illness in a population, researchers would have to make direct psychiatric examinations. The population to be studied would have to subject itself to the necessary examinations and tests. If incidence were added to the research design, the population would have to be examined at least twice, at the beginning and again at the end of the interval of observation, to ensure that all new cases were located, not just the new cases that reached a treatment center. These conditions could not be met by our research team. Indeed, to our knowledge, they have not been met by any research team.

In view of the great practical difficulties inherent in empirical research in mental health and the need for information on the extent of mental illness, our study was limited to cases being treated by a psychiatrist, or cared for in a psychiatric institution. The known psychiatric case is the primary unit around which our tests of *Hypothesis 1* are built. However, to see if the prevalence of treated mental illness in the population of the New Haven community is related to class status, we compare the clinical cases in each class in the population with persons in the appropriate class who are not patients. Speaking broadly, we compare the mentally "sick" with the mentally "well."

Figures on the prevalence of treated psychiatric illnesses in the population under study are stated either as percentages or rates. Percentages are used in the earlier parts of this chapter because we are concerned with both the presentation and analysis of data from the Psychiatric Census and the 5 percent sample. The use of percentages enables us to do both operations at the same time. Rates are used in the latter part of the chapter, but only after we have given the reader the essential data upon which they are based. When we change from an examination of the data, expressed as percentages, to the use of rates, we will define what we mean by the term "rates."

All tests of *Hypothesis 1* are made by comparing the general population in each class with the number of psychiatric patients in the class. Throughout the analysis, class status is considered to be the antecedent or independent factor and treated mental illness is assumed to be the consequent or dependent factor.

Six different factors are considered in the examination of possible interrelationships between class position and the prevalence of psychiatric patients in the population. Three are biological in origin—sex, age, and race—and three are social in nature—social class, religion, and marital status; but we shall consider all of them as social factors for present purposes. Sex, age, race, religion, and marital status are included, along with class, to learn whether class status is the salient factor in prevalence as we presumed, or if a combination of several biological and social factors confuses the assumed linkage between class status and treated mental illness. The six factors are examined first singly and then in combinations to determine what effect each one, or all of them, exerts on the assumed interdependence between class position and the presence or absence of treated mental illness in the population of the community.

CLASS STATUS AND TREATED MENTAL ILLNESS

The first test of a possible interrelation between class status and mental illness is presented in Table 8.[10] A glance at the percentages in Table 8 will show that class I has only one third as many patients as might be expected if class I individuals were distributed in the same proportion in the patient population as class I individuals are in the general population. Likewise, class II, III, and IV individuals are under-represented in the patient column, but not to the same extent as class I individuals. On the other hand, the percentage of patients in class V is more than double the percentage of class V individuals in the general population. The distribution of patients in comparison with nonpatients by class is significant.

This indicates that there is foundation in fact for our assumption that class status is a factor conditioning whether or not a member

TABLE 8

Class Status and the Distribution of Patients and Nonpatients in the Population

Class	Population, %	
	Patients	Nonpatients
I	1.0	3.0
II	7.0	8.4
III	13.7	20.4
IV	40.1	49.8
V	38.2	18.4
$n =$	1891	236,940

$$\chi^2 = 509.81, 4 \ df, p < .001$$

of the community is a psychiatric patient. However, we are not content to accept the apparent relationship between class status and treatment or nontreatment for a mental disorder without a systematic examination of the influences age, sex, race, religion, and marital status may have on the data. If it should occur that, when these factors are included in the analysis, the significant association between class status and the prevalence of treated disorders in the population shown in Table 8 disappears, then we should modify the theoretical position posited in this research. If, however, the inclusion of these factors does not efface the differences between class status and the prevalence of patients in the different classes, then we may conclude *Hypothesis 1* is tenable. Control of the five factors, in addition to class, will tell us whether the relationship we have found between class status and mental illness can be attributed to these factors.

CONTROL OF SINGLE FACTORS

Class and Sex

Let us examine the question: If the sex variable is controlled, will class status be a significant factor in the prevalence of treated psychiatric disorders? The data pertinent to this question are presented in Table 9. An inspection of the percentages for each class in Table 9 shows that both male and female patients exhibit distributions very similar to those of the total population summarized in Table 8. From classes I and II [11] through class IV, the percentage of patients, male or female, is appreciably smaller than that of nonpatients. But

TABLE 9

Class Status and the Percentage of Patients in the Population—by Sex

Males

Class	Patients	Population
I–II	7.3	11.1
III	11.1	20.5
IV	38.6	50.5
V	43.0	17.9
$n =$ 969		114,100

$$\chi^2 = 425.76, 3 \ df, p < .001$$

Females

Class	Patients	Population
I–II	8.6	11.7
III	16.6	20.3
IV	41.6	49.1
V	33.2	18.9
$n =$ 922		122,840

$$\chi^2 = 126.95, 3 \ df, p < .001$$

in class V the percentage of male patients is well over twice that for nonpatients. The same trend holds for females in class V, but the difference is not as great as it is among the class V males. The connection between class status and the extent of mental illness operates with different intensity in the two sexes at different class levels. For example, there are proportionately more female patients in class III than males. On the other hand, in class V it is the males who are concentrated in the patient group. In spite of variations in the two sexes from one class to another, class status clearly is related to whether an individual is or is not a psychiatric patient, but it is less intense among females than males.

Class and Age

Age is held constant to determine if mental illness is linked to class status within specified age ranges. In this analysis, the patients and the general population are divided into six age groups: under 15 years of age, 15–24, 25–34, 35–44, 45–54, and 55 and over.

Each of these ranges reflects important age-related social and psychiatric phenomena. Individuals under 15 years of age are viewed generally as children. The years from 15–24 encompass adolescence and young adulthood; this is the phase of the maturation cycle when most young people complete school, start their work careers, marry, and in general establish adult behavior patterns. Social and physiological changes are not so marked either in the years from 25–34, or from 35–44, but they are years of social growth and emotional stress; for the average person, youth has passed and middle age has begun. The involutional period occurs normally in the decade 45–54; in these years definite endocrinological changes occur in women and probably also in men. It is during these years that the family of procreation is changed by the maturation of children. Also during the forties and fifties, the head of the household ordinarily reaches the peak of his earning power. Individuals at 55 and over are on the farther side of middle age; many are on the edge of a decline that leads eventually to the physical impairments of old age and their withdrawal from active participation in society. From a psychiatric viewpoint, the middle fifties are the years when disorders of the senium begin to make their appearance clinically.

Class status is a significant factor in the distribution of patients in the population within each age period except during the adolescent and early adult years.[12]   Classes I and II have about as many mentally ill members under 15 years of age as we would expect if the patients were distributed proportionately between all classes. Class III contributes 60 percent more patients during childhood than its proportionate share; class IV provides only one half as many patients as expected. Class V, however, contributes more than its proportionate share of mental illness. Above 25 years of age, class status becomes increasingly important as the years pass. This finding indicates that age operates concomitantly with class in the determination of who is or is not receiving psychiatric care. Therefore, age may be said to be an independent factor that confounds the effects of class status on mental illness. Consequently, we will have to control for it in later analyses. Here we are concerned only with the finding that class status is related significantly to being a patient in five of the six age periods, and its effects become greater within each period from the lower to the higher ages.

Class and Race

When the data are viewed from the perspective of race, definite relationships between class position and the distribution of patients appear.[13] Examination of the data in Table 10 shows that among

TABLE 10

Percentage of Patients in the Population by Class and Race

Whites

Class	Patients	Population
I–II	8.3	11.7
III	14.2	20.8
IV	41.1	50.1
V	36.4	17.4
$n =$	1795	226,400

$$\chi^2 = 438.49 \ p < .001$$

Negroes

Class	Patients	Population
I–II	0.0	1.0
III	6.3	4.0
IV	14.6	36.9
V	79.1	58.1
$n =$	96	10,540

$$\chi^2 = 19.91 \ p < .001$$

whites the percentage of patients in each class is smaller than the percentage of the population except in class V. In class V the percentage of patients is twice as large as the percentage of the population. An interesting point is that Negroes exhibit somewhat the same pattern as whites.

Class and Marital Status

Analysis of the possible effects of marital status on the distribution of patients in each class is limited to individuals 20 years of age and older because only a small proportion of persons are married in their teens. Persons in the general population and the patient group 20 years of age and over are divided into three categories: (1) married, (2) separated, widowed, or divorced, and (3) unmarried. The data for each of these groupings, presented in Table 11, show that in each marital category patients in the four higher classes comprise distinctly lower proportions of patients than the general population. In class V, however, the percentage of patients in each marital category is almost double that of the population.

TABLE 11

The Percentage of Patients and Population by Class and Marital Status

Married

Class	Patients	Population
I–II	10.8	12.6
III	15.3	22.1
IV	42.3	48.9
V	31.6	16.3
$n =$ 662		117,060

$$\chi^2 = 115.87, 3 \; df, p < .001$$

Separated, Divorced, and Widowed

Class	Patients	Population
I–II	5.1	8.6
III	12.9	16.7
IV	35.7	48.6
V	46.3	26.1
$n =$ 356		25,940

$$\chi^2 = 76.71, 3 \; df, p < .001$$

Unmarried

Class	Patients	Population
I–II	6.4	9.9
III	12.7	17.9
IV	40.6	50.1
V	40.3	23.0
$n =$ 791		24,740

$$\chi^2 = 135.20, 3 \; df, p < .001$$

Class and Religious Affiliation

Religious affiliation has such pervasive influence in the community that we included it as a social factor for control. Then, too, the distribution of persons affiliated with each of the three principal religious groups—Roman Catholic, Protestant, and Jewish—is very different in the class structure. This fact alone conceivably could confound the significant association between class status and treated mental illness in the population. This observation is pertinent particularly if religion is a conditioning factor in the determination of psychiatric treatment or nontreatment for mental ills.[14] If religious affiliation rather than class status is the salient factor underlying the prevalence pattern, the previously demonstrated relationship between class status and prevalence should disappear when religious affiliation is controlled.

Table 12 shows that the percentage of Protestants is lower than the general population in each of the four higher classes. Again, in class V the number of patients is approximately two and one half times larger than the comparable figure for the population; that is 31.9 percent in comparison with 13.0 percent. Roman Catholics present a similar pattern except that there are strikingly lower percentages in the patient column from classes I through IV, but the

TABLE 12

Percentage of Patients in the Population by Class and Religion

Protestants

Class	Patients	Population
I–II	15.4	17.3
III	18.6	24.6
IV	34.1	45.1
V	31.9	13.0
$n =$ 558		77,380

$$\chi^2 = 177.80, 3 \; df, p < .001$$

Roman Catholics

Class	Patients	Population
I–II	2.3	5.4
III	8.2	16.8
IV	42.6	54.6
V	46.9	23.2
$n =$ 1021		134,720

$$\chi^2 = 335.86, 3 \; df, p < .001$$

Jews

Class	Patients	Population
I–II	14.4	25.1
III	27.0	28.8
IV	45.6	38.9
V	13.0	7.2
$n =$ 215		22,160

$$\chi^2 = 22.55, 3 \; df, p < .001$$

class V percentage of patients is more than twice as great as the nonpatients.

Jews present a pattern different from the two Christian groups. In classes I and II, the disparity in the percentage of Jews who are patients is much greater than among the Protestants, but not so great as it is among Roman Catholics. In class III there is no essential difference between the figures for the Jewish patients and the general population, 27.0 and 28.8 percent. The proportion of class III patients is much lower in the Protestant and Roman Catholic groups than among the Jews. In class IV, the percentage of Jewish patients is higher than in the population. In class V, the percentage of Jewish patients is approximately double that of the population.

The salient point in these analyses is that class status is an important factor in each religious group. The two higher classes are under-represented in the patient population in all religious groups; whereas on the other end of the status structure, class V has at least twice as many patients in each religious group as this segment of the population should contribute on a proportionate basis.

Simultaneous Control of Two Factors

The series of comparisons we have made between the patients and the population with age, sex, race, marital status, and religion controlled indicate that treated mental disorders follow a pattern that is linked with class. Let us now examine the question: Will class continue to be important in mental illness when two factors are controlled simultaneously?

This is a deceptively simple query. To answer it, eight different factors have to be manipulated statistically: (1) class, (2) patients, (3) nonpatients, (4) sex, (5) age, (6) race, (7) marital status, and (8) religion. When only three factors are considered simultaneously without any controls, for example class status, patients, and nonpatients, we are able to examine their interrelationships in a single matrix. (This was done in the analysis of the data presented in Table 8, p. 199.) When four factors are examined and one is held constant, at least three matrices are necessary (as in Table 12, p. 204), but when the patient and the general populations are compared, with age controlled, six different matrices are involved. When five factors are studied and two are controlled simultaneously, at least six matrices have to be analyzed and possibly as many as twelve.

To be brief, we made 192 analyses of the data [15] before we were convinced that we had a satisfactory answer to the question of the significance of class status when two factors are controlled simultaneously. Of these analyses, 10 percent do not show a significant association between class status and some facet of the prevalence pattern. The other 90 percent are significant. In short, nine analyses out of ten show a significant relationship between class status and the prevalence of treated mental illness when two of the selected factors are held constant simultaneously. The results of only two sets of the analyses with two factors controlled simultaneously will be discussed here. They involve interdependencies between (1) class status and mental illness when sex and age are controlled and (2) class status and mental illness when sex and race are controlled.

Class, Sex, and Age

Significant associations exist between class position and mental illness for both sexes and for all adult age groups. The connection between class and mental illness is significant also for males under 15 years of age but not for females. Class III boys show a strong tendency to be in treatment. On the other hand, the percentage of class IV boy patients is only one half as large as it is for the population.[16] Class V, however, has over twice as many boys in treatment as could be expected proportionately. In passing, we shall note that the class III boy patients are largely Jewish and they are concentrated in a voluntary private treatment clinic, whereas the class V boys are in a public clinic. The class V boys are all Roman Catholics or Protestants. They are sent to the public clinic either by the Juvenile Court or social agencies. Apparently no association exists between class position and mental illness for either males or females in the ages 15–24.

Between the ages of 25–34, the percentage of males who are patients is slightly higher in classes I and II than in the population; in class III the percentage of patients is only two thirds higher than the population. There is little difference between the patients and population in class IV, but in class V there are proportionately twice as many patients as population. The percentage of class V female patients is double that of the population, but in classes I and II, the balance tips slightly on the side of the patient group; that is, 13.6 percent of the female patients are in classes I and II, whereas only 11.9 percent of the nonpatients are in these strata.

In each older age group, the illness pattern by class is relatively stable. The higher classes have a disproportionately lower proportion of patients than population, but the differences become smaller from class I to class IV: even at the class IV level the patient group is smaller than the population. Class V is dramatically different from the higher classes at each successive age level and in both sexes. In class V, the percentage of patients is at least twice as large as the population in each age group; between ages 35 and 44, it is three times larger.

The data discussed here establish two points: (1) When sex and age are held constant simultaneously, significant relationships exist between class position and the prevalence of mental illness with the exceptions noted in the younger age groups, and (2) the differences between the classes follow the same pattern as when only one factor is held constant; namely, the lower the class, the greater the proportion of psychiatric patients. There is in each age group below 15 and above 24 a disproportionate concentration of mentally ill persons in class V.

Class, Sex, and Race

Significant associations exist between class and mental illness among both white and Negro males, but only among white females. This finding has to be interpreted cautiously because there are only 39 female Negro patients in the study. These females are distributed as follows: class III—3, class IV—9, and class V—27. The fact that so few Negro females in classes III and IV are patients limits the reliability of the lack of association between class status and mental illness among Negro females. The same caution must be applied to the finding on Negro males. Although a significant association is found between class status and mental illness among Negro males, the number of patients is small.[17] Only 57 Negro males were enumerated in the Psychiatric Census. By class they are: class III—3, class IV—5, and class V—49.

When class and sex are controlled and comparisons are made between the number of mentally ill whites and Negroes in the population who are in treatment, it is only in class III that a significant difference appears between the two races.[18] The number of Negroes in classes III and IV is too small to hold race constant along with other variables such as age and marital status. *Therefore, Negroes will be included with whites in the remainder of the tests of* Hypothesis 1 *and all other discussions of the different aspects of this study.*

Three Factors Controlled Simultaneously

The control of three factors simultaneously enables us to work with six variables, and it reduces the number of possible combinations because more variables are included in a single matrix. Thus, when we ask: Is mental illness related significantly to class status when sex, age, and marital status are controlled? we face the task of organizing the data into 12 complicated tables. But if the answer is "yes," we increase the likelihood that the relationship is a true or real one rather than an artifact of the concatenation of the factors.

The analyses we made with three factors under control showed that in 10 out of the 12 matrices required there is a significant linkage between class status and mental illness. The two matrices that do not show a significant association involve separated, widowed, or divorced males between the ages of 20 and 49 and unmarried females between 20 and 49 years of age. Individuals in these two groups combined compose only 12.7 percent of the patients. Each sex and marital status category, from 50 years on, shows a significant association between class position and mental illness.[19]

In each significant matrix analyzed with three factors held constant, the characteristic pattern of an extreme concentration of patients in class V reappears. In these analyses class V patients comprise a higher percentage of the total patient group than class V individuals in the population.

Tentative Conclusions

The procedure we have followed of stating the data in percentages of patients and nonpatients for each class, and then dividing each of these categories into subgroups by age, sex, race, religion, and marital status, has enabled us to demonstrate that class is a significant factor in the prevalence of treated mental illness. When the selected factors were partialed or controlled, class status continued to be linked significantly to mental illness. We conclude from the preceding analyses that *Hypothesis 1* is tenable. However, the reader should not infer that the factors controlled may not be linked also with the prevalence of mental illness. They may be, but we are concerned here *only* with discovering if class, as postulated in the hypotheses under examination, is associated significantly with mental illness. The procedures used have established that the prevalence of treated mental illness is linked in very definite ways to social class.

CLASS AND RATES OF MENTAL ILLNESS

The Concept of Rates

The ratio of cases of a disease active in a population during a specified interval of time in relation to the size of the population at risk is stated usually as a *rate*. A rate is computed by dividing the number of cases of the disease by the population. The major advantage of rates is that they enable us to summarize the relationship between class status and mental illness with several factors controlled in a *single* analysis.[20]

The procedure of stating the findings in terms of rates enables the reader to see how many patients would be contributed by the population or a subgroup of the population if the proportion of patients in the population or subgroup were applied to a population of some standard size. We will use 100,000 as the "standard unit." The statement of the findings in terms of this standard unit permits us to make easy comparisons of the numbers of patients in population subgroups of different sizes.

Rates are easily obtainable and understood. For example, the class I and II population in the New Haven community is 27,000, and there are 150 patients in classes I and II. Expressed in terms of the number of patients per 100,000 population, the class I and II rate is *556*. There are more patients (260) in class III, but the population is considerably larger (48,360), and the class III rate is lower, *538* patients per 100,000 population.[21] Similarly, rates are computed for the other classes or for age and sex groups. (They may be computed also for the subgroups defined on the basis of more than one factor; for example, among class V males between 15 and 24 years of age there are 19 patients and 3780 nonpatients which produces a rate of *503* per 100,000.)

Crude and Adjusted Rates

The rates we have given are *crude rates*. Crude rates for the various classes do not take into consideration the fact that such factors as sex and age which we have found to be associated with the prevalence of mental illness may be confounded with class status. It is possible, however, to *adjust* crude rates on the basis of age or sex or both by holding one or both factors constant statistically.[22] The adjusted rates may then be compared and used in tests of significance without the variations in age and sex distributions in the several classes complicating the analysis. This procedure for handling the problem of possible confounding of interrelated variables is more efficient than analyzing separately each sex-age subgroup, since it enables us to determine if class is a real factor within the limits of a single analysis. This adjustment in rates may be described briefly as a procedure of weighting the crude rates for the age and sex subgroups within each class in the same ratio as the distribution of these subgroups in the total population.[23]

Differences between crude and adjusted rates are illustrated in the following tabulations. The crude rate for treated psychiatric illness in the population is:

	Crude Rate per 100,000
Class	
I–II	556
III	538
IV	642
V	1659
Total Population	798

When these rates are adjusted for age and sex, slightly different rates emerge.

	Adjusted Rate per 100,000
Class	
I–II	553
III	528
IV	665
V	1668
Total Population	808

The adjusted rates do not differ greatly from the crude rates because the sex and age distributions of the various classes are similar. If there were marked differences among them, however, and if the crude rates of these age and sex subgroups were very different, the adjustment of rates would have a considerable effect. The important point is that by expressing the ratio of patients to the population in terms of the "standard unit" of 100,000 and then adjusting the rate for each class to control for age and sex, we are able to see the relationship between class position and the prevalence of treated mental disorders in a single table. The adjusted rates are used as the basis for tests of significance.[24]

Both the crude rates and the adjusted rates per 100,000 given above are associated significantly with class status.[25] The differences between the classes become greater as we move down the class status scale; again, the greatest difference is between class IV and class V. This is exactly the pattern we found in the controlled comparisons procedures used in the preceding section. Both procedures demonstrated that *class status is a real or true factor in the prevalence of treated mental illness in this community*.

COMPONENTS IN PREVALENCE

In the introduction to this chapter we pointed out that prevalence is a measure of the extent of a specified disease in a population. Included within it are active cases of a disease: (1) in existence before and during the interval of observation; (2) existing prior to the beginning of the interval, but terminating during the interval; (3) new cases arising within the interval and still active at its close; and (4) new cases that arise in the interval, but are terminated before the end of the interval.

Prevalence, as an inclusive concept, does not differentiate between these four types of active cases. Incidence, as a restrictive concept, does. As we pointed out earlier, incidence is a measure of the way a disease attacks a population during an interval of time. Thus, to compute an incidence rate one focuses upon the new cases that become active in the population during an interval of observation.

In the discussion of prevalence in the two preceding sections, no differentiation is made between patients who have been in treatment for a week and those who have been under psychiatric care for a number of years. When the data are viewed in relation to the length of time each patient has been in treatment, we find patients who had entered psychiatric treatment for the first time in their lives shortly before the Psychiatric Census was taken, others who had been in treatment at one time, were discharged, and have re-entered treatment, and still others who have been in continuous treatment for a number of years.

The interval of observation used in this study extended from June 1, 1950 to December 1, 1950, the dates of the Psychiatric Census. All patients in treatment on June 1, 1950 were traced to determine if they were continuing in treatment or had been discharged. Detailed questions were asked about the temporal aspects of each patient's illness: the date when he entered treatment for the first time, the duration of his treatment, the date of discharge, the date or dates of re-entry into treatment, discharge a second or third time, and so on. The information yielded by these questions enables us to differentiate among patients in terms of the duration of treatment.

Patients who were in treatment on May 31, 1950 and continued in treatment until December 1, 1950, are categorized as continuous cases. Individuals who entered treatment for the first time between May 31, 1950 and December 1, 1950 are categorized as new cases. Individuals who had been psychiatric patients at some previous time and re-entered treatment between May 31, 1950 and December 1, 1950 are called re-entry cases. The continuous, new, and re-entry cases make up the aggregate of cases we have been concerned with heretofore.

Incidence of Mental Illness and Class

Is class status related to the incidence of treated mental illness? To answer this question we separated the patients who entered treatment for the first time between June 1, 1950 and December 1, 1950 from all other patients. These are the new cases that presumably became active in the time interval under observation. Age and sex adjusted rates were then computed for these new cases. The incidence rate per 100,000 by class is:

Class	Rate
I–II	97
III	114
IV	89
V	139
Total	104

$$\chi^2 = 8.41, 3 \; df, \; p < .05$$

These figures tell us that class status is a significant factor in the way mental illness attacks the population of the New Haven Community. In a word, class status is linked to the incidence of treated mental illness.

Re-entry into Treatment

Patients who were known to have been under the care of a psychiatrist or a psychiatric institution before June 1, 1950, but who were discharged and re-entered treatment during the six months of the Psychiatric Census are a second component in the prevalence figures we are discussing. We are interested in seeing if re-entry into treatment is linked with class status. To do this, we separate pa-

tients in the re-entry category from the others and compute age
and sex adjusted rates per 100,000 for each class. The rates for re-
entry into treatment by class are:

Class	Rate [26]
I–II	88
III	68
IV	59
V	123
Total	76

$$\chi^2 = 17.84, 3 \; df, p < .01$$

These rates tell us class status is associated significantly with re-entry
into treatment. More class I and II patients, and fewer class III's
and class IV's re-enter treatment than chance would indicate, but
almost two thirds more class V's than their proportion of the population would indicate came back into treatment during the six
months of observation.

Continuous Treatment

Patients in treatment before June 1, 1950 who remained in treatment throughout the next six months represent the third component
in prevalence. This is the largest single group of patients. The age
and sex adjusted rates for the continuous cases are:

Class	Rate
I–II	368
III	346
IV	516
V	1406
Total	638

$$\chi^2 = 533.72, 3 \; df, p < .001$$

These rates reveal continuity of treatment is connected also with
class status.

Interrelations between the Components in Prevalence

The preceding analyses demonstrate that a significant association
exists between class and each of the components in prevalence: incidence, re-entry into treatment, and continuous treatment. The
sum of these comprises total prevalence, by class. Now we shall
examine interrelations of these rates during the six months interval

of observation. How each component is linked to class status as well as prevalence of treated cases is depicted in Figure 1.[27]

A glance at the curves in Figure 1 will reveal sharp differences in

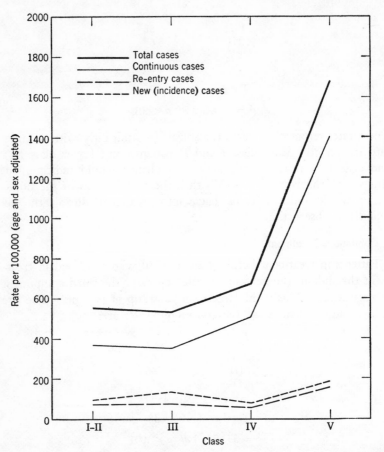

Figure 1. Age and Sex Adjusted Rates by Class Status and Components in the Prevalence Pattern.

the way one component is related to another. The curve for total cases is similar to that for continuous cases, but the distance between the lines is much less in class IV than it is for classes I–II and III. This indicates that there are proportionately fewer class IV patients in the re-entry and new (incidence) categories. The gap between total and continuous cases is wider for class V than it is for the higher classes. The rates in class V are also some two and one half to three times higher than in class IV. The rates for total cases, as we have pointed out previously, are associated strongly with class position. The rates for continuous cases are related even more strongly to class.[28]

The curves for both re-entry into treatment and incidence are dramatically different from those for total and continuous cases. The incidence and re-entry into treatment curves parallel one another with little variation from class to class except that the rate for incidence in class III is almost double the rate for re-entry into treatment, namely, 114 per 100,000 versus 69 per 100,000. In class V, by way of comparison, the incidence rate is 139 per 100,000; for re-entry into treatment the rate is 123 per 100,000. Although the variations in incidence and re-entry rates from class to class are not as spectacular as the rates for continuous cases, the differences are significant.

Classes I and II contribute almost exactly the number of new cases (incidence) as could be expected on the basis of their proportion of the community's population. Class IV had a lower number than could be expected proportionately, whereas class V had an excess of 36 percent. The clustering of new cases in class V is congruent with the data we have presented on total cases and continuous cases. Clearly, class V is contributing disproportionately to the complex of psychiatric patients entering treatment for the first time, as well as an accumulation of continuous cases. Moreover, class V patients re-enter treatment in disproportionately large numbers. On a proportionate basis there is an excess of 61 percent of class V patients who re-entered treatment in the six months prior to the Psychiatric Census. Class IV, by way of contrast, had a deficiency of 15 percent; and classes I and II had the expected number of re-entry cases.

When the three components in the curve for total cases are viewed both in relation to one another and to class status, the difference in rates between class I–II and class V changes markedly. The rate for continuous cases in class V is 3.8 times higher than in classes I and II, namely 1406 per 100,000 against 369 per 100,000. The differential rate for new cases (incidence) from classes I and II to class V is less (97 cases per 100,000 in classes I and II compared to 139 cases per 100,000 in class V); this is an increase of 43 percent. The difference in rates for re-entry cases between classes I and II and class V is likewise limited in magnitude (88 per 100,000 and 123 per 100,000); this is an increase of 39 percent. Even though the age and sex corrected rate per 100,000 for each component is related significantly to class status, the dramatic differences in rates from the higher to the lower classes are highlighted by the cases in continuous treatment.

The curves depicted in Figure 1 provide the first clue that class position is connected with what happens to psychiatric patients in a given period of time. The varying magnitudes of the differences in rates produce the gap between the continuous and the re-entry into treatment curves. The widening gap between these two curves as one's eye descends the class scale indicates that *something is happening to patients in the two lower classes.* The increase in the total patient load in classes IV and V clearly cannot be explained on the basis of the rates for the new cases and re-entry cases.

We infer that there is an accumulation of cases in class IV, and especially in class V, who have been in continuous treatment for more than six months. The question of how much longer than six months will be discussed in Chapter Nine where we will present data on the number of years the patients have been under the care of psychiatrists. Here we are concerned only with the question of how the prevalence of treated cases is related to class from the perspective of its principal components: cases in continuous treatment for six months, new cases that entered treatment within the six months of the Psychiatric Census, and those that re-entered treatment in this interval.

SUMMARY AND CONCLUSIONS

The series of analyses we have presented in this chapter have been focused on a step-by-step examination of the tenability of the first hypothesis around which this research was designed. This hypothesis was premised on the assumption that the prevalence of psychiatric patients in the population of the community studied is related significantly to social class. The search for a clear-cut answer to this proposition was carried through six progressively more difficult steps. The first involved a direct comparison of the patients with the general population. This comparison revealed three things:

(1) A definite association exists between class position and being a psychiatric patient.

(2) The lower the class, the greater the proportion of patients in the population.

(3) The greatest difference is between classes IV and V in that class V has a much higher ratio of patients to population than class IV.

To assure ourselves that the strong association between class status and mental illness is not produced by variables other than class, the data were analyzed, in the second step, with selected factors controlled—sex, age, race, religion, and marital status. When each of these factors was held constant, the association between class status and mental illness reappeared. We next held two factors constant, and the association of mental illness with class continued to reappear with one exception: No significant difference was found between mental disorder and class position for individuals aged 15 through 24. The fourth analytical step entailed holding three factors constant. Once again the association between class and the prevalence of mental illness reappeared with few exceptions. The fifth step was taken when the previously demonstrated relationship between class and the prevalence of mental illness was viewed in terms of rates. The sixth step was taken when the components in prevalence were analyzed by class: incidence, re-entry into treatment, and continuous treatment. The rates for each of these components in the general picture of treated mental illness are linked in significant ways to class status.

The several procedures followed enable us to conclude that *Hypothesis 1* is true. Stated in different terms, a distinct inverse relationship does exist between social class and mental illness. The linkage between class status and the distribution of patients in the population follows a characteristic pattern; class V, almost invariably, contributes many more patients than its proportion of the population warrants. Among the higher classes there is a more proportionate relationship between the number of psychiatric patients and the number of individuals in the population.

NOTES

[1] John E. Gordon, Edward O'Rourke, F. L. W. Richardson, and Erich Lindemann, "The Biological and Social Sciences in an Epidemiology of Mental Disorders," *American Journal of the Medical Sciences,* Vol. 223 (March 1952), pp. 316–343.

[2] Erich Lindemann, John E. Gordon, Warren T. Vaughan, Jr., and Johann Ipsen, "Minor Disorders," in *Epidemiology of Mental Disorders,* Milbank Memorial Fund, New York, 1950, p. 12.

[3] John E. Gordon et al., *op. cit.*, p. 320.

[4] Harold F. Dorn, "Methods of Measuring Incidence and Prevalence of Disease," *American Journal of Public Health* (March 1951), pp. 271–278.

[5] *Ibid.*, p. 272.

[6] Morton Kramer, "A Discussion of the Concepts of Incidence and Prevalence as Related to Epidemiological Studies of Mental Disorders," a paper read at the Joint Session of the Mental Health and Epidemiology Sections of the American Public Health Association at Atlantic City, New Jersey, November 15, 1956.

[7] Paul V. Lemkau, "Prevention of Psychiatric Illnesses," *The Journal of the American Medical Association*, Vol. 162 (October 27, 1956), pp. 854–857.

[8] Paul V. Lemkau, Christopher Tietze, and Marcia Cooper, "A Summary of Statistical Studies on the Prevalence and Incidence of Mental Disorder in Sample Populations," *Public Health Reports*, Vol. 5, No. 53 (December 31, 1943), pp. 1909–1927.

[9] For a detailed review of the literature pertinent to this point, see Fredrick C. Redlich, "The Concept of Health in Psychiatry," in Leighton, Clausen, and Wilson (editors), *Explorations in Social Psychiatry*, Basic Books, Inc., 1957.

[10] Seventy-two of the 1963 patients enumerated in the Psychiatric Census are not included in the detailed analyses for one of two reasons: (1) Essential clinical or social data are missing on particular cases, or (2) the person was seen for diagnosis only. The schedules are relatively complete on the items needed in the many analyses for the 1891 patients included in the tables of this chapter and subsequent ones.

[11] Classes I and II are combined because the number of class I patients is too small for statistical manipulation when specific factors are controlled.

[12] The specific figures for each age group by sex are given in Table 1, in Appendix Four, pp. 409–411. The total figures by age may be computed from the separate figures for each sex in the various tables if the reader desires. Here we will record only the chi squares for each age period and show their level of significance for three degrees of freedom.

$$
\begin{array}{lll}
0\text{–}14: & \chi^2 = 18.4, & p < .001 \\
15\text{–}24: & \chi^2 = 5.03, & p > .05 \\
25\text{–}34: & \chi^2 = 43.98, & p < .001 \\
35\text{–}44: & \chi^2 = 136.67, & p < .001 \\
45\text{–}54: & \chi^2 = 164.82, & p < .001 \\
55 \text{ and over}: & \chi^2 = 223.26, & p < .001
\end{array}
$$

[13] Whites and Negroes are the only races represented in the study.

[14] Bertram H. Roberts and Jerome K. Myers made a special study of the religious factor in the data from the Psychiatric Census. See their detailed report, "Religion, National Origin, Immigration, and Mental Illness," *American Journal of Psychiatry*, Vol. 110, No. 10 (April 1954), pp. 759–764.

[15] The work tables referred to here are filed in Hollingshead's laboratory. They are not published because of the detail in each one.

[16] Figures on the distribution of the patients in the population by class, sex, and age are given in Appendix Four, Table 1, pp. 409–411.

[17] $\chi^2 = 18.18$, 2 df, $p < .001$.

[18] For class III, $\chi^2 = 10.78$, $p < .01$; class IV, $\chi^2 = .08$; class V, $\chi^2 = 2.47$; 1 df, $p > .05$ in each analysis.

[19] The data for the analyses are given in Appendix Four, Table 2, pp. 411–414.

[20] Since we are primarily concerned with the factor of *class*, no further attention will be given to other social factors, such as marital status or religion. The controlled comparisons procedure used in the preceding section of this chapter demonstrates that class rather than religion or marital status is the primary conditioning factor in the prevalence of mental illness at a given class level. Race, too, must be ignored in most of the analyses because of the small number of nonwhite cases. The basic biological factors of age and sex, however, will be considered and, whenever possible, controlled.

[21] For a detailed computation of rates see Appendix Four, Table 3, p. 415.

[22] This is another application of the principle of controls used in the previous section where separate analyses were made for various population subgroups.

[23] The procedures for adjusting rates are described and illustrated in Appendix Four, Table 4, pp. 416–417.

[24] This procedure is described and illustrated in Appendix Four, Table 5, p. 518.

[25] The chi square for the crude rates comparison is 509.81, df 3, $p < .001$; for the adjusted rates comparison, $\chi^2 = 497.16$, df 3, $p < .001$.

[26] The numerator of the rate given here represents the number of patients in each class who re-entered treatment during the interval of observation. The denominator is the total population of the class. Technically, we should have used the *number* of *former* mental patients in the population as the denominator. However, this is an unknown quantity; therefore, the total population was relied upon as a substitute. These rates would undoubtedly have been much higher had the proper figures been available.

[27] The number of cases and the rates per 100,000 in each category are given in Appendix Four, Table 6, p. 419.

[28] For all cases, $\chi^2 = 497.16$, 3 df, and for the continuous cases, $\chi^2 = 533.72$, 3 df. In both analyses $p < .001$.

class position
and types
of mental illness

chapter eight

INTRODUCTION

This chapter is concerned with the examination of *Hypothesis 2* which postulated the existence of significant relationships between the types of disorders patients exhibit and their positions in the class structure. If this hypothesis is not true, the patients' disorders should be distributed in the status structure in a random manner. However, if it is correct, we will find that class status is connected with the kinds of disorders patients present to psychiatrists.

The essential difference between the first and the second hypotheses is this: In the first we were interested in learning whether class status is connected with the fact that residents of the community are or are not psychiatric patients; in the second we examine the nature of the patients' illnesses to see if they are associated with class status.

Tests of *Hypothesis 2* are of two different types: The first involves *internal* comparisons of the patient population by class and diagnosis. The second entails comparisons *between* the patients and the general population. In both types of tests age and sex differences are adjusted by the procedures described in Chapter Seven. The relationship, if any, between class status and each type of mental illness is tested for significance. The level of probability that the relationship found between class position and a particular type of mental illness is significant is included with the presentation of the data.

The Diagnostic Scheme

The validity and the reliability of the diagnosis of a patient's symptoms by the psychiatrists are crucial to *Hypothesis 2*. Psychiatrists place great emphasis upon diagnosis, and they often disagree on the subject. For these reasons we repeat that the diagnostic scheme used in this study was the one developed by the Veterans Administration.[1] This was the best nosological system available when we planned and executed the Psychiatric Census. After our data were collected, the system developed by the Veterans Administration was replaced by a modified system approved by the American Psychiatric Association. We decided to hold to the scheme developed by the Veterans Administration because of the similarity of the two systems.

The many specific diagnoses of the Veterans Administration system were grouped into categories of reactions and disorders for three reasons: First, the psychiatrists on the team believed that specific diagnoses were unwarranted because they had not examined the patients themselves. A diagnosis made from the record and from the material given by the patient's therapist raised questions in their minds. Nevertheless, they believed that the patients could be grouped into diagnostic categories that reflect with reasonable accuracy the kind of disorder the patient exhibited. For example, the probability is high that most persons classified as neurotic are in fact neurotic and not psychotic patients. On the other hand, there is a lesser probability that a neurotic patient can be placed as precisely in a category of neurotic disorders.

Second, when a patient is seen by several different psychiatrists in different psychiatric agencies over a considerable span of time, it is questionable whether a precise diagnosis or a series of diagnoses are reliable. Two psychiatrists, each with a different theoretical orientation, may diagnose the symptoms of the same patient differently. We attempted to minimize this problem by having the diagnoses made by two or more psychiatrists on the team. But there was still the problem of whether the symptoms in the clinical record or given by the therapists in personal interviews with the team psychiatrists presented an accurate picture of the patient's difficulties. Thus, it appeared prudent to group the specific diagnoses into types or categories, of a relatively small number, thereby increasing the reliability.

Third, the problem of dealing with numerous diagnostic categories had to be faced. Some diagnostic categories used by the Veterans Administration scheme did not yield a single patient in the Psychiatric Census. Others yielded only from two to five or six patients. Clearly it was impossible to analyze such a small number of cases subdivided by class, age, and sex, but by grouping the diagnoses into a relatively small number, meaningful statements could be made about the type of disorder the patient presented to the psychiatrist. As a result of this decision the patients' illnesses were grouped into two major types: the *neuroses* and the *psychoses*. The neuroses are divided, in turn, into seven subgroups and the psychoses into five subgroups. The principal identifying characteristics of each of the subgroups will be described during the presentation of the appropriate analysis of *Hypothesis 2*.

CLASS AND TYPE OF MENTAL ILLNESS

Neurosis versus Psychosis

We will not attempt the ungratifying task of defining neurosis and psychosis, but simply describe, in the following paragraphs, the subcategories. The percentage of patients in each class diagnosed as neurotic or psychotic is shown in Figure 2. This figure shows a striking connection between class position and the distribution of neurosis and psychosis in the class structure. In classes I and II, some 65 percent of the patients are diagnosed as neurotic; in class III the percentage drops to 45, in class IV to approximately 20, and in class V to 10 percent. The differential distribution of neurotic and psychotic patients by class is significant beyond the .001 level of probability.

The sharp differences between the percentage of neurotic and psychotic patients in the several classes may be attributed to the differential use of psychiatric facilities by the population in the New Haven community. We know that many neurotic patients handle their difficulties without taking them to a psychiatrist. Therefore, the larger percentages of patients with neurotic difficulties in the higher classes may be the result of the fact that individuals in classes I and II, for example, perceive the psychiatrist in a different way from persons in class IV. Class I and II persons may go to psychiatrists when they have less severe disorders than class IV persons. If this is true, the percentage of class I and II individuals in psychiatric treatment would be higher than in the lower classes. In sum, the

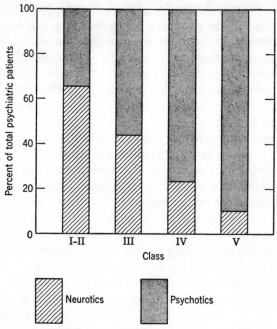

Figure 2. Percentage of Neurotics and Psychotics among Total Psychiatric Patients—by Class (Age and Sex Adjusted).

differences shown in Figure 2 could possibly be an artifact of the ways psychiatrists are utilized in the different classes. On the other hand, if a significant difference is found in the distribution of patients *within* the neurotic and psychotic grouping by class, we will have empirical evidence of a real relationship between class position and either the *kind* of disorders patients present to psychiatrists or the *way* psychiatrists diagnose the disorders of their patients. In either instance, if significant differences are found between class and type of disorder the position postulated in *Hypothesis 2* will be verified.

The Neurotic Disorders

The seven groups of neurotic disorders will be described briefly before we present the data on the distribution of each type in the patient population. The seven types are characterized thus:

1. ANTISOCIAL AND IMMATURITY REACTIONS. This group of illnesses is characterized by unapproved and intolerable behavior with minimal or no overt sense of distress to the patient. In most in-

stances, the disorder is manifested by a lifelong pattern of "acting-out" behavior. These disturbed personalities are unable to maintain an adult emotional balance and independence under normal circumstances because of faults in "emotional development." This subgroup includes the infantile personalities, sexual deviates, addicts without psychosis, and individuals who are inadequate socially and emotionally. Many of these persons are relatively unaware of their problems.

It is a moot point whether antisocial reactions should be grouped with the neuroses. Many antisocial reactions are borderline illnesses between neurosis and psychosis. However, when we separated the anti-social reactions from the other neuroses, no significant differences were found between them and the other neurotic subgroups. Therefore, they were considered to be neuroses.

2. CHARACTER NEUROSES. This diagnostic label is used to describe patients who do not belong in one of the specific reaction types classified in the Veterans Administration scheme. We realize that all neuroses could be, and probably should be, viewed as "character neuroses." Patients placed in this category exhibit a number of different symptoms. It is difficult from the data presented by the psychiatrists and the clinical records to state that these patients are troubled by a single type of reaction. They exhibit mixed symptoms as well as relatively mild character and, to a lesser extent, some behavior disturbances.

3. PHOBIC AND ANXIETY REACTIONS. This group includes acute and chronic anxiety, fear, asthenic, and phobic reactions. The symptomatology appears to be associated with some precipitating distress in the immediate life experiences of the individual, but often no such experience can be found unless the search is very thorough and skillful. In the phobic individual, anxiety tends to be focused upon a specific situation, such as fear of crowds, darkness, etc. Reactions where anxiety is the predominant factor in the symptomatology are clear-cut. Anxiety may be represented in a number of different ways such as the phobic reactions, by its somatic concomitants, or certain types of character and symptomatic defenses; some of these can hardly be differentiated from character neuroses.

4. DEPRESSIVE REACTIONS. This category includes patients burdened with emotional reactions to some social situation in which feelings of grief, guilt, shame, and anxiety are internalized in a specific way. In the main, we used this category in the way specified by the Veterans Administration scheme.

5. OBSESSIVE-COMPULSIVE REACTIONS. This category includes patients with compulsive behavior and obsessive ideation. The obsessive-compulsive patient is not able to account for his behavior, although he may consciously realize that it is unreasonable and meaningless. Nevertheless, he carries out his rituals in a systematic manner.

6. PSYCHOSOMATIC REACTIONS. Six reactions are placed in this group: psychogenic gastro-intestinal reaction, psychogenic cardiovascular reactions, psychogenic genitourinary reaction, psychogenic respiratory reaction, psychogenic skin reaction, and unspecified psychogenic reaction with somatization symptoms. The differentiation from hysterical conversion reaction and also from anxiety reaction is often difficult to make, and at times it is arbitrary.

7. HYSTERICAL REACTIONS. Dissociative and conversion reactions are grouped under this rubric. The responses are not exactly the same, but in all of them anxiety has disorganized the patient's personality to the point where he attempts to dissociate himself from the source of his anxiety. In some cases, particularly in a dissociative reaction, the individual may respond by an amnestic reaction. In conversion, the individual changes his anxiety into sensory or motor reaction and derives some secondary gain from his symptoms. Symptomatologically, anxiety in hypochondriacal reactions is manifested by many complaints about physical health, and it may be focused upon a number of different organs and organ symptoms. In all hysterical reactions, anxiety seems to be converted into some symbolic behavior meaningful to the individual.

CLASS STATUS AND THE NEUROSES

We are now ready to present the crucial *internal* test we made of the proposition that class status is related to neurotic illnesses. The data essential for the examination of this proposition are summarized in Table 13.

The data in Table 13 demonstrate that a significant relationship does exist between class position and the kind of diagnoses psychiatrists place upon their patients. Anti-social and immaturity reactions are concentrated in classes III and V, whereas phobic and anxiety reactions cluster in class IV. Character neuroses focus in classes I and II; relatively few character neuroses are found in classes IV and V. The depressive reactions are scattered, but classes I and II have 50 percent more depressives than class V.

TABLE 13

Percentage of Patients in Each Diagnostic Category of Neurosis—by Class (Age and Sex Adjusted)

	Class			
Diagnostic Category of Neurosis	I–II	III	IV	V
Antisocial and immaturity reactions	21	32	23	37
Phobic-anxiety reactions	16	18	30	16
Character neuroses	36	23	13	16
Depressive reactions	12	12	10	8
Psychosomatic reactions	7	9	13	11
Obsessive-compulsive reactions	7	5	5	0
Hysterical reactions	1	1	6	12
$n =$	98	119	182	65

$$\chi^2 = 53.62, \, df \, 18, \, p < .001$$

Psychosomatic reactions, by way of contrast, are related inversely to class. The class IV's and the class V's somatize their complaints to a greater extent than class I, II, and III patients. On the other hand, obsessive-compulsive reactions are directly related to class position. The obsessive-compulsives are concentrated in classes I and II. The gradient for hysterical patients runs in the opposite direction; in this illness there is an extreme concentration in class V.

Psychotic Disorders

The severe mental disorders are divided, for purposes of our analysis, into five types: affective psychoses, alcoholic and addictive psychoses, organic psychoses, schizophrenic psychoses, and senile psychoses:

1. AFFECTIVE PSYCHOSES. Since the etiology of this group of illnesses is obscure, a diagnosis is made essentially on a patient's symptomatology. A particular diagnosis is based upon symptoms at a particular time. At one phase of a patient's illness his behavior may be manic, whereas at another he may be in a severely depressed state, overwhelmed by feelings of guilt and unworthiness to the point where he distorts reality to such an extent that there is no connection between what he feels and thinks and what the situation is in fact. Involutional melancholia is a type of depressive reaction with delusions and severe anxiety and grief.

2. PSYCHOSES RESULTING FROM ALCOHOLISM AND DRUG ADDICTION. This diagnostic group includes patients with symptoms of chronic

alcoholism with psychotic reaction, confused type; chronic alcoholism with psychotic reaction, deteriorated type; chronic alcoholism with psychotic reaction, pathologic intoxication type; psychoses due to chronic alcoholism, undefined; psychoses due to exogenous poisons and drugs with psychotic reaction.[2] This, in the main, is a departure from the scheme used by the Veterans Administration. For purposes of this study, all chronic alcoholics and drug addicts are treated as psychotic patients.

3. ORGANIC PSYCHOSES. The organic psychoses encompass a miscellaneous group of disorders with an organic etiology: mental deficiency with psychotic reactions; psychoses traceable to a trauma; psychoses due to infectious disease (syphilitic and metasyphilitic infections, tuberculin infections, such as tuberculosis meningitis, unspecified meningitis, encephalitis, and other infectious diseases manifested by a psychotic reaction). Epileptics who developed psychotic reactions and are being treated by psychiatric agencies rather than by nonpsychiatric medical agencies are placed in this group.

4. SCHIZOPHRENIC PSYCHOSES. This category includes six schizophrenic reactions: latent, simple, hebephrenic, catatonic, paranoid, and unclassified types plus two paranoid disorders, paranoia and paranoid state. These psychoses are close enough in symptomatology to be grouped together for our purposes. In these disorders there are fundamental disturbances of ideation, emotion, and volition, but it is not often easy to say whether a particular patient is a paranoid, a hebephrenic, or a catatonic because undifferentiated schizophrenics predominate. We believe that only in exceptional cases can precise diagnostic subcategories be validly established even if there is an extensive personal examination by a psychiatrist. Examination of the records indicated that the symptoms of patients who had been ill for several years often changed, and the psychiatrist treating them changed his diagnosis in accordance with changes in symptomatology. For these reasons, all schizophrenics were placed in a single diagnostic category.

5. SENILE PSYCHOSES. Senile disorders arise in the later years of life and are caused mostly by circulatory and metabolic disorders of the brain. This statement does not imply that psychological and social factors are unimportant in the etiology of the disorders.

Class Position and the Psychoses

Now that we have described the five diagnostic categories established for the psychoses, we are ready to test the applicability of

Hypothesis 2 to these severe mental disorders. The essential data for this examination are summarized in Table 14.

TABLE 14

Percentage of Patients in Each Diagnostic Category of Psychosis—by Class (Age and Sex Adjusted)

	Class			
Diagnostic Category	I–II	III	IV	V
Affective psychoses	21	14	14	7
Psychoses resulting from alcoholism and drug addiction	8	10	4	8
Organic psychoses	5	8	9	16
Schizophrenic psychoses	55	57	61	58
Senile psychoses	11	11	12	11
$n =$	53	142	584	672

$\chi^2 = 48.23$, df 12, $p < .001$

The figures given in Table 14 reveal a significant association between the five types of psychotic disorders and class status. The effective disorders are linked directly to class position: The higher the class, the larger the proportion of patients who are affective psychotics. The proportion of affective psychotics in classes I and II is three times greater than in class V, but the percentage is the same in class III and class IV. The alcoholic and addictive psychotics show few class differences except in class IV where the percentage is only half that in classes I and II and class V. The organics exhibit a reverse of the distribution observed among the affective psychotics. Only 5 percent of the class I and II patients have an organic disorder, whereas 16 percent of the class V's suffer from one. The schizophrenic and senile psychotics show *no* appreciable percentage differences from class to class. We believe that this is a very important finding. In all classes schizophrenics make up well over half the patients. The senile psychotics represent a relatively small proportion, but this proportion is also constant from class to class.

In all classes schizophrenia is the predominant psychotic disorder. The next most frequent group is the affective one, but it tends to be concentrated more highly in classes I and II than in the other strata. The two functional psychotic groups, affectives and schizophrenics, make up well over two thirds of the patients in the four higher classes; but in class V these disorders total only 65 percent of the patients.

The three *internal* tests we have made of *Hypothesis 2*, namely, (1) the distribution of the patients into neurotic and psychotic groups, (2) the division of the neuroses into seven subgroups, and (3) the division of the psychoses into five subgroups, demonstrate that class status is a real factor in the kinds of illnesses the patients present to psychiatrists. The data we have presented lead us to conclude *Hypothesis 2* is true.

Even though we have reached this conclusion by the use of *internal* analyses, it is theoretically possible that when the patients in the several diagnostic groups of neurosis and psychosis are compared with the general population by class we may not find any relationship between class status and types of mental illness. The differences we have shown to exist between class and types of disorders may apply only to the patient group. Strictly speaking, this is all we are testing in *Hypothesis 2*.

TYPES OF MENTAL ILLNESSES IN THE POPULATION

The association between class position and type of mental illness, demonstrated in the three preceding analyses, may disappear when *external* comparisons are made between the patients and the general population; likewise, the association may be substantiated. With these theoretical possibilities before us, we will answer the question posed in this discussion: Is neurosis *or* psychosis associated with class in the population of the community? We shall present the data essential for an answer in three parts. First, we will compare the rates for neurosis and psychosis by class; second, we will examine the distribution of the seven neurotic reactions in each class; and third, we will analyze the five psychotic disorders to determine if they are related to class status. The data necessary to discover if persons being treated for neurotic or psychotic illnesses are differentially distributed in the class structure are plotted in Figure 3.

The curve in Figure 3 depicting the prevalence of neurotic patients in the population shows a direct relationship between class position and neurotic illness from classes I and II through class IV; then there is a change in direction from class IV to V. On the other hand, prevalence of the psychoses increases consistently as one moves down the class scale. The sharpest increase occurs from class IV to

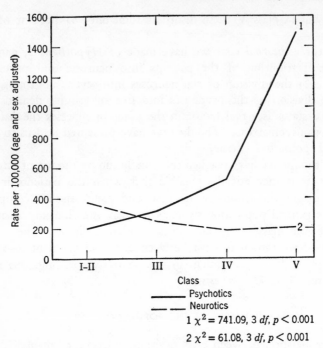

Figure 3. Prevalence of Neurotic and Psychotic Disorders per 100,000 Adjusted for Age and Sex—by Class.

class V. Between these adjacent classes, the rate almost triples, namely, 518 to 1504 per 100,000.

Comparison of the neurotic rate with the psychotic rate from one class to another reveals some interesting changes. The difference between the rate for the neuroses and the psychoses is greater for class I–II than for class III. At the class III level there are fewer neurotics than psychotics, 237 neurotics per 100,000 in comparison with 291 psychotics. This differential becomes greater in class IV; here the rate is 146 for neurotics and 518 per 100,000 for psychotics. In class V there are 9 psychotic patients to one neurotic patient; stated in rates, there are 1504 psychotics to 163 neurotics per 100,000. The marked differences in the magnitudes of the rates for the neuroses and the psychoses from one class to another indicate that separate analyses should be made for each of the twelve diagnostic groups. If significant differences are found from class to class when the data are analyzed for each of the seven neurotic and the five psychotic diagnostic groups, then we will have presumptive evidence of the impact of class status upon the various types of mental illness.

Class and the Neuroses

The association between class status and the extent of illness in each of the seven categories of neuroses is summarized in Figure 4. The linkage between class status and the distribution of treated neuroses in the population is significant for each diagnostic group. However, the effect of class varies from one type of disorder to another. There is a strong direct relationship between class position and the prevalence of character neuroses. The rate for these disorders drops from 130 in class I–II to 21 in class IV; but there is no change from class IV to class V. The rate for phobic-anxiety reactions

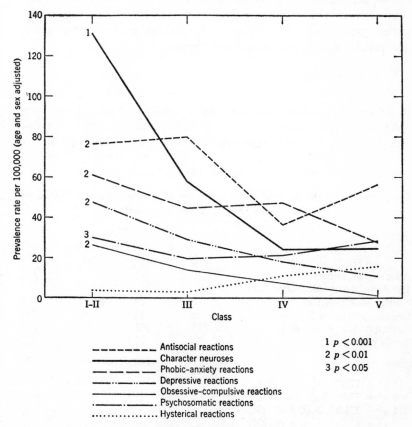

Figure 4. Class Status and Types of Neuroses.

drops from class I–II to class III; it remains stable to the class IV level; it again drops sharply to class V. The greatest difference between adjacent classes for these reactions occurs at the bottom of the status structure. A glance at the curve for the phobic anxiety reactions in Figure 4 will establish this linkage for the reader. The rate of depressive reactions declines in almost a straight line from classes I–II to class V. However, the depressive reactions are not encountered as frequently as the three types of neurotic reactions we discussed previously. The obsessive-compulsive reactions are rare in all classes, but they are so rare in class V that for practical purposes they are nonexistent. Hysterical reactions, unlike the other neurotic disorders, show an inverse relationship with class position. They are found predominantly in classes IV and V, rather than in the higher classes. Psychosomatic reactions show the least association between class position and the rate of their frequency in the patient population. Nevertheless, the linkage between class status and psychosomatic reactions is significant.

Class and the Psychoses

The distribution of the five subgroups in the several classes is given in Table 15. An examination of the age and sex adjusted rates per 100,000 will show that class status is an important factor in the distribution of each type of disorder in the community's population.

TABLE 15

Class Status and the Rate of Different Types of Psychoses per 100,000 of Population (Age and Sex Adjusted)

	Class			
Type of Disorder	I–II	III	IV	V
Affective psychoses *	40	41	68	105
Psychoses due to alcoholism and drug addiction †	15	29	32	116
Organic psychoses ‡	9	24	46	254
Schizophrenic psychoses §	111	168	300	895
Senile psychoses ‖	21	32	60	175
$n =$	53	142	585	672

* $\chi^2 = 17.49$, 3 df, $p < .001$.
† $\chi^2 = 77.14$, 3 df, $p < .001$.
‡ $\chi^2 = 231.87$, 3 df, $p < .001$.
§ $\chi^2 = 452.68$, 3 df, $p < .001$.
‖ $\chi^2 = 88.36$, 3 df, $p < .001$.

The probability statements given in the footnotes in Table 15 reveal that the age and sex adjusted rates are significant for every type of disorder from one class to another. Each type of psychosis is related inversely to class status, but the magnitude varies from one type to another. The affective disorders show the least variation from class to class, but even in this group the rate in class V is more than two and one-half times greater than it is in class I–II, namely, 105 in class V versus 40 in class I–II. Organic disorders show the greatest amount of increase from the higher to the lower classes. In this group of disorders the rate is 28 times greater in class V than in class I–II. Variation between the two extremes of the class structure for the alcoholic, schizophrenic, and senile psychoses falls between the affective and the organic disorders.

The age and sex adjusted rates presented in Table 15 are portrayed graphically in Figure 5. The curves in Figure 5 depicting the linkage of class status with the different types of psychoses are based upon the logarithms of the rates given in Table 15. These rates are transposed into logarithms so that the relationships between the different classes and groups of disorders can be shown in a single chart.

The curves in Figure 5 show that a relatively uniform tie exists between class position and the prevalence of each type of disorder in the population. The curves for schizophrenic, senile, and organic disorders are almost straight. We infer that the effect of class is greatest in the organic disorders because the slope is the steepest for this curve; and it is least in the affective disorders.

The schizophrenias are the most common mental illnesses in our population at all class levels. The next most frequent disorders are the affectives. The rates for the prevalence of treated alcoholic, organic, and senile disorders in the population at any class level are similar. The greatest differences are in the proportionate distribution of these disorders from one class to another.

COMPONENTS IN PREVALENCE AND TYPES OF ILLNESS

The comparisons we have made between the kinds of mental illnesses the patients have and their distributions in the population indictate that class status is a real factor. However, before we draw any further conclusions we shall re-examine the data to see if the associations between class and types of disorders are connected with components in prevalence: new cases, re-entry into treatment cases, and cases in continuous treatment. The reader should remember that the interval of observation covers six months. New cases refer to those persons who entered psychiatric treatment for the first time during the interval of observation and are the ones used in the

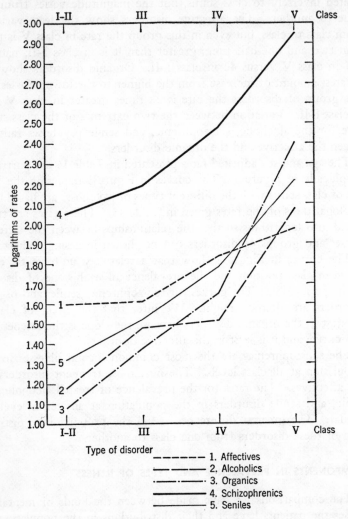

Figure 5. Class Status and the Prevalence of Psychoses.

figures on incidence. Re-entry cases represent those who had received psychiatric care at some time before June 1, 1950, but came under the care of psychiatrists again before December 1, 1950. Continuous cases were in treatment throughout the study period.

The rates for incidence, re-entry into treatment, continuity of treatment, and prevalence for the neuroses and psychoses are shown in Table 16. The neuroses and the psychoses are not separated into diagnostic groups because the number of new and re-entry cases are too few to be reliable statistically. The only exception to this generalization is the schizophrenic group. The schizophrenics will be discussed separately.

TABLE 16

Incidence, Re-entry, Continuous, and Prevalence Rates per 100,000 for Neuroses and Psychoses—by Class (Sex and Age Adjusted)

Neuroses

Class	Incidence	Re-entry	Continuous	Prevalence
I–II	69	44	251	349
III	78	30	137	250
IV	52	17	82	114
V	66	35	65	97
$\chi^2 =$	4.40	8.64	69.01	56.05
df	3	3	3	3
p	> .05	< .05	< .001	< .001

Psychoses

Class	Incidence	Re-entry	Continuous	Prevalence
I–II	28	44	117	188
III	36	38	217	291
IV	37	42	439	518
V	73	88	1344	1505
$\chi^2 =$	12.37	15.73	748.47	741.09
df	3	3	3	3
p	< .01	< .01	< .001	< .001

Table 16 shows that *incidence for the neuroses is not linked to class*. However, the rates for re-entry into treatment and prevalence are related significantly to class status. It is worth noting here that the direct relationship between class and the prevalence of neuroses is traceable, in large part, to the cases in treatment before and throughout the interval of observation. This inference is applicable particularly to classes I, II, and III.

Among the psychotic disorders each component in prevalence is related significantly to class. The *incidence* of the psychoses is almost three times greater in class V in comparison with classes I and

II, and it is double the rate for class IV. The same type of sudden increase at the class V level occurs for re-entry into treatment; the rate for class V is more than double the rate in class IV. The rates for cases in continuous treatment form a very sharp gradient that is inversely related to class status; the lower the class, the higher the rate. The cases in continuous treatment are the largest component in *prevalence* at each class level, but particularly so in class V.

Each type of rate shown in Table 17 is related to class. This

TABLE 17

Incidence, Re-entry, Continuous, and Prevalence Rates per 100,000 for the Schizophrenics—by Class (Age and Sex Adjusted)

Type of Rate per 100,000

Class	Incidence	Re-entry	Continuous	Prevalence
I–II	6	14	97	111
III	8	20	148	168
IV	10	21	269	300
V	20	46	729	895
$\chi^2 =$	8.50	13.46	355.62	452.68
df	3	3	3	3
p	$<.05$	$<.01$	$<.001$	$<.001$

means that incidence, re-entry into treatment, and continuity of treatment for the schizophrenics are linked to class status. Each of these components in prevalence are inversely related to class position. The intensity of the relationship is approximately the same for incidence and re-entry into treatment from class I–II to class V, that is, as one is to three. Incidence, however, differs from re-entry into treatment in that it increases regularly as one goes down the class scale. Nevertheless, the greatest difference is between classes IV and V. Between these two classes the ratio is as one is to two. This ratio also holds between classes IV and V for the re-entry into treatment rates. The rates for continuous treatment reveal the same pattern as incidence, except that they are much higher. They differ from both the rates for incidence and re-entry into treatment on the class IV and class V levels in that the rate for continuous treatment in class V is more than three times higher than the rate for class IV.

The series of comparisons we have made of rates for components in the prevalence patterns of the neuroses, the psychoses, and the schizophrenias demonstrate that class is a persistent factor that influences each kind of rate except the incidence of the neuroses. We have demonstrated the validity of our presuppositions in so far as *Hypotheses 1* and *2* are involved. Additional studies will be necessary to specify the conditions and processes which give rise to the facts and linkages we have substantiated with the data gathered to elucidate these hypotheses.

SOME FURTHER QUESTIONS

The Neuroses

The *internal* and the *external* analyses demonstrate that the psychological symptoms and interpersonal manifestations which are pathognomic of neurosis are linked intimately with the class position of the sufferers. In these analyses, we use the term neurosis to describe a condition of subjective malaise and disturbed social interaction. We take the position that a neurosis is a state of mind not only of the sufferer, but also of the therapist, and it appears likewise to be connected to the class positions of the therapist and the patient. A diagnosis arises from a number of conditioning factors: the experiences of the patient, the training and techniques of the doctor, as well as the social values of the community. Stated otherwise, a diagnosis of neurosis is a resultant of a social interactional process which involves the patient, the doctor, and the patient's position in the status structure of the community.

It seems likely that the most important role in diagnosing "neurosis" is played by the individual who bears the label. Just how and why he accepts this designation is a fascinating question. In a very literal sense, the individual usually decides whether he is neurotic. The old saw, "Anyone who goes to a psychiatrist should have his head examined," is applicable here. The degree to which he accepts or rejects the role he plays or is assigned in his social milieu often determines whether or not he considers himself neurotic or accepts others' appraisals of his being disturbed. One might even speculate that an adequate understanding of self-definition of neurosis versus community definition would guide us not only to a better understanding of prevailing attitudes within the social group concerning psychological sickness and health, but also to seemingly moral questions concerning sin and virtue and apparently political questions such as the degree of individual self-realization permitted under a certain form of government and nonconformity tolerated as compared to how much conformity and group immersion is demanded. In sum, we believe that certain distinguishing characteristics of the social classes are reflected in the neurosis itself. We pointed out in Chapter Six that who becomes a psychiatric case, particularly if neurotic behavior is involved, depends in large part upon where one is in the class structure.

The criteria for assumption of the neurotic role probably differs significantly from class to class, and it is quite likely that group attitudes, in turn, vary and are affected by cross-class acculturation. From our data it would appear that there is an apparent difference in the concept of self as a patient in the several classes (a) if one is uncomfortable, (b) if one's body hurts or functions poorly, (c) if one is unable to be effective in one's work, (d) if one is in trouble with his family and friends, or (e) if one is in difficulty with the law.

In a sense, the doctor-patient relationship is a symbolic one. Who chose whom is not an easy question to answer. Each party to the therapeutic transaction requires the presence, at least the agreement, in all probability, of the other in order to carry out the procedures, if not to their mutual satisfaction at least to allow them sufficient contiguity, comfort, and sense of "rightness" to proceed. In short, the same frame of reference must obtain between the psychiatrist and the patient, or one must indoctrinate the other.

Neither our data nor our inclination lead us to question the assumption that unconscious mechanisms may be common to all classes. Nor do we doubt that psychogenetic developmental elements such as identification, oedipal conflicts, sibling rivalry, and psychosexual developmental patterns are basic to people in all classes. Certainly, the phenomenon somewhat vaguely designated by the term "anxiety" is ubiquitous in the nonpsychiatric population. Recent research indicates that there are no differences in anxiety from class to class.[3] Nor are we prepared to question seriously the possibility that there would be different results if analysts examined our class V patients and directive-organic physicians treated our class I subjects. But the point is that *they do not*. Treated neurosis is a conceptual abstraction of particular elements of behavior and feeling, and those who apply the concepts define the neurosis.

Our data show there are widely varying responses on the part of physicians to the same varieties of behavior. For example, class IV or V persons arrested by the police for antisocial behavior may be treated by physicians for their complaints of bodily aches with an organic therapy and never be diagnosed as neurotic, whereas class I persons who seek psychiatric help, stimulated by an inner sense of malaise and treated by infinitely subtle and prolonged verbal communication, are diagnosed as neurotics. When we discover that certain psychiatrists consistently describe a characteristic symptom complex and treat it with equal uniformity of method and other psychiatrists persistently describe other symptoms and attempt to cure them with quite different techniques and when we finally ascertain that their patients fall into definable groups bearing common social and behavioral characteristics, similarity to organic diseases as we traditionally conceive them, is remote.

We showed in Chapter Six that agencies concerned with public order and morality, the courts and the police, serve as transmitters of class IV and V social deviants to psychiatrists. Thus, the problem of conformity or nonconformity is shifted in a particular subculture from a legal question to a psychological problem. In a similar way, ministers by their referrals conceptually alter a problem from one of sinfulness to one of neurosis, and physicians in a like manner from physical pain to psychological conflict. The significance of neurosis as a concept in a particular culture at a stated time is hardly amenable to overstatement. The sinfulness of the Bible, the *Angst* of the Kierkegaardians, the "nausea" of the existentialists, and the "stress" of the internists are all syndromes which may be and have been subsumed under the term neurosis by some experts.

The variations in types of neuroses from class to class may be a function of selective perception and focus of interest of the therapist. Raines and Rohmer [4] have shown the importance of the role of the psychological refraction of the personal therapist. They refer to the "projective" elements in diagnosis and describe how the social background, technical training, and personal proclivities of the doctor affect his emphasis. In our data, we found that a psychiatrist tends to diagnose according to his professional orientation or ideology. It is quite possible that a psychoanalyst does not report a complaint of abdominal pain in favor of sexual anxiety, whereas a directive-organically oriented therapist might emphasize the former. It is also possible that the differences we have found are reflections of the fundamental social differences that set one class off from another. In this sense, the neurosis is a part of each person's definition of his class position. It is a description of his internalization of past social experiences. It may also be said to be an expression of the way persons live within themselves and their effective social groups.[2] If this position is correct, and we are inclined to believe it is, it would be a serious conceptual error to think of certain types of neuroses as being "correlated" with class position as though they were phenomena superimposed on a "class." Thus, there appear to be significant *class-typed neuroses*, some characteristics of which may be due principally to the manner of referral, and others to the sociological characteristics of the class. Stated another way, the class V neurotic is often hailed before the psychiatrist because he is externally maladjusted (acts out, is alloplastic), and the class I–II patient most frequently comes because he is internally maladjusted (acts in, is autoplastic).

We may indulge ourselves in the following generalizations as viewed by the psychiatrist: the class V neurotic behaves badly, the class IV neurotic aches physically, the class III patient defends fearfully, and the class I–II patient is dissatisfied with himself. Thus, we have a psychosocial pattern of community dislocation, a "body language" of pain and malfunction, social anxiety, and verbal symbolic dislocation, all called neurosis.

The Psychoses

Our finding of an inverse relationship between class status and the incidence of psychotic disorders is in accordance with the results of other studies.[5] Although the studies cited have reported an inverse relationship between socioeconomic status and the incidence of psychoses, direct comparisons cannot be made because of differences in definitions of mental illness and socioeconomic groups in the various studies. The recently reported study by Kaplan, Reed, and Richardson is pertinent to this discussion so we will comment on it at some length.

Kaplan, Reed, and Richardson investigated the incidence of psychotic disorders in the population of Wellesley, Massachusetts, a prosperous suburb of Boston, and the "Whittier Street area" of Boston. The Whittier Street area is ecologically below the average residential area in Boston. They first computed incidence rates for admission of psychotic persons to mental hospitals from Wellesley between 1936 and 1950 and for the Whittier Street area during 1949. They then divided these areas into relatively homogeneous subareas of contrasting types by subtracting the lowest socioeconomic areas in Wellesley and the highest socioeconomic areas in the Whittier Street area from the population and patient totals. This left the upper and upper-middle socioeconomic areas in Wellesley for comparison with the lower-middle and lower socioeconomic areas in the Whittier Street area. The incidence rates per 10,000 person years of exposure for first psychotic admissions to mental hospitals for persons 15 years of age and above from these two areas were:

Wellesley—upper and upper-middle socioeconomic areas 9.3
Whittier Street area—lower-middle and lower socioeconomic
   areas .... 22.8 [6]

The rate of 22.8 per 10,000 person years of exposure in the Whittier Street area is almost two and one-half times higher than the comparable rate in Wellesley.

The interesting point about these rates is that they reveal somewhat the same differential between "good" and "poor" ecological areas as we found for psychotic incidence between classes I and II and class V. Kaplan, Reed, and Richardson, in addition, interviewed residents in each area to learn how many persons developed psychotic disorders but were not hospitalized. They report an incidence rate of 6.7 per 10,000 person years of exposure in Wellesley and 2.0 in the Whittier Street area for nonhospitalized psychotics. This is a remarkable reversal from what they found for psychiatrically ill persons admitted to mental hospitals. However, they admit that their case-finding procedures were more thorough in Wellesley than in the Whittier Street area. Unfortunately, the non-committed rate in Wellesley is not strictly comparable to the non-committed rate in the Whittier Street area because the "Wellesley rate is given for the whole community since non-hospitalized cases could not be computed for Wellesley minus the lowest socio-economic areas." [7] Moreover, Kaplan, Reed, and Richardson do not tell us whether the nonhospitalized patients they are reporting from Wellesley or from the Whittier Street area are in ambulatory treatment. It is entirely possible that all or a portion of the nonhospitalized psychotics in Wellesley are receiving ambulatory treatment from private practitioners. If this is the case, we would expect that they come from the best or better areas. Therefore, we would expect to find proportionately more non-committed psychotics in Wellesley than in the Whittier Street area because higher class persons who may be diagnosed as psychotic frequently receive ambulatory care from private practitioners; it is extremely unusual for lower class psychotics to receive ambulatory care from either private practitioners or clinic doctors. This situation plus the admittedly poorer case-finding in the Whittier Street area may account for the reversal of non-committed rates for the two areas.

In spite of possible weaknesses in the Kaplan, Reed, and Richardson study, when the nonhospitalized and hospitalized psychotics from the two areas are combined the inverse relationship between socioeconomic status and the incidence of psychotic disorders continues to hold true. However, the differential between the better and the poorer socioeconomic areas is reduced. The "total incidence of psychosis in Wellesley," expressed as a rate per 10,000 person years of exposure, was found to be 17.2; the comparable rate in the Whittier Street area "minus the highest socio-economic areas" was 24.8.[8] Thus, the rate in the Whittier Street area remains 44 percent greater than in Wellesley.

The problem of hospitalized versus nonhospitalized psychotics is not the same as treated versus untreated psychotics in a population, but the two questions are related one to another and to the question of how we should interpret the persistent linkages between class and psychotic illnesses reported here and implied in other studies. If we assume that the nonhospitalized psychotics found in Wellesley are receiving ambulatory treatment, as we might infer from practices in New Haven, they should be counted as treated cases. If we assume further that they come from positions higher in the status structure than the nonhospitalized psychotics from the Whittier Street area who probably were not receiving psychiatric care because of their lower status positions, one could expect to find a lesser differential in incidence between Wellesley and the Whittier Street area. But even when such hypothetical allowances are made, the differences between the better and the poorer areas remains. Lower class living appears to stimulate the development of psychotic disorders. We infer that the excess of psychoses from the poorer area is a product of the life conditions entailed in the lower socioeconomic strata of the society. This point will be developed and documented by Myers and Roberts in their report on the Controlled Case Study phase of this research.

Total Prevalence versus Treated Prevalence

The question of possible differences between the findings reported in our study for patients in treatment and what might be found if we had figures on the total or "true" prevalence of psychoses in the population must remain unanswered. All we can do is to compare our results with those reported in studies similar to ours. The study most pertinent to the problem of total versus treated prevalence of psychosis was made by Lemkau, Tietze, and Cooper in the Eastern Health District of Baltimore for the year 1936.[9]   These researchers attempted to locate all persons who were mentally ill sometime during 1936.   They included patients in ambulatory treatment, those in hospitals, and persons either neurotic or psychotic who were known to be ill during the year.[10]   The Eastern Health District, socioeconomically, is poorer than the city of Baltimore as a whole, and it is certainly poorer than a cross section of the New Haven community. Its racial composition is definitely different from that in New Haven. Some 21.5 percent of the adult population in the Eastern Health District is Negro; in New Haven, the comparable figure is slightly more than 4 percent.   However, the two populations are both urban, and they are supported mainly by industrial work.

The researchers in the Eastern Health District attempted a complete count of the mentally ill persons in the area during one year. We strove to enumerate persons in psychiatric treatment only during a six-month interval.   Lemkau, Tietze, and Cooper think they missed few persons resident during the year.[11]   We are convinced that we did not overlook an appreciable number of *psychotics* who were in treatment during the Psychiatric Census.   If the two teams of researchers are correct in their contentions that each of their counts is "almost complete," we should expect to find that the prevalence of psychotic illnesses is higher in the Eastern Health District of Baltimore than in the New Haven community.   This hypothesis, of course, assumes that a total count of prevalence will reveal a substantial number of persons who are psychotically ill, but not in treatment.

Lemkau, Tietze, and Cooper reported a one-day age-adjusted *total prevalence* rate of psychosis per 1000 of the population in the Eastern Health District of 5.44.[12] The adjusted rate of psychosis for *treated prevalence* in the New Haven community per 1000 of the population is 6.09.   The age-adjusted rate for the total prevalence of psychosis in the Eastern Health District of Baltimore is thus lower than the rate of treated prevalence is for the New Haven community.   When only white psychotics in the two areas are compared, a similar relationship prevails.   The age-adjusted rate of one-day total prevalence per 1000 of the population in the Eastern Health District is 5.78;[13] in the New Haven community, it is 6.25.   The comparisons we have made between *total prevalence* rates of psychosis in the Eastern Health District and *treated prevalence* in the New

Haven community lead us to conclude that our case-finding methods were as thorough, if not more so, than those used in the Eastern Health District.

Lemkau, Tietze, and Cooper's analysis of interrelations between socioeconomic status and psychotic illnesses are pertinent also to the question under discussion. They computed rates by family income for 180 white psychotics who were hospitalized in 1936. The essential points of their study on this topic are summarized in Table 18.

TABLE 18 *

Family Income and Hospitalization for Psychotic Illnesses (Age and Sex Adjusted Rate per 1000 of Population), Whites Only, 1936

Family Income	Number of Cases	Rate
Relief	20	6.53
Nonrelief under $1000	69	4.70
$1000 to $1500	52	3.85
$1501 to $2000	27	3.79
$2000 and over	12	3.02

* Adapted from Lemkau, Tietze, and Cooper, *op. cit.*, Vol. 26, 1942, Table 4, p. 106, by permission.

Their data cover only the lower portions of the income scale, but the definite connection between relative poorness among poor people and hospitalization for a psychotic illness is clear. The consistent increase in the rate of psychosis with each step down in income among whites in the Eastern Health District during 1936 is in accord with our findings for New Haven in 1950. We are impelled to infer some subtle connection between class status and psychotic illnesses that we cannot explain away by questioning whether the data are for all cases or only for those in treatment.

The Hypothesis of "Downward Drift"

We will consider briefly a third question raised about our findings: Have the psychotic patients "drifted down" in the status structure possibly as an effect of their illnesses? We will confine the discussion to the schizophrenic patients for two reasons: (1) This diagnostic group has been the subject of considerable controversy,[14] and (2) they comprise 58.7 percent of the psychotic patients in the study.

The possible effects of geographic and social mobility on schizophrenia were revealed originally by the finding of Faris and Dunham that schizophrenics upon first admission to a mental hospital come principally from deteriorated ecological areas.[15] Some critics of this conclusion argued that the patients drifted to these areas as a result of their disorders;[16] thus, the high rates of hospital admissions from these areas are illusory.[17] This hypothesis assumes, first, that persons who develop one of the schizophrenic disorders are so ill that they cannot maintain normal social relations and so drift downward geographically and socially. The drift hypothesis assumes, second, that schizophrenics originate in the population in a random manner. If these assumptions are correct, one should find a large concentration of geographically transient and socially downward mobile persons in the class V patient group.

We tested both the geographic and the social mobility aspects of the drift hypothesis. First, the nativity of the adult patients was compared with the nativity of the adult population of the community to see if there was an association between nativity and schizophrenia. This comparison was made because immigration represents the largest geographical movement. Conceivably, there may also be some relationship between the "culture shock" associated with immigration and schizophrenia. No significant association was found between nativity and the presence or absence of schizophrenia in the population.[18] Therefore, our data give no support to the hypothesis of a functional linkage between international migration and the prevalence of treated schizophrenia.

The second step in the test of the mobility hypothesis was an examination of the place where each native-born patient had been born and reared. This was done to determine if there is a significant relationship between class position and geographic mobility in the United States. The data in Table 19 show that movement from

TABLE 19

Birth and Rearing Place for Native-Born Schizophrenics—Percentage by Class

	Class			
Origin	I–II	III	IV	V
New Haven community	44.4	63.7	70.9	61.2
New England	25.9	17.5	15.8	18.4
United States	29.7	18.8	13.3	20.4
$n =$	27	80	301	250

$$\chi^2 = 1.89, 6 \ df, p > .05$$

community of birth and rearing to community of present residence is not a significant factor. Some 65 percent of the native-born patients had been lifelong residents of the community, and 35 percent were migrants. If the geographic transiency hypotheses were correct, these migrants should be concentrated in class V. The facts are otherwise. If the class I–II patients, born and reared in the New Haven community, are compared with the class V patients, also born and reared in the community, it is revealed that only 44 percent of the members of class I–II are native to New Haven, and that a much higher proportion (61 percent) of the class V members have been lifelong residents of the community. Thus, it may be concluded that the class V patients are not largely transients, who have drifted into the community.

The next inquiry concerns whether the class V patients have drifted to the slums in the course of their lives. The answer is crucial to the test of the downward drift hypothesis. For this purpose, the investigators obtained the residential histories of the 428 patients who had lived in the community all their lives. After the individual histories were compiled by address, we assigned to each address the ecological value of the area as determined by the studies of Davie [19] and Myers.[20] After the residential movements of the patients had been tabulated and evaluated by ecological areas, the conclusion was clear that most of the members of class I–II have always lived in the best ecological areas and the members of class V have lived in the slums all their lives. The members of classes III and IV show greater irregularities, but there is no evidence of a significant drift to the slums with the onset of schizophrenia. The present data, thus, clearly support the conclusions Faris and Dunham reached after their examination of the high commitment rates of schizophrenics from poor ecological areas,[21] namely, schizophrenic patients committed to mental hospitals from slums areas do not drift there as an effect of their illnesses.

A final test of the mobility hypothesis was made by examining data indicating whether schizophrenics are socially downward mobile. The first step was to search the family histories of the patients to learn the class positions of their families of orientation. Then the patient was located in the class system. Enough evidence was found to determine the class positions of the families of 92 percent of the patients. The data are summarized in Table 20. The salient points in Table 20 are, first, that 91 percent of the patients whose histories were adequate for our purposes were in the same class as

TABLE 20

Social Mobility among Schizophrenics through Two or More Generations—
Percentage by Class

Evidence of Mobility	Class of Patients			
	I–II	III	IV	V
Patient and family mobile	69.0	65.1	91.4	88.9
Patient upward from family	24.2	22.9	1.7	...
Patient downward from family	3.4	2.4	.9	1.0
Family history insufficient to determine mobility	3.4	9.6	6.0	10.0
$n =$	29	83	352	383

their families of orientation. Second, only 1.3 percent of the patients were in a lower class than their families, whereas 4.4 percent were in a higher class; and third, 89 percent of the class V patients came from class V families, but only 69 percent of the class I–II patients originally belonged to class I–II families. Clearly, few schizophrenics move downward in class status. The facts in Tables 19 and 20 support the conclusion that neither geographic transiency nor downward social mobility can account for the sharp differences in the distribution of schizophrenic patients from one class to another.

A recent study by LaPouse, Monk, and Terris [22] substantiates the findings presented in the preceding paragraphs. They specifically tested the drift hypothesis with schizophrenic patients. They studied all patients (587) with a diagnosis of schizophrenia on first admission from a Buffalo, New York, address to the two state hospitals in the Buffalo area between January 1, 1949 and December 31, 1951. Their study was limited to state hospitals because there were very few first admissions for schizophrenia to Veterans Administration hospitals from Buffalo, and there are no private hospitals in the area.

The socioeconomic status of the patients' residences were ranked according to the median monthly rental of the Census Tracts where they resided at the time of their admissions to the hospital. These researchers then traced the patients' previous addresses as far back as 1925. The cut-off point was 1925 because addresses before this date could not be accurately categorized in terms of economic status. The addresses of 138 white male schizophrenics were traced to 1925; the remainder were traced for shorter periods. They then matched as to age, sex, and address 114 of the patients whose addresses were traced to 1925 with three nonpatient controls drawn from the 1925 New York State Census. The researchers then attempted to trace the moves of the 114 patients and their controls from 1925 to the date the patients were admitted to the state hospital. The patients who were followed for twenty-five years, along with their nonpatient controls, do not reveal any downward drift.

The data on all 587 patients, when analyzed by socioeconomic area, reveal an annual age-adjusted rate per 100,000 population that is related inversely to socioeconomic areas beyond the .001 level for white males and .01 for white females. LaPouse, Monk, and Terris conclude:

> The findings of this study show quite conclusively that for the first admissions of schizophrenics to state hospitals from Buffalo the concentration in low economic areas is not the result of downward drift from higher areas. Nor is there any evidence that the concentration in the poor areas is the result of a recent migration into these areas of *mobile men who live alone*.[23]

SUMMARY AND CONCLUSIONS

The *internal* tests made of *Hypothesis 2* reveal significant associations between class status and the proportion of patients who suffer from different types of psychiatric disorders. The *external* tests show that when the neurotic disorders are grouped together, a direct relationship appears between class status and the extent of treated neuroses in the population. The reverse is true for the psychotic disorders. Separate analyses of the subgroups of neurotic reactions show significant associations between class position and the distribution of patients in each of the seven categories used.

Examination of each type of psychotic disorder shows a true linkage between class position and the rate of treated cases in the population, but the relationship is indirect: The lower the class, the higher the rate. The increases in rates are relatively small from class I–II to class IV for the alcoholic, the organic, and the senile disorders. Between classes IV and V, each of these disorders shows a sharp increase in each rate: incidence, re-entry into treatment, continuity of treatment, and prevalence. There are no appreciable differences in the amount of affective disorders from class I through class III, but from class III to class V there is a straight-line indirect relationship between the rate for affective disorders and class status. The sharp increases in the rates for each type of psychotic disorder between classes IV and V indicate clearly that something is operating in the society that gives rise to remarkable increases in the various kinds of rates at the class IV and V levels. *Hypothesis 2* is valid, but the data do not explain why the differences exist. The problem of interpreting these differences remains.

NOTES

[1] For a complete description of this diagnostic scheme, see Veterans Administration Technical Bulletin TB 10A-78, *Nomenclature of Psychiatric Disorders and Reactions*, October 1, 1957, Washington 25, D. C.

[2] For a systematic discussion of these problems, see A. H. Leighton, "Psychiatric Disorder and Social Environment," *Psychiatry*, Vol. 18, No. 4 (November 1955), pp. 367–383. F. C. Redlich, "The Concept of Normality," *American Journal of Psychotherapy*, Vol. VI, No. 3 (July 1952), pp. 551–576.

[3] Thomas A. C. Rennie and Leo Srole, "Social Class Prevalence and Distribution of Psychosomatic Conditions in an Urban Population," *Psychosomatic Medicine*, Vol. 18 (November–December, 1956), pp. 449–456.

[4] G. N. Raines and J. H. Rohmer, "The Operational Matrix of Psychiatric Practices I: Consistency and Variability in Interview Impressions of Different Psychiatrists," *American Journal of Psychiatry*, Vol. 111, No. 10, pp. 721–733, April, 1955.

[5] Robert E. L. Faris and H. Warren Dunham, *Mental Disorders in Urban Areas*, University of Chicago Press, Chicago, 1939; Clarence W. Schroeder, "Mental Disorders in Cities," *American Journal of Sociology*, 48 (July 1942), pp. 40–48; Robert W. Hyde and Lowell V. Kingley, "Studies in Medical Sociology I: The Relation of Mental Disorders to Community Socio-Economic Level," *The New England Journal of Medicine*, 231 (October 1944), pp. 543–548; Robert E. Clark, "The Relationship of Schizophrenia to Occupational Income and Occupational Prestige," *American Sociological Review*, 13 (June 1948), pp. 325–330; Benjamin Malzberg, "Mental Disease in Relation to Economic Status," *The Journal of Nervous and Mental Disease*, Vol. 123 (March 1956), pp. 257–261; Bert Kaplan, Robert B. Reed, and Wyman Richardson, "A Comparison of the Incidence of Hospitalized and Non-Hospitalized Cases of Psychoses in Two Communities," *American Sociological Review*, 21 (August 1956), pp. 472–479.

[6] Kaplan, Reed, and Richardson, *op. cit.*, Table 2, p. 476.

[7] *Ibid.*, footnote 4, p. 476.

[8] *Ibid.*, Table 4, p. 477.

[9] Paul Lemkau, Christopher Tietze, and Marcia Cooper, "Mental Hygiene Problems in an Urban District," *Mental Hygiene*, Vol. 25 (October 1941), pp. 624–646, also Vol. 26 (January 1942), pp. 100–119.

[10] *Ibid.*, p. 100.

[11] *Ibid.*, p. 101.

[12] *Ibid.*, p. 108, Table 6 and discussion.

[13] *Ibid.*

[14] Morris S. Schwartz, "The Economic and Spatial Mobility of Paranoid Schizophrenics and Manic-Depressives" (Unpublished Master's Thesis, University of Chicago, 1946); D. L. Gerard and L. G. Houston, "Family Setting and the Social Ecology of Schizophrenia," *Psychiatric Quarterly*, Vol. 27 (January 1953), pp. 90–101; J. A. Clausen and M. Kohn, "The Ecological Approach in Social Psychiatry," *The American Journal of Sociology*, Vol. 60 (September 1954), pp. 140–151.

[15] R. E. L. Faris and H. Warren Dunham, *Mental Disorders in Urban Areas*, University of Chicago Press, Chicago, 1939.

[16] See the review of *Mental Disorders in Urban Areas* by A. Myerson, *American Journal of Psychiatry*, Vol. 96 (January 1940), pp. 995–997.

[17] A. J. Jaffe and E. Shanas, "Economic Differentials in the Probability of Insanity," *American Journal of Sociology*, Vol. 44 (January 1935), pp. 534–539.

[18] The figures were: patients, native-born—643, foreign-born—193; general population, native-born—135,568, foreign-born—34,900. $\chi^2 = 3.48$, $p > .05$.

[19] M. R. Davie, "The Pattern of Urban Growth," in *Studies in the Science of Society*, G. P. Murdock (Editor), Yale University Press, New Haven, 1937, pp. 133–161.

[20] J. K. Myers, "Note on the Homogeneity of Census Tracts: A Methodological Problem in Urban Ecological Research," *Social Forces*, Vol. 32 (May 1954), pp. 364–366.

[21] For a discussion of these points, see Robert E. L. Faris, *Social Disorganization*, The Ronald Press, New York, 1948, pp. 230–231.

[22] Rama LaPouse, Mary A. Monk, and Milton Terris, "The Drift Hypothesis and Socio-Economic Differentials in Schizophrenia," *American Journal of Public Health*, Vol. 46 (August 1956), pp. 978–986.

[23] *Ibid.*, p. 984.

class status and treatment

part four

part four • class status and treatment

Part Four traces interdependencies between class position, the agencies which cared for 1891 psychiatric patients whose records were relatively complete, and the kinds of psychiatric therapies administered by psychiatrists. Dollar expenditures on psychiatric treatment are calculated for the several classes, diagnostic groups, agencies, and phases of illness. The pervasive effects of class loom large over the data discussed in these pages.

the treatment
process

chapter nine

INTRODUCTION

The preceding three chapters traced the paths followed by persons who came in due course under the care of psychiatrists. The materials presented in those chapters showed that the illnesses of psychiatric patients are related to their positions in the social system. This chapter will focus attention on the treatment patients receive after they have reached a psychiatrist and their difficulties have been diagnosed. The data presented and discussed here will be concerned with the examination of the third hypothesis in this research. *Hypothesis 3* postulated that the type of psychiatric treatment a patient receives is connected with his position in the class structure. If this presupposition is tenable, we should find significant associations between the two major dimensions of the treatment process, namely, (1) *where* the patients are treated and (2) *what* kinds of therapy psychiatrists prescribe for them. Tests of *Hypothesis 3* will be confined to the patient population; comparisons will not be made between the patients and the general population.

Treatment Facilities

The major types of treatment facilities available to mentally ill persons were described in Chapter Five. Briefly, these facilities are:

(1) private psychiatric practice, (2) private mental hospitals, (3) state hospitals, (4) veterans hospitals, and (5) psychiatric clinics.

Private practitioners and private hospitals are, with rare exceptions, available only to individuals able to pay their fees. The state hospitals admit patients on a voluntary and involuntary basis; payment is not a factor. The veterans hospitals are open only to veterans, but this is a considerable segment of the adult male population. Two clinics are open to individuals under 18 years of age, and three clinics are open mainly to adults if the family income is below $5000 a year. One clinic is limited to veterans, and one is for alcoholics. The number of each kind of facility and the percentage of patients treated in each type are summarized in Table 21.

TABLE 21

The Type and Number of Treatment Facilities in the Study and the Percentage of Patients in Each

Type of Facility	Number	Percentage of Patients
Private practitioners	42	19.0
Private hospitals	10	1.9
Public clinics	7	8.2
State hospitals	6	66.6
Veterans hospitals	5	4.3
$n =$ 70		1891

Table 21 indicates *where* the 1891 patients enumerated in the Psychiatric Census are located. This is interesting information, but from the viewpoint of testing the first dimension of *Hypothesis 3*, additional information is necessary. We need to ask: *Is there a significant relationship between the class status of a person being treated and the psychiatric facility where he is treated?* Before we add this perspective to the problem, however, we shall sketch in the second dimension of *Hypothesis 3*, namely the *kinds* of psychiatric therapy prescribed for the patients.

Types of Treatment

Psychiatrists assume that the selection of a particular psychiatric treatment for a given patient depends upon a number of factors. The principal ones are the doctor's diagnosis and prognosis of the patient's condition and the somatic and psychological suitability of the patient for a particular type of therapy; age is also an important factor. Further considerations are the desires of the patient and the patient's family, the availability of the therapist and the patient for treatment, the ability of the patient to pay for his treatment, and the patient's eligibility for free treatment or a reducion of fees. The training and treatment orientation of the psychiatrist also enters the picture. Although these are the factors psychiatrists talk about, class status may also be a real factor in the determination of the *kind of therapy* a psychiatrist prescribes for a patient.

The therapies prescribed for the patients studied fall into three main types: psychotherapies, organic therapies, and custodial care.

PSYCHOTHERAPIES. The specific types of *individual psychotherapy* used by different practitioners and in different agencies include: psychoanalysis, analytic psychotherapy, and directive psychotherapy. These therapies are based on the assumption that a patient's difficulties may be eliminated through discussion and re-education.

Psychoanalysis is the classical Freudian method, practiced by a member or an advanced student of an approved institute of psychoanalysis. It incorporates particularly Freud's concept of the unconscious, transference, and resistance and is aimed at a reintegration of the total personality; the therapists are maximally "analytic."

Analytic psychotherapy utilizes some of the basic principles of psychoanalysis, such as insight into unconscious forces, transference, and resistance and defenses; adherence to these concepts is less rigid than in classical analysis, but the practices used must be justifiable by psychoanalytic principles and theories. The practices do not rely on "merely" analyzing and may contain a certain amount of directiveness. For instance, if reassurance is used, it must be based on psychoanalytic insights about unconscious behavior which indicate that reassurance is important to the character structure of the patient. It is practiced by psychiatrists who are not necessarily trained in psychoanalysis, although many psychiatrists using this method are trained psychoanalysts. It is not aimed at the total reintegration of the personality, but it is satisfied to deal with focal problems or, as Felix Deutsch puts it, "goal limited psychotherapy." [1]

Directive therapy involves the authoritarian therapist. The techniques are: (1) supporting the patient's ego and reducing his anxiety by consolation, reassurance, and suggestion, (2) advising the patient on various life problems, occasionally using coercive measures, and (3) attempting to help by deliberate manipulation of his environment. These techniques are not based on analytic insight of the patient or therapist; rather they stem from the authoritative position of the therapist, his general clinical experience ("I have seen a case just like that one in Koenigsberg," the great Kraepelin used to say),[2] as well as the dependent and trustful role of the patient. *Eclectic psychotherapy* usually means any combination of the analytic and directive approaches. An eclectic psychotherapist uses concepts and treatment devices from many sources, such as the psychoanalytic school, the psychobiological school, individual psychology, Rogerian client-centered therapy, and directive therapy; some of the truly independent thinkers in the field might also be included in this category. Eclectic psychotherapy is usually an empirical[3] procedure and it is often difficult to say what theoretical concepts, if any, underlie its practices. Most of all, we believe that true eclectics are very "rare birds" and that this category, at this stage of psychiatric knowledge, barely exists. We do not list it as a special category of psychotherapy.

Group psychotherapy is an adaptation of the theory and techniques of individual psychotherapy. The general procedure is to form a group of six to ten patients under a trained therapist who serves as a leader and moderator. The therapist makes only limited suggestions as to topics of discussion and how they are to be developed. He will try to draw the silent members of the group into the discussion, and occasionally he will make interpretations and answer questions. The patients carry the discussion and are permitted to become verbally aggressive. At the end of each session, the therapist usually sums up what the patients have been trying to say. Many group therapists have basically an analytic orientation. (The group therapies observed in this study were "gripe sessions" and orientation talks for small groups of state hospital patients.)

ORGANIC THERAPIES. Organic therapies are directed principally toward an organ or organ system and are based on the assumption that the patient's symptoms may be eliminated or at least controlled by some form of chemical or physical intervention. They include many types of medical and surgical therapy, neurosurgical procedures such as lobotomies and topectomies and various shock treatments such as electro-convulsive therapy and insulin coma therapy. Sedation, physiotherapy, and hydrotherapy are listed as organic treatments even though, strictly speaking, hospital authorities ordinarily resort to these techniques to keep a patient quiet and to maintain order on the wards rather than as aids to the patient's rehabilitation. At the time of our field study, tranquilizing drugs were barely used; psychiatrists depended upon sedatives and some alkaloids.

CUSTODIAL CARE. Custodial care rests on the assumption that little can be done for a mental patient beyond providing him a place to sleep, food, and physical care until he either recovers spontaneously or dies. It refers exclusively to hospitalized patients who receive no organic therapy or psychotherapy as defined above, but who do receive essential medical, surgical, and nursing care. Patients who participate in the maintenance of the hospital but who do not receive specific therapy are included in this category, even though their work in the kitchen, dairy, garden, or shops may be a valuable therapeutic experience.

Combinations of Therapy

Patients who are prescribed two or more types of therapy are categorized here by the dominant one. For example, a depressed patient may receive analytic psychotherapy and, in addition, two or three electro-convulsive treatments. Another depressed patient may receive a series of twenty electro-convulsive treatments and attend two or three group psychotherapy sessions in the course of a month. The principal treatment of the first patient is recorded as analytic psychotherapy; secondary treatment is electro-convulsive treatment. The principal treatment of the second patient is recorded here as electro-convulsive therapy; the secondary treatment as group psychotherapy.

The three principal types of therapy are distributed almost equally within the patient population, but specific forms of psychotherapy vary within each group as the accompanying tabulation shows:

Principal Types of Therapy	Percent
1. Psychotherapy	32.0
Psychoanalysis	1.0
Analytic psychotherapy	3.8
Directive therapies	20.6
Group therapy	6.6
2. Organic therapies	31.7
Electro-convulsive therapy	18.7
Insulin shock treatment	1.5
Lobotomies	6.2
Drug therapy *	4.3
Other organic treatments	1.0
3. Custodial care †	36.3

* Before the era of tranquilizing drugs.
† No differentiation as to type.

PROBLEMS IN TESTING *HYPOTHESIS 3*

Theoretically, a patient's symptomatology should determine, in large part, *where* and *how* he is treated. If he is able to manage his interpersonal relations and function reasonably well in his family and the community, or if the psychiatrist diagnoses his symptoms as a form of neurosis, the probability is high that he will not be hospitalized. On the other hand, if a patient is so disturbed that he cannot control himself or if he is diagnosed as psychotic, the probability is high that he will be hospitalized. Therefore, if we find that diagnosis is related to both the *agency* where the patients are being cared for and the *therapy* administered to them, we must control both of these factors in our tests of *Hypothesis 3*.

Table 22 summarizes the data necessary for a test of the proposi-

TABLE 22

Percentage of Neurotic Patients in the Different Treatment Agencies

	Diagnostic Group	
Treatment Agency	Neurotics	Psychotics
Private practice	63.6	5.4
Private hospitals	1.8	2.0
Clinics	23.2	3.3
State hospitals	9.8	84.2
Veterans hospitals	1.6	5.1
$n =$	449	1442

$$\chi^2 = 1076.40,\ 4\ df,\ p < .001$$

tion presented in the preceding paragraph, that where patients are cared for is related to the diagnoses psychiatrists make of their symptoms. The fact that 87 percent of the neurotics are cared for on an ambulatory basis, whereas 91 percent of the psychotics are hospitalized, indicates that a diagnosis of neurosis or psychosis is an important determinant of where a patient is treated. The strong relationship between diagnosis and the agency where the patients are treated implies that diagnosis needs to be controlled in our tests of *Hypothesis 3*.

The data on the linkage of a neurotic or a psychotic diagnosis with the principal type of therapy prescribed for a patient are presented in Table 23. Table 23 shows that psychotherapy is administered to 83 percent of the neurotic patients; relatively few receive any organic therapy, and even fewer receive custodial care. On the other hand, the predominant form of therapy given to psychotic patients is custodial care, followed closely by organic therapy; only 16 percent receive one of the psychotherapies. The very marked correlation of diagnosis with principal form of therapy proves the need to control for diagnosis in our examination of the validity of the hypothesis under review.

TABLE 23

Percentage of Patients Diagnosed as Neurotic or Psychotic and the Principal Types of Psychiatric Therapy Administered

Type of Therapy Administered	Diagnosis of Patients	
	Neurotic	Psychotic
Psychotherapy	82.9	16.4
Organic therapy	11.1	38.8
Custodial care	6.0	44.8
$n =$	449	1442

$$\chi^2 = 696.59, \, df = 2, \, p < .001$$

The strong linkages between treatment agency and diagnosis, on the one hand, and between diagnosis and principal form of therapy, on the other, attest to the need to analyze the treatment process with four factors in the matrix: (1) the agency where the patient is treated, (2) the principal form of psychiatric therapy administered, (3) the diagnosis of the psychiatrist, and (4) the class position of the patient. The inclusion of these four variables in the series of analyses to follow will enable us to learn if the assumed relationship between class status and psychiatric treatment is sound. If we find significant differences in the ways patients with the same diagnosis are cared for within a given type of treatment agency and these differences are associated with class status, we may conclude that *Hypothesis 3* is tenable. If no linkage appears between class position and where or how patients are cared for we must reject the hypothesis.

THE TREATMENT OF NEUROTIC PATIENTS

Diagnosis and Therapy

Psychiatrists stress the importance of careful diagnosis of a patient's illness, presumably to ensure appropriate treatment. With this idea as a point of departure, we compared the seven different kinds of diagnoses the psychiatrists made of their neurotic patients' disorders with the principal form of therapy they prescribed for them to determine if a significant relationship does exist, in fact, between the psychiatrists' formulation of the patients' difficulties and how they treat them. The data on this point are summarized in Table 24. A glance at the probability statement at the bottom of the table shows that no association exists between the over-all diagnosis of the neuroses the psychiatrists make and the over-all kinds of therapy the patients receive. This is a surprising finding in view of the emphasis psychiatrists place on diagnostic formulation.

When no association was found between the diagnoses of the patients' ills and the principal forms of therapy administered to them by the psychiatrists, the data were examined for six other variables which we thought might be related to the type of therapy the patients receive: race, age, sex, the patient's psychiatric history, treat-

TABLE 24

Percentage of Neurotic Patients in Specified Diagnostic Groups Who Receive a Specified Type of Psychiatric Therapy

Diagnostic Group	Psycho-therapy	Organic Therapy	Custodial Care	n
Character disorders	81.2	11.7	7.1	112
Phobic-anxiety reactions	85.3	8.8	5.9	102
Antisocial reactions	87.6	7.3	5.1	97
Depressive reactions	77.6	16.3	6.1	50
Somatization reactions	76.1	17.4	6.5	46
Obsessive-compulsive reactions *	81.8	13.6	4.6	21
Hysterical reactions *	85.7	9.5	4.8	21

$$\chi^2 = 5.96, 10 \ df, \ p > .05$$

* The obsessive-compulsive and the hysterical reactions are combined in the χ^2 test.

ment agency, and class position. This series of analyses showed that no association exists between type of therapy patients receive and race, sex, age, and a previous course of psychiatric treatment.[4] However, highly significant associations appeared between the principal types of therapy prescribed and (a) where the patients are cared for and (b) their positions in the class system. We may conclude that when a neurotic individual comes under the care of a psychiatrist, the kind of treatment, in the gross classification such as psychotherapy, organic therapy, custodial care, that he receives is independent of the over-all diagnosis the psychiatrist makes of his disorder as well as of his race, his age, his sex, and his previous experiences with psychiatrists. We will now focus attention on the two significant factors governing the type of psychiatric therapy he receives; namely, his class position and the agency where he is treated.

Treatment Agencies

Theoretically we might expect that disturbed individuals who are diagnosed as neurotic would be accepted for treatment in any available agency. Practically, however, the problem revolves around the question of which agency is available to what patient.

The principal restrictions on each type of agency were pointed out earlier. Nevertheless, we shall repeat the essential eligibility requirements for each one. Veterans Hospitals and Clinics are open only to former members of the Armed Forces. Private practitioners' services and private hospitals are limited to those able to pay their fees. Clinics tend to be restricted to certain groups according to age, economic status, or diagnosis, such as the guidance clinics for children, psychiatric dispensaries for lower income groups, and the clinics of the Commission on Alcoholism for alcoholics. The state hospitals are available only to residents of the state. These limitations mean that particular kinds of treatment agencies are, in fact, more or less restricted to certain segments of the community's population.

Precise knowledge of the many practical considerations involved in the implementation of a decision to refer a disturbed person to a psychiatrist led us to suppose that class status is a meaningful factor in the determination of who is accepted where for treatment. In order to test this idea, the clinical record of each patient had to be studied to learn where his first psychiatric treatment occurred. The results of this phase of the research are summarized in Table 25. A glance at the probability statement for Table 25 will show that where neurotic patients are treated first is linked distinctly with class status. Individuals in classes I–II and III go, in large part, to private practitioners; class IV's go, in about equal proportions, to private and public agencies; class V's go, in very large part, to public agencies. Hospitalized neurotic patients are in the minority in all classes, but the lower the class, the higher the percentage who are hospitalized. Class I–II patients are attracted to private hospitals; class III's go, in about equal numbers, to both private and public hospitals; some

TABLE 25

Percentage of Neurotic Patients Treated for the First Time in Specific Types
of Psychiatric Agencies—by Class

Treatment Agency	I–II	III	IV	V
Private practitioners	85.7	67.0	47.4	9.8
Private hospitals	9.2	5.3	...	...
Public clinics	5.1	20.9	30.9	57.4
Military or V.A. hospitals	...	6.1	14.3	13.1
State hospitals	...	0.7	7.4	19.7
$n =$	98	115	175	61

$$\chi^2 = 131.20, \; 12 \; df, \; p < .001$$

two out of three class IV patients first enter a military or veterans
hospital; the class V neurotics go to the state hospitals or the veterans hospitals.

Changes in Treatment Agencies from First to Current Treatment

Thirty-eight percent of the patients are in their second or third
experience with psychiatric care, and some have had even more contacts. An examination of where these patients were treated first and
where they are treated currently shows a significant change in the
use of treatment agencies in each class from the first to the present
phase of their illness. In class I–II there is little change in the use
of treatment agencies from the first to the current course of treatment, except for patients who received their first treatment in private hospitals. Although only six patients had their first treatment
in a private hospital, five of the six changed to other agencies. Two
are treated currently in public clinics, one is in a veterans hospital,
and two are in state hospitals. Thus, 83 percent of the class I–II
patients who were treated first in a private hospital, then were discharged, and at a later time re-entered treatment, are now in a public
agency. Private mental hospitals appear to be patronized mainly by
persons from class I–II who are in treatment for the first time. Private practitioners hold their class I–II patients from the first to subsequent periods of treatment.[5]

Class III individuals are loyal either to private practitioners or to
clinics. If a patient starts with a private practitioner, he tends to
stay with a private practitioner in later courses of treatment, although not necessarily with the same one. Likewise, when a class
III person starts in a clinic he returns to a clinic when he feels in

need of treatment. The private hospitals lose over nine out of ten class III patients who find it necessary to re-enter treatment. Some 76 percent of the class III patients who do not return to private hospitals enter state hospitals. The remainder are treated largely by private practitioners, but a few are in clinics. Among veterans, the largest shift is from first treatment in a military setting to current treatment with a private practitioner. At the time of our field work, not a single class III neurotic patient was in a veterans hospital. In class III the two significant changes in the use of psychiatric facilities between the first treatment and the current treatment involve moves from private to state hospitals among the nonveterans and from military hospitals to private practitioners among veterans.[6] The bills for the private treatment of these veterans are paid by the Veterans Administration.

In class IV there are two marked changes in the use of psychiatric agencies between the first course of treatment and the present one. First, almost every veteran who received his first treatment in military service is cared for now by a private practitioner on an ambulatory basis at the expense of the Veterans Administration. Second, patients who first came into psychiatric treatment either with private practitioners or in clinics are now in state hospitals.[7]

In class V, the same changes occur but in even more marked ways. Specifically, 83 percent of the veterans who are treated currently by private practitioners at Veterans Administration expense had their first psychiatric experience in military service. Class V patients who are treated for the first time in clinics either return to them or go to the state hospitals when a second course of treatment is necessary. If a clinic cannot care for them, the probability is that they will be taken to a state hospital.[8]

These data tell us in a general way what treatment facilities are available to which patients and in what phases of mental illness. Classes I–II and III turn for help to private hospitals and private practitioners when they first become ill. As chronicity develops, they go elsewhere or possibly "shop around." All three classes rely upon private practitioners in later illnesses, but only class I's continue to patronize private hospitals. In classes II and III, the shift from the first to later courses of treatment is from private hospitals to public hospitals. Class IV's tend to utilize clinics and private practitioners first, rather than private hospitals. Later they turn to the state hospitals out of necessity. Class V's are wholly dependent upon public agencies in all phases of their illnesses.

Class and Treatment Agencies

We have seen that each of the five types of treatment agencies are utilized by sharply different proportions of patients in the classes who have had one and more previous courses of psychiatric treatment. We will now examine the way they are used by all the patients, that is, those who are in treatment for the first time as well as those who have a history of previous treatment. By way of introduction, we shall note that no class I neurotic patient is treated in public clinics, state hospitals, or Veterans Administration hospitals. Conversely, no class V patient is found in a private hospital. Between these extremes a series of significant associations exists between the class status of the patients and the use they make of the different treatment agencies.

Class I individuals are treated exclusively by private practitioners or in private hospitals. Class II persons, for the most part, are treated by private practitioners or private hospitals. Class III's are treated predominantly (71 percent) by private practitioners, but 21 percent are cared for in the clinics; 2 percent are in private hospitals and 6 percent in state hospitals. The percentage of class IV patients treated by private psychiatrists is lower than in class III, as is the percentage in private hospitals. The proportion in clinics is only slightly larger, but the percentage in the state hospitals is twice as great as in class III. Some 20 percent of the class V's are treated by private practitioners. The remainder are treated in public agencies, 52 percent in the clinics, 5 percent in Veterans Administration hospitals, and 24 percent in the state hospitals.

The class profiles of patients in each type of institution (see Figure 6) show that each type of institution draws its patients from selected segments of the status structure. The state hospital is utilized in sharply increasing percentages as the class status scale is descended. The use of Veterans Administration hospitals is not as closely linked to class as the state hospitals. Nevertheless, the proportion of class V patients in Veterans Administration hospitals is almost three times greater than in class IV. The veterans hospitals are used proportionately by many more lower than higher status veterans. The differential increase from class II to class V in veterans hospitals is as one is to five.

The profile for the clinics is similar to that of the state hospitals, but the differential between classes II and III is not as large. However, the increases between classes II and III and classes IV and V

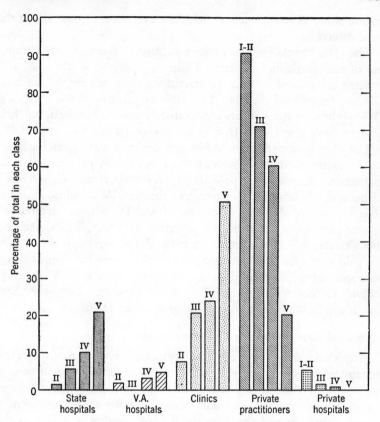

$\chi^2 = 87.98$, df 9, $p < 0.001$ (State hospital combined with V.A. hospital and private practitioner combined with private hospital for the χ^2 analysis.)

Figure 6. Percentage of Neurotic Patients in Different Treatment Agencies—by Class.

are of approximately the same magnitude. For example, 2 percent of the class II's are in the state hospitals, but of the class III's there are 6 percent; thus, the proportion of class III's in the state hospitals is three times larger than class II's. Likewise, 7 percent of the class II's are in the clinics, but 21 percent of the class III's. Between classes IV and V the differences in the percentage of patients in the clinics and the state hospitals is as one is to two, with the larger proportion belonging to class V. In brief, there is a marked increase in the proportion of patients in the clinics and state hospitals as one goes down the class scale. The gradient for the Veterans Administration is not as steep, but it is, with the exception of class III, in the same direction.

The class profile for the patients in private agencies is the opposite of that in public agencies. Eighty-six percent of the class I–II patients are treated by private practitioners, 71 percent of the class III's, 62 percent of the class IV's and 20 percent of the class V's. Only eight neurotic patients are treated in private hospitals, but half of them belong to class I–II; two are in class III and two in class IV.

The class gradient for neurotic patients in private agencies is far steeper when their use is viewed in terms of who pays the costs of treatment. All class I–II patients pay for their treatment, but only 63 percent of class III's, 39 percent of the class IV's, and none of the class V's do so. Patients in classes III and IV who are treated by private practitioners, but do not pay their own bills, are financed by the Veterans Administration. In class V the private patient's bills are paid either by the Veterans Administration or by compensation insurance carried by employers. In short, when class V neurotic individuals receive treatment it is at public expense. This generalization is applicable also to 60 percent of the class IV neurotic patients.

Principal Form of Therapy and Class Status

Interrelationships between the principal types of psychiatric therapy administered and the class status of the patients who receive each type of therapy are examined from two perspectives. First, we shall view the data without controlling for treatment agency; then we shall control for it to see if class position is linked to the kind of therapy psychiatrists prescribe for their patients within a treatment agency. The data essential for the first analysis are given in Table 26.

Some form of psychotherapy is the predominant treatment method in each class, but there are distinctly different percentages of patients in the several classes who do or do not receive a particular type of psychotherapy. Psychoanalysis and analytic psychotherapy are concentrated in class I-II. Directive therapy is clustered disproportionately in classes III and IV. Only a small number of patients receive group therapy, but the largest percentage is in class V (all group therapy was administered in a state hospital). When the individual psychotherapies are summed, a clearly defined class gradient emerges: All class I's receive it, 97 percent of the class II's, 84 percent of the class III's, 75 percent of the class IV's, and 59 percent of the class V's. The organic therapies, shock, operations and drugs, are relatively

TABLE 26

Principal Type of Psychiatric Therapy Received by Neurotic Patients—by Class

Type of Treatment	Class			
	I–II	III	IV	V
Classical analysis and analytic psychotherapy	46.9	20.9	5.1	4.9
Directive psychotherapy *	50.0	62.6	69.7	54.1
Group psychotherapy	1.0	2.6	2.9	8.2
Organic therapy (shock, drugs, operations)	2.0	9.6	16.6	9.8
Custodial care	0.0	4.3	5.7	23.0
$n =$	98	115	175	61

$$\chi^2 = 128.72, \ 9 \ df, \ p < .001$$

* Directive and group psychotherapy combined for χ^2 analysis.

rare in all classes, but the class V neurotics receive an organic therapy five times as frequently as the class I's and II's. Custodial care is limited largely to class V. When the patients who are administered an organic therapy are combined with those receiving custodial care, a definite inverse association appears between class position and the receipt of one of these kinds of treatment, namely, class II—2 percent, class III—14 percent, class IV—23 percent, class V—33 percent. These dramatic differences show clearly that the lower the class, the greater the proportion of neurotic patients who are administered therapies which dynamically oriented psychiatrists do not approve. In class V, at least two out of five patients do not receive one of the active therapies developed in this century that are believed to aid in the solution of neurotic difficulties.

Types of Therapy within Agencies

We will now analyze the therapies patients receive within three groups of treatment agencies, private practitioners, the clinics, and the public hospitals, to see if class position is a significant factor in the kind of therapy when the agency where they are treated is held constant.

PRIVATE PRACTITIONERS. Forty-two private practitioners are caring for 65.5 percent of the neurotic patients. Individual psychotherapy is the predominant therapeutic method used. The particular subtypes administered, analytic psychotherapy and directive psychotherapy, are related definitely to the patient's position in the status structure. Psychoanalysis is limited entirely to classes I and II. Analytic psychotherapy also is confined, in large part, to the same strata. Directive psychotherapy, by way of contrast, is inversely related to class status. It increases from 53.4 percent in class II to 86.4 percent in class V. This is the only form of psychotherapy which class V patients receive from private practitioners. Even though 90 percent of the private practitioners' patients are treated by some form of individual psychotherapy, the remaining 10 percent who are prescribed some form of organic treatment exhibit class-linked therapy patterns, as a glance at Table 27 shows. The lower the class, the higher the percentage receiving an organic therapy.

TABLE 27

Percentage of Private Practitioners' Patients in Each Class Treated with a Specific Type of Therapy *

	Class			
Psychiatric Therapy	I–II	III	IV	V †
Psychoanalysis and analytic psychotherapy	45.4	19.0	1.8	0.0
Directive psychotherapy	53.4	72.7	88.7	86.4
Shock and sedation	1.1	8.3	9.5	13.6
$n =$	88	84	110	12

$$\chi^2 = 89.33, 4 \; df, \, p < .001$$

* Includes eight patients in private hospitals.
† The class V patients are combined with the class IV patients in the χ^2 analysis.

Observation of the data on the types of psychiatric therapies administered to patients leads to the conclusion that the private practice of psychiatry in our community is highly correlated with class status. To test the certainty of this idea, the private practitioners' patients were divided according to the therapeutic orientation of the practitioners to see what strata are represented in the practice of each one. The procedure gave us three groups of practitioners: (a) psychoanalysts, 22 in number, (b) analytically oriented psychiatrists, but not analysts, 11, and (c) psychiatrists who utilize either directive, supportive, suggestive techniques or organic therapies.[9] The psychoanalysts draw 77 percent of their patients from classes I and II, 17 percent from class III, and 6 percent from class IV.

The analytically oriented therapists draw 52 percent of their patients from classes I and II, 39 percent from class III, and 9 percent from class IV. Forty-eight percent of the directive-organic therapists' patients are in class IV, 34 percent are in class III, and only 15 percent belong to class I or II. These figures [9] indicate that private practitioners have "class" practices for the most part. Therefore, it is not surprising to find that the type of therapy a practitioner administers to his patients is correlated with the patient's social position.

Psychotherapeutic treatment is aimed toward the re-education of the patient. This is believed to occur as a patient "works through" his personal problems with the therapist or, in the directive psychotherapies, when he accepts and follows the therapists' notions. To rehabilitate a neurotic patient through the use of individual psychotherapy takes the time of the patient and the psychiatrist. The amount of time they actually spend with one another is measured here in three different ways: (1) the number of meetings the patient has with his therapist each month, (2) the length of each psychotherapeutic session, and (3) the length of time the patient has been receiving care from his present therapist.

The number of therapeutic visits per month made by patients receiving individual psychotherapy from private practitioners is definitely linked to class status. As a rule, the higher the class the more frequently treatment is administered. The class gradient is steepest

TABLE 28

Percentage of Private Practitioners' Patients * Receiving Individual Psychotherapy Who See Their Therapists a Specified Number of Times Each Month—by Class

Number of Meetings	Class		
	I–II	III	IV–V
1	17.2	18.9	30.4
2	12.6	25.7	39.2
3–4	23.0	31.1	25.5
5–8	13.9	18.9	3.9
9 and more	33.3	5.4	1.0
$n =$	87	74	102

$$\chi^2 = 69.39, 12 \; df, p < .001$$

* Patients in private hospitals receiving individual psychotherapy included.

for the patients who see their doctors nine or more times per month. These patients are being treated by an intensive form of psychotherapy. A glance at Table 28 will show that they are heavily concentrated in classes I–II. This is what one would expect from the previously demonstrated strong association between high class status and the prescription of analytic psychotherapy or psychoanalysis. Patients who see their therapists less than once a week are clustered in classes IV and V. Patients who see their therapists once or twice a month certainly are not participating in "re-education" with the same intensity as those who see their psychiatrists more than twice a week.

The folklore of psychiatric practice tells us that the optimal length of a psychotherapeutic session is a "50-minute hour." [10] We are not interested in determining what the length of a psychotherapeutic session ought to be. Our interest is in seeing if the amount of time psychiatrists spend with their patients on each visit is related to the class position of the patients. The answer is embodied in Table 29.

TABLE 29

Percentage of Neurotic Patients Treated by Private Practitioners—by Class and Length of Sessions

Length of Sessions	Class			
	I–II	III	IV	V
50–60 minutes	94.3	81.3	75.8	45.4
30–49 minutes	3.4	17.3	20.9	18.1
15–29 minutes	2.3	1.4	3.3	36.4
$n =$	87	74	91	11

$$\chi^2 = 47.09, 6 \ df, \ p < .001$$

This table demonstrates that class position is a definite factor in the determination of the amount of time private practitioners spend with their patients. Approximately 94 percent of the class I–II patients see their therapists for a 50-minute hour. At the other end of the status structure, only 45 percent of the class V's receive treatment for 50 minutes, whereas less than 6 percent of the patients in class I–II are treated by "short time." We infer that this is another manifestation of the subtle intrusion of class status into the practice of psychiatry.

The number of months patients have been in treatment is related directly to class position. In class I–II, two patients out of five have been in continuous intensive treatment with their present psychiatrist for more than three years. In class V, no patient has received any form of treatment for as long as two years. In class IV only one patient out of 14 has received continuous psychotherapy for as long as two years.[11] Unfortunately, we cannot conclude that lower class patients are cured more quickly or do not require long-term intensive psychotherapy. Moreover, we do not know if they would remain in long-term therapy or benefit from twice the amount of time per treatment session.

Differences in the length of time patients remain in treatment with private practitioners may be attributed, at least in part, to the kind of psychotherapy being administered, but the personality characteristics of the class V patient, such as impulse gratification, inability to verbalize, and short span of attention, probably also enter into the process. However, who gets what kind of therapy is a class-linked variable. For example, a psychoanalyst may prescribe either psychoanalysis or intensive analytic psychotherapy for his patients, but these therapies are limited largely to classes I and II. Supportive therapy, by way of contrast, may be prescribed by directive psychiatrists for their patients. It is not a matter of chance that the patients who receive this form of treatment are almost exclusively in either class IV or V. These are the patients who see their psychiatrists once or twice a month for 15 to 30 minutes and drop out of treatment within a few months. In short, class status is inextricably interlinked with what kinds of treatment patients receive from private practitioners.

THE CLINICS. Seven different clinics treated the 104 patients whose treatment experiences will be examined now. Approximately two thirds of these patients were cared for in the large community clinic. Two other clinics treated most of the remainder. Because of the concentration of so many patients in a single clinic, the general statistical picture will be overshadowed by what occurs in the large clinic. Analytically oriented individual psychotherapy is the acknowledged treatment in this clinic; three of the other clinics also stress analytic psychotherapy, two have a directive-organic orientation, and the orientation of one, at the time of the field work, was indefinite. Unfortunately, the number of patients is too small for us to examine the clinics individually. However, we will present some data in later paragraphs from the large clinic in the community hospital. One final word about the clinic patients: No class I individual is among them.

Within the clinics the class position of the patients is related in significant ways to the types of therapy psychiatrists administer. A glance at Table 30 will show that the higher the class, the greater

TABLE 30

Percentage of Neurotic Patients in Clinics by Principal Type of Psychiatric Therapy in Each Class

Psychiatric Therapy	Class			
	II *	III	IV	V
Analytic psychotherapy	71.4	33.3	17.0	6.3
Directive psychotherapy	28.6	45.9	65.9	59.3
Shock therapy †	0.0	4.2	7.3	3.1
Sedation	0.0	16.7	9.8	31.2
$n =$	7	24	41	32

$$\chi^2 = 18.03, 4\ df, p < .01$$

* Class II is combined with class III in the χ^2 analysis.
† Shock therapy and sedation are combined in χ^2 analysis.

the percentage of patients who are prescribed analytic therapy. While directive psychotherapy is distributed rather evenly in the three lower classes, only a small percentage of class II's receive it. Relatively few patients receive an organic therapy, but in class V over one third are given either sedation or shock.

The significant association of class with the type of therapy psychiatrists give within the clinics is of particular interest, because the treatment prescribed is not connected with the economic factor as it is in private practice. The patients are treated free, or for nominal fees determined by administrative personnel who have no direct connection with the patient's therapy. We may infer, therefore, that the type of therapy given to a clinic patient is related more to social factors than to economic costs. The doctor-patient relationship and communication between the physician and his patient appear to be related, in turn, to the class of the patients and of the doctors.

The intensity of individual psychotherapy, as measured by the number of times a patient sees his clinic therapist per month, is not linked significantly with class position. Nevertheless, there is a tendency for class V patients to see their therapists, once, twice, or three times a month, whereas the class II and class III patients see their therapists once a week. Specifically, 71 percent of the class II patients in clinics, but only 57 percent of the class V patients in clinics, see their therapists more than once a week; none see him as often as twice a week.

The clinics are structured around a 50-minute hour; therefore, there is no association between class position and the length of time patients are seen. Only four patients receive less than this amount of psychiatric time, but three of these four are in class V; the other is in class IV. This slight tendency to give a class V patient less time and attention than a higher status patient is another bit of evidence of the generalized nature of class differences.

The length of time the clinic patients have been in treatment is related to class. The higher the class the longer the patients have been in continuous treatment. For example, 62 percent of the class II patients have been in treatment for more than one year; whereas 79 percent of the class V's have been in treatment for less than six months. Classes III and IV fall into their characteristic intervening positions along this gradient.[12]

Two members of our team, Myers and Schaffer, studied the large clinic in the community hospital to learn as much as possible about interrelations of social factors and the practice of psychiatry within one institutional setting.[13] They found that of neurotic patients in their first course of treatment, who are prescribed analytic psychotherapy, 59 percent of the class II's are treated more than 10 weeks, but only 14 percent of the class V's.[14] They also found that a patient's class status determines the professional level of the therapist who treats him. Class II patients are treated by fully trained staff psychiatrists; resident trainees select class III and IV patients; and class V patients receive treatment from undergraduate medical students or social workers.

TREATMENT IN PUBLIC HOSPITALS. The 12 percent of neurotic patients who are in state and Veterans Administration hospitals do not exhibit the class-associated therapy patterns found among private practitioners and in clinics. However, the data in Table 31 reveal some interesting treatment practices in the public hospitals. Only two patients are treated by analytic psychotherapy, one in class II and one in class V; both are in veterans hospitals. Group psychotherapy, on the other hand, is found only in one state hospital, and it is unduly concentrated in class III. Electro-convulsive therapy is limited, likewise, to the state hospitals. Custodial care and routine administration of sedation are little used, and they are found in about the same proportion in each of the two lower classes.

TABLE 31

Percentage of Neurotic Patients Treated in State and Veterans Administration
Hospitals by Principal Types of Psychiatric Therapy—by Class

Psychiatric Therapy *	Class			
	II	III	IV	V
Analytic psychotherapy	66.7	0.0	0.0	5.9
Directive psychotherapy	0.0	14.3	12.7	17.6
Group psychotherapy	0.0	42.8	20.8	29.5
Shock treatments and lobotomies	33.3	28.7	45.7	29.4
Custodial care	0.0	14.3	20.8	17.6
$n =$	3	7	24	17

$$\chi^2 = 6.52, 6 \ df, p > .05$$

* Class II is combined with class III and Analytic and Directive psychotherapy are combined in the χ^2 analysis.

Re-entry into Treatment

Approximately 32 percent of the neurotic patients have experienced one or more previous courses of psychiatric treatment. Re-
entry into treatment within a year of the time previous treatment
was completed is not related to class position although there is a trend
toward more re-entry into treatment in classes IV and V than in the
higher classes. However, when the interim between courses of treatment is 12 months or longer, there is a distinct inverse relationship
between class and the percentage of patients who re-enter treatment.
In classes I and II, 12 percent of the patients return to treatment
after an interval of at least a year, but 28 percent of the class V's
re-entered treatment after a year had elapsed since their previous
course of treatment. The intervening classes show percentages between these extremes. It would appear that a functional connection
exists between lower class status, short periods of treatment, and
periodic recurrences of disturbed behavior requiring further psychiatric care.

Summary

The place where neurotic patients are treated is strongly associated with class status; the higher the class, the higher the percentage of disturbed patients treated by private practitioners. Treatment in public agencies is related inversely to class position; the
lower the class, the greater the proportion of patients treated in

public agencies. How patients are treated also is linked to class position. Individual psychotherapy is a major treatment in all classes, but the lower the class, the greater the tendency to administer an organic therapy, shock treatment, lobotomy, or treatment with drugs. When the agency where treatment takes place is held constant, the status factor continues to be important. Private practictioners administer analytic psychotherapy to the higher classes and directive therapies to the lower classes. The same class-linked gradient exists in the clinics, but not in the public hospitals. The number of times patients see their therapists per month, as well as the length of the visits, is significantly different from one class to another. The higher classes receive more frequent and longer treatments than the lower classes; the disparity is most marked between classes IV and V.

THE PSYCHOTIC PATIENTS

We will now examine the clinical histories of the 1442 psychotic patients in the study to learn if their class positions are determinants in where and how they are treated. The where phase of the analysis will be developed in four separate but related steps. First, we will investigate which treatment agencies are utilized by what classes when psychotic individuals come under the care of psychiatrists for the first time. Second, we will see if the 51 percent of psychotic patients who have had at least one previous course of psychiatric care are now utilizing the same treatment agency as in their first episode. This analysis will be made to see if patients with a history of a previous treatment shift from one kind of agency to another when they re-enter treatment. The third step in the examination of the treatment records of the psychotics will be focused on where the patients are being treated now. Finally, we will explore the possibility that the use of treatment agencies is influenced by the kind of mental disorder the patient has, rather than by his class position.

The statistical procedures used to test the treatment hypothesis on the psychotic patients are essentially the same as those we followed with neurotic patients, but the emphasis is different. This is dictated by the differential use of treatment facilities in these diagnostic groups. For example, 87 percent of the psychotics are hospitalized in state and Veterans Administration hospitals. This means that the more rigid tests of *Hypothesis 3* are limited to psychotic patients in public hospitals. Whereas, among the neurotics the large concentration of patients treated by private practitioners indicated that the most rigid statistical tests of the treatment hypothesis should be focused on the patients of the private practitioners. The very fact that so many psychotic patients are in state hospitals presents a unique opportunity to subject *Hypothesis 3* to a critical test. There are hundreds of patients in the state hospitals who are being treated, presumably for their illnesses, in relatively similar ways. If the factor of class status is linked to the kinds of treatment these patients receive, we shall conclude that the hypothesis under examination is valid.

Agency of First Treatment

Information on the agency where psychotically disordered individuals receive their first psychiatric treatment will give us some insight into what agencies are available to whom. It also will tell us if class status is correlated with the utilization of therapeutic agencies. The data essential to provide an answer to these facets of the treatment process are given in Table 32.

TABLE 32

Percentage of Psychotics Treated for the First Time in Specified Types of Psychiatric Agencies—by Class

Treatment Agency	Class			
	I–II	III	IV	V
State hospital	7.7	39.7	77.5	89.0
Military or V.A. hospital	0.0	5.5	6.2	3.2
Private hospital	67.3	39.7	5.2	0.6
Public clinic	1.9	8.9	9.0	6.8
Private practitioner	23.1	6.2	2.2	0.5
$n =$	52	146	581	663

$$\chi^2 = 610.43, 12 \; df, \; p < .001$$

The most striking impression gained from an examination of the percentages in Table 32 is the confirmation of our common sense expectation that the higher classes turn to private hospitals, whereas the lower classes go to the state hospitals. The different percentages tell us, in a way, what kinds of treatment facilities are relied upon by different classes when a psychotic illness strikes. For example, all class I psychotics received their first psychiatric treatment in private hospitals or from private practitioners, and only four class II's were treated first in a state hospital. A brief statement of the circumstances involved in the commitment of these class II's to the state hospital will indicate that this psychiatric agency is not regarded as suitable for the mentally ill members of high-status families. One who had cancer became severely disturbed after the cancer treatment failed. This patient and the family members resisted the idea of going to the state hospital, but the lack of funds to support the patient in a private hospital forced the family to accept the state hospital, but with reluctance. This family still feels humiliated, because a member died in the state hospital. A second was treated for syphilis by private physicians for several years before he became disturbed. His mental disorder was perceived first after a fight he had with several neighbors. His wife had kept the fact that her husband was suffering from syphilis from the neighborhood both before and after the fight. She feels her husband's commitment to the state hospital is "a terrible disgrace."

The third class II patient was estranged from his family and was living at a local hotel. He became involved in a fight with other guests and employees. The manager realized that the guest was disturbed and called a psychiatrist to the hotel. The man's estranged wife, who was then called, would not help him so he was sent to the state hospital. The man's mother later denied that she had a son in the state hospital. The fourth person was a teacher in a boys' private school. When he developed psychotic symptoms, the principal called a psychiatrist who diagnosed the man's behavior as schizophrenic. This man had no funds, his parents were dead, and a married sister living in a distant state refused to assume the responsibility of his care. The headmaster and several of the masters were embarrassed because this teacher was taken to the state hospital. These four cases document the fact that the state hospital, in classes I and II, is a taboo institution to be utilized only as a "last resort." Entry into the state hospital is the antithesis of what high-status persons should do when mental disturbances occur.

Class III exhibits a distinctly different pattern of where its psychotic members are first treated. Some two out of five patients go to private hospitals, but an equal proportion go to state hospitals. A third pattern of response to psychosis is observable in class IV, in which some three out of four go directly to state hospitals and private hospitals; only 2 percent are cared for by private practitioners. Class V turns to the state hospitals in some 9 out of 10 cases. The 1 percent who are treated first either in private hospitals or by private practitioners are as distinct exceptions as the four persons in class II who went to the state hospital. It is by chance that four class V persons had their first psychiatric contact in a private hospital, but it is not chance that they entered the same hospital and that none of them stayed longer than six days. Three of the four were employees of the Community Hospital at the time they became psychotic. The house staff of the Community Hospital referred them to the University psychiatric hospital. They were kept there for a few days and then transferred to the state hospital. The fourth patient was admitted to the psychiatric hospital from her home upon the advice of a general practitioner, but when the family became aware of the economic burden entailed, the woman was taken to the state hospital.

The data summarized in Table 32 demonstrate that class status is correlated with the utilization of different types of treatment agencies when persons become psychotically disturbed. The use of private mental hospitals is related directly to the higher class positions, whereas reliance upon the state hospitals is connected with the lower classes.

First Agency Compared with Present Agency

We will now focus attention upon the 743 patients, 51 percent of the psychotics, who are known to have received one or more previous courses of psychiatric treatment to see what agencies are treating them currently. We are asking three questions of the data in this phase of the research: (1) Have these patients returned to the agency where they were first treated? (2) Is class status involved in who does or does not return to a given type of treatment center? (3) Are the psychiatrists' diagnoses related to who uses what agencies in different phases of psychotic illness?

Some 82 percent of the patients with a history of previous treatment were cared for first in a public agency; the other 18 percent were treated originally by a private agency. During their present illness, 90 percent are cared for in public agencies, and 10 percent are in private agencies. A glance at Table 33 will show that 12 percent were cared for first in clinics, but currently only 3 percent are treated in clinics. The number treated in the military services first but currently in a Veterans Administration hospital is about the same. In both the first and the present illness, the state hospitals carried the largest part of the load. Private practitioners treated

TABLE 33

Psychotic Patients with a History of Psychiatric Treatment by Agency of First Treatment and Current Treatment

	Treatment	
Agency	First	Current
Clinics	12.1	3.4
Military and/or V.A. hospitals	6.3	7.5
State hospitals	63.5	79.0
Private practice	2.1	7.2
Private hospitals	15.9	2.9
$n =$	728 *	734

$$\chi^2 = 136.086,\ 4\ df,\ p < .001$$

* Agency of first treatment is unknown for 6 patients.

a negligible part of the patients in their first illness, but the percentage is still small. Private hospitals lost 82 percent of their cases between the first and current treatments. Changes in the utilization of the five kinds of treatment agencies in different phases of mental illness are of general interest, but from our perspective the salient question is this: Are the shifts in treatment agencies linked to the class position of the patients involved in them?

This query can be answered by controlling for class position and then comparing the agency of first treatment with the agency of current treatment. The detailed results of this procedure are given in Table 8, Appendix Four, pp. 420–421. This table shows that significant relationships exist between class status and what agencies are patronized in the different phases of psychotic illnesses. No class I, and only one class II patient was seen first in a clinic; this patient is also being treated there now. No class I or II psychotic patient was brought into treatment for the first time in the military service. Approximately 23 percent of the class I's and II's were treated first by private practitioners; 21 percent are seen by private practitioners currently. Three fourths were treated first in private hospitals, but only 36 percent are treated there currently. Class I and II psychotic patients who shift out of private hospitals are absorbed by state and Veterans Administration hospitals.

Sixty-five percent of the class III patients were treated first in private hospitals, but only 5.7 percent are treated currently in these centers. This is a 91 percent loss by the private hospitals. Class III

patients who shift out of private hospitals are absorbed either by the
state hospitals or by private practitioners. A shift occurs also from
the clinics to the state hospitals, but the proportion of patients who
were seen first in a military hospital is the same as that being treated
now in veterans hospitals.

In class IV, exactly two patients out of every three with a psychiatric history were treated first in state hospitals. The clinics
treated 15 percent, 10 percent were seen in the military service, and
9 percent were treated in private hospitals. Less than 1 percent were
treated by private practitioners. Currently, 81 percent are treated
in state hospitals, 4 percent in clinics, 6 percent in veterans hospitals,
8 percent by private practitioners, and .05 percent in private hospitals. The marked shifts in class IV are first from private hospitals
to state hospitals and second from clinics to state hospitals.

Class V's utilize the state hospitals both in the first and current
treatment. However, there are significant shifts from clinics and
military hospitals into the state and veterans hospitals. Only 1 percent were treated first in private hospitals. Currently, 2 percent are
being treated by private practitioners, but these patients are veterans
whose bills are paid by the Veterans Administration. Our data reveal that each social class follows a pattern in its shifts from one
agency to another between the first and the present course of treatment. The pattern of each class is so characteristic of that particular status level that we are inclined to believe that this, too, is a
facet of the culture of the class.

Treatment Agencies, Diagnosis, and Class

First Treatment. We will carry the analysis of where patients
are treated first one step further. In this analysis we will hold the
patient's diagnosis constant to see whether class or diagnosis is the
factor determining where patients are first treated. When diagnosis
is held constant, we find that private hospitals and private practitioners attract patients from classes I and II irrespective of diagnosis.
All patients from these two classes with affective and senile disorders
were treated first in private hospitals, as were 67 percent of the
alcoholics and 64 percent of the schizophrenics. The remaining
cases were treated first by private practitioners on an ambulatory
basis.

In class III, 80 percent of the affectives, 83 percent of the alcoholics, 100 percent of the seniles, but only 17 percent of the organics
were treated first in private hospitals. The remaining cases in each

diagnostic group were distributed among private practitioners and public agencies. Schizophrenics constituted the largest number of patients (58) with a psychiatric history. Sixty-two percent of this diagnostic group were treated first in private hospitals. Of the remaining 38 percent, 3 percent were treated by private practitioners, 16 percent in state hospitals, 10 percent in the military service, and 9 percent in clinics.

A few class IV affectives, schizophrenic, and senile patients were treated in private hospitals for a few weeks, but these patients comprise only 9 percent of the class IV psychotics. In class IV, irrespective of diagnosis, the state hospital is the predominant agency of first treatment.

State hospitals are *the* major treatment agency for all diagnostic groups in class V. More than 80 percent of each diagnostic group, with the exception of the alcoholics, first went to a state hospital; 65 percent of the alcoholics were treated first in state hospitals. Public clinics care for the remainder in all diagnostic groups.

The figures given in preceding paragraphs reveal clearly that class position determines where patients with psychotic disorders go for their treatment when the kind of illness they have is controlled. The private hospitals are used mainly by classes I and II, but in class III the use of Veterans Administration and state hospitals is notable. In classes IV and V the use of state facilities is the rule.

CURRENT TREATMENT. When we look at these patients, with diagnosis and class controlled, to see where they are being treated in their current illness, we find that private hospitals and private practitioners continue to be relied upon by classes I and II, but there is a definite shift from them to state and veterans hospitals. This is particularly true for schizophrenics who have been in treatment for long periods and whose families are not able to support them longer in private facilities. The impact of class position on a family with a psychotic member who needs to be re-hospitalized is shown dramatically in class III. In class III, from 83 percent to 100 percent of each diagnostic group originally treated in private hospitals shifted into other agencies in their current treatment. Almost all of these patients are now in state or veterans hospitals; a few are treated in clinics. The private hospitals are definitely institutions of first treatment for class III psychotic individuals irrespective of diagnosis.

In class IV, affective patients move from the clinics to the state hospitals between their first and current treatments. Patients with organic diseases shift from clinics to military hospitals and then into state hospitals. Schizophrenic patients exhibit two patterns: a shift from clinics into state hospitals and a move out of private hospitals into state hospitals. The private hospitals lost 95 percent of their class IV schizophrenic patients between the first and current treatments. All senile patients who were treated first in private hospitals are currently in state hospitals.

In class V, affective, organic, schizophrenic, and senile patients exhibit a marked shift from the clinics into the state hospitals. The state hospitals are the predominant agency for alcoholics at all times, but 40 percent are carried in public clinics upon re-entry into treatment.

The figures presented in the preceding paragraphs demonstrate that class is *the* important factor in the determination of where a patient with a chronic psychotic disorder is treated. State hospitals are the predominant agencies of current treatment for all diagnostic groups in class III, IV, and V; but in classes I and II private hospitals and private practitioners hold their positions as major treatment agencies between the first and current periods of treatment. Nevertheless, there are marked shifts from private hospitals into public agencies even in classes I and II.

Current Treatment Agency

Our discussion of where the psychotic patients are treated currently does not differentiate between those who have been in treatment at some previous time and those who are in treatment for the first time, because all are in treatment. The percentage of patients in each class who are cared for in each type of treatment center is symbolized in Figure 7. Figure 7 shows two things: first, the state hospitals are caring for the vast majority of psychotic patients, and, second, the several classes contribute distinctly different proportions to each agency.

Approximately 33 percent of the class I and II, 70 percent of the class III, 80 percent of the class IV, and over 90 percent of the class V psychotic patients are in the state hospitals. There is clearly a strong inverse relationship between class status and whether a psychotic patient is in the state hospitals. There is no significant relationship between class position and the proportion of patients in the Veterans Administration hospitals or the clinics. However, a direct relationship is found between class position and the distribu-

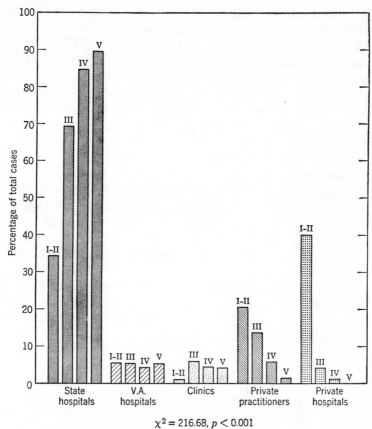

$$\chi^2 = 216.68, p < 0.001$$

(Class I–II and class III combined for the χ^2 analysis.)

Figure 7. Percentage of Psychotic Patients in Different Treatment Agencies—by Class.

tion of patients under the care of private practitioners and private hospitals.

The psychotic patients in a given class are distributed disproportionately between each of the five types of treatment agencies. More class I's and II's are treated in private hospitals than in any other agency (38 percent); the state hospitals are next with 33 percent; the private practitioners are third with 21 percent; 6 percent are cared for in Veterans Administration hospitals, and 2 percent in the clinics. Class III shows a very different distribution. Some 71 percent of the class III patients are cared for in the state hospitals; 14

percent are treated by private practitioners; 4 percent are in private hospitals; 5 percent are in clinics; and 5 percent in Veterans Administration hospitals. Eighty-five percent of the class IV's are cared for in state hospitals; 6 percent by private practitioners; and 4 percent are in Veterans Administration hospitals; 3 percent are in the clinics, and less than 1 percent in private hospitals. Ninety percent of the class V's are in state hospitals; none are in private hospitals; 1 percent are treated by private practitioners, 6 percent are in veterans hospitals, and 3 percent are seen in clinics.

The data summarized in Figure 7 shows that each agency draws its patients largely from selected portions of the population. Classes I and II are attracted to private hospitals and private practitioners. Class III goes to the state hospitals in much larger numbers than class II, but there is a marked tendency to turn to private practitioners and private hospitals. Class IV, in large part, uses the state hospitals, but a considerable number turn to private practitioners, veterans hospitals, and clinics. A few use private hospitals. Class V persons, for all practical purposes, have only two possibilities open to them—state and veterans hospitals. Only a relatively small proportion are eligible for Veterans Administration hospitals and thus the vast majority turn to state hospitals when a severe mental illness strikes.[15]

Treatment Agency, Class, and Diagnosis

We will now take the fourth of the steps listed at the beginning of this section relating to where the patients are treated. This step will examine the data with diagnosis held constant to determine if class is the important factor in the distribution of patients in each agency. Our tests of relationships between class and treatment agency within each of the five major diagnostic categories are summarized in Table 34. Each of the five parts of this table will be discussed separately.

AFFECTIVE DISORDERS. The 160 patients diagnosed as affectives are distributed unequally among the treatment agencies. Two distinct class gradients appear among these patients; first, the lower the class, the higher the percentage in state hospitals; and second, the higher the class, the greater the proportion treated in private agencies. Few affectives are treated in clinics and Veterans Administration hospitals.

ALCOHOLICS. The association of class status with agency of treatment is shown clearly among the alcoholics. The lower the class,

TABLE 34

Percentage Distribution of Psychotics in Different Agencies by Diagnosis
and by Class

Affectives

Treatment Agency	Class			
	I–II	III	IV	V
Public				
Clinic	0.0	0.0	0.0	2.1
V.A. hospital	9.1	0.0	1.2	0.0
State hospital	45.4	71.4	87.6	93.6
Private				
Practitioner	18.2	23.8	9.9	4.2
Hospital	27.3	4.8	1.2	0.0
$n =$	11	21	81	47

Alcoholics

Treatment Agency	Class			
	I–II	III	IV	V
Public				
Clinic	25.0	50.0	52.0	31.2
V.A. hospital	0.0	7.1	0.0	0.0
State hospital	0.0	28.6	40.0	66.7
Private				
Practitioner	75.0	14.3	8.0	2.1
Hospital	0.0	0.0	0.0	0.0
$n =$	4	14	25	48

Organics

Treatment Agency	Class			
	I–II	III	IV	V
Public				
Clinic	0.0	0.0	0.0	0.0
V.A. hospital	0.0	0.0	2.0	2.8
State hospital	50.0	83.3	92.1	95.4
Private				
Practitioner	0.0	16.7	5.9	1.8
Hospital	50.0	0.0	0.0	0.0
$n =$	2	12	51	109

TABLE 34 (*Continued*)

Percentage Distribution of Psychotics in Different Agencies by Diagnosis
and by Class

Schizophrenics

	Class			
Treatment Agency	I–II	III	IV	V
Public				
Clinic	0.0	1.2	1.7	1.0
V.A. hospital	6.9	8.4	6.8	8.9
State hospital	34.5	71.1	84.6	89.3
Private				
Practitioner	20.7	14.5	5.7	0.8
Hospital	37.9	4.8	1.1	0.0
$n =$	29	83	352	383

Senile

	Class			
Treatment Agency	I–II	III	IV	V
Public				
Clinic	0.0	0.0	0.0	0.0
V.A. hospital	0.0	0.0	0.0	0.0
State hospital	16.7	93.8	97.2	100.0
Private				
Practitioner	0.0	0.0	2.8	0.0
Hospital	83.3	6.2	0.0	0.0
$n =$	6	16	72	76

the greater the probability that an alcoholic patient will be cared for in the state hospital; the higher the class, the greater the tendency for alcoholics to be treated by private practitioners.[16] Patients cared for in the clinics are predominantly classes III and IV, but one third of the class V's are treated in clinics. No alcoholic is treated in a private hospital.

ORGANIC DISORDERS. Psychotic patients whose disorders are attributed to an organic illness are treated, in large part, in the state hospitals. Those who are not in the state hospitals tend to be cared for by private practitioners. The lower the class, the smaller the proportion of organic patients treated by private practitioners.

SCHIZOPHRENICS. No association exists between class position and the percentage of schizophrenic patients treated in either the clinics or the Veterans Administration hospitals. The other treatment agencies exhibit distinct class gradients. The state hospital reveals a strong inverse relationship between class position and the percentage of schizophrenics under its care. On the other hand, private practitioners and private hospitals show direct relationships between class position and the proportion of schizophrenics they are treating.

SENILES. This diagnostic group reveals the characteristic inverse relationship between class position and commitment to state hospitals. Some 6 out of 7 class I and II senile patients are in private hospitals, but in class III only 1 out of 16 is in a private hospital; in class IV 97 percent and in class V 100 percent are in state hospitals.

The series of analyses presented in Table 34 demonstrate clearly that class status is a determining factor of where most psychotic patients are treated, irrespective of the kind of psychotic disorder. Speaking generally, the lower the class, the greater the probability that a psychotic patient will be treated in the state hospital, and if not in the state hospital, in a clinic, irrespective of the diagnosis the psychiatrist makes of his illness. This is what we might expect on theoretical grounds, because disturbed individuals are taken to the kind of agency available to them. Class I and II persons look to private practitioners and private hospitals for help. Class III persons prefer private practitioners and private hospitals, and attempt to be treated in these agencies, but their resources are so limited they soon turn to public agencies. The clinics and veterans hospitals are preferred over the state hospital, but many persons who prefer private practitioners and private hospitals are discouraged from using these agencies, both because of the high cost and the attitudes they encounter in them. Class V persons must turn to public agencies, and the state hospital is their major reliance when psychiatric illness strikes. They both fear and hate the "loony bin," but no other resource is open to them.

PSYCHIATRIC THERAPIES AND THE PSYCHOSES

The psychiatric therapies administered to the psychotic patients represent the *how* dimension of the treatment process. We will begin our analysis of this dimension of treatment by ignoring status. We will focus attention first on diagnosis and psychiatric therapies to learn if they are associated with one another. If we find that diagnosis is related to therapy, diagnosis must be controlled in the analyses where relations between class status and the kinds of ther-

apy are tested. Otherwise, possible linkages between class status and
the kinds of therapy prescribed may be confounded by the diagnosis.

The data in Table 35 show that diagnosis is related in highly significant ways to the kind of therapy the psychotic patients receive.

TABLE 35

Percentage of Psychotic Patients in Specified Diagnostic Groups Receiving a
Principal Type of Psychiatric Therapy

Diagnostic Group	Psycho-therapy	Organic Therapy	Custodial Care	n
Affective psychoses	18.8	63.8	17.5	160
Alcoholic psychoses	52.7	25.3	22.0	91
Organic psychoses	10.9	46.0	43.1	174
Schizophrenic psychoses	14.3	40.6	45.1	847
Senile psychoses	10.6	6.5	82.9	170

$$\chi^2 = 228.53, p < .001$$

In actual practice, psychotherapy is administered to relatively few
psychotic patients except for the subcategory of alcoholics. Organic therapy is the most widely used treatment for affective and
organic psychoses. Custodial care is given to the vast majority of
senile psychotic patients but more custodial care is administered to
schizophrenics than any other type of treatment; of course, we must
remember that we studied "treated" prevalence with a large accumulation of chronic patients. The strong association between diagnosis and principal type of therapy indicates that diagnosis must be
controlled when we look for linkages between class status and the
principal types of therapy prescribed for patients.

By holding diagnostic group constant, we can determine if class
position is associated in significant ways with the therapies patients
receive within each diagnostic group. The data necessary to test
this idea are presented in Table 36. A brief look at the findings for
each diagnostic group in Table 36 shows the following things:

Affectives do not reveal a significant relationship between class
position and the principal forms of therapy administered to them.
Psychotherapy, either individual or group, is a minor treatment,
whereas organic therapy is given to the majority of patients in all
classes. Custodial care does show a class gradient, but the number
of patients involved is too small for significance.

Alcoholics demonstrate a significant relationship between class position and the type of therapy administered. In classes I and II, all
patients receive individual psychotherapy; there is no essential dif-

TABLE 36

Principal Type of Therapy in Different Diagnostic and Class Groups, in Percent

Affectives

Type of Therapy	Class			
	I–II *	III	IV	V
Psychotherapy	18.2	23.6	19.8	12.8
Organic therapy	72.7	66.7	63.0	61.7
Custodial care	9.1	9.7	17.3	25.5
$n =$	11	21	81	47

$$\chi^2 = 5.83, 4 \ df, p > .05$$

Alcoholics

Type of Therapy	Class			
	I–II *	III	IV	V
Psychotherapy	100.0	71.4	72.0	33.0
Organic therapy	0.0	21.4	24.0	29.2
Custodial care	0.0	7.1	4.0	37.8
$n =$	4	14	25	48

$$\chi^2 = 19.20, 4 \ df, p < .001$$

Organics

Type of Therapy	Class			
	I–II *	III	IV	V
Psychotherapy	0.0	27.3	11.3	9.2
Organic therapy	50.0	36.4	47.2	46.3
Custodial care	50.0	36.4	41.5	44.4
$n =$	2	11	53	108

$$\chi^2 = 2.43, 4 \ df, p > .05$$

Schizophrenics

Type of Therapy	Class			
	I–II	III	IV	V
Psychotherapy	51.7	20.5	15.3	9.1
Organic therapy	24.1	48.2	47.7	33.7
Custodial care	24.1	31.3	36.9	57.2
$n =$	29	83	352	383

$$\chi^2 = 74.53, 6 \ df, p < .001$$

TABLE 36 (*Continued*)

Principal Type of Therapy in Different Diagnostic and Class Groups, in Percent

Seniles

Class

Type of Therapy	I–II *	III	IV	V
Psychotherapy	50.0	18.8	8.3	7.9
Organic therapy	0.0	12.5	4.2	7.9
Custodial care	50.0	68.8	87.5	84.2
$n =$	6	16	72	76

$$\chi^2 = 9.08, 4 \ df, p > .05$$

* Classes I–II combined with III in χ^2 analysis.

ference between classes III and IV, but only one third of the class V's receive it. Organic therapy is given to about the same proportion of the patients from class III through class V. Custodial care is concentrated largely in class V.

Patients with organic disorders do not exhibit any association between class status and the prescribed forms of therapy.

Schizophrenic patients show a clear-cut association between class position and the types of therapy they receive. The mode is psychotherapy or custodial care in classes I and II, organic therapy in classes III and IV, and custodial care in class V.

Senile patients do not show a significant relationship between class status and type of therapy administered, but class I–II patients tend to receive more psychotherapy than the lower status patients. Custodial care is the lot of the vast majority of the old people in classes IV and V.

The highly significant relationship between class position and the type of therapy prescribed for alcoholics and schizophrenics may be related to treatment agencies as well as to class status. To learn which of these possible factors is responsible, both diagnosis and treatment agency will be controlled in the next test of *Hypothesis 3* which stated that the *kind* of *psychiatric treatment* administered is associated with the patient's position in the class structure.

Treatment Agency, Diagnosis, Type of Therapy, and Class

Hypothesis 3 can be tested stringently by holding both diagnosis and treatment agency constant and making comparisons between class position and the principal form of therapy prescribed for patients. Unfortunately, from the perspective of statistical methodology, when the data are analyzed with treatment agency, diagnosis, principal form of therapy, and class position interacting, the number of patients in any one cell of the tables is too small for reliability.[17] To meet this problem, we grouped treatment agencies into three categories: (1) private practitioners and private hospitals, (2) clinics, and (3) public hospitals. The data on patients in each of these groups of treatment agencies were then analyzed with diagnosis held constant. The findings on this series of analyses are presented in subsequent paragraphs.

Private Practitioners and Private Hospitals

No significant relationship appears between class position and the principal forms of therapy administered by private agencies in any diagnostic group. This finding is a product of three sets of factors: First, practically no class V psychotics are treated by private practitioners and none are treated in private hospitals. Second, patients treated by private practitioners, irrespective of their class position, tend to receive individual psychotherapy. Custodial care is not applicable to the patients of private practitioners. Third, the patients treated in private hospitals and by private practitioners represent a relatively narrow range of class positions. These considerations practically eliminate the possibility of a significant relationship between class position, diagnostic group, and the type of therapy administered. In sum, if a class I, II, or III psychotic patient is treated in a private agency, irrespective of his diagnosis, he is likely to receive individual psychotherapy. Nevertheless, 14 percent of the affectives and 27 percent of the schizophrenics in private facilities are treated by an organic therapy. This is of interest because current psychiatric folklore holds that organic therapy, especially electro-convulsive therapies, are significantly helpful in many of the affective disorders; the same body of theory denies that there is a similar degree of benefit by any known therapy except possibly prolonged intensive psychotherapy for the schizophrenic psychoses. Incidentally, only two thirds of the schizophrenics but 76 percent of the affective patients in these agencies are being treated by psychotherapy. In each disorder, psychotherapy is concentrated in classes I, II, and III; both diagnosis and therapeutic theory are subordinate to class position.

Clinics

So few psychotic patients are treated in the clinics that no reliable statement can be made about interrelationships among diagnostic groups, therapy, and class position. No seniles or organics, and only one affective, are treated here. The 11 schizophrenics treated in the clinics all receive psychotherapy. Of the 36 alcoholics treated in the clinic, 34 receive individual psychotherapy, and the remaining 2 receive an organic therapy.

Public Hospitals

Schizophrenic patients are the only psychotic group large enough (60 percent of all psychotics in public hospitals) to enable us to test *Hypothesis 3* with both diagnosis and treatment agency controlled. Nevertheless, so few of the schizophrenic patients are in classes I and II (1.5 percent) that patients in these classes have to be combined with class III in the chi square tests. This requirement increases the severity of the test of assumed relationships between class status and the kind of treatment prescribed for the patients. If significant relationships do appear between class status and the principal form of psychiatric therapy prescribed, we may conclude that class position is a true variable operating in the treatment process within the public hospitals in the one diagnostic group that is large enough to enable us to analyze the data with some measure of reliability.

Table 37 shows that a significant association does exist between class position and the type of therapy prescribed for schizophrenic

TABLE 37

Principal Form of Therapy Administered to Schizophrenic Patients in State and Veterans Administration Hospitals—Percentage by Class

	Class			
Type of Therapy	I–II *	III	IV	V
Psychotherapy	16.7	12.1	9.6	8.5
Organic therapy	25.0	53.6	50.6	33.8
Custodial care	58.3	34.3	39.8	57.7
$n =$	12	66	322	376

$$\chi^2 = 27.14, 4 \; df, \; p < .001$$

* Classes I–II were combined with class III in the computation of χ^2.

patients in the public hospitals. Only a small proportion of the schizophrenic patients receive psychotherapy but the class I–II patients receive it twice as frequently as the class V patients. The proportion receiving organic therapy varies unevenly from class II to class V with classes III and IV receiving more than the adjacent classes. On the other hand, custodial care is prescribed for the highest proportion of the cases in classes I–II and in class V. The reader should remember there are only seven persons in class I–II, whereas there are 217 in class V. Moreover, every class I–II patient has been ill for a long time and has experienced two or more previous hospitalizations. All these patients are "burned out." The state hospital is indeed the "end of the road" for them. By way of contrast, 64 percent of the patients in class V who are receiving custodial care have had no previous treatment.

Additional Tests

After the significant relationship between class position and the types of therapy prescribed for schizophrenic patients in the public hospitals was found, we made an additional series of analyses to see if the association between class position and the principal type of therapy found for the total group would hold for selected subgroups. In these analyses, we held constant sex, age, psychiatric history, and the number of years since first psychiatric contact.

It was found that the significant linkage between class position and the type of therapy administered held for (1) males and females separately and (2) age within each sex with a particularly significant relationship between class position and the type of therapy administered to males and females between 35 and 54 years of age. Significant relationships exist also for patients who have had a previous course of psychiatric treatment as well as for those who are in treatment for the first time. Finally, the significant association between class status and therapy holds for patients who have been in treatment from less than one year to fifteen years. After fifteen years of treatment there is no significant difference from one class to another. Practically all patients who have been in a hospital this long are on chronic wards where custodial care is the prevailing type of treatment.

It is of interest to note that in classes III, IV, and V there is a higher percentage of cases in treatment for the first time receiving custodial care than there is among the patients who have been hospitalized previously. This series of analyses reaffirmed the finding that class status influences in real ways the kind of psychiatric therapy schizophrenic patients receive in public hospitals.[18]

DURATION OF TREATMENT

It is difficult, if not impossible, to determine the time at which a mental illness develops even if a detailed history is available. This is true especially of the neuroses. In the psychoses, when the onset appears to be acute, many acts and symptoms may foreshadow the dramatic event that calls attention to the disturbed person. These may cover a number of years, but this fact can only be established when anamnesis is sufficiently detailed, and detailed clinical material has been collected on the patient. The kinds of data gathered in the Psychiatric Census do not enable us to estimate how long the patients were ill before they entered treatment. However, we did collect information on (1) the number of courses of treatment each patient had experienced, (2) the length of treatment in each episode, (3) whether the treatment was ambulatory or in a hospital, and (4) the amount of time that elapsed between each course of psychiatric treatment. We will draw upon this information to see if there is an association between class position and (1) re-entry into treatment among the psychotic patients and (2) the number of years the psychotic patients have been under the care of psychiatrists.

Experiences in Treatment and Class

The definitions used here are different from those given in Chapters Seven and Eight. A re-entry into treatment always follows a discharge from an earlier course of treatment both as used here and earlier. However, for present purposes, a re-entry into treatment is applicable to any patient with a previous history of psychiatric treatment who experienced a remission of symptoms for more than a year, then re-entered treatment. This could have occurred years before, not just in the six months of observation discussed in Chapters Seven and Eight. A patient who has been in continuous treatment since his first contact with a psychiatrist has, by definition, never experienced a re-entry into treatment. These patients are categorized as continuous, irrespective of how long they have been in treatment. A "short remission" is a period of less than one year between two or more periods of psychiatric care.

When the psychotic patients' experiences with treatment agencies were divided into these three categories and then subdivided by diagnosis, only schizophrenics showed a significant association between class position and re-entry into treatment. The findings for the schizophrenics are given in Table 38. A sharp inverse relationship exists between class status and continuous care from the date the schizophrenic patients entered treatment to the present. Both short remissions and re-entry cases show gradients sloping in the opposite direction. The percentage of class I–II schizophrenics who

TABLE 38

Percentage of Schizophrenic Patients in Each Class Who Have or Have Not Re-entered Treatment *

	Class			
Type of History	I–II	III	IV	V
Continuous case	15.4	32.0	37.9	56.3
Short remission (one or more)	46.2	35.9	35.0	20.4
Re-entry (one or more)	38.4	32.0	27.1	23.3
$n =$	26	78	343	378

$$\chi^2 = 44.48, 6 \; df, \; p < .001$$

* Only patients whose treatment history is known are included.

have had at least one short remission is more than twice as high as in class V. The same trend holds for the re-entry into treatment cases, but the differences are not as great from one class to another.

From the findings in Table 38, we may infer that schizophrenics in the higher classes shuttle in and out of treatment more frequently than those in the lower classes. This inference is confirmed by an examination of the number of courses of treatment schizophrenic patients in the several classes have experienced. The mean for each class is:

Class	Re-entry into Treatment
I–II	3.9
III	2.6
IV	2.1
V	0.6

This tabulation reveals that the lower the class, the greater the tendency for schizophrenic patients to be kept under psychiatric care without remission of symptoms. In the case of class V persons, this means state hospital care largely at public expense. A class V schizophrenic may be discharged from treatment once, and about half these patients experience this, but if he is returned to the hospital, the chances are very high that he will remain there indefinitely. We believe that this is one of the outstanding findings of this study. When it is connected, on the one hand, with the data on components in prevalence for the psychoses discussed in Chapter Eight and, on the other, with the material we will present in the next section on the length of time psychotic patients have been in their *present courses* of treatment, one can begin to understand why there has been a constant increase in the number of patients in public mental hospitals as the years have passed.

YEARS IN TREATMENT AND CLASS

The length of time the psychotic patients have been continuously under the care of psychiatrists is related to class status. This generalization is applicable to each diagnostic group. However, the affectives differ markedly from the other diagnostic categories in the following two respects. First, the patients in class I and II are older than patients in the other classes and second, there is wide variability in the length of time they have been in treatment. After the adjustment of the class means for differences in present age by the use of covariance analysis,[19] the mean duration in years of treatment ranges from 7.3 in classes I–II to 4.2 in class V. The other psychotic groups reveal a consistent inverse relationship between class status and the length of time they have been in treatment. This linkage between class position and duration of treatment is symbolized by the several curves shown in Figure 8.

Class I and II alcoholics have been in treatment for two years but the average class V alcoholic has been in treatment for five years. This is a mean difference of three years. Although the schizophrenics have been in treatment longer than the other diagnostic groups, the class V's have been under the care of psychiatrists much longer than the higher classes. The means adjusted by covariance analysis for class differences in age are 10.5 years in classes I and II, and 15.2 years in class V. This is a difference of almost 5 years. Classes III and IV have means that fall between those of classes I and II on the one hand and class V on the other. The consistent differences in the means of the several diagnostic categories may be attributed to the differential impact of class status on psychotic patients irrespective of the diagnoses psychiatrists make of their disorders.

CLASS AND YEARS IN TREATMENT

The differential impact of class status on the mentally ill members of the community who are under the care of psychiatrists for the

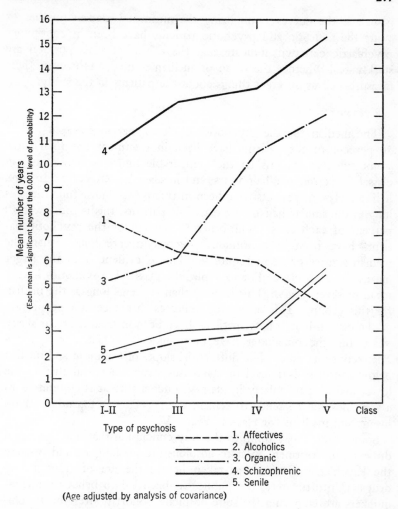

Figure 8. The Mean Number of Years Different Types of Psychotic Patients Have Been in Their Present Course of Treatment.

first time is depicted trenchantly in Figure 9. The curves in Figure 9 reveal that the number of years both the neurotic and psychotic patients have been in their present courses of treatment is linked to class status. However, the class gradient runs in opposite directions in these diagnostic groups. Among the neurotic patients, the higher the class, the longer the patients have been in treatment. The opposite association prevails among the psychotic patients; that is, the lower the class, the longer the patients have been in treatment. A glance at the curves symbolizing the mean and median number of years the neurotic and psychotic patients have been in continuous psychiatric care will indicate that the effects of class position are starkly real whether the mean or median is used. However, these measures tell us different things about the patients in the study.

Psychotics

The median for the psychotics discloses that in classes I and II 50 percent of the patients have been in treatment less than three years, whereas in class III the comparable figure is four years; in class IV, six and one-half years; and in class V, ten years. In sum, half the class V patients have been in treatment almost four times as long as the similar half of the class I–II patients; this is the lower 50 percent of each class. The other 50 percent of the psychotic patients have been in continuous psychiatric care longer than the median figures given in Figure 9. This is evident from the larger means for each class. For example, the class I–II psychotics have a mean of seven years. This is more than twice as long as the median for this group. This difference indicates that a certain proportion of the class I–II psychotic patients have been in treatment for many years, but the remainder have been under psychiatric care for a relatively short time. The differential slopes of the mean and median below the class I–II level of the status structure reveal that in the lower classes, particularly in class V, once a patient is committed to a state hospital he tends to remain there. This fact produces high means and medians for classes IV and V.

Some readers may jump to the easy conclusion that our figures on duration of treatment in state hospitals are no longer valid because the Psychiatric Census was taken before the era of tranquilizing drugs. Unfortunately, the public has been led to believe the tranquilizers are emptying the state hospitals. Shortly after the Psychiatric Census was completed we selected a random sample of 100 state hospital patients in their first course of treatment for follow-up purposes. These patients were followed until March 1, 1956, or for five years and four months after the Psychiatric Census was taken. Of the 100 patients, 54 were still in the hospital when the field work ended; 30 had died in the hospital, and 16 had been discharged. The 54 patients still in the hospital five years and four months after the Psychiatric Census date had been there a long time. When the follow-up stopped, the mean number of years these patients had been in continuous psychiatric care was: classes I through III—14, class

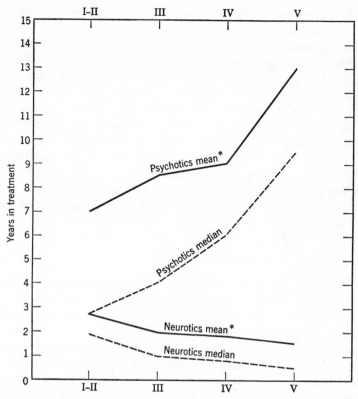

*Mean years in treatment are significant, $p < 0.001$.

Figure 9. Mean and Median Number of Years Neurotic and Psychotic Patients Have Been in Their Present Course of Treatment—by Class.

IV—18, class V—22.5. The experiences of these patients during the present years of the "tranquilizing era" do not lead to the conclusion either that the new drugs are emptying the state hospitals, nor that the class differences in duration of treatment are growing shorter with the passage of the years.

Neurotics

The duration of treatment curves for the neurotic patients are not as dramatic as are those for the psychotic patients. Nevertheless, the differences in the length of time the neurotics have been under psychiatric care are highly significant. The mean in class I–II is 33 months. It declines rather consistently to 18 months in class V. The median shows greater variation from one class to another; it is 23 months in class I–II, but only six months in class V. The differences in the mean and median measure the tendency of patients to remain in treatment or to drop out of it. In classes I–II, the neurotic patients remain in treatment much longer than in classes III and IV. The vast majority of the class I–II neurotic patients are in ambulatory treatment with private psychiatrists. On the other hand, the class V neurotics are either clinic patients or they have been committed to the state hospital. Those treated in the clinics tend to drop out of treatment shortly after they begin, but the neurotics in the state hospital tend to be retained in hospital indefinitely. These counter trends result in the relatively large disparity between the mean and the median figures below the class II level. The fact that class V patients receive less treatment unfortunately does not mean that they are cured.

SUMMARY AND CONCLUSIONS

This chapter has been focused on a series of tests of the proposition that class status is a significant factor in the treatment of mentally ill patients. We have found real differences in *where, how,* and *how long* persons in the several classes have been cared for by psychiatrists. The many statistical tests made, even under the most rigid controls, demonstrate the validity of *Hypothesis 3.*

The data presented lead to the conclusion that treatment for mental illness depends not only on medical and psychological considerations, but also on powerful social variables to which psychiatrists have so far given little attention. It is certainly true that not enough psychiatrists are trained to handle patients in the way good psychotherapy prescribes, and that the process of psychotherapy in particular is complex, not easily mastered, and inevitably costly. This cost, as we will show in Chapter Ten, with the exception of a few clinics, is assumed only rarely by third parties for those who cannot afford to pay themselves. Here, however, we want to point out that we controlled economic factors by dealing with treatment agencies separately and still found that distinct class differences prevail within agencies. Psychotherapeutic methods and particularly insight therapy are applied in disproportionately high degrees to higher status neurotic patients being treated by private practitioners. Organic therapies tend to be applied most often to neurotics in classes III and IV. Among the psychotic patients treatment differences among classes are most marked for the schizophrenics contributing, in no small part, to the large number of chronic patients in class V who remain in state hospitals year after year. Class as a factor in the length of treatment is also marked in the affective disorders. The bulk of these patients receive organic therapy, that is, electro-convulsive treatment. This suggests that if, for a given disorder, there is a treatment available which is relatively effective, inexpensive, and technically simple, class differences may be reduced, but not eliminated.

This lack of availability becomes enhanced when the social and cultural backgrounds of the patients differ from that of the psychiatrists. This should not be interpreted to mean that the lower class patients are not able to participate in or benefit from any kind of psychotherapy, but we believe that obstacles which have their roots in certain aspects of the social structure are quite formidable. Such practice is not just a social injustice; even if the lower class patient were to be given the same opportunity, much effort in research and therapy will have to be exerted before the situation will change. It is deeply rooted in certain habits of therapist and patient and their social value systems. A number of lower status patients are treated in mental hygiene clinics and in hospitals of the Veterans Administration. Yet we have serious doubts that the application of insight therapy to patients is effective unless considerable modifications of therapeutic techniques are undertaken. Any changes in technique and orientation must consider the phenomenology and dynamics of social stratification. Finally, on the basis of our data, we think that new approaches are indicated in order to bring psychotherapy to lower class patients with mental and emotional disorders. This may point to group therapy, new techniques for certain groups, such as adolescents and children, and the use of less expensive personnel, such as social workers and clinical psychologists in carrying out certain aspects of psychological intervention, for which they are trained.

We wish to reiterate that value differences between high status psychiatrists and lower status patients are a serious obstacle in psychotherapy, even if psychiatrists were to widen their cultural and social horizons and learn to understand the class IV and V patient. The mere suggestion of the existence of such a bias may offend psychiatrists who, like most professional practitioners, do not like to think in terms of social differences. Nevertheless, a number of different social and cultural factors operate on the psychiatrist, the patient, his family, and the community to produce the relationships reported here. Relevant factors include differential evaluation of psychiatrists by different classes, the attitudes of patients toward psychiatrists, and the ability of the persons in various classes to pay for psychiatric care. Another major factor is the different ways members of the several classes conceive of the nature and treatment of mental disorders. Finally, differing perceptions create communication problems for both the doctor and the patient. Needless to say, the practices we have highlighted in the preceding tables and charts are not the result of deliberate policy, but the unanticipated consequences of complex and tacit sociocultural and psychosocial processes of expectancies and role assignments. Powerful social processes keep many psychotic patients, particularly schizophrenics, in public mental hospitals; neither the family and community nor the hospital facilitate rehabilitation. However, they substantiate the assumption we built into the research design, namely, that latent social factors besides claimed medical criteria are influential in the determination of who is treated *where, how* and for *how long.* We will return to these sociocultural factors in Chapter Eleven.

NOTES

[1] Felix Deutsch, *Applied Psychoanalysis,* Grune and Stratton, New York, 1949.

[2] Verbal communication by Eugen Kahn.

[3] In medical terminology, any therapy that is not based upon some theoretical system is referred to as "empirical."

[4] For principal form of therapy and race, $\chi^2 = 2.743$, 2 df, $p > .05$; for principal form of therapy and sex, $\chi^2 = 4.731$, 2 df, $p > .05$; for principal form of therapy and age, $\chi^2 = 7.677$, df 8, $p > .05$; and for principal form of therapy and a history of previous psychiatric treatment, $\chi^2 = 3.660$, 2 df, $p > .05$.

[5] A comparison of first and current treatment by public versus private agencies in class I–II gave a $\chi^2 = 5.46$, 1 df, $p < .05$.

[6] $\chi^2 = 15.40$, $p < .01$, 4 df, for class III.

[7] $\chi^2 = 42.34$, $p < .01$, 3 df, for class IV.

[8] $\chi^2 = 9.38$, $p < .05$, 3 df, for class V.

[9] $\chi^2 = 86.075$, 4 df, $p < .001$.

[10] This is a heritage from the Freudian practice of scheduling appointments an hour apart.

[11] $\chi^2 = 25.523$, 4 df, $p < .001$.

[12] $\chi^2 = 10.56$, 4 df, $p < .05$.

[13] See Jerome K. Myers and Leslie Schaffer, "Social Stratification and Psychiatric Practice," *American Sociological Review,* Vol. 19 (June 1954), pp. 307–310.

[14] $\chi^2 = 17.503$, 6 df, $p < .01$.

[15] The distribution of psychotic patients in the different treatment agencies by class depicted in Figure 7 are given in Table 7 of Appendix 4, p. 419.

[16] The one class II patient treated in the state alcoholic clinic had been treated by a private practitioner for a number of years; when his funds were exhausted he had turned to the clinic.

[17] The data referred to here are included in Table 9, Appendix 4, pp. 421–423.

[18] $\chi^2 = 8.61$, 2 df, $p < .05$. In the preceding chi square, classes III and IV were combined and compared with class V. (1) Affectives: the type of therapy administered to affective patients is not related to class status. However, two points need to be considered in evaluating this finding. First, the major form of therapy is organic treatment, and there are only seven affective patients in classes I and II. Second, custodial care is increasingly frequent in classes IV and V, but the numbers are too small for significance. (2) Organics: The therapy administered to organic patients is not associated with class status, but only two class II and nine class III organics are in public hospitals. Therefore, comparisons of the types of therapy are limited to classes IV and V. (3) Seniles: Among senile patients no significant relationship exists between class status and the principal form of therapy, because the vast majority of senile patients simply receive custodial care. Their organic needs are cared for while they wait for time to take its toll of them. (4) Alcoholics: A significant relationship exists between class status and the type of therapy administered to alcoholics, even though only classes III, IV, and V are represented. Forty percent of the class III's are given psychotherapy, but only 9 percent of the class V's. On the other hand, only 20 percent of the class III's are given custodial care, but 56 percent of the class V's receive it.

[19] Analyses of variance and covariance were used as more appropriate tests of significance of the length of treatment than chi square, because they enable us to deal with time in treatment as a variable controlled by using covariance whenever there are (1) marked class differences in the distribution of present age and (2) sizeable intraclass correlations between age and the duration of treatment.

expenditures
on treatment

chapter ten

INTRODUCTION

This chapter is focused on providing an answer to two general questions: (1) How much does psychiatric treatment cost? (2) Are expenditures on psychiatric care linked to the class status of the patients? Every person who has experienced a severe illness in his family knows that medical treatment is expensive. Mental illness is particularly expensive because of the chronic nature of emotional and mental disturbances. In spite of the importance of the problem, there is little known about the economic burden of mental illness on the population as a whole or to individuals and families. Moreover, no systematic studies have been made to determine the connection between class status and expenditures on the treatment of the mentally ill.

Computation of the over-all costs of psychiatric illnesses ought to encompass at least ten different kinds of economic burden, each calling for an expenditure that must be borne by someone—the patient's family or public or private agencies—and each should be charged to the cost of mental illness. These direct and indirect costs include:

(1) *The amounts spent for practitioners, treatments, and medicines during the preclinical phase of a mental illness,* such as the sum paid

to a gynecologist by a neurotic female for treatment of a condition which is emotional rather than organic

(2) *Legal costs,* which enter the picture when a mentally disturbed individual is arrested, jailed, tried in court, and, in due course, committed to a mental institution

(3) *The cost of property damage or attack* on other persons committed by a disturbed individual

(4) *Capital expenditures* on mental hospitals, clinics, and other treatment agencies which need to be computed and amortized on a per patient basis

(5) *The costs of training personnel* directly or indirectly engaged in patient care, including psychiatrists, psychiatric nurses, psychiatric social workers, research personnel, technicians, and attendants, and the cost of research

(6) *The cost of home or nonpsychiatric institutional care* which does not include any psychiatric therapy for mentally disturbed individuals

(7) *The effects of mental illness on productivity* (which ought to take into consideration the possible inefficiency of a patient for a considerable time before he becomes too ill to work at his accustomed job), the effects of an ill person in an organization on his associates, and even the difficulties created for a person who is working by a disturbed individual not in the labor force, as, for example, an ill wife

(8) *The care of dependents* during a patient's illness

(9) *Expenditures of re-establishing the patient* in his family, his social group, and his job after release from a mental hospital

(10) *The direct cost* of psychiatric treatment.

The data and discussion in this chapter are confined to *the direct costs* of psychiatric care and treatment, because the calculation of the over-all costs of mental illness can be achieved only in a study where close cooperation continues over a long span of time between diverse persons and institutions. The difficulties of collecting data on direct expenditures in caring for mentally ill persons forces us to limit our interests to a single aspect of the general problem of the costs of mental illness in the New Haven community.

TREATMENT COSTS

Sources of the Data on Expenditures on Treatment

The data on costs of treatment were gathered in four separate ways: a private practitioner's schedule, a clinic schedule, a private hospital schedule, and a state hospital schedule. These schedules were designed to supplement the Psychiatric Census. When the information gathered on each schedule was collated, we were able to determine the costs of treatment in different kinds of agencies and who pays for it. In addition, we were able to calculate such items as how much of the daily cost of in-patient care is spent on therapy, how much on board and room, and what portion of the costs of a clinic patient's treatment is paid for by the patient or by others.

Cost per Unit in Different Agencies

The mean dollar cost of one unit of treatment in each type of treatment agency during 1950 is the basic figure used to calculate expenditures on treatment. We define a unit of treatment as one day of in-patient care in a mental hospital or one treatment administered by a psychiatrist to an ambulatory patient.

The cost of one day of patient care in each state hospital is computed biennially by the state comptroller's office.[1] The cost of one unit of treatment in the veterans hospitals is a simple arithmetic average for the net costs of maintaining one patient one day in the neuropsychiatric hospitals of the Veterans Administration from which we collected cases. It was calculated from the net per day costs of in-patient care regularly computed by the Veterans Administration for each hospital in the system. The daily in-patient costs in veteran and state hospitals are based on "total ordinary recurring expenses." They include expenditures for housing, feeding, and caring for the patients, maintenance of the hospitals, and medical, surgical, and psychiatric treatment. They do not include the original costs of the plants or replacement costs amortized on a daily per patient basis.

The cost of one day of patient care in private hospitals was computed from detailed financial data furnished by hospitals where 94 percent of the privately hospitalized patients are treated. All types of current expenditures reported by the hospitals are included in the total figure used to compute the mean daily cost per patient. This includes the expenditures for salaries, upkeep of the plant, food, and even such items as limousine service, facial massages, and other services provided for the patients. If the original cost of the plants and amortization of them were included, the mean costs per patient day would be higher than those we report.

The cost of a unit of treatment in the clinics was computed by dividing the total reported costs of operating the clinics during 1950 by the number of therapeutic visits they reported their patients had made during the year. The dollar costs per treatment for patients carried in private practice were computed from data furnished by psychiatrists who treated 95 percent of the private patients. As such, it is comparable to the figure for the cost per visit in the clinics.

The mean cost per unit of treatment in each type of agency presented in Table 39 is computed without consideration of social variables. It is strictly a dollar figure, and, as such, it is applicable to

TABLE 39

Mean Dollar Expenditures for One Unit of Treatment in Different Agencies

Daily Costs for Hospitalized Patients

State hospitals	$ 2.70
Veterans hospitals	7.85
Private hospitals	29.04

Costs per Treatment for Ambulatory Patients

Public clinics	$12.29
Private practitioners	15.28

every patient in each type of agency. For computational purposes, we assume that the costs of a single unit of treatment is the same for a paranoid schizophrenic as for a senile with a simple deterioration regardless of the class of the patient. Moreover, no consideration is given to the question of who pays the bill. Ignoring social factors enables us to apply the cost of a unit of treatment in each agency to all patients in the agency irrespective of class position or diagnostic group. Thus, the mean cost of a unit of treatment is a standard measure. It is used as a yardstick to determine if expenditures on treatment are linked to class position.

Estimates of Treatment Costs

The figures presented in the following pages are estimates of how much is expended on the average patient in different classes, agencies, and diagnostic groups. Each figure is computed by multiplying the cost of one treatment unit in a given type of agency by the number of known treatment units administered to each patient in the agency in a given period of time. For example, a clinic patient may have received seventeen units of treatment from the time he became a patient until the Psychiatric Census was taken. The computed estimate of his treatment costs to that time would be $12.29 × 17 = $208.93. These seventeen treatments may have been administered over a 15-month period. All these treatment units would be included in the total estimated expenditure on his treatment. However, only those administered between December 1, 1949 and November 30, 1950 would be included in the estimate of treatment costs for 1950. Multiplication of the mean cost per treatment unit by the number of known treatment units administered to patients in the different types of treatment agencies between December 1, 1949 and November 30, 1950 enabled us to estimate the amount of money expended on treatment in each class and diagnostic group in one year. Where treatment was received in more than one agency the expenditures were allocated according to the amount of treatment the patient had received.

Estimates of the total known expenditures on treatment in the patient population were computed by extrapolation. In this procedure, the mean cost of a unit of treatment in 1950 was multiplied by the number of treatments each patient was known to have received in each type of agency throughout the history of his illness. More detail will be given on this procedure in the section in which total estimated expenditures on treatment are discussed. Cost estimates were computed separately for each type of agency and class, as well as other appropriate subcategories, for example, diagnosis, but for purposes of presentation they are grouped into public and private agencies in some tables; in others, only the total figures are given.

EXPENDITURES ON TREATMENT IN 1950

Estimates on the costs of treatment in the patient population during 1950 are presented from four points of view: (1) the mean cost per patient, (2) the magnitude of the treatment bill, (3) the cost per capita, and (4) the effect of diagnosis on treatment costs. The factor of class is held constant in all analyses, and in most analyses comparisons are made between private and public agencies. Data to illumine each of these facets of the problem will be given and discussed in the foregoing order.

Expenditures per Patient

Are expenditures on treatment related to class position when diagnosis and treatment agency are controlled? The answer is given in the data summarized in Table 40. Examination of this table will

TABLE 40

Mean Expenditures per Patient for Neurotics and Psychotics in Private and Public Agencies—by Class

	Neurotics		
Class	Private Agencies	Public Agencies	Total
I–II	$2,564	$200	$2,765
III	1,688	370	2,059
IV	1,038	807	1,844
V	53	903	956
Total	$1,404	$576	$1,979

	Psychotics		
Class	Private Agencies	Public Agencies	Total
I–II	$3,477	$ 514	$3,961
III	630	1,074	1,704
IV	154	1,193	1,347
V	13	1,276	1,289
Total	$ 256	$1,195	$1,450

show six different sets of figures, three for neurotics and three for psychotics. Each set will be discussed separately.

We will focus attention first on expenditures by class for neurotic patients in private versus public agencies. A strong inverse relationship exists between class position and the amount spent on the treatment of neurotics in private agencies, but a reverse relationship appears in the public agencies. The cost of treating class I–II neurotics is $2564 for private agencies, but it is only $200 for public agencies. On the other end of the class status scale, $53 are spent on the class V neurotics in private agencies; in public agencies the cost is $903. In spite of the reversal of the class gradient in public and private agencies, the total cost of treatment per patient is inversely related to class, because such a large proportion of the expenditures is in private treatment agencies.

The per patient expenditures by class and agency for psychotic patients is similar to that for neurotics, but the differences are even greater. The cost of caring for the class I–II psychotic in private facilities in 1950 was $3447; the cost for the average class V psychotic patient was $13. A reverse relationship holds true for psychotic patients treated in the public agencies, but the differences are not as great. The total average per patient expenditures on psychotics followed the same pattern for neurotics, namely, the lower the class, the less the amount spent.

The mean per patient expenditures on treatment during 1950 are definitely a function of class position when agency and diagnostic group are controlled. In private agencies, the average annual expenditure per patient is inversely related to class level; in public agencies the association is direct. Although class position, as measured by dollars spent on patient care, is more apparent in private than in public agencies, it is significant in each type of agency.

The Treatment Bill

Approximately three million dollars were spent on the care of the 1891 patients studied in the twelve months preceding the taking of the Psychiatric Census. The division of expenditures on treatment among the different classes is shown in Table 41. The strong rela-

TABLE 41

Estimated Expenditures for the Care and Treatment of Patients in Private and Public Agencies during 1950—by Class

Class	Number of Patients	Private Agencies	Number of Patients	Public Agencies	Number of Patients	Total
I–II	117	$430,554	33	$ 46,364	150	$ 476,919
III	111	285,443	150	198,388	261	483,831
IV	150	271,214	606	836,752	756	1,107,966
V	20	12,066	704	899,496	724	911,562
Total	398	$999,277	1,493	$1,981,000	1,891	$2,980,278

tionships between class position and average per patient expenditures in both private and public agencies revealed in the preceding analysis appear again in the total estimates given in Table 41. In private agencies the reverse is true.

The figures in the column on total expenditures may appear to be a contradiction of the linkage between class position and expenditures on treatment because the treatment bill is almost as large in class I–II as in class III. However, we must remember that the number of patients is sharply different in these two classes. Actually the 150 patients in class I–II have almost as many dollars spent on them as the 261 patients in class III. The total expenditure figure is a product of the class pattern of spending combined with the number of patients in treatment.

Per Capita Expenditures

The average per capita expenditure on the treatment of mental illness in 1950 (see Table 42) was computed by dividing the popu-

TABLE 42

Estimated per Capita Expenditures for the Care and Treatment of Patients in Private and Public Agencies during 1950—by Class

Class	Private Agencies	Public Agencies	Total
I–II	$15.95	$ 1.72	$17.67
III	5.90	4.10	10.00
IV	2.30	7.09	9.39
V	0.28	20.64	20.92
Total	$ 4.22	$ 8.36	$12.58

lation of the community by the estimated total spent on care and treatment given in Table 41. The total figure at the bottom of the right-hand column of Table 42 means that the treatment of mental illness cost every person in the community, irrespective of sex, age, or social condition, at least $12.58 during 1950. This procedure was repeated to obtain the per capita expenditures of $4.22 in private agencies and $8.36 in public agencies.

The per capita estimates for each class were computed by dividing the total expenditures in each class and type of agency by the population of the appropriate class. For example, in class I–II, $430,544.20 are spent in private agencies (see Table 41), and there are 27,000 persons in these classes: $430,544.20 divided by 27,000 = $15.95 per capita.

This procedure is repeated for each class and agency type with the appropriate totals substituted in the formula. By reading across Table 42, one can readily see how much is spent in private and public agencies as well as the per capita expenditure in each class. For example, in class I–II, $17.67 are spent per capita; of this amount, $15.95 are spent in private agencies and $1.72 in public agencies.

Per capita expenditures by class and treatment agency reveal the familiar gradients. They are inversely related to class in the private agencies, but in the public agencies, the association between class and the amount spent is direct.

Diagnostic Group and Expenditures on Treatment

If diagnosis is held constant, will class be a meaningful factor in determining the amount that is spent on treatment? This question is answered by comparing mean dollar expenditures for care and treatment in 1950 by class for each of six diagnostic groups. The neurotic reactions are grouped into one category for computational purposes.

Examination of the figures in Table 43 shows that the amounts expended are functions of both diagnosis and class. The largest ex-

TABLE 43

Mean per Patient Expenditures on Care and Treatment during 1950—by Diagnostic Group and Class

	Class				
Diagnostic Group	I–II	III	IV	V	Total
Neurotic reactions	$2,765	$2,059	$1,844	$ 956	$1,979
Affective disorders	4,114	1,703	1,356	1,107	1,518
Alcoholic disorders	1,689	1,037	854	903	942
Organic disorders	642	1,450	1,229	1,303	1,284
Senile disorders	8,052	1,645	1,161	1,171	1,454
Schizophrenic disorders	3,599	1,844	1,443	1,376	1,536
Total	$3,478	$1,623	$1,313	$1,136	$1,450

penditures are the rule in class I–II for each diagnostic group,[2] but there is wide variation from one type of disorder to another. There is a markedly lower amount spent on class III patients than on the class I–II patients, but it is more than is spent on class IV patients. With the exception of the organics, more is spent on class V patients than on the class IV patients. In classes IV and V diagnosis has little effect on the amount spent for care and treatment because most patients are committed to public hospitals and the costs of treatment vary little from one class and diagnostic group to another. It may be concluded that class is far more important than diagnosis in determining the size of the treatment bill.

Who Pays for Treatment?

Direct expenditures on care in 1950 totaled almost three million dollars. Did the patients and their families bear this expense or did third parties help to meet it? Is a patient's class position a significant factor in who pays for his treatment? The data to answer these questions are summarized in Table 44.

TABLE 44

Percentage of Patients in Private and Public Agencies—by Sources of Support and Class

A. Private Agencies

	Class			
Sources of Support	I–II	III	IV	V
Patient and/or family	95.7	85.6	67.3	...
Veterans Administration *	0.9	11.7	30.7	70.0
Free treatment *	3.4	1.8	1.3	5.0
Private welfare *	...	0.9	0.7	5.0
Compensation insurance *	...	...	...	20.0
$n =$	117	111	150	20

$$\chi^2 = 66.51,\ df = 3,\ p < .001$$

* All types of third party payments were combined in χ^2 analysis.

B. Public Agencies

	Class			
Sources of Support	I–II	III	IV	V
Patient and/or family	15.1	14.7	6.3	1.6
Town, state, family	51.5	56.0	47.4	23.7
Town and state	21.3	22.7	41.3	68.7
Veterans Administration *	12.2	5.3	4.5	5.7
Private welfare *	...	1.3	0.5	0.3
$n =$	33	150	606	704

$$\chi^2 = 205.15,\ df = 9,\ p < .001$$

* These categories were combined in the χ^2 analysis.

A strong association exists between class positions and whether treatment is paid for by the patient and his family or a third party in both private and public agencies. The bills of some 96 percent of class I–II patients are paid by the patient and/or his family, whereas in class V all patients cared for in private agencies are supported by third parties—the Veterans Administration, private welfare agencies, compensation insurance, or psychiatrists. The proportion of the treatment bill underwritten by the Veterans Administration for patients in private practice in each class is: class I–II—5.4 percent, class III—13.4 percent, class IV—36.4 percent, class V—87.2 percent.

Private practitioners treating patients at public expense are, with one exception, directive-organic in orientation. Only one patient whose bill is paid by the Veterans Administration is treated by an analytically oriented therapist. This patient's bill comprised 1 percent of the total bill paid by third parties at public expense; thus 99 percent of the money paid by public agencies, mainly the Veterans Administration, to private practitioners goes to directive-organic therapists.

The folklore of medical practice fosters the belief that a considerable portion of patients are carried free by practitioners. This belief may be true in the general practice of medicine, but it needs to be modified before it fits the facts of private psychiatric practice. Only nine patients were carried free by private practitioners, and no psychiatrist carried more than one free patient. These free patients were given only periodic treatment and for short periods. The psychiatrists involved reported that they "gave the patient a little free time" when he dropped into the office "from time to time." These free patients are carried by directive-organic psychiatrists who give them supportive therapy. Not a single psychoanalyst or analytically oriented private practitioner is treating a patient free, although a few patients are treated at slightly reduced fees.

The state has long accepted the responsibility of caring for mentally ill residents, but it prefers to charge the patient's family part of the established costs of maintaining patients in the state hospital. When a family can afford to pay for its ill member's care, the state bills the responsible relatives for whatever portion of the established costs welfare officers judge is fair to both the family and the state. When the family cannot meet any portion of the patient's support, the town where the patient resides shares the expense with the state. In rare instances a patient may have his treatment bill paid by a lodge, a church, or some other type of private association. Patients in Veterans Administration hospitals, of course, are supported by the Federal government, but here class is not a significant factor.[3]

Section B of Table 44 summarizes the several sources of support for patients treated in public hospitals and clinics. These figures bring into focus four relationships between class and who pays the patient's bill. First, there are no differences between classes I–II and III in the percentage of patients supported in part by their families or wholly by the town and state. In these classes some 15 percent of the families pay for the patient's treatment; in an additional 52 to 56 percent of the cases, the families pay some part of the cost; less than 25 percent of these cases are supported entirely by the town and state. Second, there is a sharp break in the pattern of support between classes III and IV. The percentage of patients in class IV who are supported by their families is less than half that in class III; moreover, the percentage of partial family support drops sharply between classes III and IV; conversely the percentage of patients supported wholly by the town and state almost doubles in class IV in comparison with class III. Third, class V exhibits a distinctly different support pattern from class IV. The percentage of class V patients whose bills are paid by their families is less than one third as large as in class IV. Fourth, the percentage of patients supported wholly at public expense increases from 41 percent in class IV to 68.7 percent in class V. These differences indicate the existence of clear-cut class-related patterns, insofar as interrelations of the patients, their families, the state welfare department, and mental institutions are concerned.

The data summarized in Table 44 demonstrate that class position determines in large part who pays the treatment bill. Bills for treatment in private hospitals are paid by the families. Class I–II and III patients of private practitioners pay for their own treatment for the most part, but in classes IV and V, the probability is very high that the bills are paid by the Veterans Administration. In all public agencies—clinics, veterans, and state hospitals—the costs of treatment are borne mainly by the public at large. One might not expect to observe the presence of class as a potent factor in payment of treatment bills in these agencies. However, the Veterans Administration hospitals are the only institutions where class is not a significant factor in who pays the bill, in whole or in part, simply because the public pays all of it. A percentage of treatment bills in the state hospitals are paid by the patient's family in all cases, but the lower the class, the higher the percentage of patients who are supported wholly at the public's expense. Clinic patients are supported overwhelmingly by public agencies, but, as we shall see later, there is a distinct inverse relationship between class position and the amount expended on patient care from public funds.

ESTIMATED TOTAL EXPENDITURES

Estimates of how many dollars had been expended from the time each patient entered treatment until the Psychiatric Census date were prepared by extrapolation from the 1950 data. In this procedure the cost of a unit of treatment was multiplied by the number of known units of treatment administered to a patient throughout the history of his illness. All agencies where a patient is known to have been treated from the first time he entered treatment until the Psychiatric Census date are included in the total.

It is important for the reader to remember that we are now discussing *estimates*. They are computed from a base that is undoubtedly higher than it would have been had the Psychiatric Census been taken in 1940, but not as high as it would have been in 1955. Moreover, they deal only with amounts of treatment patients have had. If a patient's record is not complete or accurate, the estimates are in error by this unknown quantity. However, these estimates give some idea of the accumulated burden of direct treatment costs in a patient population. These estimates are presented from the viewpoints of treatment agency, costs per capita, and costs by diagnostic groups.

Total Estimates by Agency

We estimate that more than 26⅓ million dollars have been spent on treatment from the time the patients entered treatment until the Psychiatric Census date. This total is divided between public and private agencies. Patients in classes II and III, and to a lesser extent in class IV, are taken to private agencies during the early phases of their illness. In classes I and II a much higher proportion of the estimates of treatment costs is expended in public institutions in the total treatment picture than is true for 1950. However, estimated expenditures in private institutions are only four times greater than in public institutions. As time passes and the need for care on a continuing basis becomes apparent, the patient is taken to a state hospital. In these cases, the longer the period of treatment, the greater the probability that the patient will be cared for at public expense.

In class III, estimated expenditures are greater in public than in private agencies; in class IV the ratio is more than 10 to 1 in favor of public agencies; and in class V it is 178 to 1. The extreme disparity between estimated expenditures in private and public agencies in class V, shown in Table 45, is produced by the use of public

TABLE 45

Estimated Total Expenditures for the Care and Treatment of Patients in Private and Public Agencies—by Class

Class	Private Agencies	Public Agencies	Total
I–II	$1,744,258	$ 401,087	$ 2,145,345
III	1,162,643	1,590,706	2,753,349
IV	795,341	8,375,935	9,171,276
V	68,700	12,228,316	12,297,016
Total	$3,770,942	$22,596,044	$26,366,986

agencies at this level and the accumulation of class V psychotics in the state hospitals. Clearly, the lower the class, the greater the ratio of estimated expenditures in public institutions.

Estimated per Capita Expenditures

The total estimated costs of treatment in each class, presented in Table 45, divided by the number in each class provides estimates of the per capita amounts that have been expended on the care of patients in public and private agencies summarized in Table 46.

TABLE 46

Estimated Total per Capita Expenditures for the Care and Treatment of Patients in Private and Public Agencies—by Class

Class	Private Agencies	Public Agencies	Total
I–II	$64.60	$ 14.86	$ 79.46
III	24.04	32.89	56.93
IV	6.74	70.98	77.72
V	1.58	280.59	282.17
Total	$15.92	$ 95.37	$111.29

We estimate that $15.92 have been spent on patients in private agencies and $95.37 in public agencies. Thus, the direct estimated cost of treating these patients totals $111.29 for every person in the community. Per capita estimates within the private agencies vary greatly from one class to another: $64.60 in class I–II, but only $1.58 in class V. The pattern in public agencies is the reverse; less than $15 per capita have been spent on class I–II patients, but over $280 on class V patients. The estimated total per capita expenditures by class and type of agency given in Table 46 show the characteristic direct relationship between large expenditures in private agencies and high class position and the inverse association between high expenditures and low class position.

Even though class I–II patients are treated mainly in high-cost private agencies, the total estimated per capita expenditures on this segment of the population are only 28 percent as great as in class V, namely, $79.46 in comparison with $282.17. Although the state hospitals are minimum-cost institutions, the accumulation of hundreds of class V patients in the chronic wards over a long span of years raises per capita expenditures on these patients to the highest figure in the series. It would appear that high-cost treatment, such as is experienced in private agencies, costs society less in the long run, but we must remember that social rather than strictly economic factors are involved in the treatment process.

The class V patient is supported almost entirely at public expense whether he is treated in a clinic, a veterans hospital, a state hospital, or by a private practitioner. On the other hand, the class I–II patient's treatment is supported mainly by his family whether he is in a private or public institution. Nevertheless, the class V patient is an indirect charge upon the elements of the population who pay for their own treatment, because they are the ones who pay the largest proportion of taxes into the state and Federal governments. In short, we may conclude that the higher classes support both their own and the treatment of the lower classes. Moreover, we may infer that the long-run treatment bills of the patients in the lower classes are higher than those of the patients in the upper strata because influential people in the higher classes do not insist upon more adequate care for patients in public institutions. Numerous individuals in the core group are opposed to more adequate care of the mentally ill in public institutions, because by raising state appropriations to provide adequate care, taxes might possibly be raised to meet the assumed added expenses.

Diagnosis and Estimated Expenditures

It is of interest to note the effect of the type of mental illness a patient has on the long-run cost of his treatment. Do patients in some diagnostic groups cost more than those in others? Is class a factor when diagnosis is controlled? The data to answer these and similar questions are presented in Table 47. When the data in Table

TABLE 47

Estimated Average per Patient Cost of Total Treatment—by Diagnosis and Class

Diagnostic Group	Class *				
	I–II	III	IV	V	Total
Affectives	$35,497	$ 4,888	$ 9,471	$ 8,015	$10,216
Alcoholics	2,859	3,264	3,691	6,097	4,583
Neurotics	10,077	6,341	5,680	3,301	6,486
Organics	2,247	11,614	16,018	16,018	16,017
Schizophrenics	18,575	20,031	17,370	23,754	20,559
Seniles	35,455	5,340	5,273	6,908	7,075

* The figures in this table are significant beyond the .001 level for each diagnostic group by class.

47 are examined from the viewpoint of estimated total cost of treatment, we see that alcoholics, neurotics, and seniles are relatively low-cost patients in comparison with affectives; whereas organics and schizophrenics are high-cost patients relative to affectives. These figures need to be interpreted because the vast majority of the neurotics and alcoholics are ambulatory patients. Moreover, more than half the neurotics and nine tenths of the alcoholics are treated in clinics or public hospitals. The seniles are in state hospitals except in class I–II where they are cared for in private institutions. Practically all seniles irrespective of class status are chronic care cases. Where affectives are hospitalized is a function of class, but they experience remissions of symptoms more frequently than either organics or schizophrenics for various lengths of time. During their intervals of remission, they normally do not receive treatment. Class I–II affectives are extremely high-cost patients largely because they are treated repeatedly in private hospitals. The class III affective is a low-cost psychotic in comparison with the class I's and II's on the one side and the IV's on the other; but the class IV affective costs appreciably more than the V. The net result is that the typical affective patient's treatment costs, in the long run, are only about half as much as the average schizophrenic's.

The neurotics and alcoholics are the only diagnostic groups that show consistent associations between class position and estimated total average treatment costs. In these groups, the class gradient runs in opposite directions. Among neurotics, the higher the class, the greater the treatment cost, but for alcoholics, the lower the class, the higher the expenditures for treatment. The class I–II senile, like the affective of the same status level, has many thousands of dollars spent on him. This is a function of the use of private mental hospitals in these classes for all types of patients. Below the class II level, there is little difference in average estimated costs among seniles until class V is reached. Class V senile patients cost distinctly more than class IV's, primarily because they are placed in the hospital at an earlier age. Class IV and V organic patients cost about the same because they are in state hospitals and are continuous care cases. The low figure for class I–II must be interpreted carefully because only one patient is involved. The class III figure is more reliable, but even here there are only four patients. Schizophrenics are high-cost patients in all classes; but definitely highest in class V. These patients represent the major burden of care because they constitute such a high percentage of patients in the state and veterans hospitals. We estimate a total of $17,413,473 spent on the treatment of schizophrenics in the patient population from the time they entered treatment until the Psychiatric Census was taken.

EXPENDITURES ON A SINGLE COURSE OF TREATMENT

Calculation of the amount of money spent on a single course of treatment by patients, their families, or third parties in different agencies was a major interest. To accomplish this goal a series of patients in their first course of psychiatric treatment who were cared for by private practitioners in private hospitals, clinics, or state hospitals were followed from the time they became psychiatric patients until each one's dismissal or until March 1, 1956. The number of patients followed in each agency is:

Private practitioners	117
Private hospitals	107
Public clinics	68
State hospitals	100
Total	392

Different procedures are used in selecting the patients to be followed in each type of agency. A stratified random sample of private practitioners' patients, who were paying for their own treatment, was selected from the patient population enumerated in the Psychiatric Census. It included enough patients from each class for statistical reliability. The number of patients treated in private hospitals was too small to meet our needs. Therefore, we included patients in cooperating private hospitals enumerated in the Psychiatric Census and, in addition, a number of cases who entered these hospitals between December 1, 1950 and June 30, 1952. All clinic patients were followed from the date of the Psychiatric Census until their cases were closed. The state hospital patients are a random sample of cases without a previous psychiatric history from the Psychiatric Census population. Patients in the private and state hospitals were followed until their release, death, or to March 1, 1956.

Private Practice

Cooperative psychiatrists furnished data on the cost of treatment for the 117 patients selected for follow-up study. These psychiatrists represent treatment orientations that range from classical Freudian psychoanalysis to a directive-organic orientation. This point is raised here because there is a marked relationship between the therapeutic orientation of a practitioner and the size of the bill for a course of treatments. A psychoanalyst's patients are treated four or five hours a week for two, three, or four years and sometimes longer. The patient pays a fee ranging approximately from $15 to $40 for each 50-minute hour. A directive-organic psychiatrist sees his patients half an hour perhaps once a week for a month, two months, maybe as long as six months, and he may charge approximately $10 to $20 for each visit.

When the costs of a single course of treatment are viewed from the perspective of class, clear-cut differences appear as a glance at Table 48 will show. The differences demonstrated here are a function of the interdependency between the therapeutic orientations of the practitioners and the class status of their patients. The psychoanalysts' patients are in class I–II; 81 percent are in class I, and 19 percent are in class II. The analytically oriented practitioners' patients are predominantly in class II and class III; 47 percent are in class II, 33 percent in class III, 11 percent in class I, and 9 percent in class IV. Patients of practitioners with a directive-organic orientation show a distinctly different distribution: 84 percent are in class IV, 14 percent in class III, and 2 percent (one patient) from class II. Not a single class I patient in the series is treated by a

TABLE 48

Mean Expenditures on a Single Course of Treatment with Private Practitioners—by Class

Class of Patients	Number of Patients	Mean Expenditure
I	13	$6,202
II	17	4,137
III	38	1,505
IV	49	368
Total	117	$1,932

directive-organic psychiatrist. These figures show that class I patients spend their money on psychoanalysis for the most part. This
is a long, expensive form of treatment as the mean of $6202 reveals.
Class II patients tend to patronize analytically oriented practitioners
who see them two or three times a week for a year to fifteen months.
The pecuniary consequent is a mean expenditure of $4137 on a
course of treatments. Class III patients divide their patronage between analytically oriented and directive-organic practitioners; they
are not seen as often or as long as the class II patients, and their mean
expenditure is $1505. The class IV patients are treated predominantly
by directive-organic practitioners once or twice a week for twelve
to fifteen weeks; their mean expenditure is consequently only $368.
Class V patients are not treated by private practitioners if they have
to pay for their care.

Private Hospitalization

One hundred and six patients in private hospitals were followed
from the time they entered the hospital until they were discharged;
one additional patient was still in treatment when the field work
ended on March 1, 1956. Some 70 percent were admitted to the
hospital upon the advice of a physician who had been treating them
for ailments presumably not psychiatric in nature. The remainder
were sent to a hospital by a psychiatrist who had them in treatment
before hospitalization. Expenditures on their illnesses before they
entered the hospital and after their discharge are not included in
the computations on the cost of private hospitalization. The figures
in Table 49 are based only upon what was paid for current care to
a private hospital.

TABLE 49

Mean per Patient Expenditures on a Single Private Mental Hospitalization
—by Class

Class	Number of Patients	Mean Expenditure
I	23	$3,265
II	20	1,682
III	33	1,264
IV	31	831

The definite inverse relationship between class position and mean dollar expenditures on a single hospitalization is highly significant. This association results from the operation of two class-linked factors: the length of time patients are hospitalized and discount practices in the hospitals. These factors, however, produce opposite effects. The longer a patient remains in hospital the larger his bill, unless the time factor is neutralized by a larger discount. With these points before us, we will present data to demonstrate how class status is related, first, to the length of time patients remain in private mental hospitals, second, to the frequency with which discounts are given to patients, and, third, to the size of the discounts they receive.

The data summarized in Table 50 reveal that hospitalization in

TABLE 50

Mean Number of Days Patients are Privately Hospitalized—by Class

Class	Number of Patients	Mean Number of Days	Standard Deviation in Days
I	23	138	114
II	20	57	34
III	33	43	20
IV	31	27	20
Total	107	61	43

class I is longer and variations in the length of hospitalization are greater than in class II. The class II patients remain in the hospital longer than the class III patients, and their hospital stay is more variable. The class III patients are in the hospital 37 percent longer than the class IV's, but there is no difference in the distributions around the mean. Clearly, a patient's class status is linked to the length of time he remains in a private mental hospital.

Financial arrangements between the "front office" and a patient's family are highly confidential. Therefore, who receives a discount and how large are "delicate subjects." Departures from quoted fee schedules are made for a number of avowed reasons—"inability to meet the full schedule," "professional courtesy," "to help the patient's recovery," "for business reasons," "an interesting case"; no administrator is willing to state that a patient's status influences the patient-hospital relationship. Nevertheless, a definite connection exists between class position and (a) those who receive discounts and (b) in what amounts discounts are given. These conclusions are supported by the data presented in Table 51.

TABLE 51

Discounts in Private Mental Hospitals—by Class

Class	Percentage of Patients Receiving Discounts	Percentage of Bill Discounted
I	57	30
II	25	21
III	21	16
IV	7	2

These data reveal that the discount system operates to the distinct advantage of class I. Interestingly, only small differentiations are made between class II and class III, both in the percentage of patients who receive discounts and the proportions of the bills that are discounted. Class IV, in comparison with class III, is treated in a more singular manner than is class I when compared with class II. The discount system does not apply to class V since these people do not utilize private mental hospitals.

The frequency and the size of the discounts could be attributed to the length of time patients remain in hospital rather than to class status. To determine if this were true, the data were analyzed by covariance procedures with the number of days patients remained in the hospital controlled.

The data given in Table 52 show that class I patients pay significantly less for their hospitalization than the class II, III, or IV patients. In short, the analysis summarized in Table 52 demonstrated that the observed mean differences in daily costs are functions of class position rather than of the length of time patients remain in the hospital.

The patient-centered orientation of these hospitals meets with the

TABLE 52

Average Daily Cost of Private Hospitalization—by Class

Class	Adjusted Mean Payment per Day	Standard Deviation
I	$23.76	$7.37
II	29.66	5.87
III	29.88	5.92
IV	31.11	5.11

$$F (3, 102) = 2.690, p < .05$$

most approved psychiatric conceptions of procedure, but it is accompanied by the pricing practices shown in Table 52. What this table does not show is that class I patients begin to receive discounts after the first week and, in an appreciable number of cases, from the hour of their admission, because many class I patients are not charged for the examination given to patients upon admission to the hospital. Lower ranking patients are charged routinely for this examination. The class II and III patients do not begin to receive discounts until their families are sorely pinched by the financial drain of the patient's illness. The class IV patient who receives a discount does not have it applied to his bill until his family has insisted upon it. To be sure, the sizes and frequencies of discounts vary from hospital to hospital.

An ironical aside relevant to the discounts granted to the higher classes is the tie between class status and the kind of therapy that is prescribed for the patients by hospital psychiatrists. Approximately 93 percent of the class I's receive analytic psychotherapy, but only 19 percent of the class IV's. The class IV's are treated predominantly by electro-convulsive therapy. Analytic psychotherapy is a slow, time-consuming form of treatment, but it is believed to be effective in cases where (a) the therapist is well trained, and (b) it is applicable and acceptable to the patient. A psychiatrist can treat only twelve patients by this method, whereas electro-convulsive therapy is rapid and inexpensive; one psychiatrist may treat forty to fifty patients. Moreover, the latter is a controversial form of therapy with very narrow indications. The contrast between who is prescribed which therapy, both from the perspective of the class position and the costs to the hospital, are too great to be ignored.

Private mental hospitals are oriented primarily toward the aristocratic tradition. The best ones are designed to present the appearance of luxurious estates if in the country or gracious town houses if in the city to which one may retire from the world to a Shangri-La type of existence. The front office in both settings is furnished with elegance and taste. The comfort, welfare, and treatment of patients within the genteel tradition is the acknowledged function of the institution. The administrators and the staff know the patients pay for these surroundings, and they are aware of the manifest and latent values in this setting. Administrators, receptionists, psychiatrists, nurses, maids, aides, groundskeepers, and chauffeurs know the earmarks of high and low status from long experience. In unguarded moments they may state this fact plainly. For example, a chief nurse in a noted private hospital summarized her status awareness in these words:

> I can tell from their grooming, their clothes, their luggage, and the way they talk what they are. One has to be aware of these things or you will be in difficulty all the time. Good care means knowing who the patients are and how they expect you to regard them.

We may infer that while many private hospitals are oriented toward class I patients they are maintained, in good part, by the high-paying, low-cost class III and class IV patients. To use a metaphor, private hospitals are designed for the "carriage trade" but they are supported by the "shock box." Exceptions to this rule are institutions where psychotherapy predominates; however, practically no class III or IV patients are treated in these hospitals.

It may be noticed in Table 52 that two patients are missing from the covariance analysis. These patients merit special mention. Both are class I individuals; they represent the range of hospitalization in the series. One was hospitalized only six days; the other had been hospitalized more than nine years when the field work ended. The patient with the brief hospitalization was brought to the hospital in an acute panic by her family. After a few days, the decision was reached to discharge her for ambulatory treatment. No charge was made for examination, therapy, or maintenance during the time this patient was in hospital. The reasons for this action are obscure, but it is known that a relative has been a benefactor of the hospital in recent years. Since no charges were made, the patient was eliminated from the covariance analysis.

The long-run case was not used because the treatment is not completed, and there are four hospitals involved. This patient had a schizophrenic break during his freshman year in college. He was given intensive analytic psychotherapy in the first hospital for approximately a year and a half. His family then decided that a change of therapist and scene was essential. He was transferred to a second hospital and given further analytic psychotherapy. He had been in this hospital almost two years when the Psychiatric Census was taken. Between the Census date and the close of field work he had been treated in two other hospitals. This patient's father and mother come from distinguished families. Each was the recipient of substantial trust funds from their parental families. The father was influential in bringing several million dollars in endowment to a famous eastern university. They conceive of themselves as patrons of education, the arts, and the humanities. They make sure the son is cared for by the standards they believe are theirs by right of position. If the son does not receive the courtesy and attention they believe is his "natural due" they are in a position to use their connections with other wealthy families to withhold funds from institutions where they feel they have been slighted. They use their influence to have appointments made for them with psychiatrists when they desire. The parents have interviewed three university presidents and the deans of their medical schools about their problem. This family has received discounts from each hospital where the son has been treated. Nevertheless, it spent approximately $160,000 on treatment during the nine years we followed this patient.

Clinics

The cost of treatment in a clinic has two sides: how much the patient pays and how much the treatment administered costs the clinic. The clinics have fee schedules that range from nothing to $10 a visit. Each patient's fee is determined by the size of the family's income and the number of persons supported by it. The responsible heads of the clinics do not expect the patients to support the clinics with their fees. The fees paid are assessed simply to help defray some of the costs. Often they appear to be assessed more for psychological than for economic reasons.

The mean charge for each clinic visit ranges from $2.10 in class II to $2.02 in class III. Class V has to be treated separately, because only four patients were carried beyond their diagnostic interviews, and of these only two paid for their visits: 25 cents each. When class V is ignored, there is no association between class position and the fees the patients pay. On the other hand, the amount of money the clinics spend on the average patient is related to his class status. This is clear from the data in Table 53.

TABLE 53

Gross and Net Treatment Costs per Patient in Clinics—by Class

Class	Number of Patients	Mean Gross Costs per Patient	Mean Amount Paid by Patient	Mean Net Cost to Clinic
II	11	$467	$77	$390
III	29	246	42	204
IV	24	110	18	93
V	4	49	1	48
Total	68	$222	$37	$187

The gross cost of a patient to a clinic was calculated by multiplying the number of visits he made to the clinic by the mean cost of each visit. Then the amount the patient paid was subtracted from his estimated gross cost to determine his net cost to the clinic.

A glance at Table 53 shows that the clinic's net mean estimated expenditure on class II patients is almost twice as large as it is for class III patients, $390 versus $204. Class III patients, in turn, cost the clinics more than twice as much as class IV patients, $204 versus $93. Finally, class IV patients cost the clinics almost twice as much as class V patients, $93 versus $48.

Interrelationships of class status, gross costs, the amounts patients pay, and net costs are functions of the way the different classes use the available clinic facilities. The average class II patient receives almost twice as much treatment as the average class III patient; he personally pays more for it, but he costs the clinic proportionately more because he stays in treatment longer. The same principle applies to class III in comparison with class IV and particularly to class IV in comparison with class V. The net results of the differences between the length of time patients are treated in clinics and class position is this: Class II patients receive the most therapy and class V patients the least. If we consider that clinics are established primarily to help lower status patients, presumably badly in need of help, this is, in the words of a colleague who is himself a psychiatrist, "a startling finding."

The treatment received in the clinic by class II patients may prevent far more expense in a hospital at a later time. On the other hand, the relatively low cost of the class V patient may be compounded by expensive care in a state hospital in a later phase of his illness. These are speculations; only carefully designed research can give an answer to them. It is not speculation, however, to infer that the subtleties of status enter into the practice of psychiatry in clinics as well as in private hospitals and in private practice.

State Hospitals

The 100 state hospital patients in the series are almost exclusively public charges. The state sends bills to the families of patients who are able to pay all or a part of the computed mean daily cost of the patient's hospitalization, but relatively few of these families are billed; of those who receive statements, a still smaller percentage pay the bill. Therefore, for present purposes, we will assume the public is bearing the entire costs of hospital care.

The computation of the cost of a single course of treatment in the state hospital was complicated by the fact that 54 percent of the patients followed were still in hospital on March 1, 1956; 16 percent had been discharged, and 30 percent had died in hospital. In view of this situation, we analyzed the data in terms of how much had been spent on the patient's hospitalization up to the time of his discharge, death, or to March 1, 1956.[4] The results of this analysis are summarized in Table 54.

TABLE 54

Mean per Patient Expenditures in State Hospitals until Discharge, Death, or to March 1, 1956—by Class

Patient	Class		
	II–III	IV	V
Discharged from hospital	$ ...	$ 6,296	$10,728
Died in hospital	1,926	12,306	15,866
Still in hospital	22,865	16,487	28,549
$n =$	6	46	48

The mean expenditures on each patient's hospitalization given in Table 54 show two things: first, maintenance of mental patients in a state hospital is expensive, and second, class V patients are far more expensive than patients from the higher classes. Since no class differences exist between mean daily hospital costs, the mean aggregate costs shown in Table 54 are the product of the differences in the length of time patients in each class have been hospitalized.

When we examined the data on this point, we found that the class IV patients who were discharged spent an average (mean) of 5 years in a hospital before their release. The class V patients spent 12⅓ years in hospital before moving back into the community. The one class III patient who died in the hospital had been there 18 months at the time of his death; the deceased class IV's and V's had been in the hospital from 10 to 13 years when death came.

The patients still in hospital when the field work closed had been there a long time. The mean number of years by class is: class III— 18 years, class IV—13 years, and class V—22 years. On the basis of the low percentage of discharges experienced during the 64 months that elapsed between the Psychiatric Census and the end of the field work, it appears safe to infer that patients hospitalized continuously for as long as these have been are not likely to be discharged in appreciable numbers. These patients have been a continuous expense for many years, and public and private funds will continue to be expended on their care for indefinite periods in the future. The few who have been discharged may even return to the hospital. The only patients whose costs can be computed definitely are those who have died; their accounts are closed.

SUMMARY AND CONCLUSIONS

The data in this chapter establish that expenditures on treatment are linked in highly significant ways with class status in each type of psychiatric facility. In private practice, the higher the class, the greater the mean per patient expenditure. In private hospitals, the higher classes spend more than the lower classes because they are hospitalized longer. However, the mean cost per day is significantly less for the higher classes. This is attributable to discriminatory discounts granted to high status persons. In the clinics, the fees paid by classes II, III, and IV are not significantly related to class status. On the other hand, the cost to the clinic of treating patients is related inversely to class status. The clinics spend eight times as much treating each class II patient as they do each class V patient. This differential results from the varying amounts of treatment administered to patients in these classes. Public expenditures on patients in state hospitals are related to class position. This association is produced largely by the differences in the ways the state hospitals are used by each class. In classes II and III, the patients are sent to the state hospitals as a "last resort," and usually only after their families have exhausted their resources in private facilities. Class IV uses the state hospital as a treatment center as well as a place for custodial care. The state hospital is the one psychiatric facility available to class V persons who become so disturbed that they have to be separated from the community. Ordinarily, these persons are not wanted by their families, and they are viewed as useless, obnoxious, and occasionally as dangerous to society, if not to themselves. The sequel to rejection by the family and isolation from the community is long-range custodial care. Thus, although the state hospital is a minimum-cost institution on a per diem basis, it is a maximum-cost institution in the long run because it functions in large part as a "dumping ground" for psychotic individuals in the two lower classes, especially class V. In sum, the class status of the patient influences expenditures on treatment in each type of psychiatric facility in highly significant ways.

NOTES

[1] *State of Connecticut, Public Document #1,* Report of the Comptroller to the Governor for the Fiscal Year Ended June 30, 1950, pp. 206–213.

[2] The apparent exception of the organics involves only one case; this case was in treatment only part of the year.

[3] Although the percentage of class I–II patients supported by the Veterans Administration is more than twice that in the other classes, only four individuals are involved.

[4] The computed cost per patient day for each year the patients have been hospitalized was obtained from the State Comptroller's office. This figure was then multiplied by the number of days in a given year each patient was hospitalized.

discussion
and
application

**part
five**

part five • discussion and application

The attitudes of patients, family members, and psychiatrists toward mental illnesses are discussed herein. The research problem is restated and the results are summarized. The state of research in social psychiatry is viewed critically, and proposals are put forward which may lead to controversy. However, we believe that our ideas on the need for a new type of therapist are warranted by the facts we have presented.

attitudes toward mental illness and treatment

chapter eleven

INTRODUCTION

The statistical data presented in the five preceding chapters demonstrate that significant interrelations exist between class status and the ways patients reach psychiatrists, how their difficulties are diagnosed, how they are treated, and expenditures on treatment. Early in the data-gathering phase of this research we saw that patients, members of their families, and the psychiatrists treating them possess different attitudes toward the problems with which they must cope. This chapter summarizes our observations and conclusions on the part attitudes contribute to the statistical materials.

Attitudes Defined

We use the term "attitude" to designate the presence of an intervening variable in a social situation that is inferred primarily from action responses.[1] Attitudes may be inferred from verbal or written statements, subliminal cues, and overt acts.

We infer attitudes primarily from behavior observed in and around psychiatric treatment situations rather than from hypothetical questions presented to persons in interview situations. For example, we did not ask a parent, "To whom would you send your son if he developed mental illness?" giving the respondent a series of multiple choices. Instead we drew inferences from what was done when a difficulty developed. We did ask questions to ascertain patients' sentiments toward their illnesses and their treatment. We also asked members of their families similar questions, but we placed greater emphasis upon actual behavior than upon statements made in response to direct questions.

Attitudes toward Psychiatry and Treated Illness

We infer from the sources of referral discussed in Chapter Six that persons in the higher classes hold more favorable attitudes toward psychiatrists than those in the lower classes. This inference is supported by the responses of a stratified subsample of 517 persons, drawn from the 5 percent sample, to questions about their willingness to turn to psychiatrists for help in emotional difficulties. These respondents corroborated hunches gained from patients and members of their families. Some seven out of eight class I respondents in the subsample have a fair grasp of the psychiatrist's functions; practically all know he is a medical doctor. In class V, by way of contrast, less than one person in sixteen knows that a psychiatrist is a medical doctor, and even fewer have more than the vaguest idea of how a psychiatrist functions in our society. Twenty percent of the class I's say that they would be willing to "go to a psychiatrist for help" for "emotional" or "mental" problems, but less than 1 percent of the class V's think a psychiatrist could help them with emotional or mental problems. The intervening classes occupy positions between these extremes on both questions. These respondents' answers indicate that each class has a distinctly different conception of the role of the psychiatrist in our society.

Class differences in the acceptance of psychiatry may account, in large part, for the direct relationship between class status and the rate of treated neuroses in the New Haven community. This point may be made by referring briefly to materials we have discussed in earlier chapters. For example, in classes IV and V the neurotic patients in treatment, with few exceptions, are being treated because of the pressures brought to bear by social agencies or the police.

In the severe disorders, which correspond roughly to the psychoses especially when they break out suddenly and violently, there is considerable urgency for intervention. There may be danger for the life and safety of the patient as well as for persons in his environment unless intervention is immediate. Intervention in these cases usually consists of, more or less forced, hospitalization. The mandate of society to psychiatrists is reasonable and clear: Remove the disturbed person from the environment where the disturbance occurs. Society has legal safeguards in its commitment and certification laws to ensure that removal may be prompt. This is done by exerting pressures through family, friends, employers, responsible and authoritative persons in the community, and, if necessary, especially in classes IV and V, through the enforcement of laws often with the aid of the police. Society and not the individual makes the basic relevant decisions and ensures their execution; here the psychiatrist acts under customary practices and laws. Cooperation between the patient and the psychiatrist is desirable but not considered necessary in these cases. Theoretically, this kind of "help" is available to all classes. Only if help beyond the minimal requirements is desired *for those who can afford it* are treatment arrangements between psychiatrists and patients made privately.

In the less severe disorders, that is, the neuroses, there is no comparable urgency or obligation to submit to treatment. This is true particularly for disorders without a clear line of demarcation which blend into essentially "normal" states. In these disturbances the agreement between psychiatrist and patient is entirely voluntary, and the decision to obtain treatment is based on a rather critical self-appraisal and a strong urge for maximal self-realization. Treatment in these cases is not an emergency; often enough it is not essential as compared with the need for treatment in the severe disorders. These patients are not too sick to pursue their jobs or minimal obligations to family and community. Treatment for such persons does not take place in hospitals but in private practitioners' offices and in psychiatric clinics. Generally speaking, a cooperative attitude on the part of the patient is considered essential. This does not preclude unconscious resistance, but what is necessary is the voluntary effort to analyze one's troubles and conflicts, the desire to change, and willingness not to "act out." There are cases in which individuals seek treatment as a formal or informal requirement for professional training. Actually, psychiatrists, psychologists, nurses, social workers, artists, other professional workers, and persons in the communication businesses make up a considerable percentage of the class I and II neurotics in this study.

Treatment in these cases depends on the proximity of the patient's to the therapist's values. It is a specific, highly individualized effort directed toward the emotional re-education of the patient; it is designed to free the patient from any signs and symptoms of mental illness. The goal, although commonly referred to as a "cure," is an attempt to reintegrate the patient's drives and defenses so that he may achieve maximal self-realization. Such personal re-education in its most intensive form—psychoanalysis—sets an ambitious goal for the patient. In most cases, it is only approximated; for this reason, criteria for the end of an analysis are not definite. At best, the psychoanalyst can say when maximal benefit has been reached, and the analysand may continue the process by himself. Analysis is an interminable process. Not many persons can afford this or will avail themselves of this method of self-improvement.

Class and Availability of Treatment

Differences in the number of neurotic patients enumerated in the Psychiatric Census may be explained also, in part, by the relative ease with which the higher classes get what they want while the lower classes do not. Class I persons know better than others how to use experts and how to get their attention. Moreover, they are able to buy professional services in many areas of life—civic matters, law, and health to name only a few instances.

The techniques persons use to obtain psychiatric therapy differ from one class to another. Class I relies upon techniques that are casual, "gentlemanly," occasionally even devious, but effective. Many approaches are made through an influential "middleman," often but not always a physician, who approaches what he believes to be the "best" psychiatrist and intervenes for his client. For example, a busy general practitioner recently made an appointment with a prominent psychiatrist solely to tell him about the influence and power of one of his patients whom he wanted to refer to psychiatric treatment. The practitioner made it very clear that the psychiatrist could not "afford" not to accept this member of the core group as a patient. In another instance, a leading class I individual complained to the trustees of a private institution because a relative was being treated by the best psychiatrist on the staff instead of by the director himself.

Class II and III persons often utilize techniques that are not approved of publicly in order "to get things done." Their greatest reliance is upon "political" influence. Public hospital psychiatrists often receive red-margin letters from local politicians who make special requests for persons having access to them. Only class IV persons depend on direct demands. The proverb "The squeaking wheel gets the grease" is particularly true for this class. Class V

persons tend to be resigned to their fate; they seldom "squeak."
For example, an old Italian woman always dressed in black regularly
visits her schizophrenic son who is assigned to a back ward in a
nearby state hospital. She shyly keeps her eyes to the floor when
she walks by the doctor's office; she never dares to talk to a doctor
or nurse. She accepts whatever she is told on the rare occasions
when she is told anything.

NEUROTIC PATIENT'S KNOWLEDGE OF PSYCHIATRY

Knowledge of psychiatry in nearly all intensively studied neurotic
patients in every class is inadequate. Psychiatrists do not expect
patients to have a professional level of information, but they do
expect them to have sufficient knowledge to cooperate with their
therapists and, to some degree, understand their efforts. We found
that, with the exception of some class I and II persons who understood principles of dynamic psychiatry before they entered treatment, patients know very little about psychiatric theory or practice. Even those whose knowledge might be rated as "fair" usually
know little more than that psychiatry deals with mental illness and
that psychiatrists heal their patients not only with drugs and surgery,
but also by "mental" methods. How mental methods work and how
emotional stresses or problems are related to emotional and physical
symptoms are not understood, even after months of psychotherapy.
This may be attributed to resistance and, in part, to the difficulty
psychiatrists have in communicating simple, clear, and meaningful
explanations to their patients.

One woman whose therapist was convinced that she understood
what he was doing after a year of "insight" therapy was asked during an interview by a different psychiatrist what she thought was
occurring in her treatment. She stated, "The doctor is wonderful;
he tells me how to forget." It is difficult for patients in every class
to explore their emotional problems. But less than 2 percent of
the class V patients understood the aims or techniques of psychotherapy. Over 90 percent of the class IV patients remained so upset
that real participation in exploratory psychotherapy was never possible. Even among the class III's who were able to talk about their
problems there were some who never grasped the meaning of psychotherapy and hoped that after "all the talking" comes the "treatment." In some patients, this hurdle is never overcome.

The majority of neurotic patients in classes III and IV are adverse initially to the idea of psychiatric intervention. Practically all class V patients are antagonistic. In many instances, hostility to psychiatrists is rooted in fear of mental illness and lack of understanding of the function of the psychiatrist. This may be illustrated by such comments as, "Psychiatry is fine for crazy people, but it can't help me," or, "People think you are crazy when you come to see a psychiatrist."

Class V persons know less about mental illness than patients who have had a better education, and they know less about how to get help than persons in the higher classes. They are most likely to be dumped into the laps of psychiatrists by authorities in the community, often accompanied by aggressive gestures. When this occurs, they passively expect to be cared for in some way. Class V patients accept professional procedures which have no meaning to them and which often arouse their anxiety. If they remain in treatment, they submit unquestioningly to orders they do not grasp rather than rebel or stubbornly refuse to cooperate. Even class IV persons, in treatment for some time, with the exception of a few "who get the idea," gain little from the kind of psychiatric treatment they receive. Practically all class V neurotics soon drop out of treatment. The few who remain beyond the intake period are unable to understand that their troubles are not physical illnesses. They continue to hold these attitudes even when their therapists change from insight therapy to directive-supportive psychotherapy. These patients are disappointed in not getting sufficient practical advice about how to solve their problems and how to run their lives. They express in word and action their lack of confidence in a "talking treatment." They retain rigid attitudes toward mental illness and consider the psychiatrist a magical doctor who can miraculously cure their "physical ills." They expect "pills and needles" and, also as a gratuity, sympathy and warmth, and they are disappointed at not having such demands gratified.

Knowledge of psychiatry does not increase with the length of time neurotic patients in the two lower classes are in treatment. Only a few patients in class IV learned anything about the "human mind," unconscious conflict, psychological mechanisms, and how individuals express themselves in emotional and somatic symptoms. The class V patients did not grasp the principle that they could be helped if they obtained "insight" into their problems. Their inflexible attitudes toward mental illness and psychiatry served as barriers to learning. Their therapists were unable to communicate with them for reasons we will discuss in the section on the attitudes of psychiatrists toward patients.

Family's Knowledge of Mental Illnesses of Relatives

The knowledge of family members in all classes with regard to the mental illnesses of their relatives is similar to those the neurotic patients held before the onset of their illness. Knowledge of mental illness among the members of the families of patients in classes I and II was higher, more detailed, and more rational than among those in class III. It was less, as one might expect, in class IV and least in class V. As far as any expressions about the causes of illness are made by relatives, members of classes I and II stress "strain on the nerves," "fatigue," and "overwork." Class III's mention such things as "brain disease." The majority of class III relatives are unable to accept a psychogenic explanation of their relative's difficulties. Such an etiological explanation is beyond the grasp of most class IV and almost all class V persons. Class IV and V family members regard mental illnesses as somatic diseases and think they are caused by such things as "bad blood," a "bump on the head," and "too much booze."

Class I and II persons are inclined to inform themselves about theories of mental illness to a much greater extent than class III or class IV persons. In classes I and II, information about mental illness has been gained from courses in college or from systematic reading of books and magazine articles. Sources of information in the three lower classes are hearsay, motion pictures, and least of all, systematic reading of books on the subject. In the last decade, mental illness and its treatment have become acceptable topics in motion picture, radio, and television programs. Some impact through these channels of information should be expected in the not too distant future. But, to date, ideas of mental illness based on the notions of dynamic psychiatry and spread by the Mental Health Movement have not penetrated to the two lower classes. So far, the Armed Forces and the Veterans Administration have contributed the most to an understanding of mental hygiene and psychiatry to classes IV and V.

There is a marked tendency on the part of relatives to be secretive about the occurrence of mental illness in the family. Efforts to conceal illness differ from one class to another. Motivations for secrecy also are different from class to class. Class V families guard themselves against "prying," "snooping," and "interference" from outside "agencies" regardless of whether the intruders are physicians, social workers, nurses, or police. When it becomes impossible to hide the existence of trouble, the resistance of a family often collapses completely. Then relatives allow the authorities to take over the patient. They watch the ensuing events in an outwardly passive way; they may be burning inwardly with resentment towards the patient, themselves, and the authorities. In class IV, shame is the mainspring for secrecy. Concern over what the neighbors, friends, and employers will think if they hear about the existence of mental illness in the family is a common source of anxiety. In classes II and III, the relatives are worried about such things as how mental illness in the family will affect the children, their chances to "get ahead in the world," their marriages, and opportunities to "get a good job." Class I families show the least overt concern about their mentally ill relatives. They tend to accept the fact that some people have emotional difficulties, and a psychiatrist is the person to see when such trouble strikes. We want to point out, however, that our observations on class I families do not adequately portray family efforts to conceal psychiatric treatment, because we have data only on patients who permitted us to contact their families. The families of patients we were not able to interview might have expressed different attitudes.

In general, members of the families of psychotic patients regard their mentally ill relatives with mixed feelings of fear, shame, guilt, pity, and resentment. These sentiments, however, are differently distributed in the class structure. As a rule, the lower the class, the greater the feelings of fear and resentment; the higher the class, the more pronounced the feelings of shame and guilt. During the course of treatment, resentment in the families of patients in the two lower classes are replaced by feelings of helplessness, apathy, and lack of cooperation. In class I, II, and III families, such feelings are less marked. Interest in the sick member is stronger, more realistic, and the negative emotions are less rampant.

These sentiments are more difficult to detect in the families of neurotic patients. Most neurotic patients continue to function in the community and there is less opportunity to seize upon the illness as an excuse to express anger, guilt, fear, and shame. Ambulatory neurotic patients often cause as much trouble for their relatives as psychotic persons, but the behavior of neurotics is not identified, usually, as illness by members of their families.

The attitudes of the family toward its psychotic member are responsible, to a significant degree, for the determination of who goes to a hospital, who stays home, who improves in hospital, who "deteriorates" and eventually stagnates in a chronic ward. This generalization is applicable particularly in a disease like schizophrenia where there is a marked, though variable, tendency toward "deterioration." In this situation, interaction between patients, families, and hospital staff is particularly important for the outcome of the illness and the fate of the patient. The great discrepancy in the rates of chronic schizophrenia between classes I and II, on the one hand, and classes IV and V, on the other, may be explained, at least in part, by these differences in attitude.[2] The attitudes of family members toward the patient are strong and ever-present factors from the first day of hospitalization on through the active and less active phases of treatment, and, in fact, until the patient returns home and adjusts in the community.

Patients are not discharged just because they are well; neither are they retained in hospital just because they are sick. Their discharge is the result of many factors and events, among them being the nature of the illness, whether adequate benefit resulted from hospitalization, attitudes of the family toward the patient and of the patient toward the family, relationships of the patient with the hospital staff, and of the hospital staff with the family. To be sure, the behavior of the patient is a major factor in what happens. Undoubtedly, there are many patients who are not discharged because nobody wants to take care of them in the home. In class V, such occurrences are frequent. Once a class V person is committed to a mental institution, the likelihood of his return to the family is small. Class V patients tend to be dropped by their families as injured limbs are cast off by some organisms. In class IV three families out of five are interested in their hospitalized members, and they are prepared to reaccept them into the home. Class III families tend to be closely knit, concerned about their sick relatives, and the possibility of reacceptance into the family is high. In class II, the family tries to do "the right thing" for the patient. In class I, the advice of professional experts is relied upon commonly in any crisis, and turning to the psychiatrist or a psychiatric hospital is no exception. In addition, "influential" people with "know-how" are more likely to rally to a friend in distress. The fact that these families have adequate means enables them to gain access readily to private practitioners and private hospitals and to receive "better" treatment.

Attitudes of Psychiatrists toward Patients

The attitudes of psychiatrists toward their patients are determined by subtle psychic and social pressures. Included in this network are such things as why one person likes another and what a particular relationship does for its participants on a conscious level, as well as transferences and countertransferences on an unconscious level. We interviewed seventeen psychiatrists to learn how they felt on the "surface" toward their patients. Five were private practitioners, nine were residents, and three were staff physicians. We tried to assess whether: (a) these psychiatrists held similar views toward life and society with their patients, (b) they noticed differences in social class between themselves and their patients, and (c) they liked their patients. The attitudes of these psychiatrists were all expressed toward neurotic patients in ambulatory treatment. After these psychiatrists had expressed their views toward their patients to psychiatrists on our team, we rated the attitudes as "like" or "dislike."

The numerical ratings of "likes" and "dislikes" of patients in class I through class III in contrast to class IV and V patients are significantly different. The class I through III patients were the ones who were "liked" and the class IV and V patients were "disliked." Some of the "dislikes" were due to the frustration of therapists who had to work with "bad" cases, patients whose desperate environmental conditions and personality characteristics made their work difficult. Practically all the therapists interviewed disapproved of the dominant behavior patterns in the class V patients. They were repelled by their crude, vulgar language, their outbursts of violence, at times by their passivity and apathy, or by their acceptance of such behavior as a husband beating his wife and the wife taking the beating for granted, and their endurance of poverty and economic insecurity. The therapists were puzzled and upset over the sexual mores of their class V patients. As a group, the psychiatrists were irritated by the patients' inability to think in their terms. They complained about the dullness and stupidity of these patients and particularly of their apathetic dependency. The following remarks are illustrations of such attitudes: "Seeing him every morning was a chore; I had to put him on my back and carry him for an hour." "He had to get attention in large doses, and this was hard to do." "The patient was not interesting or attractive; I had to repeat, repeat, repeat." "She was a poor, unhappy, miserable woman—we were worlds apart."

The therapists and the class V patients *are* worlds apart socially.

None of the therapists thought that friendships between these patients and themselves could be possible. They voiced hostile feelings toward the patients' values, especially when the therapist was upward mobile from a class III or IV background. These differences were more marked toward male than female patients. The therapists, at least, understood class III values; this cannot be said regarding the values of classes IV and V. The lack of understanding between therapists and patients is a major reason why neurotic patients in the two lower classes drop out of treatment much faster than in the higher classes. The gulf between psychiatrist and patient may be explained, in part at least, by the lower status patients' lack of education.

Modern psychotherapy is most likely to succeed when communication is relatively easy between the therapist and the patient. Optimal conditions prevail when the therapist and the patient belong to the same social class. All too often, psychotherapy runs into difficulties when the therapist and the patient belong to different classes. In these instances, the values of the therapist are too divergent from those of the patient, and communication becomes difficult between them. The greatest difficulty we observed occurred among relatively untrained psychiatrists. The one exception was a novice who, at times, established a surprisingly good man-to-man contact with a patient, regardless of class. As the psychiatric residents gained in their knowledge of the psychotherapeutic process and of social and cultural differences, communication with members of classes other than their own became less difficult, but in no instance was the difficulty overcome completely. Even inexperienced men discerned, when the patients and therapists did not belong to the same class, social factors which accounted for difficulties in the therapeutic process.

The most frequent source of difficulty between the lower status patient in psychotherapy and the therapist is the patient's tacit or overt demand for an authoritarian attitude on the part of the psychiatrist, and the psychiatrist's unwillingness to assume this role because it runs counter to certain therapeutic principles. "Insight" therapy is less likely to be grasped by lower class patients than physical therapy or a therapy employing "magical methods." This should not be construed as a recommendation of supportive, suggestive, or coercive techniques for these classes.

The essential principles underlying insight therapy are shared most frequently by psychiatrists and patients in classes I and II, for a number of reasons: Patients in these classes are inclined more than the lower classes—because of their education—to seek and follow professional advice. Their capacity (this varies from person to person) to think in symbolic terms, to view interpersonal relations with some interest, and their desire to reach their potential in efficiency leads them to be disposed more favorably toward psychotherapy, particularly insight therapy. Class V patients are least likely to accept any type of psychiatric treatment unless they are committed to a mental hospital, but, as our data show, when this occurs they tend to receive custodial care.

The need and value of insight therapy is not appreciated by lower class patients. Class IV and V persons seek material help in the form of pills, needles, obscure rays, and ritual; some actually seek support and sympathy. This is certainly not the kind of cooperation the psychiatrist needs who attempts to administer psychotherapy. Finally, only a few persons in the two lower classes enter treatment voluntarily; hence, they can hardly be expected to feel an obligation to cooperate with a psychiatrist. The professional closeness necessary to help a patient in psychotherapy rarely takes place between a mobile class I or II therapist and a non-mobile class IV or V patient. When the patient fails to cooperate, he is blamed and labeled a "bad" patient by the psychiatrist. The reasons for the patient's failure to fulfill the expected obligation is not appreciated by the therapist. The psychiatrist expects patients from the two lower classes to accept his ideas of how they should behave in the therapeutic situation, or they are viewed as just "no good."

To help the patient achieve self-realization the psychiatrist must understand the patient. It is not the patient's job a priori to understand the psychiatrist, but it is the psychiatrist's job to understand the patient. This principle is particularly important in a more active dynamic psychotherapy where the therapist engages in a significant interaction and is not a mere mirror image of the patient's emotional and cognitive reflections. Our main thesis is that the psychiatrist should not overlook the social differences between himself and his patients, but he should understand them, face them squarely, and deal with them in the therapeutic situation. When therapist and patient are far apart in their basic values and views, they have little to say to each other. When the role expectation on either side is uncertain, goals are not clearly stated, and the relationship is distant, both the therapist and the patient feel lost. To help persons of all classes, psychiatrists will have to learn about the way of life of patients of all classes and ethnic groups. Before they can do this, psychiatrists will have to face some of their professional biases, just as the analyst in training learns to face unconscious and irrational personal sentiments through analytic scrutiny. Knowledge of the social worlds which surround us and analysis of some of the therapist's prejudices may pave the way for proper treatment of mental patients in all classes.

This discussion runs counter to a dictum important to psychiatrists, namely, that they treat any patient regardless of his race, religion, ethnic background, or cultural and social values. Our observations do not negate this ideal altogether; nevertheless, certain difficulties are likely to appear when psychotherapists and patients of different classes encounter each other. Difficulties involving class status are much less pronounced when upward mobile psychiatrists meet upward mobile patients, especially successful ones, with whom the psychiatrist can identify socially. Differences arising from divergences in class status may be less disturbing when a deeper level of therapy is reached; but to get started on a psychoanalytic [3] excursion into the depths is the problem. We would like to caution the reader that the values of therapist and patient need not be alike or even similar; they merely cannot be too far apart socially and psychologically unless the therapist has a real and sympathetic understanding of the patient's class culture.

Class-linked factors facilitate or inhibit the prescription of psychoanalysis and other variants of dynamic psychiatry. Psychoanalysis is limited almost exclusively to classes I and II for economic and social reasons. The two higher classes are the only ones where individuals are not preoccupied with overwhelming external pressures and conflicts. Only when such pressures are relatively small can the patient afford to dispense with direct advice, the manipulation of the external situation, and work his problems through by the application of analytical methods. Obviously, only a few persons with considerable means or willingness to spend large sums, often as a sacrifice to themselves or their families, can afford the high fees analysts charge, and analysts, as one of them put it, "cannot afford lower fees." Even analysts in training charge high fees as they are pushed into practice to earn the fees charged them by senior analysts. Yet senior analysts earn less than other medical specialists of a comparable level of competence. This is a serious dilemna.

The capacity for verbalization and symbolization, which is important though not indispensable in dynamic psychotherapy, is not exclusive to classes I and II. Nevertheless, it is mostly in the higher classes where we encounter the necessary incentive and opportunity for optimal self-realization. The patients in classes I and II strive to live according to values which are not too far removed from the values of the psychiatrist. These values are neither "high" nor "low"; they are simply the values of the higher classes. These values include ethical norms and esthetic tastes, such as concern for achievement, skill, order, beauty, and, to a certain extent, needs for psychological intimacy and insight. In these classes we find more definite attempts in the direction of sublimation.

In contrast to the higher classes, the reality situations of the lower classes are tough, threatening, and, in many respects, hopeless. Lower class patients who have an insoluble reality situation often have little desire to get better. Moreover, they are not able to understand how thinking and talking can help them. Lower class persons have not learned to verbalize and symbolize in the same way higher class persons have. Neither have they learned to sublimate present needs for the realization of future goals. The class V individual, especially, is not trained to look at his troubles as if they were possibly the result of his own doing, and then undo them after the proper insight is reached. Insight therapy is "inside" therapy, and the vast majority of individuals in the two lower classes want "outside" therapy. If reality cannot be changed for them, at least they want advice and some tangible intervention, such as pills, shots, warmth, or radiation. Techniques providing merely "insight" may not be the best or only method; another approach may have to be found.

At present, psychotherapy seems to work when a "good" therapist meets a "good" patient. There are not enough good therapists, and we need to train more. In due time, we may be able to treat even those who cannot be called good patients. A good patient is a person who can cooperate with the therapist, one who understands his objectives, and what he is doing to attain them. A good patient is similar in cultural background to the good psychotherapist. The two can communicate with one another. In principle it is possible for any psychiatrist to understand any patient. In application, it is unlikely that any psychiatrist fully understands patients who have very different value systems from the ones he holds. This constitutes a challenge to psychiatry to find appropriate methods to treat patients in all classes.

One might argue that difficult patients should get the most skillful therapists. Pursuant to this thesis, we are aware that most class V patients fall, by and large, into the category of difficult patients, but their therapists are the least experienced. It is established practice to assign indigent patients in clinics to trainees without sufficient regard, at times, for the skill which is required to treat a particular problem.

At the end of this discussion of the reasons for the concentration of insight therapy in the higher classes, we would like to stress, in order to avoid misunderstandings, that insight therapy is not restricted of necessity to these classes. There are lower class individuals who are capable of it, and there are psychiatrists who are capable of understanding lower class individuals. All this is hardly more surprising than the fact that individuals in the upper and lower classes, in rare instances, marry each other and that a few of these marriages are harmonious.[4] Likewise, therapeutic relationships between lower class patients and upper class psychiatrists sometimes occur. We are aware also of the fact that the ultimate criterion for insight therapy is what might be referred to as being "psychologically minded"; and of course there are many individuals in the upper classes who are not psychologically minded, and there are some lower class people who are.

We shall add two factors so far not mentioned which probably influence the data we presented in Chapter Nine on relationships between class status and the type of therapy psychiatrists administer to their patients. Treatment will be more readily available to a wider spread in the status structure if it is inexpensive, relatively uncomplicated in technique and application, and reasonably certain to work. Unfortunately, generally speaking, no such treatment exists in psychiatry today. Psychotherapy is expensive and complex, and we have no absolutely convincing proof that it "works" beyond the therapist's and the individual patient's convictions in cases which were benefited. Organic treatments are simple, and, once hospitalization is provided, inexpensive, but they have only a very limited indication and their therapeutic efficiency at present leaves much to be desired. It is interesting that differences in treatment which are attributed to social "causes" are greatest in diseases like schizophrenia and the psychoneuroses and smallest in the manic-depressive group. The tentative explanation we offer is that electro-convulsive therapy for the depressive psychoses offers an inexpensive, simple method which is successful in a considerable proportion of the causes where it is used. Public Health men, some psychiatrists, and persons concerned with welfare and health legislation are aware of this and express definite interest in a treatment which is economical, simple, and efficient. Some of the enthusiasm for the tranquilizing drugs and efforts to develop psychopharmacological therapy can be understood in terms of such demands. Freud is said to have remarked that the man with the syringe stands behind the psychoanalyst; ultimately, we hope to develop more effective and more democratic methods of psychiatric treatment. However, it is unrealistic to expect that such methods will solve all man's emotional problems, that is the ones we usually call neurotic.

Social inequalities in treatment are seen most clearly among schizophrenic patients. The class IV or V schizophrenic, once cast off by his family and community, may receive one or two series of organic treatments in a public hospital. If these treatments do not succeed, the patient drifts to the back wards where in stultifying isolation he regresses even more into a world of his own. Rarely, however, do we see in the class I or II schizophrenic patients in private hospitals, who may get the benefit of psychotherapy and environmental treatment, deterioration comparable to what we see regularly in the chronic wards of the state hospitals. Indeed, in wealthy families who can afford to provide show farms and boat yards as occupational therapy for their schizophrenic scions we have observed over a period of years unmistakable schizophrenic symptomatology, but little deterioration. We have, in view of our clinical observations and of newer experiences on "isolating" individuals,[5] every reason to believe that to expose schizophrenics to a "back ward atmosphere" is the worst thing we can do to them. These differences add up to deep social fissures in psychiatric treatment, such as we do not encounter in the rest of medicine with the possible exception of peacetime cosmetic surgery.

Economic as well as social factors are important determinants in who is or is not a psychiatric patient and how he is treated. It is not easy to differentiate between the importance of economic and social considerations. Nevertheless, our observations, in different settings where the economic factor is negligible, convinced us of the importance of social class in relation to economic aspects of this question. For example, in the large clinic in the community hospital, no patient is refused treatment because he cannot pay. There is no deliberate policy to treat patients differently depending on whether they pay five dollars per treatment, nothing, or any amount in between. Nevertheless, a very strong preference exists for patients from classes II and III. When we examined this clinic we found that, to begin with, it is much more difficult for a class IV or V person to be admitted to treatment than it is for persons in classes II or III. When a class IV individual is admitted, the likelihood of his dropping out after a few treatments is much greater than it is for a class III person. The class IV patient is more apt to get short-term supportive psychotherapy instead of prolonged intensive psychotherapy than is the class II or III patient. Moreover, class IV patients tend to be treated by medical students, class III patients are assigned to residents, and class II patients are selected by the senior staff members.

This finding came as a "bolt out of the blue" for the men who determined the policies of this clinic. It was certainly not planned. A similar situation is found in the public mental hospitals where, also without regard to the ability of the patients' families to pay, the acute schizophrenics in class III are more likely to get psychotherapy than class IV and V patients in the same disease group who entered the hospital at approximately the same time.

The lack of rapport found between most of the therapists and class V patients in the clinic may be attributed, in part, to the fact that they are beginners. But beginners *are* the therapists who deal with patients in clinics all over the country. Although psychotherapy of class V patients is by no means impossible, new techniques need to be developed to reach and to communicate to them both the goals of therapy and the rationale of the psychiatrist who is trying to reach these goals.

ATTITUDES AND SOCIAL ROLES

The Patients

The preceding discussion leads us to a brief consideration of how attitudes toward mental illness are related to the "sick" role, on the one hand, and to the professional role of the psychiatrist on the other. Talcott Parsons has stated that there are four institutionalized norms associated with the roles of sick persons in our society: (1) The sick person is exempted from normal social role responsibilities. (2) The sick person is not held morally responsible for his illness; therefore, he needs to be cared for. (3) The sick person is obligated to "get well." And (4) the sick person has a moral obligation to seek "technically competent" help, that is, a physician, and to "cooperate with him" in trying to get well.[6]

When these theoretical norms are applied to psychiatric disorders, our data show: first, that most persons with neuroses are not exempted from normal social obligations. A cold, for instance, is a recognized excuse to be absent from work on a given day, but a neurosis is not an acceptable excuse for the same behavior. The lower classes, in particular, do not recognize the legitimacy of neurosis as an excuse for failure to meet normal obligations. Psychotics in all classes, however, are exempted from social obligations, but as a consequence of radical disenfranchisement, provided their state of mind is recognized and they are placed in a mental hospital. When we examine the data in relation to Parsons' second point, we find that the neurotic person is held responsible for his behavior, in contrast to an individual who is organically ill. Under the impact of modern psychiatric theory, there is a partial conviction in classes I and II that persons with neuroses are not completely responsible for their behavior. But even in these classes there is a widespread conviction that neurotics bring their suffering on themselves, and they could have prevented it if they so chose. Even the viewpoints of psychiatrists on these questions, particularly concerning antisocial behavior, are often confusing to other professional persons; they could hardly be expected to be any clearer to the general public. Our data on the psychoses are in accord with Parsons' theoretical position; the psychotic person is not considered to be responsible for his illness.

With respect to Parsons' third point we shall ask: If a neurotic person's difficulties are not recognized as illness, how can the individual be expected to "get well"? The psychoses are recognized as illnesses in our society, but there is little or no obligation placed upon the psychotic person to "get well." Popular attitudes toward the psychotic individual are such that he is far more likely to be removed from society than he is to be made to feel he should "get well."

When the data are viewed in terms of Parsons' fourth point, namely, the obligation to seek "technically competent" help, incongruities reappear. The neurotic patient, once he enters treatment, is expected to cooperate with the therapist even more than a patient with an organic illness is expected to cooperate with his physician. But the neurotic patients in classes I, II, and III evaluate their problems differently from persons with similar disorders in classes IV and V. For example, neurotic patients receiving ambulatory treatment present a great variety of complaints at their first psychiatric interview. We divided these into somatic and emotional and interpersonal complaints. Patients in classes I and II especially, but even a majority of the class III patients, are able to accept a psychogenic explanation of their difficulties. Class III patients present their complaints in terms of emotional and interpersonal difficulties more frequently than class IV patients: 85 percent versus 37 percent. Some three out of four class V neurotics present somatic symptoms when they first enter psychiatric treatment. These patients express an organic orientation not only at the beginning of therapy, asking their therapists for "shots" or pills, but they continue to hold these attitudes and express their lack of confidence in a "talking treatment" throughout therapy. Parsons' theoretical conceptions of the "sick role" in our society are clearly only partially applicable to psychiatric disorders.

The Roles of Psychiatrists

The roles psychiatrists play in relation to patients and other family members vary according to whether they are private practitioners, salaried employees in private hospitals, public hospitals, or clinics, or in teaching and administration. A private practitioner who treats primarily classes I and II is the protector and expert "friend" of his patient and the patient's family, even though he does not engage in social relations with them. Such patients, especially when their families are prominent and influential, often make their psychiatrists feel uncomfortable by exercising pressures and influences which are a hindrance in treatment.

The expectancies of the patient in the class I core group are stated in no uncertain terms. Usually these patients and their families make more demands of psychiatrists than other patients. As far as they are concerned, psychiatrists are no different from physicians in general practice or other medical specialties. These patients and their families usually view the psychiatrist as middle class. In such relationships the psychiatrist is not in a position to exert social power; he is lucky if he is able to rely on professional techniques successfully. All too often he has to carry out complicated maneuvers vis-à-vis a critical, demanding, sometimes informed, and sometimes very uninformed "VIP." Some VIP's push the physician into the role of lackey or comforter, and some psychiatrists fall into such a role. The psychiatrist who faces a demanding and manipulating patient, or the family member of such a patient, labors under considerable anxiety at times. When this occurs, the psychiatrist mobilizes aggression to counter the patient's behavior. The psychiatrist has to think hard to understand the relationship socially and dynamically to do his job even reasonably well. Psychiatrists are inclined to discuss such behavior in professional circles in psychodynamic rather than in social terms.[7]

If there is a split between the interests of the patient and those of his family, the psychiatrist's primary loyalty is usually on the side of the patient. If payments, however, come from the family and not from the patient, an ambiguous and unfavorable constellation arises which often blocks treatment; at least it is apt to create complications.

The role of the psychiatrist in the private hospital is very similar to that of the private practitioner except that the average institutional psychiatrist is tempted to show more loyalty to the family than to the patient, especially when the patient has been placed in the institution after committing antisocial acts in the family or the community. In public hospitals loyalty relationships are often divided between the community and the patient. Unless careful thought is given to this problem, the position of the psychiatrist may be very difficult in his relations to the patient and to the institution that employs him. A divided loyalty, at times, complicates the psychiatrist's relationships with the patient. Psychiatrists dealing primarily with interpersonal relations will do better when their loyalties are on the patient's side, and, if this is at all possible, they should not be divided.

In adult clinics and in practically all children's clinics, psychiatrists treat the patient and a social worker treats the family. This division of function is rare in classes I and II; family members in these strata show a great deal of resistance and often aversion to a social worker and demand the undivided attention of the psychiatrist. In the clinic, however, where psychiatrist and social worker are expected to cooperate, the basic situation is very similar to private practice except that factors other than money decide whether patients are accepted. Value judgments as to whether patients are worthwhile, whether they will make a contribution to society through functioning adequately, or if possible at a superior level, whether they are intelligent, sincere, and attractive, play a decisive part in the disturbed individual's efforts to find a "place in the sun." An opportunity to obtain psychotherapy is often highly coveted, and, as there are few such opportunities, the struggle for it may be intense.

The administrator in public hospitals [8] has essentially the characteristics of other public servants in the field of health and welfare and an orientation and role assignment which is closely akin to that of psychiatrists in clinics. The academic psychiatrist—the "professor"—is oriented toward teaching and research with less emphasis on administration of a complicated institution. The woes of today's patients may take his time, but his thoughts are upon the profession's larger problems.

SUMMARY

One might speak of psychiatry's role as being in a state of transition, bridging the functions of several other institutions which are inadequate by themselves to handle the complexities of living in urban communities. It is not our task to predict the future of a young and growing profession and its social functions. These will be shaped in some measure by the attitudes of members of the society toward mental disorders and the professional persons who must cope with them.[9]

NOTES

[1] This usage follows that developed by Carl I. Hovland, Irving L. Janis, and Harold H. Kelly, *Communication and Persuasion*, Yale University Press, New Haven, 1953.

[2] Newhouse, in a short story, sketched the problem in a fascinating manner; E. Newhouse, "Come Again Another Day," *The New Yorker*, April 15, 1950, p. 26. For a systematic study see Ozzie G. Simmons, James A. Davis, and Katherine Spencer, "Interpersonal Strains in Release from a Mental Hospital," *Social Problems*, Vol. 4 (July 1956), pp. 21–28. F. C. Redlich, "The Psychiatrist in Caricature: An Analysis of Unconscious Attitudes toward Psychiatry," *American Journal of Orthopsychiatry*, Vol. 20 (July 1950), pp. 560–571.

[3] H. Hartmann, E. Kris, and R. Loewenstein, "Some Psychoanalytic Comments on Culture and Personality," in *Psychoanalysis and Culture*, Wilbur and W. Muensterger, International Universities Press, New York, 1951.

[4] A. B. Hollingshead, "Cultural Factors in the Selection of Marriage Mates," *American Sociological Review*, Vol. 15 (1950), pp. 619–627.

[5] John C. Lilly, "Mental Effects of Reduction of Ordinary Levels of Physical Stimuli on Intact Healthy Persons," *Research Techniques in Schizophrenia*, Psychiatric Research Reports, No. 5, American Psychiatric Association, June 1956, pp. 1–9. W. H. Herm, W. H. Benton, and D. O. Hebb, "Cognitive Effects of a Decreased Variation to the Sensory Equipment," *American Psychologist*, Vol. 8, No. 8 (August 1953), p. 366.

[6] Talcott Parsons, *The Social System*, The Free Press, Glencoe, Illinois, 1951, pp. 436–437.

[7] Jurgen Ruesch, "Social Factors in Therapy," in *Psychiatric Treatment, Procedures of the Association for Research in Nervous and Mental Diseases*, Vol. 31 (1953), pp. 59–93. M. Gill, R. Newman, and F. C. Redlich, *The Initial Interview in Psychiatric Practice*, International Universities Press, New York, 1954, p. 70.

[8] For a brilliant and forthright treatise on this subject see Ivan Belknap, *Human Problems of a State Mental Hospital*, McGraw-Hill Book Company, New York, 1956.

[9] For an interesting discussion of this point, see J. Spiegel, "The Social Roles of Doctor and Patient in Psychoanalysis and Psychotherapy," *Psychiatry*, Vol. 17 (November 1954), pp. 369–376.

social implications
of psychiatric
practice

chapter twelve

INTRODUCTION

This research was undertaken with two questions in mind: First, is the presence of mental illness in the population related to class status? Second, is the treatment which a mentally ill member of our society receives affected by his class position? To answer these questions we formulated five hypotheses. In successive chapters we have presented the data we gathered to test the first three of the five hypotheses. In this chapter we will review our findings. In addition, we will discuss briefly *Hypothesis 4*, which assumed that psychodynamic factors in the development of psychiatric disorders are correlative to an individual's position in the class structure, and also *Hypothesis 5*, which postulated that mobility in the class structure has some influence on certain psychiatric disorders. Finally, we will point to the application of our findings in psychiatric practice and make some pertinent recommendations.

THE FINDINGS IN BRIEF

The many systematic tests we made of the first three hypotheses demonstrate that our original assumptions are correct. Highly significant associations do exist between class status and (*a*) the prevalence of psychiatric patients in the population, (*b*) the types of disorders mentally ill individuals present to psychiatrists, and (*c*) the kinds of treatment psychiatrists administer to their patients. These hypotheses are clearly tenable in the setting described in this book. However, many readers may ask: Does the same situation prevail in my community or any other community? It may, but only additional research can give a meaningful answer. Before our results are applied to another community, the following limitations should be kept in mind.

First, our data were gathered at mid-century in *one* New England metropolitan community. To be sure, there are a number of similar communities in the northeastern urban industrial region that stretches eastward from Chicago to the Atlantic Ocean, south of the Great Lakes, and north of the Ohio River, but generalizations about the relationship of social class to the treatment of mental illness in our community when applied to other communities in this region, let alone to other regions of the United States, need to be made with care. Cross-community comparisons of psychiatric disorders and treatment by social class will be necessary before our findings are applicable to the larger society. Such studies should be similar to this one if the findings presented here are to be tested in different community settings.

Second, and we cannot repeat this too often, this study dealt only with patients under the care of psychiatrists. Therefore, it is a study of the prevalence of *treated* mental illness. It is not a study of true prevalence. Our data do not permit inferences as to true or endemic prevalence of mental illness in the population.

Third, this research was not designed to determine the true incidence of psychiatric disorders. Future research should be able to achieve one or more of the specific objectives mentioned here. They represent crucial next steps in the development of an epidemiology of mental illness.[1]

SOME TENTATIVE INFERENCES

Phenomenology of Mental Illnesses and Social Class

In spite of the limitations listed, certain tentative inferences may be drawn from this study. First, each type of mental and emotional disorder occurs in all classes, but in different proportions. This discovery indicates that social and cultural conditions do influence the development of the various types of psychiatric disorders at different class levels in important ways.

The significance of sociocultural factors in the etiology of severe functional neuroses and psychoses is illustrated by culture-specific syndromes, such as the Lata of the Javanese [2] and Imu of the Ainus.[3] Most of the functional psychoses and neuroses clearly reflect a specific color from the social setting in which they occur. For example, some continental clinicians colloquially refer to certain depressions in Eastern European Jews as *melancholia agitata Hebraica*. In the days when we observed patients with general paresis, euphoric patients in Vienna and depressed patients in Boston seemed to be the rule rather than the exception. Some hysterical reactions and specific paranoid states, such as being bewitched or under the influence of the evil eye (*mal occhio*) are particularly frequent in New Haven's lower status southern Italian first-generation immigrant population. Related to such observations, psychiatrists have noticed by way of clinical observations that gross hysterical reactions in the Armed Forces are more frequent among enlisted personnel than among officers. Currently, no research explains how these culturally and socially specific syndromes develop.

Second, some of the differences in the distribution of the various groups of disorders may be related to conditions in the several hospitals and clinics catering to particular status levels. For example, we rarely see extremely regressed schizophrenics in good private institutions; we see them often on the chronic wards of bad public hospitals. Psychiatrists noticed how quiet, docile, and gentle chronic Japanese schizophrenics appear in their clean, neat hospitals with a well-defined hierarchy role assignment. In contrast to this, under the vile and violent mental hospital conditions of Korea and Okinawa immediately after the war Redlich observed that schizophrenic and organic psychotics seemed particularly regressed.

Third, cultural and social conditions are reflected in the content of mental illnesses. To give a simple example, in a republic, megalomanic patients imagine themselves president and not emperor. Shortly after World War II, Japanese and American psychiatrists noticed that some Japanese patients changed their paranoid delusion of being Emperor Hirohito to being General MacArthur. In our culture, symptoms of being influenced by spirits and demons have been replaced by beliefs that one is controlled by electricity and, most recently, by radar or atomic energy. Culture probably determines the external shape and form rather than the essential nature of the phenomenon. The deeper relationship between symptom and culture is not understood. Exploration of the influence of social factors on the development of the ego is still ahead of us.[4]

Fourth, perception of mental health varies from class to class. From the viewpoints of both theory and clinical practice the measure of mental health or illness is not who is "normal" or "abnormal," but who is normal for what and for whom in each class.[5] Research furnishing data on parameters of gratification, frustration, success-failure, and deviation-conformity would be. of great importance. At present we lack such data, just as we do not know enough about the balance of unconscious-preconscious-conscious forces which according to Kubie determine the normality of the single act in any status level.[6] Good phenomenological and etiological data are needed on the psychopathology of everyday life in all classes. Once such data are accumulated, the problem of the distribution of mental health and illness should fall into its place.

Fifth, confusion prevails over the relationship of the "external" event to the "internalized" experience and the impact of the two on the mental health of the individual. H. Murray[7] speaks, for instance, of external presses and internal stresses. The relative significance of presses has been grasped by poets for generations. As the Viennese playwright Raimund put it: *"Da ist der alleraermste Mann dem andern viel zu reich"* (The poorest man is much too rich for his neighbor). In our search for the etiological components of disorders, we would like to know the stresses and presses, as well as the conflicts, the rewards, and punishments of primary and secondary groups, particularly as far as they are related to social class. While our data indicate that sociocultural factors are important in the prevalence of treated disorders in the population, we cannot conclude they are the essential and necessary conditions in the etiology of mental disorders.

SOCIAL CLASS AND THE LIFE CYCLE

We pointed out in Chapter One the complexity and difficulty of assessing the importance of hereditary, organic, and social factors in the development of psychiatric disorders. Nevertheless, a brief sketch of psychogenetics and psychodynamics bearing on *Hypothesis 4* may provide a frame of reference for future research on the importance of sociocultural factors for understanding disturbed behavior. We shall do this by suggesting the influence of social class in the life of individuals. In our discussion we shall divide the life cycle into the following phases: (1) early infancy, (2) late infancy, (3) early childhood, (4) late childhood, (5) puberty and adolescence, (6) early adulthood, (7) maturity, and (8) decline. Psychogenetics is the study of unconscious forces operating on the individual during the course of his life. Psychodynamics is concerned with current unconscious conflict. Both psychogenetics and psychodynamics deal with the importance of unconscious forces and conflicts in the phenomenology and etiology of psychiatric disorders.

Psychogenetics

1. EARLY INFANCY is a period of extreme dependency. It covers approximately the first year of life. Psychoanalysts refer to it as the period of early orality. The infant is totally dependent upon the mother or mother-substitute. The existence of a loving, protective, and stable environment is of paramount importance for the child's healthy development. Lack of loving care and protection at this age may produce catastrophic consequences.[8] A number of psychoanalysts believe that major environmental disturbances at this period may result in schizophrenia, but this has never been proved. However, it is quite possible that severe disturbances in later life may be traced back to traumatic experiences in early infancy. Lifelong dependency and characterological states of dejection, apathy, and a lack of trust in others may be related to damage in this phase of the life cycle. We postulate that the presence or absence of these characteristics is related to the child-rearing practices associated with families in the different social classes. For instance, a loveless infancy is more likely in a class V family than in a class II family.

2. LATER INFANCY is concentrated mainly in the second year of life. This is the period of orality and anality of psychoanalytic theory. The infant has become much less dependent; this is a time of crucial learning. In this period the young child learns to speak and to move about in the erect position, and, in our culture, toilet training is begun. The child expresses unmistakable aggression and begins to perceive some differentiation between the world and his own emergent ego. According to psychoanalytic theory, a fixation in this phase of development is related to the later development of a compulsive character with traits such as orderliness, rigidity, punctuality, cleanliness, perfectionism. It is of some interest that such traits as well as the prevalence of obsessive-compulsive neuroses are

more frequently encountered in the higher classes. Persons in classes I and II often complain about the lack of these traits in lower class people, unaware of the fact that such "anal" traits may be class-specific.

3. EARLY CHILDHOOD covers the third through the sixth years of life. During this phase, object relationships become widened and intensified, particularly toward parents and siblings. Also infantile sex drives, by now of a much more genital character, become intensified. Freud spoke of a flowering of infantile sexuality during this period with the parent of the opposite sex as the main love object and the parent of the same sex as the chief rival. Such object relationship is experienced with anxiety and later guilt; much of the anxiety is derived from a fear of injury to the genitalia. Most of these processes are unconscious and reveal themselves only by symbolic substitutes and residuals. These phenomena appear to be intensified in the class III family, whereas in the all-too-often-broken class V home or in some core group class I families with loose internal ties, the conflicts are less stormy and the ensuing object relationships are less intense. The significance of the primal scene (observation of parental intercourse) probably varies considerably from class to class, and it is probably much less important in American families than it was under the spatially tight living conditions of the European continent at the beginning of the twentieth century. We also think that identity formation concerning sex, and possibly also dominance, emerges more clearly defined in middle class families where the dissolution of the oedipal conflict is more apt to take its classical course than in lower class families.

4. LATE CHILDHOOD begins with the dissolution of oedipal conflicts ordinarily in the sixth to the seventh year of life and ends with puberty. In psychoanalytic theory, this is referred to as the *latency phase,* because in most children the intensity of the infantile sex drive has diminished, or, as analysts postulate, has been repressed. The child, it is assumed, has learned under the impact of the pressures of his culture to relinquish his sexual wishes concerning the beloved parent of the opposite sex and to identify, to a considerable extent, with his former competitor the parent of the same sex. With such identification, what used to be "social anxiety" has been internalized; the child at this stage has developed a conscience and its unconscious counterpart, a superego. There are, of course, children in all classes in which this theoretical development for many reasons has been rudimentary.

A defective superego—an already severe disturbance in identity formulation—is clinically more prominent in lower class children than in the higher classes. Possibly the large number of antisocial reactions of class V boys and girls who aggressively "act out" may be related to disturbances in identification in this phase of the developmental cycle. It is also possible that more intensive sexualization plays a role in the class V child's inhibition to learn in school. However, the lack of proper identification with "good" social models is probably a more pertinent explanation. Differentiation of elementary sexual, aggressive, and dependency drives have become marked along class lines. We see this most clearly in the aggressive behavior of children in different classes. Formal schooling divides children along class lines. This differentiation begins at a time when, according to psychoanalytic theory, the foundations of personality are established. This is the time when the neighborhood and the school determine whether "good" manners, that is, manners of classes I, II, and III, will replace "crudeness" and violence or whether official restraints imposed by teachers and juvenile authorities check uninhibited instinctual gratification. "Nice" children of the upper and middle classes become differentiated from the "bad" children of the lower classes. Faulty identity formation or malignant identity diffusion may impel "bad" children unconsciously into juvenile delinquency, and in a later phase into the gangland of the underworld. It is not coincidence that the public psychiatric clinic for children in this community is filled, in large part, with class V boys and girls sent there by the juvenile court or school authorities. These children come mainly from a domiciliary institution caring for children from disorganized homes. Furthermore, it is not a matter of chance that the state reformatory and other prisons are filled by a disproportionately large percentage of young adults, males and females, from classes IV and V. In fact, some 95 to 98 percent of the inmates in the state prison are from classes IV and V.[9]

5. PUBERTY AND ADOLESCENCE, with their marked physical and psychological changes, shifts in values, and particularly the strong resurgence of the sex drive now of a more definite genital character, are experienced in different ways in the several social classes. Social class has become a fact of life by the time of puberty; the customs of teenagers are almost as differentiated along class lines as those of adults. The teenager has a very strong tendency to live his social life in a clique. One of the important characteristics of cliques is the narrow range of classes represented in the membership.

Dominance of petting, necking, and masturbation in classes I, II, and III adolescents may be compared with actual intercourse in classes IV and V.[10]   In the lower classes, full sexual activity starts early with or without marriage.   Bernfeld[11] coined the term "stretched puberty" (*gestreckte Pubertät*), and Erikson[12] speaks of a "psychosexual moratorium"; both refer to the delay of sexual gratification in young men and women of our culture who are physically capable of procreative activity.   They imply that such delay permits higher learning and inner refinement and is of the greatest importance for the transmission of culture.   This psychosexual moratorium persists in classes I and II until late into young adulthood.   It is accompanied in both young men and women by a definite feeling of being "unfinished," in a "student" category, of being "immature," and not fully responsible.   This feeling, in some professions with long training, such as psychoanalysis, may last into the thirties.

6. A YOUNG ADULT has achieved, or is expected to achieve, three major goals: psychological and economic independence from his parents, a personal status in the community appropriate to his sex, age, and class, and marriage or approaching marriage.   Parenthood and the possession of reasonable long-term goals are also necessary elements in the life space of a normal young adult.   When, how, and if these goals are realized differ markedly from one class to another.   Regardless of age, maturity is reached when the individual has attained a reasonable mastery of his occupation and has assumed his full obligations toward community and family.   Late adolescence and young adulthood are not differentiated in the two lower classes. Most young people in classes IV and V pass directly from childhood to the occupational, social, and marital responsibilities of adulthood. In doing so, they miss, in varying degrees, what we have come to refer to as sublimation.   Their sexual, aggressive, and dependent impulses remain much more pronounced and more primitive than those of classes I and II.

7. ADULTHOOD is the time of full differentiation into the various patterns of living characteristic of each class.   The subcultural ways of life described in Chapter Four are the warp and woof of society in these years.

Deviations of behavior from social norms must be considered within the frame of reference of each class.   For example, if a class I husband beats his spouse, this needs to be evaluated quite differently from similar occurrences in class V.   Class V adults have a strong propensity to physical violence.   Aggression in classes I and II is more apt to be expressed verbally, directly or through rumor, gossip, and slander. The need for "independence" is more marked in the upper and middle classes; an unabashed dependence without conflict is found more frequently in the lower strata. Exceptions to this are individuals from the bottom of the social heap—tramps, prostitutes, habitual criminals, "rebels without cause," as Lindner called them—who try to escape from all social obligations.

We believe also that *presses* to the mature individual are stronger in the lower strata, whereas *stresses* appear to be more marked in the upper strata. Throughout the mature years, the external problems of lower class individuals, as well as threats to their economic, social, and physical security, are much stronger than to members of the higher classes. Sensitivity to internal threats, fears, guilts, and conflicts, however, appear to be greater in classes II and III than in the other strata. The mature years are also a time of intense interclass conflicts and emotional trauma for upward mobile individuals. Our society places high regard upon upward mobility, particularly in adolescence and in early adult life. But in the mature years, "background" is brought home to the arriviste in painful ways.

8. THE TRANSITION FROM MATURITY TO OLD AGE is imperceptible. Some signs of physical decline occur early in the adult years and they increase with age. The loss of physical vigor may be balanced by an increase in judgment and experience, and by the emoluments of status in the higher classes. The benefits of status in the later years of life are particularly impressive in class I. Mature individuals in classes I, II, and III protect themselves with an elaborate system of private insurance which buys physical and, to some extent, psychological security against the hazards of old age. Individuals in the lower classes have many reasons to dread old age and its two most important manifestations—disease and unemployment. Elderly class IV and V persons are threatened continuously by the fate of becoming dependent; often this threat produces a passive and resigned attitude. Even though minimal needs may be met by public or private charity, there is no system of insurance that can possibly underwrite an individual's feelings of personal failure if he has to depend upon public welfare. No matter how emotionally painful the experience, he must resign himself to the unavoidable. The social differences among men do not disappear when death occurs. The members of each class try to perpetuate status in their funeral arrangements and the monuments they erect over the graves of their late-departed relatives.

Psychodynamics

We gathered considerable material about the relationship of conscious and unconscious conflicts to social status, but we are not ready to make a definitive statement on the subject. We will merely point out here that conscious conflicts, and in all likelihood preconscious conflicts, between moral and social values and instinct-drives differ in the various classes. Lower class patients express their instinct-demands more directly and with less restraint, whereas higher class patients are more likely to check their aggressive and sex drives or express them by way of compromise. The higher classes are also, generally speaking, the ones who either sublimate their unconscious needs or express their conflicts in neurotic reactions. We realize that this does not assert any more than what Freud stated, in a general way, half a century ago; unfortunately we cannot furnish any quantitative corroboration nor any striking examples of carefully matched cases. At present, we assume that unconscious conflicts in all classes are similar; the girl in the finishing school, discussed in Chapter Six, who was promiscuous and became pregnant presented similar dynamics to those of her counterpart in class V. We must point out, however, that the psychiatrist's observations were better on the girl from the elite family than on the class V girl from the street. Our knowledge of lower class psychodynamics, unfortunately, are particularly inadequate. This fact stems from the psychiatrist's focus on classes I and II, principally class I. We can only hope that future research will provide better data on the influence of social class on ego development and structure.

Such future work might explore systematically our impression that members of the lower classes, particularly of class V, have a weaker ego than members of the higher classes. Many of them seem to be less able to check their own impulses, and they are more passive in their attempts to master the harsh reality aspects of their lives. Such ego weakness seems related to the greater difficulties these patients present in attempts to treat them in intensive ambulatory psychotherapy. There also seem to be marked differences in the superego structure of members of the different classes. Although lower class children are exposed to more external methods of discipline, such as physical and often brutal punishment, they are less inclined to internalize social inhibitions. As we stated earlier, the lower class patient is more likely to "act out," while the patient in the upper classes is apt to "act in." These differences seem to be mediated more indirectly through early experiences within the family than through the direct impact of the social structure itself. However, much more needs to be learned about personality structure and dynamics and social and cultural variables. Erik Erikson's concept of identity is a very important construct for such research.

SOCIAL MOBILITY

The fifth hypothesis upon which this research was predicated assumed that mobility in the status structure of our society is connected with the development of functional mental illnesses. We will not encroach upon the material presented by Myers and Roberts in their book *Social Class, Family Dynamics, and Mental Illness,* by summarizing the findings they will discuss on this hypothesis. Here we are interested only in pointing out that an understanding of some of the elementary principles of mobility are important to the practice of psychiatry.

Psychiatrically, the preconscious and unconscious motivations which provide the psychic energy necessary to move ahead are more important than the conscious goals. The principal motivations probably are the needs to replace a rejected parent or parent substitute or to be loved by a parent or parent-image for this particular behavior, thus fulfilling the expectations of the parental figure. The ambitions of a parent whose aspirations have not been realized but whose fantasies are conveyed to a child are often also strong stimuli for behavior that may lead to mobility in later years. It is important to keep in mind that the unconscious expectation, or the ego ideal of the parent, is more important as a motivating stimulus than conscious or overt imitation. For example, one of our patients became an outstanding chemist—something his father, a clerk in a drug store, always dreamed of being; another became a dancer, realizing the unconscious wish of an ambitious, exhibitionistic, unsuccessful, and very neurotic mother. We also observed cases where the individual moved not only overtly very differently from the parent but even appeared to act against the ego ideal of the parent. These negative identifications are beset with deep conflicts even if the achieved mobility appears to be successful to outsiders. It must be remembered, too, that both positive and negative identifications usually coexist. Such identifications occur with both parents, and they can be, and often are, contradictory. The ideals of parents and of parental figures are more important in determining the orientation of the individual than overt behavior of the parent; this is true in general and certainly true of the status and mobility orientations of the individual.

Social Mobility and Mental Illness

We observed two types of mobile neurotics among the patients: the "climber" who appears to move more or less successfully and the "strainer" who does not move successfully.[13] To a certain extent, all our mobile patients are strainers, probably most mobile people are, because their achieved mobility is less than their aspired mobility. This generalization is true especially if one is not satisfied with "surface" statements made by patients or persons who are not patients. The climber may impress an observer as pleasant, successful, and very able if he *is* successful and appears well integrated. Only on longer acquaintance and after a deeper search does one become aware of the climber's conflicts and defenses. His deeper anxieties become manifest when his mobility drive becomes blocked; then his defenses do not function properly. We saw this reaction most markedly among the extremely upward mobile individuals who attempted to penetrate the inner core of class I. When these social climbers were rejected by those who "are there" socially, their reactions were characterized by severe anxiety, depression, sometimes by antisocial acting out, and in some extreme cases by suicidal attempts which were related, in part, to blocked mobility.

The relatively low achievers, the strainers, with high aspirations are unable to compensate for their efforts by recognized successes in the social groups where they function. The defensive nature of their mobility drives are much more apparent than in the "high" achievers. The strainers tend to be ambitious dreamers, the type James Thurber so beautifully portrayed in his *The Secret Life of Walter Mitty* and Steig in *Dreams of Glory*. If they do not dream, they constantly plan and scheme, rush from one pursuit to another, or from one "big deal" to the next hoping to succeed sufficiently to climb upward in the social system, but always disappointed and frustrated, complaining and rationalizing about what they consider bad luck and failure.

Psychiatrists and Mobility

There are three reasons why psychiatrists should be particularly interested in social mobility. First, strongly upward mobile persons, particularly the strainers, have a certain proneness for neurotic disorder and are apt to cause social troubles. They need not be highly unconventional or flout accepted values—actually, many highly mobile persons are quite conventional—but they are uncertain about their values and some of them can be, at times, obnoxious and hard on others as well as on themselves in their attempt to reach their goals. Psychiatrists encounter many mobile persons with such unpleasant character traits that, behind external conformity, they cannot get along with anybody and do not care for anyone but themselves and their goals.[14]

The second clinical reason for our concern with social mobility is the problem of downward mobility. Downward mobile persons and families are not encountered frequently in our society, but when this process occurs persons subject to it are recognized by the community as troublemakers. As their behavior becomes overtly antisocial they are referred with increasing frequency to psychiatrists when they do not obey the subtle rules of the game expected of them by persons in higher status positions. These patients present the psychiatrist with severe problems, such as alcohol or drug addiction, crime, and most of all with serious character disorders. They are labeled clinically as sadistic-masochistic characters or as destructive and self-destructive personalities. Some of their disorders present the syndrome of a "fate" neurosis. The spell of gloom, failure, and disaster which these patients exude, even when they are not depressed, makes them rather unapproachable and dreaded by therapists. Treatment of such persons is exceedingly difficult and even more so of families who like that in Faulkner's *Sartoris* march inexorably toward annihilation. Even when insight is reached in downward mobile patients by dynamic psychotherapy, their self-destructive urges in the form of negative therapeutic reactions prevent any real success in treatment.

The third clinical reason social mobility is of interest to psychiatrists is its influence on the therapist-patient relationship. In upward mobile patients, the differences in value orientation between the psychiatrist and the patient are overcome by the patient's identification with some of the values of the therapist. Such patients have a desire to sublimate, to achieve, to obey the rules of the game, and yet to enjoy. It is particularly the dynamic psychiatrist who has become the "sage" for upward mobile persons who have lost their bearings in their exhausting and frantic climb toward the "top." Lower class patients in this study who had a good relationship in dynamic psychotherapy with their psychiatrists were invariably upward mobile. The downward mobile patient, in whom the lack of a capacity to sublimate, unwillingness to achieve, often an extraordinary dependency, a tendency to regress and to destroy himself and others, makes insight therapy particularly difficult. Downward mobile patients arouse more antagonism in psychiatrists than any other single group; it is easier to accept a patient with standards different from one's own than someone who, so to speak, has abandoned and betrayed the standards the therapist values as desirable.

APPLICATIONS OF THIS STUDY

We shall conclude with some reflections on ways our findings may be used by others. We implied in Chapter One that validated knowledge in psychiatry is inadequate to meet the challenge presented by the size of the mental health problem. In view of the need for research data, we assume that any increase of knowledge, regardless of whether it is theoretical or applied, or whether it is contributed by the biological, medical, or social sciences, will help eventually in the solution of the problems we have attacked.

Future Research

We have stated repeatedly that we lack definitive knowledge on the epidemiology of mental disorders. The epidemiological problem is a formidable one. To attack it, a new type of professional worker will have to be trained. A research scientist equipped with psychodynamic, physiological, sociological, anthropological, and biostatistical knowledge is indicated. Also a type of psychiatrist who understands the necessity of controlled observation and the need for interdisciplinary collaboration will aid in this endeavor. Future research should concern itself with the task of providing sound data on *true* prevalence and incidence of psychiatric signs, symptoms, and diseases in various subcultures of our society and other societies. Once we possess adequate data on incidence and prevalence, we may draw conclusions concerning the influence of socioenvironmental factors.

Knowledge of Social Factors

At present, most psychiatrists consider in their diagnostic effort primarily somatic and psychological factors. They fuse them under catch-words, such as psychosomatic and comprehensive medicine, or try to understand the "total man," "unitary man," "the human being as a whole," and so on.   Until very recently, they did not consider putting this human being into a social system and culture.

We believe that psychiatrists need to understand the social system of the community if they are to diagnose accurately and treat their patients effectively.   They must know something of its structure and its history; they must know its churches and industries, its schools and clubs, and, most of all, they must know the values of its inhabitants.[16]   In our community, a psychiatrist should know its Yankee core culture, its southern Italian immigrant stock, tensions between the university and the community, the peculiarities of its health and welfare organizations.   In addition the psychiatrist needs to understand the norms of his own professional subculture, how he conforms or deviates from them, and how he reacts to the value systems of other professional and social groups.

The diagnosis of social class can be made in an objective fashion by utilizing education and occupation as "diagnostic" criteria.[15]   These items can be gathered easily and accurately from patients or their families and entered on the face sheet of a patient's record.   These valuable guideposts should be supplemented by less precise but more casual observations, such as a patient's general appearance, gestures, manners, clothes, and particularly his speech.   To understand the patient's exact position in the status structure, one has to know the family and the social groups with whom they associate.   The psychiatrist needs to know whether the patient is intergenerationally stable or mobile, and the psychiatrist should be aware of how comfortable he feels with his patients and whether his and the patients' statuses contribute to his and the patients' feelings of comfort or discomfort.

An explanation of the interplay of social and psychodynamic forces is a legitimate function of an emergent sociology focused on the dynamics of the interaction of individual drives and needs and the social situations which encompass individuals as they pass through the successive phases of the life cycle.   To develop this area of knowledge the sociologist and the psychiatrist should work together.   This can be achieved by appointing sociologists to major staff positions in departments of psychiatry where residents are in training.

New Treatment Methods

The data in Chapter Nine on the length of time the patients in this study have been in treatment and the dollar costs of treatment discussed in Chapter Ten indicate the desirability of more efficient and economical therapeutic methods. Clearly, no inexpensive and effective methods of psychiatric treatment exist at the present time such as treatment with antibiotics in medicine and surgery. Thus, the creation of such methods is an important and urgent task for future research. One hopeful approach (at present, there is considerable optimism in lay circles and some psychiatric groups regarding its possibilities) is to develop tranquilizing therapy beyond its present use as an adjunctive agent to other forms of care. Persons who place great faith in pharmacological therapy hope to see the day when a pill or an injection will either counteract or inhibit the assumed etiological agents that produce mental illness. Whether this can be achieved, at least in some disorders, remains to be seen. If a truly effective drug therapy is developed, it will be most helpful in the solution of a problem our society faces: *to provide treatment for all mental patients.*

A second approach, and the approaches suggested here by no means exclude each other, would be to develop more effective and shorter methods of psychotherapy. Freud, years ago, expressed his thoughts on this point:

> And now in conclusion I will cast a glance at a situation which belongs to the future—one which will seem fantastic to many of you, but which I think, nevertheless, deserves that we should be prepared for it in our minds. You know that the therapeutic effects we can achieve are very inconsiderable in number. We are but a handful of people, and even by working hard each one of us can deal in a year with only a small amount of persons. Against the vast amount of neurotic misery which is in the world, and perhaps need not be, the quantity we can do away with is almost negligible. Besides this, the necessities of our own existence limit our work to the well-to-do classes, accustomed to choose their own physicians, whose choice is diverted away from psychoanalysis by all kinds of prejudices. At present we can do nothing for the crowded ranks of people who suffer exceedingly from neuroses.
>
> Now let us assume that by some kind of organization we were able to increase our numbers to an extent sufficient for treating large masses of people. Then on the other hand, one may reasonably expect that at some time or other the conscience of the community will awake and admonish it that the poor man has just as much right to help for his mind as he now has to the surgeon's means of saving his life; and that the neuroses menace the health of a people no less than tuberculosis, and can be left as little as the latter to the feeble handling of individuals. Then clinics and consultation departments will be built to which analytically trained physicians will be appointed, so

that men who would otherwise give way to drink, the women who have nearly succumbed under their burden of privations, the children for whom there is no choice but running wild or neuroses, may be made by analysis able to resist and able to do something in the world. This treatment will be free. It may be a long time before the State regards this as an urgent duty. Present conditions may delay its arrival even longer; probably these institutions will be started by private beneficence; some time or other, however, it must come.

The task will then arise for us to adopt our technique to the new conditions. I have no doubt that the validity of our psychological assumptions will impress the uneducated too, but we shall need to find the simplest and most natural expressions for our theoretical doctrines. We shall probably discover that the poor are even less ready to part with their neuroses than the rich, because the hard life that awaits them when they recover has no attraction, and illness in them gives them more claim to the help of others. Possibly, we may often be able to achieve something if we combine aid to the mind with material support. It is very probable too, that the application of our therapy to large numbers will compel us to alloy the pure gold of analysis plentifully with the copper of direct suggestion; and even hypnotic influence might find a place in it again, as it has in the treatment of war neuroses. But whatever form this psychotherapy may take, whatever the elements out of which it is compounded, its most effective and most important ingredients will assuredly remain those borrowed from strict psychoanalysis which serves no ulterior purpose.[17]

Unfortunately, Freud's thoughts on this issue have been ignored by most of his disciples. The truth of this observation is evidenced by the fact that classical psychoanalysis has gradually become longer and longer as time has passed. Analyses of five to seven hundred hours lasting for years have become the rule.[18]

Much will have to be learned through research about the indication for psychotherapy, its techniques, and aims before an economical application will be possible. A possible approach to this issue is to make psychotherapy accessible to a larger number of patients through the development of effective group methods. It is very likely that group therapy, particularly in hospital settings, may have advantages over individual therapy as the pioneering work of Maxwell Jones and T. P. Rees indicates. To bring dynamic psychotherapy to the lower classes, important innovations in individual and group therapy will be necessary. Principles of supportive, manipulative, and suggestive techniques will have to be understood better, and probably much from current methods of psychotherapy and educational work with problem children could be borrowed to aid in the develop-

ment of more effective methods.[19] Psychotherapists who are able
to devise therapeutic techniques for schizophrenics and for children
should be able to devise techniques for mentally ill persons of various
ages, cultures, and classes.

Evaluation of Psychiatric Care

In the last two decades the range of treatable disorders has increased greatly. Today we are treating patients, on the one hand,
who are more "normal" than those who were under psychotherapeutic care only a short time ago, and, on the other, patients who
are much "sicker." In addition, our therapeutic aims have become
more ambitious and far-reaching. The recognition of particular
problems with reference to patients in the various classes is an important new development.[20] But we suggest further study of the
specific problems of the lower classes by investigators trained in
psychiatry and the social sciences. Class V needs help most—social
and psychiatric—and gets it least.

One of the most striking findings in this research was the accumulation of chronic psychotic patients in classes IV and V in public hospitals. Why do they become chronic? Why are they not
discharged? What are the psychosocial conditions under which patients are retained? Is this accumulation traceable to the kind of
psychiatric therapy they receive? It probably is; the results in the
state hospitals of Kansas after reforms introduced by Karl and
William Menninger seem to indicate this. A great deal of pains-
taking work needs to be done to find the answers to these questions
before the situation can be remedied.

In view of the increasing scope of psychiatry in our society, and
the constantly expanding recognition of the need for psychiatric
treatment in the population, it is amazing how few careful evaluative
studies of psychiatric therapies have been made. The paucity of
evaluation of the psychiatrist's efforts should not be attributed to
negligence or deliberate efforts to avoid the issue. The more probable reason is that evaluation of treatment is an enormously complex
task because so many factors are involved in each case. Nevertheless, in order to plan and to obtain adequate public support, what
psychiatrists are doing will have to be evaluated by *objective methods.* No treatment with any claim to success, regardless of whether
it is organic or psychological, whether it is simple or complex like
psychoanalysis, in the long run can be *accepted on faith* or on the
unsubstantiated claims of its protagonists. A major research job

which needs to be done is the evaluation of the principal kinds of psychiatric therapy now in use.

Professional Training

The rapidly increasing demand for psychiatrists has created acute problems for training centers and, on a broader front, for the profession as a whole. There are not enough psychiatrists to perform adequately the work our society is demanding from the profession. To be sure, nobody knows how many psychiatrists are needed; some well-informed sources suggest twice or three times the present number, but this is only a guess. The difficulty of estimating the number of psychiatrists our society needs is traceable to at least two things. On the one hand, we do not know how much mental illness there is in the population, and, on the other, there is a constantly increasing demand for more and better psychiatry.

In our community, for example, before World War II, there were only three psychiatrists in private practice. One confined his practice to neurology and organic psychiatric therapies, the others concentrated on directive psychotherapies. The psychiatrists in the University Hospital saw a few private patients, but on a sporadic and desultory basis—only one of them was in half-time practice. At the end of World War II, when a former resident returned to the city with the intention of establishing a practice, he was advised, in strong terms, to go elsewhere. Why? Because the community was "overcrowded with psychiatrists." Today, by way of contrast, twenty-four psychiatrists are in full-time private practice, and thirty-three are in practice part time. In addition, there are thirty-two residents in training who treat patients in the clinics, in a Veterans Administration hospital, and in a private psychiatric hospital. Every newcomer with intentions to settle here is told by psychiatrists in practice that the community is "saturated." He is advised either fearfully or angrily to go elsewhere. Nevertheless, everyone who has settled here, in spite of such protests, builds a busy practice after a short time. This extraordinary demand for psychiatric help has been created in this community in the last ten years, and, surprisingly, the demand has not been filled. The "psychiatric market" has expanded with the increasing supply of psychiatrists. Classical psychoanalysis, which relatively few patients can afford, is the only saturated practice. The training analysts are the only ones in this field fully booked with patients undergoing psychoanalysis. Most of their patients are professional persons, many in psychoanalytic training. We do not know how many psychiatrists are needed to meet the expanding demand for good psychotherapy, but we do know that more are needed.

The crucial question from the viewpoint of public health is this: Will psychiatrists be able to supply the needs of all patients, not only those who can afford to pay the high fees of private practitioners, but also those who cannot afford them, particularly persons in classes IV and V? The only persons in our society who do not get what they need and do not even know it are in class V. However, the vast majority of class IV persons in need of psychiatric help cannot afford the fees of private practitioners. We are aware, too, that all too often class III persons, as well as the "genteel poor" in class II cannot afford their fees. Numerous class II persons, who could not afford psychiatric help at the current prevailing fees, though they needed it badly, were seen during the course of this research.

The impact of the costs of psychiatric treatment is undoubtedly sharper on the individual family than in other specialties and illnesses for two reasons: first, existing insurance systems provide very limited benefits for psychiatric patients; second, adequate psychiatric treatment is expensive because it is so slow and indefinite in its outcome. Psychiatrists cannot be accused of antisocial attitudes, but serious economic problems in providing private care cannot be denied. Although psychiatrists are not prone to treat their private patients in psychotherapy for low fees, they are paid less well than their colleagues in organic psychiatry or in other medical specialties. This situation arises from the nature of the psychotherapy process and the structuring of psychotherapists' ideas of good procedure. A dermatologist, for instance, can see four or five patients in one hour, and each patient will pay him $10 quite willingly for his services. A psychiatrist who conscientiously follows good professional procedures can see only one patient an hour. He may charge the patient $25 per visit, but few patients can afford a fee of this size two or three times a week for a year or more.[21]

The most acute problem from the viewpoint of diluting the "pure gold," to use Freud's expression, of psychoanalysis to a larger segment of the population involves the cost of training a psychoanalyst and the support of the psychoanalyst after he has completed his training. Complete training in psychoanalysis costs approximately $20,000 in the United States today. This estimate covers only the psychoanalytic training; if the preceding professional training is added, this figure would need to be doubled. Thus, candidates with low incomes are not accepted easily in psychoanalytic institutes, or they are forced into debt or into a "money-making" practice to earn the $15 to $25 per hour fees charged them by their training analysts. The analysand's need to earn fees to pay the fees charged him by his training analyst results in an extreme emphasis upon remunerative practice in psychoanalytic circles, rather than research and training. In the long run, estrangement of analysts from scientific research will prove to be a detriment to analysis and to scientific progress in general. We also think that psychoanalysis limited to a "luxury" practice is not likely to survive in the face of the great demands for a psychiatric therapy that will meet the medical needs of the majority of the population.

What is the answer to the problem we have posed here? First, so far as psychoanalysis is concerned, we believe that psychoanalytic services, research, and training need the same public assistance as other psychiatric institutions. Such support is more likely to come if psychoanalytic institutions conform to the general and established principles of higher learning and become part of them. A short while ago this was not possible; today it is, at least in the United States. Second, and this is an even larger and more complex problem, we believe that steps must be taken to provide more psychiatric therapy at a lower price. One might jokingly say that what America needs is a "good five-dollar psychotherapist." This may be true, but psychiatric time is of necessity expensive; it is the time of a highly trained medical specialist who usually is in his middle thirties before he can earn his "salt." From a social and economic viewpoint, we are obliged to think of training a less expensive therapist. American medicine has opposed strongly and correctly the lay practice of medicine, and psychiatry is a medical specialty. This has resulted, among other things, in staunch opposition to lay therapy in the American Psychoanalytic Association and in the American Psychiatric Association. It has led to undercover hostility as well as open quarrels between psychiatrists and clinical psychologists who are interested more in therapy than in their traditional pursuits.

We do not expect to solve this difficult problem in these pages, but we would like to repeat the question: Do we need more therapists? If we do, we ought to train more. If we cannot train a sufficient number of psychiatrists, we ought to train other therapists in the mental health field. Some might be in the field of medicine, such as internists dealing with psychosomatic problems or pediatricians dealing with emotional problems of children. Others might be in clinical psychology or social work, or in educational, occupational, or pastoral counseling. As long as these counselors, and with some courage we might call them therapists, are well trained and do not dabble in fields beyond their training, there should be no meaningful objection to such a venture.

To be sure, therapy, at least since the days of pure magic, has been the prerogative of the medical profession, but why should a nonmedical problem, such as emotional re-education in work and family life, remain in the domain pre-empted by the medical profession? Why should we not train a new professional specialist? A large part of the subject matter and experience in traditional medical training is superfluous and expensive for someone limited to psychotherapy notably in nonmedical problems. Therapies which demand basic medical knowledge should remain the prerogative of the medical profession, but outside of this medical orbit, psychiatrists and medical analysts have little right to block attempts to train an adequate number of therapists to do the job our society needs.[22] The public would get used to such a profession, and the profession, in due time, would develop the sense of responsibility and regard for human welfare and dignity which have rewarded the medical profession with such high prestige in our society.

The profession of social work has come closest to the ideals and tasks of such a profession; some social workers, in a way, have functioned as "lower class psychiatrists" for some time, although they, in their loyalty to psychiatry and medical psychoanalysis, like to deny such a role. Possibly, out of the professions of medicine, social work, psychology, and sociology, a new discipline providing us with the needed therapists might emerge. Such a profession might help us solve the *urgent* need for good psychotherapy in classes IV and V.

Better Public Mental Hospitals

To provide more therapists, however, is not the only problem of a better application of psychiatric therapy to the population in need of help. During the last few years there has been an increasing awareness of the inadequacy of our public mental hospitals,[23] which, alas, so often are more custodial places for the undesirable and unwanted than "therapeutic communities" from which patients are likely to return to their families and lead a normal life.[24] There also has been an increasing emphasis on psychiatric therapy in wards and clinics of general hospitals, in community clinics, and in the offices of psychiatrists in the last few years. This trend should lead eventually to marked changes in public mental hospitals as we know them. As we learn more about mental illnesses, the present type of mental hospital is likely to become an historical anachronism just as the medieval asylum and the debtor's prison have passed into disuse.[25] The present institution with its back wards of paupers and unwanted people should disappear when emphasis on the care of institutionalized mentally ill persons is shifted from commitment to treatment. The enormous accumulation of chronic lower class patients should disappear as our knowledge of etiology and treatment increases and active efforts are made to help these unfortunate victims of society's life processes.

One last and eminently practical point: To do better therapy in a modern hospital or clinic and not in an asylum will take a great deal of money. It will be difficult to prove what results such an "investment" will have before we know more about evaluation. It is even possible that we will never know how much unhappiness such money will prevent and how much happiness it will buy. Yet, such money for "the greatest single health problem" will have to be spent. We believe that a society which can afford atomic bombs can afford good psychiatry. The point we want to stress is the necessity to inform the decision-makers and money-spenders who can bring about such changes. To find and provide funds for psychiatric work has always been a difficult and unpopular task. Science can provide the tools, but only people can translate dissatisfaction with a state of affairs into action.

Mental Health Education

Opinion polls, attitude research, and clinical experience indicate how little lay persons know about psychiatry. Not only ignorance, which can be overcome by instruction, but unconscious resistance to knowledge about mental disorders are impediments to learning. Ignorance and resistance also have prevented the dissemination of psychiatric knowledge into the ranks of lawyers, legislators, and, to a lesser degree, educators and ministers.

A good many "self help" books, which probably help little in most cases, and a few well-written popular volumes by experts, for example, Karl Menninger's *The Human Mind*,[26] have brought some understanding to the "reading public"; but the reading public is limited in numbers. Recently, films, radio and television programs, and articles in popular picture magazines have drawn attention to the mental health problem and to the potentialities of psychiatry, particularly psychotherapy.

The most effective demonstration for medical and lay persons of the role of psychiatry in our society were the achievements of psychiatrists in the Armed Forces during World War II and the Korean War. New and fascinating demonstrations of the effects of prevention and early treatment of psychiatric disorders are being carried on in American communities.[27] Such research training in our field has developed in many centers and particularly through the direct and indirect influence of the United States Public Health Service. Popular education toward the proper use of psychiatry has just begun. In a country where the mental health movement was initiated and where economic resources are large, our hope to achieve the necessary enlightenment of the public is high.

In conclusion, we want to emphasize that there are difficult and important tasks ahead in the new fields which have been called social psychiatry and dynamic sociology. The definition of psychiatry is neither fixed nor clear. The whole field is in a stage of transition. We do not know whether more people are psychiatrically ill today than a generation ago, but we do know that more people are treated today than were considered in need of treatment a decade ago. Psychiatry is becoming a major trouble shooter in modern society; promises and hopes are great, at times too great; fulfillment of them will come only if we are guided by the spirit of science and by a strong social conscience. Our scientific knowledge is rapidly increasing and shifting emphasis on our ideas about mental illness. Theories which were considered true and accepted yesterday are disproved today and forgotten tomorrow. Solution of the mental health problem is one of the great challenges of our time. Is our society ready to meet this challenge?

NOTES

[1] J. Clausen and M. Kohn, "The Ecological Approach in Social Psychiatry," *American Journal of Sociology*, Vol. 60 (1954), pp. 140–151; S. H. Kramer, *Therapy of the Neuroses and Psychoses,* Lea and Fabiger, Philadelphia, 1947; Marvin K. Opler, *Culture, Psychiatry and Human Values,* Charles C. Thomas, Springfield, Illinois, 1956; P. V. Lemkau, C. Tietze, and M. M. Cooper, "A Survey of Statistical Studies on the Prevalance and Incidence of Mental Disorder in Sample Populations," *Public Health Reports,* Vol. 58 (1943), 1909–1927; R. H. Felix and R. V. Bowers, "Mental Health Hygiene and Socio-Environmental Factors," *Mil-*

bank Memorial Fund Bulletin Quarterly, Vol. 26 (1948), pp. 124–127; Thomas A. C. Rennie, Leo Srole, Marvin K. Opler, and Thomas S. Langner, "Urban Life and Mental Health," *American Journal of Psychiatry*, Vol. 113 (March 1957), pp. 831–836; E. M. Gruenberg, "Community Conditions and Psychoses of the Elderly," *The American Journal of Psychiatry*, Vol. 110 (1954), pp. 888–896.

2 P. M. Yap, "Lata Reaction: Its Pathodynamics and Nosological Position," *Journal of Mental Science*, Vol. 98 (October 1952), pp. 515–564.

3 Y. Uchimura, "Psychiatric Studies of the Ainu, Particularly Imu," quoted in T. Muramatsu et al., "Letter From Japan," *American Journal of Psychiatry*, Vol. 110 (1954), pp. 641–643.

4 Erik H. Erikson, "The Problem of Ego Identity," *Journal of the American Psychoanalytic Association*, Vol. 4 (1956), pp. 56–119.

5 Robert N. Wilson, verbal communication.

6 Lawrence S. Kubie, "The Fundamental Nature of the Distinction between Normality and Neurosis," *Psychoanalytic Quarterly*, Vol. 23 (1954), pp. 167–204.

7 Henry A. Murray, *Explorations in Personality*, Oxford University Press, New York, 1938.

8 Rene Spitz and Katherine M. Wolf, "Auto-Eroticism: Some Empirical Findings and Hypotheses and Three of its Manifestations in the First Year of Life," *Psychoanalytic Study of the Child*, Vols. 3 and 4 (1949), pp. 85–120.

9 A member of our team, Dr. Lawrence Z. Freedman, is now studying prisoners in our state. We are indebted to Dr. Freedman for the figures given here.

10 Alfred C. Kinsey et al., *Sexual Behavior in the Human Male*, W. B. Saunders Company, Philadelphia, 1948, and *Sexual Behavior in the Human Female*, W. B. Saunders Company, Philadelphia, 1953.

11 Siegfried Bernfeld, "The Present-Day Psychology of Puberty; Critical Remarks About Its Scientific Validity," Vienna: *Int. P. V.*, 1927, p. 59, and *Imago*, Vol. 13, 1927, pp. 1–56.

12 Erik H. Erikson, *Childhood and Society*, W. W. Norton and Company, New York, 1950.

13 Jurgen Ruesch et al., "Acculturation and Illness," Washington, D. C., *Psychological Monographs: General and Applied*, Vol. 62, No. 5 (1948).

14 Henry Murray, "American Icarus" in *Clinical Studies of Personality*, Arthur Burton and Robert Harris (editors), New York, Harper Bros., 1955, pp. 615–641.

15 See A. B. Hollingshead, *Two Factor Index of Social Position* (printed privately), New Haven, 1957.

16 N. A. Cameron, "Human Ecology and Personality in the Training of Physicians" (Chapter 5) in *Psychiatry and Medical Education*, 1951 Conference, American Psychiatric Association, Washington, D. C., 1952.

17 Sigmund Freud, *Collected Papers* (Vol. II), The Hogarth Press and the Institute of Psycho-Analysis, London, 1950, pp. 400–402.

18 There are exceptions to this; among them are the efforts of Franz Alexander and Thomas French, of F. Deutsch, of E. Cameron, and of Jules Coleman to abbreviate and focus therapy, of Harry Stack Sullivan and his disciples, and also the work by Carl R. Rogers and his students.

[19] B. Bettelheim, *Love is Not Enough: The Treatment of Emotionally Disturbed Children,* The Free Press, Glencoe, Illinois, 1950; Fritz Redl and D. Wineman, *Children Who Hate: The Disorganization and Breakdown of Behavior Controls,* The Free Press, Glencoe, Illinois, 1951.

[20] T. Lidz, B. Parker, A. R. Cornelison, "The Role of the Father in the Family Environment of the Schizophrenic Patient," *American Journal of Psychiatry,* 113 (1956), pp. 126–132; John Spiegel, "The Resolution of Role Conflict Within the Family," Harvard University mimeographed publication, 1957.

[21] Barton Lawden, "Why Psychiatrists Go Mad," *Medical Economics,* Vol. 32 (November 1955), pp. 274–280.

[22] Lawrence S. Kubie, "The Pros and Cons of a New Profession: A Doctorate in Medical Psychology," *Texas Report on Biology and Medicine,* Vol. 12, No. 3 (Fall, 1954), pp. 692–737.

[23] Ivan Belknap, *Human Problems of a State Mental Hospital,* McGraw-Hill Book Company, New York, 1956, pp. 197–199.

[24] British psychiatrists, such as Maxwell Jones and T. R. Rees, have recognized the need for a "Therapeutic Community" earlier than their American colleagues. In the United States, the Menningers have set the best example for such a development in the state of Kansas.

[25] Eric Berne, "Comparative Psychiatry," *The American Journal of Psychiatry,* Vol. 113 (1956), pp. 193–203.

[26] Karl A. Menninger, *The Human Mind* (Third Edition), Alfred A. Knopf, New York, 1956.

[27] Ernest M. Gruenberg, et al., "A Project Designed to Prevent Mental Disorders in an Aged Population, Syracuse, New York," October 1957, New York.

the psychiatric census schedule

appendix
one

PSYCHIATRIC PATIENT CENSUS

Case No....................   Abstractors:....................

Hospital...................   ....

1. Code No............   2. SSI No....................................

3. Name..

4. Address..
                          (Street & Number)   (Town)

5. Occupation (specify)..

6. Age............   7. Sex M F   8. Race W N Other

9. Patient:

        ( ) unmarried   ( ) separated........... ( ) widowed............

        ( ) married........... ( ) divorced........... ( ) remarried ....

10. Education   0   1–6   7–9   10–11   12   Col.   1   2   3   4   GW

11. Specify any post-secondary training...

....

12. Place of birth...
                          (City or Town)   (State)   (Country)

13. Place reared...
                          (City or Town)   (State)   (Country)

14. Number and rank of siblings..

15. National origin, Father.................... 16. Mother....................

17. Religious affiliation   C   P   J   GrO   Other   None

18. If married, occupation of spouse (specify).................................

19. Education, spouse   0   1–6   7–9   10–11   12   Col.   1   2   3   4   GW

20. Specify any post-secondary training...

21. Number of children...

22. Occupation of patient's father...

23. Occupation of patient's mother...

24. Marital status, parents:

        ( ) unmarried   ( ) separated........... ( ) widowed............

        ( ) married............ ( ) divorced........... ( ) remarried............

25. Synopsis of Family History:..

....

....

....

....

....

....

....

26. Case rich in sociological detail: Yes   No

27. Type of referral:
    ( ) self-referral   ( ) medical clinic
    ( ) relative   ( ) psychiatric clinic
    ( ) another patient   ( ) general hospital
    ( ) friend   ( ) psychiatric hospital
    ( ) physician ....   ( ) social agency
    ( ) certification   ( ) psychologist
    ( ) commitment (probate court)   ( ) school
    ( ) medical specialist other than   ( ) minister
         psychiatrist   ( ) lawyer
    ( ) psychiatrist ....   ( ) police or court

28. Patient classification:
    ( ) hospital full rate   ( ) clinic full rate   ( ) private practice full rate
    ( ) hospital reduced rate ( ) clinic reduced rate ( ) private practice reduced rate
    ( ) hospital free   ( ) clinic free   ( ) private practice free

29. Date present treatment initiated...

30. Date of psychiatric hospitalization for present illness...

31. Number of previous psychiatric hospitalizations..

32. If patient has previous psychiatric hospital history, date patient first hospitalized.................

....

33. Total duration (in months) of previous psychiatric hospitalization...............................

....

34. Date any medical treatment for present illness..

35. Number of previous terms of treatment with psychiatrist...

36. If patient has previous psychiatric history, date patient first saw psychiatrist:.....................

37. Total duration of previous terms of treatment with psychiatrist (in months)........................

38. Type of treatment (present illness): indicate all present types applied; *double check* the principal method of treatment.

A. No treatment

( ) general diagnostic
( ) forensic diagnostic
( ) compensation diagnostic
( ) hospitalization; no treatment

C. Psychotherapy

( ) psychoanalysis
( ) analytic psychotherapy
( ) eclectic psychotherapy
( ) relationship therapy
　　( ) supportive therapy
　　( ) suggestive therapy
　　( ) directive therapy

B. Organic treatment

( ) physical therapy
( ) hydrotherapy
( ) electroshock ....
( ) insulin shock ....
( ) shock, other ....
( ) drugs ....
( ) sedation
( ) operation ....
( ) other ....

( ) hypnosis
( ) hypnoanalysis
( ) narcoanalysis
( ) other ....

D. Environmental hospital treatment

( ) industrial therapy ....
( ) occupational therapy ....
( ) educational therapy ....
( ) other ....

39. Average length of psychotherapeutic sessions...

40. Number of monthly meetings with psychotherapist...

41. Psychiatric diagnosis...
....
....
....
....
....

42. Synopsis of examination and history..
....
....
....
....
....
....

43. Case rich in psychiatric detail: Yes   No

44. Doctor in charge of case..

the index of
social position

**appendix
two**

The Index of Social Position was developed to meet the need for an objective, easily applicable procedure to estimate positions individuals occupy in the status structure of the community. Its development was dependent both upon detailed knowledge of the community's social structure and procedures social scientists have used to delineate class status positions in other studies. It is premised upon three assumptions: (1) the existence of a class status structure in the community, (2) that class status positions are determined mainly by a few commonly accepted symbolic characteristics, and (3) that characteristics symbolic of class status may be scaled and combined by the use of statistical procedures so that a researcher can quickly, reliably, and meaningfully stratify the population.

PHASES IN THE DEVELOPMENT OF THE INDEX OF SOCIAL POSITION

Background Knowledge of the Community

New Haven has been studied by historians, psychologists, and sociologists for many years. Although there is general agreement among these social scientists that the community's social structure is differentiated both horizontally and vertically, we were faced with the problem of determining how to place a given individual or family in this social system in an objective and reliable manner.

This situation is not peculiar to New Haven. Numerous studies have reported stratification in American communities, but there is little agreement among research workers as to how individuals may be placed in the status structure that impinges upon them.

Before the plethora of facts accumulated from diverse studies can have meaning they have to be conceptualized in some systematic way. Careful analysis of the discrete data on the social structure of the community indicated three things about it: First, the community's social structure is differentiated *vertically* by racial, ethnic, and religious factors, and *horizontally* by a series of strata or classes. Second, each stratum or class in a vertical division is similar in its cultural characteristics to the corresponding stratum in other vertical divisions. Third, the primary status system of each racial, ethnic, and religious group is patterned after the one prevailing in the old Yankee segment of the community, because the old Yankees provided the master cultural mold that has shaped the acculturation of each ethnic and racial subgroup in the community. For example, Italians, Jews, and Poles, in a given class, have cultural characteristics similar to Yankees in the same class and aspire to similar status positions. However, these groups are separated into different vertical divisions by religious and ethnic factors.

Cross Sectional Sample of Households

General knowledge of the community's class structure was supplemented by a study of a cross sectional random sample of 552 households. Each household drawn in the sample was interviewed in the home with a 200-question schedule designed to furnish detailed data on the family's ethnic, religious, economic, educational, social, and residential backgrounds in the New Haven community, elsewhere in the United States, and other countries. The interview lasted from two to three hours. In addition to the answers to the semistructured and structured questions, each interviewer wrote a detailed statement of his impressions of the family and how he believed the family was adjusted to the community and to one another. This study provided detailed data on the size of the family, participation in economic, religious, educational, and leisure-time institutions, as well as the members' values, attitudes, aspirations, standard of living, ideas of the future, and their frustrations, desires, hopes, and fears.

Estimates of Class Position

Two sociologists familiar with the community's social structure, August B. Hollingshead and Jerome K. Myers, studied each family's schedule in detail and the interviewer's discussion of the family. On the basis of the detailed schedule data and the interviewer's impression, Hollingshead and Myers, working independently, made judgments as to where they believed each family belonged in the stratification system of the community. Previous to the independent judgment of each family's position in the community's stratificational system, Myers and Hollingshead agreed that functionally the horizontal strata in the New Haven community could well be divided into five class or social levels.

When the process of individual estimation of class position had been completed, the tentative class positions assigned to a family by Hollingshead and Myers were compared. They were in agreement on where they thought 96 percent of the families belonged in the stratificational system of the community. On the 4 percent where there was disagreement, Hollingshead and Myers re-examined the evidence, and assigned the family to a class by mutual agreement. Their agreements and disagreements were distributed unevenly in the status structure. They agreed on thirty-five families who they judged to be in the two top classes. They disagreed on the class positions of two families immediately below these strata. Myers placed one family in the second class, and the other in the third class; Hollingshead placed these families in the opposite positions. They disagreed on the placement of ten families in the third and fourth class areas of the social structure and nineteen families in the fourth and fifth class areas. In each instance, one judge placed the family in a different class from that of the other judge. However, in no instance was the discrepancy of one judge more than one class position away from the other, and there was no consistent tendency for one judge to overplace or underplace families compared with the placements made by the second judge.

CHARACTERISTICS SYMBOLIC OF STATUS

When the work on the judgment of class positions was completed, Hollingshead and Myers discussed the criteria they thought they had followed to make their judgments. Although a number of different criteria were followed by each man, they were in general agreement that most consideration was given to (*a*) where a family lived, (*b*) the way it made its living, and (*c*) its tastes, its cultural orientation, and the way it spent its leisure time. After considerable additional discussion, the conclusion was reached that the educational level of the head of the household was probably a good single index to the general area of cultural and social values exhibited in the answers the respondents had given to questions about their associations and leisure time activities.

Scaling of Symbolic Characteristics

The next step was to abstract from the interview schedules, as specific indicators of class position, the family's address, the occupation of its head, and the years of school he had completed. These data were placed on tabulation sheets, along with the agreed estimate of the family's position in the status system. After this step was completed, the address, occupation, and years of school completed were scaled.

1. THE RESIDENTIAL SCALE. The residential scale was based upon ecological research carried on by Maurice R. Davie and his associates in the New Haven community over a 25-year span. In the early 1930s, Davie mapped the city of New Haven ecologically, and ranked residential areas on a six-position scale that ranged from the finest homes to the poorest tenements. Jerome K. Myers brought Davie's data up to date as of 1950, within the city of New Haven, and mapped the suburban towns in the same way that Davie had mapped New Haven in earlier years. This work provided a uniform scale for the evaluation of addresses.

2. THE OCCUPATIONAL SCALE. The occupational scale is a modification of the Alba Edwards system of classifying occupations into socioeconomic groups used by the United States Bureau of the Census. The essential differences between the Edwards system and the one used is that Edwards does not differentiate among kinds of professionals or the sizes and economic strengths of businesses. The scale used in the Index of Social Position ranks professions into different groups and businesses by their size and value. Without further discussion of similarities and differences between the Edwards system and ours, we will proceed to characterize each of the seven positions on the scale we used: (1) executives and proprietors of large concerns, and major professionals, (2) managers and proprietors of medium-sized businesses and lesser professionals, (3) administrative personnel of large concerns, owners of small independent

business, and semiprofessionals, (4) owners of little businesses, clerical and sales workers, and technicians, (5) skilled workers, (6) semiskilled workers, and (7) unskilled workers.

This scale is premised upon the assumption that occupations have different values attached to them by the members of our society. The hierarchy ranges from the low evaluation of unskilled physical labor toward the more prestigeful use of skill, through the creative talents, ideas, and the management of men. The ranking of occupational functions implies that some men exercise control over the occupational pursuits of other men. Normally, a person who possesses highly trained skills has control over several other people. This is exemplified in a highly developed form by an executive in a large business enterprise who may be responsible for decisions affecting thousands of employees.

3. THE EDUCATIONAL SCALE. The educational scale is premised upon the assumption that men and women who possess similar educations will tend to have similar tastes and similar attitudes, and they will also tend to exhibit similar behavior patterns.

The educational scale was divided into seven positions:

(1) *Graduate professional training.* (Persons who completed a recognized professional course which led to the receipt of a graduate degree were given scores of 1.)

(2) *Standard college or university graduation.* (All individuals who had completed a four-year college or university course leading to a recognized college degree were assigned the same scores. No differentiation was made between state universities or private colleges.)

(3) *Partial college training.* (Individuals who had completed at least one year but not a full college course were assigned this position.)

(4) *High school graduation.* (All secondary school graduates whether from a private preparatory school, public high school, trade school, or parochial high school were given this score.)

(5) *Partial high school.* (Individuals who had completed the tenth or eleventh grades, but had not completed high school were given this score.)

(6) *Junior high school.* (Individuals who had completed the seventh grade through the ninth grade were given this position.)

(7) *Less than seven years of school.* (Individuals who had not completed the seventh grade were given the same scores irrespective of the amount of education they had received.)

The Matrix of Scale Patterns

The exact scores a family head received on each of the four variables—judged class position, address, occupation, and education—were placed in a matrix, and the families were ranked from high to low on the basis of the scale patterns. Families who were judged to belong in the top social class in the community, and had a scale score of 1 on ecological area, 1 on occupation, and 1 on education were placed at the top of the listing. Families with a combination of different, but high scores on the four variables, were listed immediately below this group. For example, a family may have been judged to be in the top class if it lived in the best residential area and its head was a vice-president of a large industry and had a B.A. degree. The score pattern would be 1, 1, 1, 2. Another family head was judged to be in the top class, but he lived in an area that was graded ecologically as second class; however, he was a partner in a large brokerage firm, and had a degree from the Harvard Business School. His score pattern was, thus: 1, 2, 1, 1.

As the listing of the different scores proceeded from higher to lower sequences, the combinations of ones and twos faded out and a few cases entered the matrix where a family's score was 1 on class, 1 on occupation, 2 on address, but 3 on education. This process was carried successively lower until all the families were listed and all the score combinations were available for examination.

The listing of families by their score patterns enabled us to delineate areas of complete agreement between our clinical judgments of class position and the objective scores of a family on the three-criterion scales, as well as variations between the judgments and the achieved scale scores of the family. It indicated also where there were "pure" patterns of scores, such as 2 on class, 2 on address, 2 on occupation, and 2 on education, and "mixed" patterns where the four scale values showed a range of two or three points. For example, one family is given a class judgment of 3, but its address is scored as 1, its occupational score is 4, and its educational score is 3. The head of the family is a bank teller, who completed two years of college. His home was purchased by an inheritance, and it is maintained, in part, by income from the residue of his legacy and the man's own "do-it-yourself" efforts on weekends and evenings.

Score patterns such as these revealed heterogeneity in the different facets of social reality which we were using to measure the indirect quality of social status. They also gave us a clue as to where we might cut the continuum of scores in a meaningful way to produce operational classes we could work with in later phases of our research.

Homogeneous score patterns, at the top and the bottom of the continuum, were believed to be indicative of the existence of two clear-cut classes—an "upper" one and a "lower" one. But how were we to differentiate among the combinations of scale scores of the intervening patterns to give us the most meaningful index of an individual family's position in the community's status system? The tentative answer was to cut the continuum at the points where the greatest amount of variation existed between the four variables. We inferred these points were indicative of meaningful discontinuities in the social hierarchy of the community.

MULTIPLE CORRELATION AND REGRESSION

Multiple Correlations

The next analytical problem was to determine how the three variables, address, occupation, and years of school completed, were combined and weighted in our judgments of class position. The answer to this problem was sought by intercorrelating the four variables of judged class position, address, occupation, and years of school completed by the family's head. The essential findings on the intercorrelations of the four variables are summarized in Table 1.

Examination of the intercorrelations will show that the highest association is obtained when a combination of area of residence, education, and occupation is correlated with judged class position as would be expected in view of the high correlation of each of these variables with the criterion. Slightly lower r's are obtained when judged class position is correlated with a combination of any two of the three variables. In general, lower r's appear when judged class position is correlated with the individual factors in the matrix. However, the lowest associations appear when the criterion factors are correlated with one another.

Multiple Regression Equation

The multiple regression analysis of these data indicated the weights appropriate for each factor when estimating the class position of families in the sample.

These multiple regression weights could then be applied to fami-

TABLE 1

Intercorrelations between Judged Class Position, Ecological Area of Residence, Education, and Occupation of Sample Families in the New Haven Community, 1948

A. Intercorrelations of Scale Variables

	Correlation
Education with residence	.451
Occupation with residence	.505
Occupation with education	.721

B. Criterion Predicted from One Variable

Judged class with residence	.692
Judged class with education	.782
Judged class with occupation	.881

C. Criterion Predicted from Two Variables

	Multiple Correlation
Judged class with residence and education	.870
Judged class with residence and occupation	.926
Judged class with education and occupation	.906

D. Criterion Predicted from Three Variables

Judged class with residence, education, and occupation	.942

lies other than those in the present sample, and thus estimates of their class positions could be obtained. The computed multiple equation was:

$$X_1 \text{ (Estimated class position)} = .183X_2 \text{ (Residence)} + .154X_3 \text{ (Education)} + .269X_4 \text{ (Occupation)} + .884$$

Use of this multiple regression equation will give a distribution of estimated class positions ranging from approximately 1 to 5. For simplicity of computation, however, the constant (.884) can be omitted and the *approximate* weights of 6, 5, 9, respectively, can be used to weight the factors X_2, X_3, X_4 appropriately. This will yield a distribution of scores ranging from a theoretical low of 20 to a theoretical high of 134, and representing a continuum from the very highest class to the very lowest. This distribution can then be broken into segments or ranges of scores indicative of meaningful social positions in the class structure.

ESTIMATION OF CLASS POSITION

Index of Social Position Scores and Class

The computation of an Index of Social Position Score is only one phase of the problem of determining class. The determination of the points where the continuum of scores should be cut to differentiate among the classes of the community's social system is crucial. This problem is handled by computing Index of Social Position scores for each of the families included in the multiple correlation and multiple regression procedures discussed above.

In this operation, the factor weights of 6, 5, and 9 respectively established through the multiple regression equation were used in combination with the scale position scores (1 to 6 on residence, 1 to 7 on occupation, and 1 to 7 on education) to compute the Index of Social Position scores. When these scores were computed, each family's weighted score was compared with its position on the continuum of raw scale scores and judged class position. This comparison indicated where there was homogeneity and heterogeneity between the raw scores and the weighted scores. Where there was homogeneity in the patterns of the raw scale scores, and congruity of these scores with judged class position, we assumed that the cluster was indicative of a functional segment of the community's status system. Where there was heterogeneity in the score clusters, we assumed there was indeterminacy in the status system. Thus the inference was made that Index of Social Position scores should cut at the point of most heterogeneity in the scale score patterns. By the use of this procedure, the range of scores for each "class" was decided to be shown as follows:

Class	Range of Scores	Percentage of Total Number of Families
I	20–31	2.7
II	32–55	9.8
III	56–86	18.9
IV	87–115	48.4
V	116–134	20.2

This procedure compresses the continuum of scores into score groups. It assumes that the differences *between* the score groups are greater than the differences *within* each score group in terms of class status characteristics. Within each group differences in individual scores are ignored, and each score is treated as a unit in a cluster. This procedure assumes there are differences between the score groups. Families with scores that fall into a given segment of the range of scores assigned to a particular class position are presumed to belong to the class the Index of Social Position score predicts for it.

Determination of a Family's Index of Social Position Score

To obtain a family's score on the Index of Social Position, the researcher needs to know three things: (1) its address, (2) its head's exact occupational pursuit, and (3) the years of school he has completed. The next step is to assign the appropriate scale scores for address, occupation, and education. Once the scale scores are determined, each factor is multiplied by the appropriate weight. For example, the score of a family whose head works at a clerical job, is a high school graduate, and lives in a middle rank residential area would be computed thus:

Factor	Scale Value	× Factor Weight	= Partial Score
Residence	3	6	24
Occupation	4	9	36
Education	4	5	20
			—
Index of Social Position Score =			74

The computations for a family whose head is a semiskilled factory worker who attended high school for two years and lives in an area of two family houses would be:

Factor	Scale Value	× Factor Weight	= Partial Score
Residence	5	6	30
Occupation	6	9	54
Education	5	5	25
			—
Index of Social Position Score =			109

This definition of class position is based on three assumptions: First, a family's mode of living is mirrored in its home; second, the occupation of its head reflects the skill and power associated with maintenance functions in the society; and third, the amount of formal education the head has received reflects the tastes of the family. The combination of these factors enables a researcher to determine within approximate limits the position a family occupies in the status structure of such an industrialized community as New Haven.

The operationally determined hierarchy of scores which emerges is presumed to be an estimation of the status hierarchy which exists in the community. In short, the Index of Social Position attempts to delineate operationally the socially discriminating comparisons people make of each other in their day-to-day behaviors. How it was validated is described in Appendix Three.

social
stratification
and mass
communication *

**appendix
three**

Many studies have been made in the past decade of interrelations between stratification variables and specific types of social behavior. These studies have analyzed the data after the population has been stratified into identifiable groups. This practice has presented critical readers with the question: Are these groups merely arbitrary categories or are they in some empirical sense "real" classes? This study is focused on the examination of this question by the use of behaviorally relevant data.

The data we have examined are responses households in the 5 percent sample made to mass media of communication. Mass communication items were used because they are available to all members of the community in the sense that they are (1) relatively cheap and (2) designed to have wide appeal. The crucial question to which we addressed ourselves was: Are the responses of the members of households to mass communication items distributed evenly along a social hierarchy, or do they cluster along particular segments of it? The social hierarchy is measured by Hollingshead's Index of Social Position which is designed as a continuous scale ranging from the highest positions in the social hierarchy to the lowest ones.

The data used are drawn from the Systematic Sample of 5 percent

* Written in collaboration with Theodore R. Anderson.

of the households in the New Haven community which contains 3559 households. Each household was queried as to what newspapers and periodicals were read and what radio and television programs were heard and watched regularly. Responses were classified into 50 attributes, such as, Does any adult regularly listen to a news commentary on the radio?

The specific problems of this research were, on the one hand, to identify stratification-related patterns of response to the mass media and, on the other hand, to determine whether these patterns tended to characterize bounded intervals of the social hierarchy.

To solve these problems, the Index of Social Position scale was grouped into 33 intervals, called ISP groups, each consisting of 3 specific scores. (The grouping was made necessary by the size of the sample.) Within each of these groups, the proportion of households indicating participation in each mass media item or attribute was determined. For example, in the highest ISP group, 12 percent of the households reported that a child watched at least one children's variety program, 29 percent of the households (or at least one member thereof) watched a sports program, 51 percent of the households regularly read *The New York Times*. The collection of 50 proportions associated with each ISP group showed the pattern of response to the mass media which existed within that particular small segment of the social hierarchy.

To discover more general patterns of response, the patterns within each pair of ISP groups were correlated, and the resulting correlation matrix was factor-analyzed using Thurstone's centroid method. Each correlation coefficient measures the similarity in pattern of two ISP groups. All correlations in the matrix were positive, and most were quite high. The occurrence of high, positive correlations means that responses which are relatively common in one segment of the social hierarchy tend to be relatively common in all other segments. In other words, the norms and values governing the selection of mass media responses tend, to a considerable extent, to operate throughout the entire population studied. (If this were not true, the items would hardly be called collectively the *mass* media.) However, the correlations tend to be highest between adjacent ISP groups, and tend to decline regularly as the ISP groups become more and more distant. This fact indicates the validity of the ISP as a measure of the social hierarchy.

Factor analysis yielded three orthogonal factors, or general response patterns. That these factors in combination would accurately reproduce the pattern within each ISP group is shown by the fact that the factors, or general patterns, account for 94 percent of the variation in the original patterns.

The orthogonal factors were then rotated to an oblique simple structure. The method of extended factors was used and, since only three factors were involved, the resulting solution was quite determinate. That is, if a simple structure exists in the data, we found it. That something very much like a simple structure does in fact exist can be seen clearly from the table of the rotated factor loadings (Table 1). The loadings meet all the criteria of Thurstone using .099 as the largest "zero" loading.

These rotated factors are, as the loadings show, patterns of response which characterize different intervals of the social hierarchy. Pattern *A* correlates highly with patterns found near the top of the hierarchy and is uncorrelated with all patterns in the lower third of the hierarchy. The highest loadings for pattern *B* occur near the center of the hierarchy. Pattern *C* is most similar to patterns found at the bottom of the hierarchy.

However, it must be noted, first, that these patterns are highly intercorrelated. The correlation between pattern *A* and pattern *C* is about .75, whereas the other two correlations are about .90. Here again we can see the basic similarity of response to the mass media at all levels of the social hierarchy. Second, note that these general patterns are overlapping. For example, patterns just below the top of the hierarchy are correlated both to pattern *A* and pattern *B*. Thus, while different general patterns of response to the mass media have emerged at different levels of the social hierarchy, the structure of these patterns relative to that hierarchy is not very clear-cut.

If we are to seek points which represent boundaries between actual class status groups, we must have a criterion. Had the general patterns been non-overlapping, the criterion would have been obvious. Given overlap, however, the issue is more complicated. The best criterion for selecting boundary points appears to be the occurrence of a marked change in the combination of patterns *A*, *B*, and *C* from one ISP group to the next. Using this criterion there appear to be four major boundary points.

First, there is a sharp break between ISP groups 27 and 28 in both patterns *B* and *C*. At this point, *B*'s loadings drop to zero and *C*'s loadings rise substantially. Second, there is a definite, but not too sharply defined break somewhere between ISP groups 15 and 20. We chose to call this a break between groups 17 and 18. This

TABLE 1

Loadings of Factor Patterns After an Oblique Rotation to Simple Structure

	Factor Loadings		
ISP Group	A	B	C
1	.813	.008	−.034
2	.485	.196	.028
3	.776	−.042	.020
4	.444	.359	−.200
5	.670	.093	.022
6	.521	.164	−.022
7	.492	.221	.017
8	.515	.201	.007
9	.322	.335	−.035
10	.386	.314	−.055
11	.214	.364	−.014
12	.390	.312	−.035
13	.275	.343	−.023
14	.268	.307	.035
15	.219	.264	.089
16	.116	.295	.113
17	.203	.235	.134
18	.079	.285	.141
19	.012	.316	.127
20	.157	.216	.189
21	.033	.308	.132
22	−.003	.249	.209
23	−.021	.257	.203
24	−.059	.243	.228
25	−.017	.198	.267
26	−.009	.173	.292
27	−.010	.179	.285
28	.017	.036	.421
29	−.023	.056	.412
30	.001	−.010	.463
31	−.079	.018	.459
32	.013	.002	.453
33	.058	−.106	.539

point essentially marks the emergence and disappearance of patterns *A* and *C*. Thus, with one exception, for all ISP groups below 17, pattern *C* is present and *A* absent, whereas the reverse (*A* present and *C* absent) is true for all groups above the 18th. A similar kind of break appears between groups 8 and 9. For groups 8 and above, the loadings on A are markedly higher than those on B, whereas these loadings are about equal for groups 9 and below. Furthermore, pattern A drops somewhat between groups 8 and 9.

Finally, there appears to be a break near the very top of the hierarchy. Groups 1, 3, and 5 seem to manifest a somewhat different pattern than groups 2 and 4. This difference suggests a break, but the lack of contiguity among the similar groups makes the positioning of the break somewhat difficult. It was decided, more or less arbitrarily, to place the break between groups 1 and 2. The fact that group 1 responds in a manner more like that of groups 3 and 5 than like group 2 is a bit surprising. It may result simply from the smallness of our sample, that is, it may be simply random sampling variation. The small number of families in the first 5 ISP groups (77, 46, 29, 26, and 62) makes this idea plausible, at least. On the other hand, the lack of stability in the loadings near the top may indicate that the ISP does not measure relative social positions accurately near the top of the social structure. Such a conclusion may also be plausible. However, slight discrepancies, such as the above, are to be expected in any empirical scale when the sample is too small to be stable. Indeed, looking at the entire factor patterns, what is remarkable is that such discrepancies are as rare as they are.

The households making up the class status groups, generated by using these boundary points, possess somewhat different behavioral responses to the mass media. Details of these differences are shown in Table 2. Suffice it to say here that in general the two extreme classes (I and V) differ from the others primarily through not participating as much in exposure to the mass media. On the other hand, class II and, to some extent, class III differ from class IV through greater emphasis on magazines and the radio and less emphasis on television. Television tends to dominate the response pattern of class IV.

It is very interesting, and important, to note the essential agreement between the system of classes generated from these mass media data and the system previously enunciated by Hollingshead, largely through an internal analysis of the ISP itself (see Table 3). Thus, this research supports Hollingshead's earlier work, and does so in a rather informative way for no a priori assumptions were made in this research about the existence, the number, or the positioning of social classes. Nor was the method at all similar to that used by Hollingshead earlier. On the other hand, since the criteria for locating the class boundaries for this study were not specified before

TABLE 2

Percentage of Households Indicating Participation in Specified Type of Activity—by Social Class

1. Responses Occurring Most Frequently in Higher Class Positions

Item	Class				
	I	II	III	IV	V
Television (none)					
Radio					
News commentary	35.1	23.4	13.9	9.1	7.8
Other drama	11.7	11.7	8.1	6.0	5.0
Serious music	27.3	27.5	13.4	9.0	7.2
Magazines					
News (more than 1)	31.2	25.6	19.7	11.3	7.0
Digests	42.9	39.9	37.3	24.0	10.5
Professional and trade	16.9	7.3	6.1	3.0	0.7
Educational, literary, and information	39.0	28.9	9.6	4.1	1.2
Hobby and Crafts	9.1	4.4	4.1	5.2	2.5
(4 or more in all)	53.2	56.0	46.9	31.5	13.5
Newspapers					
New York Times	50.6	40.3	24.2	8.7	4.0
New York Herald Tribune	26.0	15.8	9.8	3.2	2.4

2. Responses Occurring Most Frequently Near Middle Class Positions

Item	I	II	III	IV	V
Television (none)					
Radio					
Variety programs	13.0	21.2	15.9	15.8	13.9
Light music	9.1	10.3	6.3	4.0	1.9
Quiz programs	15.6	23.8	23.2	17.3	17.1
Magazines					
News (only 1)	28.6	40.3	29.7	24.1	17.1
Mixed fiction and information	28.6	39.6	44.3	41.3	23.3
Women's mixed fiction and information	18.2	39.2	42.0	36.4	17.1
Home improvement and recreation	15.6	17.2	22.6	15.5	6.5
Business	1.3	5.9	5.0	1.1	0.5
Newspapers (none)					

TABLE 2 (Continued)

Percentage of Households Indicating Participation in Specified Type of Activity—by Social Class

3. Responses Occurring Most Frequently Near Lower Class Positions

			Class		
Item	I	II	III	IV	V
Television					
Western drama (child)	3.9	10.6	15.6	21.7	15.6
Other drama (child)	2.6	3.3	6.5	7.2	5.2
Variety (child)	11.7	20.9	26.0	31.1	26.4
Religious	22.1	30.8	39.8	48.7	43.1
News	26.0	46.9	59.2	66.1	55.3
Domestic drama	7.8	8.8	13.6	19.9	17.6
Crime drama	2.6	11.0	20.9	27.6	24.9
Comedy drama	23.4	28.9	35.3	40.1	38.2
Other drama	26.0	40.7	52.7	52.7	44.4
Variety	22.1	38.5	50.6	59.7	54.7
Sports	28.6	46.9	58.9	65.3	59.2
Music	13.0	20.9	25.7	25.8	20.3
Radio					
Crime drama	1.3	5.9	7.1	7.2	8.3
Magazines					
Women's escape fiction	0.0	0.0	1.2	3.4	6.9
Parent-Child relations	1.3	2.6	3.6	6.4	3.9
(1 to 3 magazines in all)	35.1	35.9	40.3	47.6	46.9
Newspapers					
New York News	1.3	6.6	9.6	16.5	15.1
New York Mirror	1.3	4.8	6.5	12.8	11.1

4. Responses Showing No Particular Relation to the Social Hierarchy

Television					
Child's information	2.6	2.6	3.0	2.7	3.4
Adult program (child)	3.9	5.9	6.5	6.8	5.9
Radio					
Western drama (child)	5.2	3.3	3.2	4.3	3.3
Other drama (child)	2.6	1.5	1.3	2.0	0.9
Variety (child)	5.2	5.9	5.0	5.3	6.7
Adult program (child)	1.3	1.1	0.0	0.9	0.3
News bulletins	31.2	32.2	26.7	21.1	23.9
Domestic drama	9.1	5.5	6.6	7.5	8.1
Sports	26.0	34.1	27.2	24.8	27.3
Popular music	9.1	7.3	5.6	7.6	6.4
Magazines					
Motion picture	1.3	0.7	1.3	2.0	3.2
Style and beauty	3.9	3.3	4.5	2.5	2.5
Comic books	1.3	0.4	0.3	1.7	1.9
Newspapers (none)					

TABLE 3

Percentage of Households in Each Class or Status Group by Present System
and Hollingshead's Earlier Analysis

Class	Present System	Hollingshead's Earlier Analysis
I	2.2	3.4
II	7.7	9.0
III	16.9	21.4
IV	44.7	48.5
V	28.5	17.7
Total	100.0	100.0

Percentage placed in same class by both systems: 78.2

the data were analyzed, and since Anderson was familiar with Hollingshead's earlier classification, the possibility of bias must be considered.

More importantly, the question always may be asked: Do these particular boundaries have any significance, or would other boundaries be just as effective? Of course, the purpose of any classification system is to produce categories which are relatively homogeneous internally and relatively heterogeneous externally. That is, the within variance should be relatively small, and the between variance relatively large. Since these two criteria cannot necessarily be maximized, simultaneously, it is reasonable to evaluate any classification system by means of the ratio of the between to the within variance. The larger the ratio, the better the classification system. To demonstrate that our boundaries are not arbitrary it was decided to test these boundaries against randomly selected ones using the above criterion.

Three different sets of 4 boundaries were chosen randomly. Using the proportion of response to a given item within each of the 33 ISP groups, the between-within variance ratio was computed for each of these random sets and for our set of boundaries. For any one item, the probability that our set of boundaries would yield the highest between-within variance ratio is .25, assuming that our system produces no better than random results. In a sample of 10 items, using a 5 percent level of significance, the hypothesis that our boundaries are arbitrary can be rejected if 6 or more of the items show our system to yield the highest between-within ratio. With this test procedure fixed, a random sample of ten items was selected and analyzed. The boundaries we have established were found to be the best in more than 6 of the 10 cases sampled. Thus, we may conclude that our system does produce class boundaries that are preferable to purely random or arbitrarily produced ones.

While this is a very important conclusion, its meaning should not be exaggerated. The test shows that factor analysis applied in the manner we have outlined can be used to establish a classification system which yields between-within variance ratios which are higher than those produced by an arbitrary classification. It also shows that for a specific set of mass media response items some points on the social hierarchy are better boundaries than other points in delimiting class status groups. That is, within our sample, and for the 50 mass media items studied, the social hierarchy is in some parts continuous and in others discontinuous in its impact on behavior.

However, before it can be concluded that class status groups exist, as other than arbitrary intervals along a social hierarchy, two types of further research are necessary. First, it must be demonstrated that our results are not specific to our particular sample. Second, the same results must be demonstrated for other behavioral domains. That is, these same boundary points must appear in other samples and in other areas of behavior before the existence of classes as functional status groups can be said to have been demonstrated. Our results suggest that "classes" do, in fact, exist in the behavior of individual families. These results also suggest that factor analysis, properly interpreted, can be used as a means of locating classes and their boundaries. Only further research can confirm or refute these suggestions.

SUMMARY AND CONCLUSION

On the basis of our analysis we have reached several conclusions: (1) It is indisputable that mass communication responses are distributed differentially along the social hierarchy despite the presence of strong over-all values and norms governing the selection of responses to the mass media. (2) There are three distinct though interrelated configurations of behavioral responses to mass communication media. (3) Each configuration is characteristic of a different segment of the social hierarchy, although the configurations overlap each other to some extent. (4) Although the five intervals are clear-cut, the boundaries separating them cannot be fixed precisely in all cases. (6) We conclude that our analysis is a further confirmation of the existence of five classes or strata in the New Haven community. (7) Our data indicate that the boundaries previously generated by Hollingshead are substantially correct. (8) Factor analysis can be used to determine meaningful boundaries. (9) As a general conclusion, we feel that when social phenomena are viewed behaviorally, it is meaningful to break the social hierarchy into distinct social strata rather than to treat it simply as a continuum. The boundaries we found yield results which are better, in the sense of internal homogeneity and external heterogeneity, than boundaries chosen at random. These conclusions are subject, of course, to further research for confirmation. We invite replication by other investigators.

supplementary tables

appendix
four

TABLE 1

Percentage of Patients in the Population—by Class, Sex, and Age

A. Males
14 Years and Younger

Class	Patients	Population
I and II	11.9	11.4
III	28.6	20.4
IV	26.2	52.8
V	33.3	15.4
$n =$ 42		31,800

$$\chi^2 = 16.02, 3 \ df, p < .01$$

Age 15–24

Class	Patients	Population
I and II	12.5	7.8
III	16.7	17.2
IV	44.4	46.3
V	26.4	28.7
$n =$ 72		13,140

$$\chi^2 = 2.26, 3 \ df, p > .05$$

TABLE 1 (cont'd)

Percentage of Patients in the Population—by Class, Sex, and Age

A. Males (cont'd)

Age 25–34

Class	Patients	Population
I and II	12.8	10.7
III	14.3	23.1
IV	50.5	53.8
V	22.4	12.4
$n =$ 210		17,580

$\chi^2 = 25.35$, 3 df, $p < .001$

Age 35–44

Class	Patients	Population
I and II	6.1	12.3
III	11.1	21.8
IV	37.8	51.9
V	45.0	14.0
$n =$ 180		18,060

$\chi^2 = 146.50$, 3 df, $p < .001$

Age 45–54

Class	Patients	Population
I and II	5.1	12.8
III	10.1	24.1
IV	34.2	47.2
V	50.6	15.9
$n =$ 158		13,940

$\chi^2 = 145.05$, 3 df, $p < .001$

Age 55 and Over

Class	Patients	Population
I and II	3.6	11.0
III	5.5	16.7
IV	33.6	47.8
V	57.3	24.5
$n =$ 307		19,580

$\chi^2 = 185.97$, 3 df, $p < .001$

TABLE 1 (cont'd)

Percentage of Patients in the Population—by Class, Sex, and Age

B. Females

14 Years and Younger

Class	Patients	Population
I and II	0.0	10.0
III	40.0	18.8
IV	30.0	53.6
V	30.0	17.6
$n =$ 10		30,840

$$\chi^2 = 5.19,\ 3\ df,\ p > .05$$

Age 15–24

Class	Patients	Population
I and II	10.7	9.1
III	28.6	16.2
IV	35.7	47.2
V	25.0	27.5
$n =$ 56		14,740

$$\chi^2 = 7.28,\ 3\ df,\ p > .05$$

Age 25–34

Class	Patients	Population
I and II	13.6	11.9
III	22.0	22.9
IV	39.0	51.6
V	25.4	13.6
$n =$ 177		20,640

$$\chi^2 = 24.33,\ 3\ df,\ p < .001$$

Age 35–44

Class	Patients	Population
I and II	10.5	12.4
III	17.0	21.1
IV	42.1	49.7
V	30.4	16.8
$n =$ 171		19,500

$$\chi^2 = 22.53,\ 3\ df,\ p < .001$$

TABLE 1 (cont'd)

Percentage of Patients in the Population—by Class, Sex, and Age

B. Females (cont'd)

Age 45–54

Class	Patients	Population
I and II	7.1	14.6
III	18.1	23.3
IV	41.3	46.0
V	33.5	16.1
$n =$ 155		16,160

$\chi^2 = 38.03$, 3 df, $p < .001$

Age 55 and Over

Class	Patients	Population
I and II	5.7	12.7
III	10.5	20.0
IV	44.2	43.2
V	39.6	24.1
$n =$ 353		20,960

$\chi^2 = 65.63$, 3 df, $p < .001$

TABLE 2

Percentage of Patients in the Population—by Class, Sex, Age, and Marital Status

A. Males

Age 20–49

Married

Class	Patients	Population
I and II	12.6	12.5
III	14.2	23.9
IV	48.6	51.3
V	24.6	12.3
$n =$ 183		36,300

$\chi^2 = 29.93$, 3 df, $p < .001$

TABLE 2 (cont'd)

Percentage of Patients in the Population—by Class, Sex, Age, and Marital Status

Males Age 20–49 (*cont'd*)
Separated, Widowed, Divorced

Class	Patients	Population
I and II	2.4	4.7
III	21.4	12.1
IV	38.1	49.0
V	38.1	34.2
$n =$ 42		2,980

$\chi^2 = 4.69,\ 3\ df,\ p > .05$

Single

Class	Patients	Population
I and II	7.8	7.4
III	10.1	17.5
IV	39.9	53.6
V	42.2	21.5
$n =$ 306		9,700

$\chi^2 = 81.63,\ 3\ df,\ p < .001$

Age 50 and Over

Married

Class	Patients	Population
I and II	7.8	12.9
III	9.4	19.0
IV	38.3	45.7
V	44.5	22.4
$n =$ 128		21,540

$\chi^2 = 38.60,\ 3\ df,\ p < .001$

Separated, Widowed, Divorced

Class	Patients	Population
I and II	3.1	7.7
III	5.1	16.8
IV	35.7	45.0
V	56.1	30.5
$n =$ 98		4,400

$\chi^2 = 33.99,\ 3\ df,\ p < .001$

TABLE 2 (cont'd)

Percentage of Patients in the Population—by Class, Sex, Age, and Marital Status

Males Age 50 and Over (cont'd)
Single

Class	Patients	Population
I and II	1.4	13.5
III	5.4	21.6
IV	27.7	39.2
V	65.5	25.7
$n =$ 148		1,480

$\chi^2 = 130.78$, 3 df, $p < .001$

B. Females

Age 20–49
Married

Class	Patients	Population
I and II	15.7	12.4
III	22.9	24.1
IV	38.1	50.7
V	23.3	12.8
$n =$ 210		37,040

$\chi^2 = 26.69$, 3 df, $p < .001$

Separated, Widowed, Divorced

Class	Patients	Population
I and II	7.6	5.4
III	21.2	9.4
IV	31.8	55.4
V	39.4	29.8
$n =$ 66		5,560

$\chi^2 = 19.01$, 3 df, $p < .001$

Single

Class	Patients	Population
I and II	9.6	9.7
III	21.1	15.8
IV	43.7	50.3
V	25.6	24.2
$n =$ 199		11,500

$\chi^2 = 5.37$, 3 df, $p > .05$

TABLE 2 (cont'd)

Percentage of Patients in the Population—by Class, Sex, Age, and Marital Status

Females (*cont'd*)

Age 50 and Over

Married

Class	Patients	Population
I and II	4.3	12.8
III	10.6	19.0
IV	44.0	45.2
V	41.1	23.0
$n =$ 141		22,180

$\chi^2 = 33.56$, 3 df, $p < .001$

Separated, Widowed, Divorced

Class	Patients	Population
I and II	6.0	11.1
III	12.0	20.9
IV	36.7	46.9
V	45.3	21.1
$n =$ 150		13,000

$\chi^2 = 54.50$, 3 df, $p < .001$

Single

Class	Patients	Population
I and II	4.3	19.4
III	13.8	17.5
IV	51.5	40.8
V	30.4	22.3
$n =$ 138		2,060

$\chi^2 = 25.13$, 3 df, $p < .001$

TABLE 3
Computation of Crude Rates

	Number of Patients	Class Population	Proportion of Patients in Class Population	Crude Class Rate per 100,000
Class I–II	150	27,000	.005556	555.6
Class III	260	48,360	.005376	537.6

Crude Rates per 100,000

$$\text{Class I–II:} \ \frac{150}{27,000} \times 100,000 = .005556 \times 100,000 = 555.6$$

$$\text{Class III:} \ \frac{260}{48,360} \times 100,000 = .005376 \times 100,000 = 537.6$$

TABLE 4

Adjustment of Class I–II Crude Rate for Age and Sex

Adjustment for Age

Males

Age Subgroup	Class Population	Number of Patients	Crude Rate per 100,000	Total Male Population
−14	3,620	5	138.1	31,800
15–24	1,020	9	882.4	13,140
25–34	1,880	27	1436.2	17,580
35–44	2,220	11	495.5	18,060
45–54	1,780	8	449.4	13,940
55+	2,160	11	509.3	19,580
Total	12,680	71	559.9	114,100

Females

Age Subgroup	Class Population	Number of Patients	Crude Rate per 100,000	Total Female Population
−14	3,080	0	0	30,840
15–24	1,340	6	447.8	14,740
25–34	2,460	24	975.6	20,640
35–44	2,420	18	743.8	19,500
45–54	2,360	11	466.1	16,160
55+	2,660	20	751.9	20,960
Total	14,320	79	551.7	122,840

Age-Adjusted Rates

Males:

$$\left(\frac{138.1}{100,000}\right)\left(\frac{31,800}{114,100}\right) + \left(\frac{882.4}{100,000}\right)\left(\frac{13,140}{114,100}\right) + \left(\frac{509.3}{100,000}\right)\left(\frac{19,580}{114,100}\right)$$

$$= \frac{664.1}{114,100} = 582.0 \text{ per } 100,000$$

Females:

$$\left(\frac{0}{100,000}\right)\left(\frac{30,840}{122,840}\right) + \left(\frac{447.8}{100,000}\right)\left(\frac{14,740}{122,840}\right) + \left(\frac{751.9}{100,000}\right)\left(\frac{20,960}{122,840}\right)$$

$$= \frac{645.3}{122,840} = 525.3 \text{ per } 100,000$$

Note that to adjust the class I–II male rate for age, we assume that the *class I–II male age structure* is the same as the age structure of the *total male population*, and we weight the six crude age rates proportionately. To adjust the class I–II female rate, we use the age structure of the *total female population* as the basis for the weighting.

We now have age-adjusted rates for both males and females in class I–II. The next step will be to combine these into a single class I–II rate which will reflect adjustment for *sex* as well as for *age*.

Adjustment for Sex

	Class Population	Age-Adjusted Rate per 100,000	Total Population
Males	12,680	582.0	114,100
Females	14,320	525.3	122,840
	27,000		236,940

Age- and Sex-Adjusted Rates

Class I–II:

$$\left(\frac{582.0}{100,000}\right)\left(\frac{114,100}{236,940}\right) + \left(\frac{525.3}{100,000}\right)\left(\frac{122,840}{236,940}\right) = \frac{1309.34}{236,940}$$

$$= 552.6 \text{ per } 100,000$$

Here the basis for the weighting of the separate age-adjusted sex rates is the proportion of males and females in the total population.

TABLE 5

χ^2 Test of Significance of Class Rates Adjusted for Age and Sex

(Age- and Sex-Adjusted)

Class	Population	Rate per 100,000	Observed Number of Patients	Expected Number of Patients
I–II	27,000	552.6	149.2	218.3
III	48,360	528.2	255.4	391.0
IV	118,000	664.5	784.1	953.9
V	43,580	1667.7	726.8	352.3
Total	236,940		1915.5	1915.5

Observed Number of Patients Is Obtained Thus:

$$\text{Class I–II:} \quad \frac{552.6}{100,000} \times 27,000 = 149.2$$

$$\text{Class III:} \quad \frac{528.2}{100,000} \times 48,360 = 255.4$$

$$\text{Class IV:} \quad \frac{664.5}{100,000} \times 118,000 = 784.1$$

$$\text{Class V:} \quad \frac{1667.7}{100,000} \times 43,580 = 726.8$$

Expected Number of Patients Is Obtained Thus:

$$\text{Class I–II:} \quad 1915.5 \times \frac{27,000}{236,940} = 218.3$$

$$\text{Class III:} \quad 1915.5 \times \frac{48,360}{236,940} = 391.0$$

$$\text{Class IV:} \quad 1915.5 \times \frac{118,000}{236,940} = 953.9$$

$$\text{Class V:} \quad 1915.5 \times \frac{43,580}{236,940} = 352.3$$

The χ^2 obtained from the observed and expected frequencies in this table is 497.16, with 3 degrees of freedom, and $p < .001$.

TABLE 6

Age and Sex Adjusted Rates per 100,000 for Each Component in Prevalence—by Class

	Type of Rate			
Class	Incidence	Re-Entry	Continuous	Total
I–II	97	88	368	553
III	114	68	346	528
IV	89	59	516	664
V	139	123	1406	1668

TABLE 7

Percentage of Psychotic Patients in Different Treatment Agencies—by Class

	Class			
Treatment Agency	I–II	III *	IV	V
Public				
Clinic	1.9	5.5	3.3	3.0
V. A. hospital	5.8	5.5	4.5	5.6
State hospital	32.7	70.5	85.4	90.2
Private				
Practitioner	21.2	14.4	6.0	1.2
Hospital	38.5	4.1	0.9	0.0
$n =$	52	146	581	663

$$\chi^2 = 216.68, \ 8 \ df, \ p < .001$$

* Classes I–II and III combined for χ^2 analysis.

TABLE 8

Percentage of Psychotics with a History of Psychiatric Treatment—by First
Treatment Agency and Present Treatment Agency—by Class

A. Classes I–II

Agency	First Treatment	Current Treatment
Clinic	2.6	2.6
Military hospital	.0	7.7
State hospital	.0	13.3
Private practice	23.1	20.5
Private hospital	74.4	35.9
$n =$	39	39

$$\chi^2 = 19.52, 3 \, df, p < .001$$

B. Class III

Agency	First Treatment	Current Treatment
Clinic	9.3	3.4
Military hospital	8.1	8.0
State hospital	12.8	64.4
Private practice	4.6	18.4
Private hospital	65.1	5.7
$n =$	86 *	87

$$\chi^2 = 82.25, 4 \, df, p < .001$$

* One case agency of first treatment "unknown."

C. Class IV

Agency	First Treatment	Current Treatment
Clinic	14.6	4.1
Military hospital	9.6	6.3
State hospital	66.6	81.4
Private practice	0.6	7.5
Private hospital	8.6	.6
$n =$	314 *	318

$$\chi^2 = 65.96, 3 \, df, p < .001$$

* Four cases agency of first treatment "unknown."

TABLE 8 (cont'd)

Percentage of Psychotics with a History of Psychiatric Treatment—by First Treatment Agency and Present Treatment Agency—by Class

D. Class V

Agency	First Treatment	Current Treatment
Clinic	11.4	2.8
Military hospital	3.1	8.6
State hospital	84.1	86.9
Private practice	0.0	1.7
Private hospital	1.4	0.0
$n =$	289 *	290

$$\chi^2 = 23.02,\ 3\ df,\ p < .001$$

* One case agency of first treatment "unknown."

TABLE 9–A

Where Patients with Affective Disorders Were First Treated—Percentage by Class

Treatment Facility *	Class			
	I–II	III	IV	V
State hospital	9.1	42.9	74.1	87.2
Military or V. A. hospital	...	...	2.5	...
Public clinic	...	4.8	14.8	10.6
Private practitioner	9.1	4.8	4.9	2.1
Private hospital	81.8	47.6	3.7	...
$n =$	11	21	81	47

$$\chi^2 = 58.80,\ 3\ df,\ p < .001$$

* The χ^2 was computed with the public treatment facilities grouped into one category, and the private ones grouped into a second category.

TABLE 9–B

Where Alcoholics Were First Treated—Percentage by Class

Treatment Facility *	Class			
	I–II	III †	IV	V
State hospital	...	14.3	52.0	70.8
V. A. hospital	...	7.1	4.0	...
Public clinic	...	28.6	36.0	29.2
Private practitioner	50.0	14.3	8.0	...
Private hospital	50.0	35.7	...	...
$n =$	4	14	25	48

$$\chi^2 = 40.62, 2 \; df, \; p < .001$$

* The χ^2 was computed with the public treatment facilities grouped into one category and the private treatment facilities into another.

† The four cases in classes I–II were combined with the class III cases in this analysis.

TABLE 9–C

Where Patients with Organic Disorders Were First Treated—Percentage by Class

Treatment Facility *	Class			
	I–II †	III	IV	V
State hospital	50.0	58.3	88.2	90.8
V. A. hospital	...	...	5.9	...
Public clinic	...	16.7	2.0	7.3
Private practitioner	...	16.7	2.0	1.8
Private hospital	50.0	8.3	2.0	...
$n =$	2	12	51	109

$$\chi^2 = 22.00, 2 \; df, \; p < .001$$

* The χ^2 was computed with the state hospital, veterans hospital, and public clinic cases grouped into one category, and the private practitioner and private hospital cases grouped into a second category.

† The two cases in classes I–II were combined with class III cases for the χ^2 computation.

TABLE 9-D

Percentage of Schizophrenics Who Were First Treated in Specified Types of Psychiatric Facilities—by Class

Treatment Facility	Class			
	I–II	III	IV	V
State hospital	6.9	36.1	75.3	89.6
V. A. hospital	. . .	8.4	8.5	5.5
Private hospital	58.6	43.4	6.5	1.0
Public clinic	3.4	7.2	8.5	3.9
Private practitioner	31.0	4.8	1.1	0.0
$n =$	29	83	352	383

$$\chi^2 = 395.91, 2 \, df, p < .001$$

TABLE 9-E

Percentage of Patients with Senile Disorders Who Were First Treated in Specified Types of Psychiatric Facilities—by Class

Treatment Facility *	Class			
	I–II	III †	IV	V
State hospital	. . .	62.5	93.1	96.1
Public clinic	. . .	. . .	. . .	3.9
Private practitioner	. . .	. . .	2.8	. . .
Private hospital	100.0	37.5	4.2	. . .
$n =$	6	16	72	76

$$\chi^2 = 57.68, 2 \, df, p < .001$$

* The χ^2 was computed with the public treatment facilities grouped into one category, and the private facilities in another category.

† The six cases in classes I–II were combined with class III in this analysis.

name index

subject index